THE
SOVIET ASSAULT
ON AMERICA'S
SOUTHERN FLANK

THE
SOVIET ASSAULT
ON AMERICA'S
SOUTHERN FLANK

By
James R. Whelan
and Franklin A. Jaeckle

INTRODUCTION BY L. FRANCIS BOUCHEY

Published by Regnery Gateway, Inc., in cooperation
with the Council for Inter-American Security and the
Inter-American Security Educational Institute

Washington, D.C.

126340

The publishers wish to acknowledge the generosity of Jameson Books, the publisher, and James R. Whelan and Patricia B. Bozell, the authors, for granting us permission to reproduce material originally appearing in their book *Catastrophe in the Caribbean: The Failure of America's Human Rights Policy in Central America*, Jameson Books, Ottawa, Illinois.

Library of Congress Cataloging-in-Publication Data

Whelan, James R. (James Robert), 1933–
The Soviet assault on America's Southern Flank/James R.
Whelan and Franklin A. Jaeckle; introduction by L. Francis Bouchey.
p. cm.
Bibliography: p.
Includes index.
ISBN 0-89526-561-3 : $17.95
1. Central America—Foreign relations—Soviet Union.   2. Soviet
Union—Foreign relations—Central America.   3. Communism—Central
America—History—20th century.   4. Geopolitics—Central America.
5. United States—National security.   I. Jaeckle, Franklin A.,
1953–   .   II. Title.
F1436.8.S65W47   1988
327.470728—dc19   88-3113
                                                                             CIP

ISBN 0–89526–561–3 (cloth)
0–89526–772–1 (paperback)

Published in the United States by
Regnery Gateway
1130 17th Street, NW
Washington D.C. 20036

Distributed to the trade by
Kampmann & Company, Inc.
9 E 40th Street
New York NY 10016

10   9   8   7   6   5   4   3   2   1

CONTENTS

v

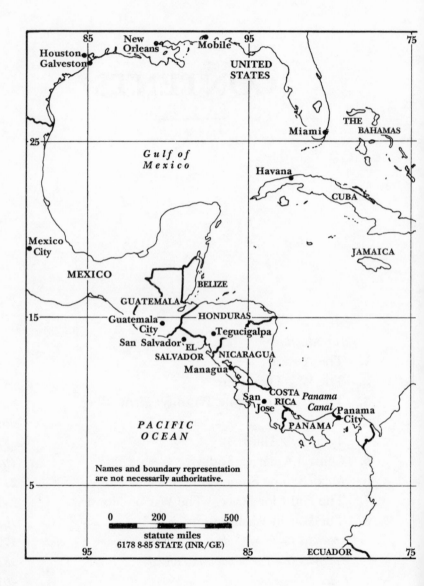

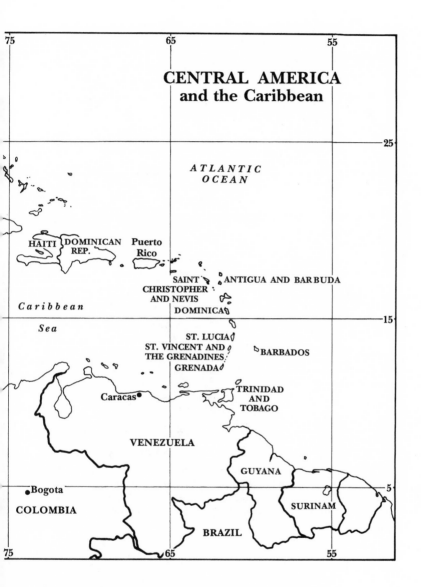

CENTRAL AMERICA
and the Caribbean

75

65

55

25

ATLANTIC
OCEAN

HAITI DOMINICAN Puerto
REP. Rico

SAINT ANTIGUA AND BARBUDA
CHRISTOPHER
AND NEVIS
Caribbean DOMINICA

15

Sea

ST. LUCIA
ST. VINCENT AND BARBADOS
THE GRENADINES
GRENADA

TRINIDAD
Caracas AND
TOBAGO

VENEZUELA

GUYANA

Bogota 5

COLOMBIA SURINAM

BRAZIL

75 65 55

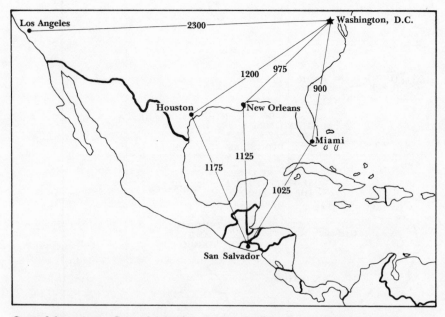

One of the reasons Central America and the Caribbean is so important is the proximity of the region to the southern border of the United States. Notice that San Salvador is about the same distance from Miami as Miami is from Washington, D.C.

INTRODUCTION

The average American may not understand—and seemingly isn't interested in—the ever-widening conflict between Communism and freedom in Central America.

Yet it is an issue on which President Reagan has spent much of his accumulated political capital since he was first elected in November, 1980. And it is an issue the President has involved himself in with such a consuming passion that many have called it the greatest risk to his place in history.

The nightly news broadcasts and the editorial pages of many newspapers are filled with a constant parade of critics calling for an end to our involvement in Central America, an end to our aid for the anti-Communist Freedom Fighters there.

This disparity of viewpoints—President Reagan on the one hand, with much of the political establishment lined up against him—has produced in this country a tremendous confusion over what exactly our goals and policies are in Central America and what they should be.

Introduction

Even as I write this introduction the United States Congress approaches still another vote on aid to the Nicaraguan Resistance. The question widely asked is "how long can the Contras last without more aid?" A more pertinent question is how long can the Leninist Sandinistas last, even if the USSR and Warsaw Pact nations continue the present level of support? For every dollar of economic aid provided by the United States to Central America during the 1980s, Cuba and Nicaragua received $10 worth from the Soviet Union and its East European allies. Soviet Bloc military deliveries—weapons, ammunition, vehicles—exceed the cumulative value of U.S. military assistance by eight to one in the region. Yet, today pitiful Nicaragua subsists economically at the sufferance of the Kremlin, because of the Sandinista Commandantes' personal corruption and because of their ideologically induced incompetence. Store shelves are bare, inflation is rampant, and political discontent is nearly as widespread as during the final months of the Somoza government.

The purpose of this book is twofold: to provide an intelligent, comprehensive overview of the situation in, and the history surrounding, Central America, and to dispel many of the myths which have often been transformed into "facts" by the national news media and some politicians in Washington, D.C., about our involvement there.

Not since the War of 1812 has the United States faced such a threat to our national security so close to our own shores. This danger will not go away overnight, and it will grow worse if we remain in our present state of confusion and near-paralysis.

This book has been distributed to all five hundred thirty-five U.S. Senators and Congressmen. Copies have been delivered to the White House, the Department of Defense, the State Department, and dozens of governmental agencies, as well as to members of the news media and the myriad special interest groups that thrive in our nations' capital.

But my greatest hope is that you will read *The Soviet Assault on America's Southern Flank* and then share it with family, friends and co-workers. As the politicians continue their debate over our next move in Central America—or whether there will even be a next move—it is of vital importance that we all participate in and understand the decision-making process.

L. Francis Bouchey
President,
Council for Inter-American Security
March 1988

THE
SOVIET ASSAULT
ON AMERICA'S
SOUTHERN FLANK

1

The Assault

WHEN Fidel Castro came to power in 1959, the Soviet Union had diplomatic relations with only three Latin American countries. Now, Soviet embassies operate in 15 countries south of the Rio Grande.

If Europe and America may be called the front, the scene of the main engagements between socialism and imperialism, the nonsovereign nations and colonies . . . should be regarded as the rear, the reserve of imperialism. In order to win a war, one must not only triumph at the front but also revolutionize the enemy's rear, his reserves.

That was written by Joseph Stalin in 1921. In the case of the United States, the rear to which Stalin was referring was Latin America, a target on which the Soviets have long focused.[1]

Americans tend to overlook the threat to our security posed by hostile forces in this hemisphere. Unlike so many other parts of the world, the United States, for more than 150 years, has not had to defend its mainland against invading armies. Unlike the West Germans, Americans do not have a border marked off by minefields, barbed wire, and guard towers, serving as a constant reminder of an enemy close at hand. The most obvious threat to U.S. security, the Soviet Union, is so powerful militarily and so vast geographically that its allies in Cuba and Nicaragua might seem insignificant by comparison.

Yet it would be a fatal mistake to overlook the dangers introduced into the American hemisphere by the Soviet Union and its allies. Indeed, by the early 1980s, the Soviets had so extended their reach into the region as to proclaim a new kind of Monroe Doctrine of their own, "repeatedly warning Washington about the repercussions of U.S. intervention" in Cuba, Nicaragua or against the Salvadoran left.[2]

Soviet-Cuban advances threaten the vital shipping lanes of the Caribbean. Nearly half of all crude oil shipped to the U.S. goes through the Caribbean. During World War II, half of all U.S. supplies to Europe went through these sea lanes. The Germans sank 150 merchant ships there in the first five months of the war.[3] Those sea lanes are no less important today than they were forty-five years ago, although the Soviets are in a much better position to threaten them than Hitler ever was.

Of more immediate concern is a threat posed by construction of a new airfield at Punta Huete, 100 miles north of Managua. With a 10,000-foot runway—longer than any needed by aircraft now in the Nicaraguan inventory, but big enough to handle anything the Soviets fly—that base could become the southern anchor the Soviets need for patrol flights they cannot now fly over Hawaii, the U.S. west coast and the Panama Canal. As Marc Liebman wrote in the *Armed Forces Journal* at mid-1987, Soviet aircraft have been intercepted in the Alaskan Air Command airspace and escorted out of the Air Defense Identification Zone for years. Although some have dipped south into the Gulf of Alaska, they cannot make the long arc that would carry them along the Pacific coast and across the Central American isthmus to bases in Cuba. Punta Huete—under construction since 1982 and now near completion—could change that. Leaving Petropavlovsk on the east coast of the Kamchatka Peninsula, Bear reconnaissance and anti-submarine aircraft could cruise past such sensitive military facilities as the Canadian Forces base at Comox, British Columbia, the U.S. Navy's Trident base at Bangor, Washington, Beale Air Force Base, California and the complex of U.S. military bases in southern California, including the missile launching facilities at Vandenberg Air Force Base—not to mention Pearl Harbor and the Panama Canal. During 1986 alone, at least nine Bear D (naval reconnaissance) and five Bear F (anti-submarine) aircraft flew from Murmansk/Archangel area bases down through the Greenland/Iceland/Norway gap, across the Atlantic and then along the U.S. east coast to bases in Cuba. The Nicaraguan base would enable the Soviets to close the ring around the U.S. on the west.[4] Caribbean shipping routes and a wealth of new reconnaissance opportunities are not the only reasons the U.S. must be concerned with the Central American region. As a global power with global commitments and security interests, the United States must be prepared to respond to threats virtually anywhere in the world. The ability of the U.S. to honor its worldwide commitments, however, depends very much on the preservation of secure borders at home. The Soviet-Cuban alliance is creating turmoil not only in Central America, but raises the specter that Mexico, a non-belligerent neighbor sprawling across two thousand miles of now-peaceful border, could become a violent cauldron menacing U.S. security.

Soviet analysts themselves believe that the real outcome of the struggle for power in the once-secure Western Hemisphere will be decided, not in Central America, but "in key countries—Brazil, Mexico, Argentina."[5] It was for this reason that the Kremlin decided on the calculated risk of dispatching Foreign Minister Edward Shevardnadze, in September 1987, to Brazil and Argentina (against the risk of encouraging demands for expanded trade-and-aid, at a time when Moscow can ill-afford either, and with the comparable risk of triggering an anti-Soviet backlash, particularly among the still-powerful and mainly anti-communist military in both countries). In part, the Soviets are exploiting the positive appeal of *glasnost*. Cole Blasier, professor of political science at the University of Pittsburgh, puts it this way:

> The democratic countries of Latin America are greatly intrigued by *glasnost*. The Brezhnev regime was no alternative to the U.S. Gorbachev is appealing because he provides an alternative, a counterbalance to the influence of the United States.

Under the spell of *glasnost*, delegations from at least a dozen Latin American countries visited Moscow in late 1986 and 1987. Principal among them: President Raul Alfonsin of Argentina, the first head of state of his country ever to visit Moscow. Among concrete results: the first ever Soviet cultural agreement with Guatemala, the first trade agreement with Honduras, and an eight-day seminar in Moscow in September 1987 attended by representatives from 145 countries discussing economic integration in the region and Moscow's possible role in it.[6]

But, while not the ultimate target, Central America is important—crucially-important—because conflict there exacerbates differences within the western alliance, in the measure that it weakens the ability of the U.S. to engage fully in other international arenas (the Middle East, Persian Gulf, western Pacific), and in the measure it brings nearer the eruption of full-blown chaos in Mexico. Should events there require the U.S. to defend its southern border, the necessary redeployment of forces would seriously weaken NATO, jeopardize the security of Europe and gravely imperil the entire worldwide balance of forces.

Nor is that reasoning far-fetched. The naval blockade of Cuba in 1982, for example, required 284 ships, including eight aircraft carriers. The entire Atlantic Fleet today has only 250 ships and 6 aircraft carriers. During naval exercises in 1983, a total of 43 warships and 204 surface combat vessels were deployed off Central America. A respected analyst,

Capt. John Moore, editor of *Jane's Fighting Ships*, wrote at the time that this stretched the U.S. Navy "desperately tight . . . the U.S. Navy simply does not have enough ships. NATO does not have enough ships."[7] Ground and air forces are similarly scarce to meet existing global commitments. A final reason for concern is the social and economic chaos that would inevitably result from a surge of Central American refugees into the southern United States. The current level of illegal immigration is already posing serious problems for the U.S. economy and social fabric, but it is nothing compared to the flood of immigrants that would result if the armed conflicts in Central America should reach Mexico. President Reagan warned in an 1983 speech that a military collapse on the Central American isthmus could produce "a tidal wave of refugees—and this time they'll be 'feet people' and not boat people—swarming into our country seeking a safe haven from communist repression to our south."[8]

It is for these reasons that the United States must be very concerned with Soviet-Cuban subversion and expansionism in the western hemisphere. This is not to argue that the East-West conflict is the only theoretical framework by which the U.S. should interpret Latin American affairs. The problems faced by most Latin American countries stem not from Soviet expansionism, but from largely internal political, economic, and social factors. These include highly uneven distribution of income, rapid societal modernization, authoritarian governments that block political avenues to change, and increasing nationalism.[9] All of these factors are responsible for creating tensions worsened in recent years by the worldwide economic crisis of the late 1970s and early 80s.

If Soviet-sponsored communism is not the cause of all the turmoil in Latin America, it is certainly a willing catalyst and beneficiary. We need to examine how the Soviet Union, primarily through Cuba, has managed to exploit the weaknesses of the societies and political institutions of Central America in order to further its own geopolitical ends.

Pre-Castro

We are internationalists. We aim at the firm union and full fusion of the workers and peasants of all nations into a single, worldwide Soviet Republic.

—V. I. Lenin[10]

Marxist doctrine teaches that the entire world is a battleground for socialist revolution, one in which the eventual triumph of communism is inevitable. This view has been reiterated time and again by the Soviet Union. Yet it is often claimed that for many years after the Russian Revolution the Soviets showed little interest in playing a public role in the political events of the western hemisphere. To the extent that this is true, it is because of the great distance between the Soviet Union and the Americas. There were no significant cultural, political, or economic ties between the two regions until the 1960s (when Fidel Castro sought Soviet help to build communism in Cuba).

In addition, the Soviets could hardly overlook the political dominance of the United States. The Monroe Doctrine had warned European powers against interfering in the western hemisphere, and the United States' own record of intervention in Latin America demonstrated a willingness to use force when necessary to guard national interests. So through the first half of the twentieth century, the Soviet Union faced serious obstacles to the successful exportation of revolution to the Americas. The Soviets did not, however, ignore Latin America. Where ambitious revolutionary adventures are impractical, subtler forms of subversion are still available.

Shortly after taking power, Lenin founded the Comintern, an international federation of communist parties dedicated to promoting communism worldwide while rendering unconditional support for the Communist Party of the Soviet Union. Much of the attention of the Comintern would focus on colonies and dependent states in search of their own national identities. Though nationalism is not consistent with Marxist aims, Lenin favored limited support for selected nationalist movements in the hope of weakening the foreign powers—especially Great Britain and the United States—that stood in the way of his long-range plans. Communist infiltration of U.S.-dominated Latin America was also an early goal.

Though restricted by logistical problems, the Comintern lost little time launching its activities in the Caribbean Basin. In 1919, it sent its agent Michael Borodin to Mexico to organize one of the first communist parties outside of Eurasia, which he succeeded in doing within a matter of weeks. The new party was not particularly stable, but when it crumbled (in part because the Mexican government deported its American members), the Comintern responded by sending another agent to oversee its rebuilding. Before long, the Communist Party of Mexico (PCM) was infiltrating the trade unions, starting youth cells, and fielding political candidates (the 1922 elections).[11]

About this time, the Soviets opened an embassy in Mexico City and began to recruit intellectuals and labor leaders, while the Comintern instructed the PCM to concentrate on creating sister parties in neighboring states. The Communist Party of El Salvador (PCS) was formed in this way in 1921, though its existence was kept secret for several years.

In 1927, the Comintern agent who led the Salvadoran Party, Augustin Farabundo Marti, saw the landing of U.S. Marines in nearby Nicaragua as a potential spark for Soviet-style revolution. Marti went to Nicaragua to join General Agusto Cesar Sandino, a Nicaraguan nationalist who had assembled a guerrilla force of several thousand to challenge the U.S.-backed regime. This marked the Soviet Union's first attempt to turn nationalist impulses into communist gains in the Americas.

Sandino was not a communist, but he was nevertheless valuable to the Comintern as an anti-imperialist symbol. The

Sixth Congress of the Comintern, meeting in 1928, adopted a resolution extending

> fraternal greetings to the workers and peasants of Nicaragua, and the heroic army of national emancipation of General Sandino, which is carrying on a brave, determined struggle with the imperialism of the United States.[12]

It was a classic guerrilla war. Sandino had no chance of defeating the U.S. forces, but by his very survival he was an embarrassment to the United States. In supporting him the Comintern associated itself with an international hero who could be used to organize Americans to oppose their government's policies. The Comintern also saw in Sandino an opportunity to intensify pre-existing anti-American sentiments through assorted propaganda efforts, such as the communist-controlled "Hands Off Nicaragua" committee set up in Mexico. The Soviets even arranged for a Sandino Division to be part of the Nanking Army, which they advised in the 1927 Chinese Civil War.[13]

In 1929, however, Sandino broke his ties with Marti and the Comintern, and was denounced by the PCM as a "traitor to the cause."

One year later, Mexico was the target, where the Soviets, growing more bold, encouraged the PCM to launch a coup against the government. They must have viewed this as an experiment, for the coup had little chance of success and no chance of installing a communist government that would be tolerated by the United States. In any event, Farabundo Marti participated in the plot, which was easily put down by the Mexican Army. The government responded by expelling two Soviet agents and severing relations with Moscow.

For several years after this failure in Mexico, El Salvador was the only place in Central America or the Caribbean to have any significant communist activity. While Marti was in Mexico, a Mexican communist named Jorge Fernandez

Anaya went to El Salvador to organize farm workers. He was well received by the peasants, and within weeks he converted Marti's secret PCS into an open, rural-based communist party. By May 1930, when Marti returned from Mexico, Fernandez Anaya had mobilized eighty thousand men for a May Day parade in San Salvador.[14]

Fernandez Anaya was not the only non-Salvadoran behind this movement. There are various accounts of Eastern Europeans posing as peddlers as they travelled about El Salvador spreading communist propaganda, and there were communist agitators among El Salvador's Palestinian immigrant population. The Comintern provided assistance through the Communist Party of the United States (CPUSA) by sending printed propaganda. In a single month in 1931, the postal authorities in San Salvador confiscated over three thousand pounds of communist publications sent from New York.[15]

Marti had plans to lead the PCS in armed revolt, and there is some evidence that a simultaneous revolt was to take place in Guatemala. In any event, the communist leaders in Guatemala were arrested in early 1932, so the PCS acted alone when, later that year, it launched a campaign of terror. As in Mexico, the radical forces were easily overwhelmed by the military. Marti was executed.

It is not entirely clear whether the Salvadoran uprising had the Comintern's backing. The CPUSA, through which the Comintern exercised nominal control over the PCS, praised the "heroic struggles of the workers and peasants of El Salvador, under the leadership of the Communist Party," but it was critical of the armed revolt.[16] This may simply be a case of 20-20 hindsight. One thing is clear: Central America saw no further armed activity by communist parties aligned with Moscow until after Stalin's death in 1953.

For two decades after the Salvadoran fiasco, the Soviet Union paid little attention to the Latin American communist parties beyond encouraging them to infiltrate labor organizations and to build "popular fronts," or political coalitions, with Leftist, non-communist parties. Fertile ground for such activity was found in Mexico. In 1934, just four years after the government had put down a communist revolt, Mexico's new president, Lazaro Cardenas not only released the Mexican communist leaders from jail, but openly consulted with them and mixed with them socially.

Another country where communists made gains working within the system was Cuba, where they were part of a coalition that elected Fulgencio Batista to the presidency in 1940. Two years later, Juan Marinello, president of the Cuban Communist Party, entered Batista's cabinet as a minister without portfolio, and after that, a young communist theoretician named Carlos Rafael Rodriguez, joined Batista's cabinet. With successes like these, it is understandable that the Soviets preferred, at least temporarily, to promote socialism through political channels.

World War II, however, brought a global redistribution of power that created new opportunities for Soviet subversion worldwide. The dismantling of European empires resulted in the creation of dozens of new states characterized by a strong sense of nationalism accompanied by an equally strong desire to exercise their new-found independence.

The nations of Latin America, for the most part, had long been not only independent of Europe, but, thanks in no small measure to the Monroe Doctrine, largely unmolested by Europe. Still, goaded mainly by intellectuals driven more by envy and resentment of the United States than an affinity for communism, they clamored for greater freedom from American dominance in the hemisphere. So the spirit of independence seen elsewhere in the post-war Third World was echoed in this hemisphere as growing anti-Americanism (which, by extension, would become anti-anti-communism; so that a regime such as Somoza's in Nicaragua would become loathsome, to an important degree, because it was anti-communist). The proliferation of small, independent states with weak governments and unstable democratic institutions provided fertile ground for communist agitation.

One way the Soviets sought to take advantage of this situation was through the creation of international front groups. The idea was not new. In 1902, Lenin had envisioned "mass organizations" that would attract unwitting supporters to communist causes. Later, when he ruled the Soviet Union, the creation of such organizations was the responsibility of the Comintern. The tactic was explained at a Comintern meeting in 1926:

> The first part of our task is to build up, not only communist organizations but other organizations as well, above all mass organizations sympathetic with our aims. . . . We must create a whole solar system of organizations . . . around the Communist Party, so to speak, smaller organizations working actually under the influence of our party.[17]

Such organizations could attract many supporters who would not openly associate with communist parties.

Joseph Stalin dissolved the Comintern during World War II, but in the late 1940s and 1950s, he created over a dozen new front groups to further develop and refine the techniques of subversion. Chief among these were the World Federation of Trade Unions, the World Federation of Democratic Youth, the International Union of Students, and the World Peace Council.

One special front was created in Mexico during the war: the Mexican-Russian Institute of Cultural Exchange. This was a bridge-building exercise between war-time allies but it naturally served as an outlet for Soviet propaganda. Through fronts operating in Mexico, the Soviets were able to infiltrate the government and actually control the Mexican teachers' union.[18]

Another country in which front activities proved successful was Guatemala, where the labor movement provided an opening in the late 1940s. The members of the Communist Party of Guatemala gained influence by posing as nationalists, in which capacity they were able to conduct "political orientation" seminars. Their leader was Jose Manuel Fortuny, a member of the World Peace Council, who was under orders from Moscow to establish a Soviet camp in Guatemala.[19] One of Fortuny's colleagues in the party was Victor Emanuel Gutierrez, a member of the Executive Committee of the World Federation of Trade Unions, who gave the Soviets considerable influence over Guatemalan labor.

By building an effective political coalition and by tapping the strength of the labor movement, Fortuny and his followers were able to elect their candidate, Jacobo Arbenz, to the Guatemalan presidency. Arbenz's government was the first in the western hemisphere to be thoroughly infiltrated and dominated by communists. Some like to deny this, noting that none of Arbenz's cabinet ministers were communists and that Guatemala maintained no diplomatic relations with the Soviet bloc. But Arbenz's wife was active in the Guatemalan Women's Alliance, the local affiliate of a prominent Soviet front, and his inner circle of friends included Fortuny, Gutierrez, and other communists, who dropped their facade after the election and openly revealed their colors. Fortuny, who wrote speeches for Arbenz, reported to the Soviets through their embassy in Mexico City, according to J. Michael Waller of the Council for Inter-American Security.[20] One contemporary observer wrote, "The Soviet conspiracy in the Caribbean was not entrusted to the domestic communists—the Fortunys and the Gutierrezes—but to Soviet technicians practiced in the art of conspiracy."[21]

Gutierrez was another who maintained ties to Moscow; he chaired the Guatemalan congressional committee that drew up an agrarian reform program based on a Communist Chinese model. The administration of this program was thoroughly controlled by communists,[22] and it became an instrument for the subversion of legal and constitutional order. Whole properties were burned so that they could be "legally" declared uncultivated and therefore subject to expropriation. In February 1953, the Supreme Court of Guatemala ruled 4 to 1 to issue an injunction preventing the program's expropriation of a small farmer, but the Congress, with Arbenz's approval, voted along party lines to remove the four errant justices. One month later, that same Congress became the only legislative body outside the iron curtain to observe the death of Joseph Stalin with a moment of silence.[23]

Other agencies of the Arbenz government which fell under communist control included the education and labor ministries, the national bank, the social security system, the press and propaganda agencies, the foreign ministry, and the police.

In the international arena, Guatemala became a base for subversion in Latin America. Panama, Colombia, Costa Rica, Nicaragua, and Honduras all expelled Guatemalan diplomats. As recorded by University of Pennsylvania scholar Ronald M. Schneider, the Soviet leadership

> exploited the Guatemalan situation to disrupt hemispheric unity, used Guatemala as a base for Communist operations in the Central American area, and presented that country as a model for other Latin American Communists to copy. Above all, the international leaders attempted to use developments in Guatemala to picture the United States as an "imperialist" power.[24]

Indeed, in June 1952, as a U.N. force consisting largely of U.S. troops was defending South Korea against North Korean communist aggression, the Guatemalan government sent the North Korean dictator, Kim Il Sung, a "Declaration of Solidarity with the Korean People," which referred to the "second anniversary of the Yankee aggression and the heroic resistance of a heroic sister people."[25]

A variety of Soviet fronts supported the Guatemalan government through propaganda. To guard against intervention, the Second Congress of the Communist Party of

15

Guatemala launched an international "Hands Off Guatemala" campaign directed at the United States. It was taken up by the World Peace Council.

Such propaganda efforts, however, could not conceal the fact that the real threat came from within Guatemala. Increasing dissent—of a peaceful kind—met with increasing repression from the government. Independent labor unions were destroyed, a labor leader was murdered, a radio station was closed, foreign reporters were expelled, and a local reporter was tortured. Even an opposition member of Congress was tortured.[26]

The entire Central American region was shocked to learn in the spring of 1954 that Guatemala had just received a secret shipment of two thousand tons of arms from the Soviet bloc. This munitions shipment, then the largest in Central American history, would make Guatemala stronger than all of its neighbors combined. But those neighboring countries were not the only parties with cause for concern. The Guatemalan military, too, saw a serious threat looming when Arbenz revealed his intention to create a "people's militia," a paramilitary force of union members under communist control.

On June 18, 1954, Castillo Armas, an exiled Guatemalan Army officer, led a small exile force in an invasion from Honduras, with support from the United States and Nicaragua. A week later, the Guatemalan Army officers refused to comply with Arbenz's demand that they distribute weapons to the "people's militia," and on June 27 they ousted Arbenz, who was replaced by an anti-communist junta. The forces of Castillo Armas never advanced more than forty miles into Guatemala.

Castro Shows the Way

The collapse of communism in Guatemala occurred during Nikita Khrushchev's second year in power. The Guatemalan failure offered little hope for communist insurrection in the Americas, so the new Soviet dictator simply continued Stalin's policy of promoting political agitation through various fronts and using propaganda to capitalize on anti-Yankee sentiment, which was especially strong in the wake of the U.S.-supported ouster of Arbenz. Communist campaigns sought to discredit U.S.-backed dictators in Guatemala, Honduras, El Salvador, Nicaragua, Cuba, and the Dominican Republic. The objective was not to gain power, but to chip away at U.S. influence in the hemisphere and gradually build Soviet influence. Indeed, Moscow discouraged armed rebellion by the local communist parties.

So it was without Soviet assistance that Fidel Castro toppled Fulgencio Batista in Cuba on New Year's Day of 1959. The Soviets had paid little attention to Cuba prior to World War II, and just before Castro's success, the country enjoyed one of the highest—if not the highest—standards of living in Latin America.

By 1958, Fulgencio Batista had become a repressive and very unpopular dictator. His downfall resulted from widespread urban violence; rural guerrilla campaigns run by Castro; the corruption, disunity, and poor morale of the Cuban Army; and the imposition of an American arms embargo. Ironically, the Cuban Communist Party had representatives in Batista's government, so it supported Batista even longer than the United States did, joining the revolution only at the end.

Because Castro was not supported by the Communist Party, it is often said that he was not a communist when he took power. This interpretation is very convenient for those who like to argue that the new regime wanted good relations with the U.S. but was "driven into the arms of the Soviets." It doesn't fit the facts, however. It is true that before taking power Castro repeatedly denied that he was a communist, but as he did so he was placing communists in charge of his guerrilla forces.[27] Moreover, in a speech given on December 2, 1961, he admitted to having been an "apprentice Marxist-Leninist" for years, announcing, "While in the Sierra Maestra I hid my way of thinking. . . . Since then, I have been, I am now and I shall always be—until the day I die—a Marxist-Leninist." And in a 1977 interview, he admitted that he had decided to become a communist in the late 1940s.[28]

Before seizing power, Castro had to conceal his ideology so as not to arouse anti-communist opposition. Even afterwards he was cautious, fearing U.S. intervention. Twenty years later, he advised the Sandinistas to use the same deception in Nicaragua, and very probably gave the same advice to Maurice Bishop in Grenada. In all three cases it worked.

Fidel Castro clearly planned from the start to align his regime with the Soviet Union. In April 1959, during his first visit to the United States, he refused to permit discussions of economic aid.[29] He himself conceded twenty-five years later that U.S. hostility was not the reason he had aligned his government with the Soviets,[30] and indeed, Andres Alfaya Torrado, a defector from the Cuban DGI intelligence organization, has revealed that the very idea was the product of a disinformation campaign. Alfaya has also reported that Cuban intelligence agents learned such disinformation tactics from 120 KGB agents who were stationed in Havana as early as 1959, even as Castro was in the United States denying any communist ties.

As this illustrates, the Soviets wasted no time welcoming this upstart into the fold. Before long they were supplying enormous quantities of aid, economic and military, to consolidate and expand Castro's power. By June 1960, Soviet engineers in Havana were building a 12,000-foot runway to accommodate military aircraft. By 1961, there were three thousand Soviet-bloc "technicians" in Cuba,[31] busily constructing a new puppet state. In 1962, Cuba received 250,000 metric tons of military equipment from the Soviet Union[32]— 125 times the size of the arms shipment to Guatemala that had so shocked Central America just eight years earlier! And this was only the beginning of a build-up that continues to the present day, accelerating in more recent years.[33]

Castro's military manpower now stands at 297,000 and is rivaled in Latin America only by Brazil, a country with more than twelve times the population of Cuba.[34] As if that were not enough, Castro has also assembled a militia of over 1.2 million.[35] With Soviet military aid on the order of $10 billion since 1961, Cuba has acquired almost 1,000 tanks, almost 200 sophisticated fighter aircraft, and a navy that includes hydrofoils, submarines, and amphibious landing craft,[36] all of which serve the aims of Soviet foreign policy.

Cuba's armed forces are not the only ones stationed on Castro's island. Soviet military personnel there include 2,800 troops, an equal number of military advisers to keep the Cubans in line, and 2,100 technicians staffing the Soviets' most sophisticated electronic listening post outside the USSR. This intelligence facility monitors U.S. communications.[37] The Soviets also use Cuba as an air base for reconnaissance flights along the U.S. coastline and over vital sea lanes.

When Soviet Premier Khrushchev attempted in 1962 to install missiles in Cuba targeted at the United States, he was forced by President Kennedy to back down and remove them, but this proved to be only a temporary setback. Since then, the Soviet military presence, and especially naval activity, has been incrementally and insidiously growing in a continual test of U.S. resolve, which has generally been lacking. Today, Soviet naval vessels, which have participated in joint maneuvers with Castro's navy, are routinely serviced in Cuban ports, sometimes in flagrant violation of agreements made with the United States.[38]

Nor is Cuban militarism limited to the island. In 1984, 74,000 Cuban troops were ranged in 24 countries around the world. In Angola alone, there were 16 motorized infantry regiments, an artillery regiment, and an antiaircraft defense brigade—a total altogether of 31,000 men.[39]

The effect of Fidel Castro's communism on Cuban society has been predictable and devastating. The economy has been destroyed, rendering the island completely dependent on the USSR. During Castro's first decade in power, economic production per capita declined in real terms by about ten percent. Troubled by poor agricultural production, lack of labor force discipline, inherently poor central planning, lagging economic growth, and a serious foreign debt problem, Cuba has had to rely on $4 billion to $5 billion a year in Soviet economic aid—exclusive of military assistance.[40] That's about $11 million a day.

In 1959, when Castro took power, Cubans enjoyed the third highest per capita income in Latin America, and although serious structural inequities remained in the socio-economic system, Cuba's middle class was expanding rapidly and was already one of the strongest in Latin America. By 1984, a quarter of a century of revolutionary enlightenment had succeeded in catapulting Cuba to 15th place among nations in the western hemisphere in terms of per capita income. Cuba was now entirely dependent upon Russian hand-outs to sustain even the ragged standard of living left.[41]

The political institutions built by Castro with this assistance have made his regime far more brutal than the one it replaced. The Communist Party is the only legal party—"the highest leading force of the society," according to Cuba's 1976 constitution, which was designed to pattern the regime after the Soviet model. Castro controls the society through a network of neighborhood spies. Everyone is required to carry an identification card, and Carlos Franqui, a former confidant of Castro, reports that even farm animals are tagged and registered in order to control the black market—farmers face stiff penalties for failing to report every livestock transaction.[42]

All political freedoms have been crushed. As one Cuban wrote in a letter (penned at great personal risk), "Here we have no human rights, no peace and not even the right to subsist. . . . Here everybody is afraid of everyone and you can't believe in no one [sic]." The press is thoroughly controlled, and according to a former Cuban intelligence agent, Juan Vives, "Police control within Cuba is so severe that there is virtually no circulation of typewritten copies of unauthorized literature such as occurs in Eastern Europe and Russia."[43]

When Castro the rebel was arrested in 1953 for attacking the Moncacda military barracks, he spent only two years in jail before being granted amnesty by Batista. But under the Castro regime, thousands have been executed or sentenced to twenty years or more in prison simply because of their political opinions. Political prisoners are beaten, ill-fed, deprived of medical care, and routinely incarcerated well beyond their sentences.

One such victim was Armando Valladares, who has described his sufferings in his book *Against All Hope*. Valladares, a government clerk who was not a political activist, was arrested and imprisoned for twenty-two years. His crime was that he criticized Marxism and refused to place on his desk a plaque that read, "If Fidel is a Communist, then put me on the list. He's got the right idea."[44] That was in 1960, when, according to liberal scholars, Castro wasn't yet a communist. During his imprisonment, Valladares was starved, beaten, crippled, burned, drenched in excrement, covered with roaches, and bitten by rats. This was Castro's socialist vision.

Though severe reprisals await Cubans who ask to emigrate, it is estimated by the State Department that two hundred thousand have so requested, and that one to two million

Cubans would leave the country (population 10 million) if permitted to do so. Castro has taken advantage of this to raise cash by charging up to $30,000 per person for the privilege of leaving the country.[45] Reports surfaced in mid-1987 that Castro might be about to encourage another exodus of people, as he had done in the past, in order to ease pressure on the country's rickety economy.[46]

In the words of Carlos Franqui, "Cuba is still a land of sugar and slavery."[47]

Castro's success at consolidating power in Cuba gave the Soviet Union good reason to take a fresh look at the opportunities for communist revolution in the western hemisphere, though in the early years of his regime they were not eager to support some of his more aggressive tactics. Castro, convinced of the efficacy of rural guerrilla warfare, lost no time sponsoring revolutionary movements throughout the hemisphere. Guerrillas trained in Cuba became active in Argentina, Colombia, Peru, Chile, Bolivia, El Salvador, Mexico, Guatemala, Uruguay, Nicaragua, Honduras, and the Dominican Republic. Special targets for armed revolt were the Dominican Republic, Venezuela, and Bolivia, where Castro's close friend Che Guevara was killed attempting to overthrow the government in 1967.

Such activities led to broken or suspended relations with Guatemala, Nicaragua, Paraguay, Haiti, the Dominican Republic, and Peru, while Cuban diplomats were expelled from El Salvador, Honduras, Venezuela, and other countries. As early as January 1962, Cuba was expelled from the Organization of American States for its policies of aggression. Not to be deterred, in 1966 Castro hosted the Tricontinental Conference, a week-long gathering of terrorist and guerrilla organizations from around the world that was described by James Reston of *The New York Times* as

an attempt by the most militant segments of the Communist Parties of the world to organize a Communist strategy that would confront the non-Communist nations, particularly the United States, with an unmanageable series of guerrilla wars.[48]

This approach was not the one preferred by the Soviets, who, especially after their embarrassment in the 1962 missile crisis, were reluctant to back guerrilla movements in Latin America. Many revolutionary movements were seen to have little chance of success, and the Soviets often saw them as ideologically unorthodox. By the late 1960s, Castro, too, had cut back his support for revolutionary movements. In part, this was due to the Che Guevara fiasco, in part to Soviet pressure. Certainly he was facing financial constraints due to a decade of communist mismanagement of the Cuban economy. Desperate for Soviet economic aid, Castro was compelled to defer to Soviet policy preferences, which tended to favor political infiltration and coalition-building.

But the hiatus in insurrectionary activities was only temporary. In 1973, an anti-communist coup in Chile ousted President Salvador Allende as he was busily constructing a Marxist-Leninist state. That coup was followed in quick succession by the ouster of Leftist regimes in Uruguay, Argentina, and Bolivia. But it was the collapse of the Allende regime that, according to scholars Jiri and Virginia Valenta,

> seems to have caused the Soviets to doubt the feasibility of following the purely parliamentary path toward socialism in Latin America. . . . The Soviets in the late 1970s once again began to promote, though guardedly, the more militant aspects of the struggle by revolutionary forces. The successful revolutions in Nicaragua and Grenada increased Soviet confidence in the militant path.[49]

But if Chile was the watershed of *la via pacifica* (the peaceful road) strategies, it was Nicaragua that would tip the balance decisively in favor of Castro and his advocacy of *la via insurreccional*, the path of armed uprising. Sergio Mikoyan,

23

editor of *Latinskaya Amerika*, characterized the Nicaraguan revolution as "an event of colossal international importance ... [demanding] a re-examination of established conceptions" of Soviet strategy. "Only the armed road has led to victory in Latin America," Mikoyan would write.

The violence that Castro had always advocated was now back in vogue. In 1974, Castro formally set up the Americas Department, in charge of masterminding revolutionary activities throughout the hemisphere. By 1986, he was known to support 31 major factions in 11 Latin countries, including the *Montoneros* in Argentina, *Movement of the Revolutionary Left* in Chile, *People's Revolutionary Movement* in Costa Rica, and *Tupamaros* in Uruguay.[50]

Cuban aggression and subversion did not, however, stiffen the resolve of the hemisphere's statesmen to keep Castro isolated. By 1975—when the Organization of American States lifted its sanctions on Cuba, many Latin American governments had already reestablished diplomatic and trade relations.

Today, Cuba's increased militancy is reinforced by the unification of Soviet and Cuban strategies that has resulted from growing Cuban dependency and "Sovietization."

Cuba has provided the Soviets with a formula for the "transition of revolutionary-prone Third World countries from the inchoate stage of 'national liberation' to the rigidly structured socialism of the Soviet brand,"[51] a military base just ninety miles from the U.S., and a staging area for renewed guerrilla and terrorist operations against Latin America, the coordination of which Castro is happy to administer—thus sparing the Soviets any direct involvement that might tarnish their international image and hinder their participation in such lofty diplomatic charades as detente.

Cuba's function as a Soviet proxy fits Moscow's strategy of maintaining a low profile for itself while expanding its influence in the hemisphere. As Soviet analyst Morris Rothenberg puts it:

> ... By relying on proxies indigenous to the area, the USSR avoids an interventionist appearance which might drive Latin American countries back toward the United States and jeopardize Soviet interests elsewhere on the continent. . . .[52]

In addition, Castro has sought to give the Soviet Union much-wanted international legitimacy and apparent respectability through his support in international forums and through his continuous harangues against capitalist "imperialism" and proclamations on the superiority of communist government. Thus he has exerted considerable influence over the so-called Non-Aligned Movement (the association of Third World nations that Henry Kissinger once characterized as "non-aligned against the United States"). In 1979, the sixth summit of non-aligned leaders met in Havana, where Castro, acting as host and president, "effectively outmaneuvered Yugoslavia and other moderates" to give the conference a distinct pro-Soviet orientation. This was achieved, in part, by providing new Mercedes automobiles for the conference participants.[53]

Castro's propaganda value to the Soviets is greatly amplified by his widespread popularity abroad. His carefully nurtured image as a charismatic Robin Hood leading his poor, little nation in defiance of the imperialist Yankee leviathan has endeared him to the hearts of many western intellectuals who ought to know better. No assessment of the success of the Cubans in disarming gullible westerners would, in fact, be complete without a glance at Mr. Castro himself. As the respected weekly *The Economist* noted in a review of three fawningly pro-Castro books:

> ... Mr. Castro has an appeal that no living Latin American leader of left or right has managed to attain. . . . Much of Mr. Castro's appeal is easy to explain. He has charisma . . . [and] has been effective in playing the role of underdog. He has not let himself be hampered in pursuit of this role by the fact that,

in negotiations with the Soviet Union after the missile crisis of 1963, America pledged not to invade Cuba—a pledge which, to the chagrin of right-wing Cuban emigres in Miami, it has scrupulously observed. Mr. Castro, though, has never let facts get in the way of fantasies. A fabled and windy orator (with a penchant for five-hour speeches), he has an instinctive ability to tell audiences what they want to hear. . . .[54]

For this reason, Cuban intelligence agents have been able to cultivate and recruit influential Americans who would never consider cooperating with the Russians. And this, despite the fact that since 1970, the Cuban DGI has been completely controlled by the KGB.

According to one recent high-level defector, Maj. Florentino Azpillaga, Cuban espionage capability is far more sophisticated than has been commonly believed—and has included infiltrating U.S. intelligence. Azpillaga—who headed Cuban intelligence operations in Czechoslovakia and worked in the American targets section of the DGI—said the Cubans managed to plant double agents in the U.S. intelligence system actually loyal to Castro. These agents compromised a number of ongoing and sensitive intelligence operations, forcing yet another review of the CIA's counterintelligence activities.[55]

The value of Cuba's propaganda apparatus is substantiated by Andres Alfaya (also a DGI defector), who has reported that the Cuban news agency *Prensa Latina* is the single most important conduit for Soviet disinformation in the Third World.

The Stage Prepared

Fidel Castro's revolution clearly set the stage for Soviet-Cuban subversion throughout Latin America, especially in Central America and the Caribbean, which are so strategically important to the U.S. While many Americans like to play down the significance of this, arguing that communism is not a particularly important force in the region, Castro has been quite clear about his intentions. "I will pursue to the end the anti-imperialist struggles of the Caribbean peoples," he told a meeting of non-aligned nations.[56] Likewise, the Soviet optimism that the Cuban and Sandinista victories provided, proving that the winds of change were in their sails—even within this hemisphere—was reflected in a 1983 Soviet pamphlet:

> ... the Sandinista revolution, being an integral part of the world revolutionary process, serves as yet one more convincing confirmation of the helplessness of imperialism to restore its lost historic initiative and to turn back the development of the modern world.[57]

The Soviets and Cubans realize that the global triumph envisioned by communist doctrine cannot be achieved overnight, so they are patient, willing to lay the groundwork by seeking to weaken U.S. influence in the region while gradually increasing their own. When opportunities for successful armed revolutions present themselves, the Soviet-Cuban alliance is prepared to take full advantage of them. As Moscow's *New Times* said in November of 1984: "The future belongs to socialism, whose triumphal march on our planet began in Russia in October 1917."[58]

To the extent that socio-economic and political conditions do, in fact, play a significant role in fostering revolutions—by now a dubious proposition at best—the economic, political, and social conditions in Central America and parts of the Caribbean have been ideal for Soviet strategy. Government corruption, the repression of political dissent, and the recession of the early 1980s, which was especially hard on the nations of Central America, have deepened popular dissatisfaction. The fact that communism demonstrably worsens, in every dimension, the lots and lives of its "beneficiaries" remains muted in the debate over the search for difficult solutions to very real problems. Although U.S. intervention in the political, economic, and military affairs of the region was not always benign or well-intentioned, the United States has generally assisted its neighbors and the rest of the world, as well. As Andre Malraux has said: "Never in history has any great power behaved more unselfishly than has the United States." Yet, as one Latin American specialist has observed:

> Many Latin Americans have come to regard world events as a contest between reactionary forces, led by "Yankee imperialism," of which they have had first-hand knowledge, and progressive forces, led, or at least assisted, by the Soviet Union, with which they have no direct experience.[59]

This situation was hardly improved by U.S.–Soviet detente in the 1970s. By improving the Soviet Union's international image, detente served only to increase Soviet influence in the western hemisphere. One indication of this is that in the decade beginning in 1972, scholarships offered to students in Latin America for study in the Soviet bloc increased by 205 percent, even as U.S. government-sponsored scholarships fell by 52 percent (although, as a direct result of the Kissinger Commission report, the Reagan administration, beginning in 1986, reversed that trend). The presence of 675 Costa Rican students in the USSR and Eastern Europe in 1981 attests to the Soviet strategy of exerting communist influence in the region for the long pull.[60]

Moreover, between 1983 and 1985, Soviet-bloc economic aid to Cuba and Nicaragua was more than three times the amount of economic aid provided by the United States to all of Central America. In military aid, the U.S. was outspent by more than three to one. (See figure 1.)

28

FIGURE 1
Economic/Military Regional Aid
The U.S. and the Soviet-Bloc in 1983-85

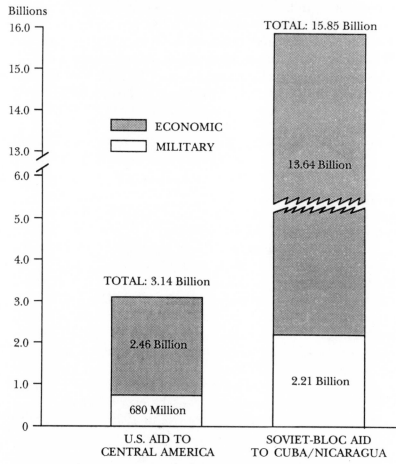

Note: U.S. Aid Figures Include Belize & Panama.

Soviet aid to Cuba and Nicaragua is five times greater than U.S. aid to all of Central America. An investment of this magnitude clearly signals the Soviets' keen interest in this area that is vital to the United States.

Source: U.S. State Department

Grenada and Nicaragua

Grenada is a tiny island on the eastern rim of the Caribbean, about ninety miles off the coast of Venezuela. It is roughly twice the size of Washington, D.C., but has a population of only about a hundred thousand people. Long part of the British empire, Grenada gained full independence in 1974. Strategically, the island is important for its proximity to shipping lanes in the southern Caribbean and to the oil fields of Venezuela (the source of about ten percent of U.S. oil imports as of 1984).

On March 13, 1979, Sir Eric Gairy, Grenada's elected (though corrupt) prime minister was ousted in a nearly bloodless coup by the New Joint Endeavor for Welfare, Education, and Liberation—or New JEWEL Movement. This was a party that had declared the United States "No. 1 enemy" as early as 1976, and whose communist orientation became more and more evident over the next two years. In 1978, the party was reorganized along Leninist principles, later sending a delegation to the founding conference of the Workers' Party of Jamaica, an organization that described itself as the ninety-first member of the Communist International.[61] But taking a lesson from Fidel Castro, the New JEWEL Movement attempted to conceal its colors. "We repeat again," it declared, "that NJM is not a communist party or movement and has no intention of bringing to Grenada what has been called 'Soviet Type' communism—whatever that is."[62]

When New JEWEL seized control in 1979, it did so with the help of a clandestinely organized military wing trained by Cuba and Guyana, and there is strong circumstantial evidence that Cubans and Guyanese actually took part in the coup. Once in power, the party established a People's Revolutionary Government headed by Prime Minister Maurice Bishop, a friend and admirer of Fidel Castro. The new government turned immediately to Cuba and the Soviet bloc for assistance, while still attempting to conceal its true intentions. The Soviets and Cubans were quick to exploit the opportunity. Grenada's 250-man militia was replaced by the People's Revolutionary Army numbering 1,500 to 2,000 soldiers and trained by more than fifty Cuban military advisers.[63]

The first Eastern-bloc arms shipment arrived when the new regime was only a month old: 3,400 rifles, 200 machine guns, 100 heavier weapons, and ammunition.[64]

That same month, *Washington Post* correspondent Karen DeYoung expressed the standard leftist interpretation of the unfolding events:

> Cuban political and military overtures to the Caribbean's newest government has [sic] provoked a strong U.S. diplomatic response that many here believe may succeed only in pushing Grenada farther to the left.[65]

Maurice Bishop and his propagandists actively encouraged this view. For the sake of appearances, he announced at an April 5 press conference that his government would seek arms from the United States, Canada, and the United Kingdom in order to defend itself against any counter-coup attempts, but he refused to issue any specific requests until April 10, by which time secret shipments of Cuban arms had already begun to arrive.[66]

Meanwhile, Bishop had suspended the constitution, given full police powers to the People's Revolutionary Army, and legalized the preventive detention of anyone "likely to endanger the public safety." The government then proceeded to monopolize political power, close the free press, gain control of the trade unions, infuse education with Marxist ideology, establish a socialist economy, and support revolutionary movements throughout the Caribbean.

One of the inevitable results was the destruction of the economy. Foreign exchange earnings from cocoa, the most important cash crop, fell from $10 million in 1979 to $4 million in 1983, and banana production declined from 26,000 tons in 1978 to 9,000 tons in 1983.[67] The government deficit rose from 3.3 percent of gross domestic product in 1978 to 16.1 percent in 1979, and 32.3 percent in 1982. Such difficulties, however, did not prevent the People's Revolutionary Government from steadily pouring 40 to 50 percent of Grenada's capital investment into a new international airport capable of accommodating high-performance military aircraft.[68] This construction project, carried out by Cuban workers, was said to be for the promotion of international tourism, though the island possessed only 300 hotel rooms.

The end of the New JEWEL Movement came quickly in 1983. An internal power struggle had been developing between Bishop and his Deputy Prime Minister, Bernard Coard. Dissatisfied with the failing revolution, Coard partisans advocated strengthening Grenada's already-close relations with Cuba and the USSR. Coard succeeded in ousting the charismatic Bishop and executing him on October 19. What resulted was chaos and civil disorder. All ports of entry and departure were closed. A 24-hour shoot-on-sight curfew was imposed, threatening, among others, the one thousand American citizens residing on the island.

This turn of events, incredibly, has been blamed on the United States. Though the extremist Coard faction had attacked Bishop for being too friendly toward the U.S., *The New York Times* editorialized on October 21:

> The United States' undifferentiated hostility to leftists in this hemisphere, has been rewarded with a hard lurch to the dogmatic and pro-Soviet left. Whether Prime Minister Maurice Bishop's regime could have been lured into moderation will never be known. But his killing suggests the inadequacy of policies that seek to influence leftist regimes by shunning them.

In the midst of the turmoil, Sir Paul Scoon, Grenada's Governor-General, confidentially appealed to the regional states to restore order in his country. The Organization of Eastern Caribbean States then formally requested the assistance of the United States. On October 25, a joint U.S.-Caribbean force landed on the island to evacuate the Americans, depose Coard, and restore order. The invasion forces were greeted as liberators by a wildly enthusiastic populace, 91 percent of whom approved of the American intervention.[69]

What the American forces found on Grenada were vast quantities of arms that were clearly not intended to preserve peace in the Caribbean. They also captured thousands of government documents. Many of these documents have been published by the State Department. They thoroughly demolish the liberal view of Maurice Bishop's regime as "annoying but essentially unthreatening."[70]

The Grenada documents revealed that the New JEWEL Movement had established formal party ties with the communist parties of the Soviet Union and Cuba; that Soviet instructors had assisted the People's Revolutionary Government in conducting a vast "ideological crash course"; that Grenadian officers were sent to the Soviet Union for training; and that Grenada had signed a series of secret military aid agreements providing for the delivery of 50 armored personnel carriers, 50 portable rocket launchers, 60 anti-tank and other heavy guns, 72 mortars, 74 anti-tank grenade launchers, 4,000 submachine guns, and enough uniforms for an army of 6,300.[71] By way of comparison, nearby Barbados, with more than twice Grenada's population, has no army, while Trinidad-Tobago, with ten times Grenada's population, then had fewer than 1,500 in its armed forces, with no heavy equipment or armored vehicles.[72]

Also revealed by the documents was a September 1982 secret speech presented to party regulars, entitled "Line of March for the Party." Maurice Bishop spoke openly of his government's effort to mask its communist ideology:

... the first set of names we announced for the ruling council was fourteen.... And these fourteen names were made up mainly ... of the petty-bourgeoisie, the upper petty-bourgeoisie, and the national bourgeoisie.... And this was done deliberately so that imperialism won't get too excited and would say "well they have some nice fellas in that thing; everything is allright [sic]."

He also made it abundantly clear that no moderates would ever exert any influence in his government:

... while we are in an alliance with sections of the bourgeoisie and upper petty-bourgeoisie, they are not part of our dictatorship. They are not part of our rule and control—they are not part of it. We bring them in for what we want to bring them in for.

In the same speech Bishop commented on the procedure for keeping the populace under control:

... consider how people get detained in this country. We don't go and call for no votes [sic]. You get detained when I sign an order after discussing it with the National Security Committee of the Party or with a higher Party body. Once I sign it—like it or don't like it—it's up the hill for them.

Domestically, the Grenadian government saw the church as a threat and sought to remove from the schools "all deeply religious head teachers." In foreign affairs, the Bishop regime was determined to curry favor with the Soviets. In July 1983, W. Richard Jacobs, the Grenadian ambassador to the Soviet Union, wrote a lengthy report to his government in which he said:

Our revolution has to be viewed as a world-wide process with its original roots in the Great October [1917 Bolshevik] Revolution. . . . We have to establish ourselves as the authority on events in at least the English-speaking Caribbean, and be the sponsor of revolutionary activity and progressive developments in this region at least.

To the extent that we can take credit for bringing any other country into the progressive fold, our prestige and influence would be greatly enhaned [sic].[73]

Regarding the airstrip that was ostensibly being built for commercial use, Bishop's "Outline of Presentation" for a meeting with Soviet Foreign Minister Andrei Gromyko included the phrase, "There is also the strategic factor which is well known!!"[74]

One of the documents offers a particularly pointed statement of Soviet intentions in Central America and the Caribbean. Grenadian Major Einstein Louison reported a conversation that he had, while he was training in Moscow, with Marshal Ogarkov, Chief of the Soviet General Staff. In Louison's reconstruction of the conversation, Ogarkov said that "United States imperialism would try to prevent progress, but that there were no prospects for imperialism to turn back history"; while "Over two decades ago there was only Cuba in Latin America; today there are Nicaragua and Grenada, and a serious battle is going on in El Salvador."[75]

The liberation of Grenada was a major setback for Soviet-Cuban strategy in Latin America. Whether it was a turning point remains to be seen. Castro didn't give up on Grenada. Only one year after the liberation, Cuba and Libya were covertly funding the Maurice Bishop Patriotic Movement.[76] But even if Grenada cannot be reclaimed, Castro can point to a major success in Nicaragua, where Cuban-supplied training, arms, soldiers, and advisers helped put the communist Sandinistas in power in July of 1979, just months after the initial success in Grenada.

Castro himself would boast, and not entirely without reason, that *he* was responsible for revolution in Central America:

> One of the great lies that the imperialists use concerning Central America is their attempt to impute the revolution in this area to the Soviet Union. . . . [The USSR] has had nothing whatsoever to do with Central America. . . . The Soviets did not know even one of the present leaders of Nicaragua . . . during the period of revolutionary struggle. . . . The same holds true for El Salvador. . . . The same goes for Guatemala. . . . We Cubans . . . have relations with the revolutionary movements. We know the revolutionary leaders in the area. I am not going to deny it.[77]

The Soviet-backed Socialist Party of Nicaragua did not support the armed struggle until 1978, shortly before it triumphed. There, as in Cuba before, the Soviets at first grumbled that it should be the Communist Party, and not "an ideologically-suspect band of guerrillas" (the Sandinistas), who should lead the revolution. Indeed, between 1979 and 1982, the Sandinistas got twice as much aid from the U.S. as from the USSR.[78] But, once it was clear that the Sandinistas had consolidated their grip on power, Soviet support, present from the beginning, came cascading in.

Of course, the Soviets were supporting Cuba's interventionist capabilities at the same time that Castro was assisting the Sandinista revolution, so they did share an indirect involvement in the course of events. But it was Castro who saw the potential for armed revolt in Nicaragua in the late 1970s. As one pro-Soviet analyst saw the Central American situation prior to 1978, "none of us would utter an optimistic phrase about the future of that struggle."[79] According to Joseph G. Whelan and Michael Dixon of the Congressional Research Service, "Only after the victory of the Sandinistas in July 1979 did [the Soviets] move from indifference to involvement—and they did so with great speed." They continue, however:

36

For the Soviets the Sandinista victory signalled a new revolutionary upsurge in Latin America and an historic watershed reversing the downturn in Communist fortunes since Allende's overthrow in Chile.[80]

Castro has visited subversion upon virtually the entire western hemisphere (not to mention Africa).[81] But since 1979, increased Soviet interest in the region and the availability of Nicaragua as a communist base on the American mainland have magnified Cuba's effectiveness. There is a real spirit of international cooperation to this communist activity. Veteran Argentine and Chilean guerrillas serve in Nicaraguan camps staffed by Cubans to train guerrillas from El Salvador and elsewhere.[82]

Chief among current targets for revolution are El Salvador, Guatemala, and Honduras. These countries, and their neighbors, are the focus of the chapters to come.

NOTES

1. Joseph Stalin, *Marxism and the National and Colonial Question* (New York: International Publishers), p. 115, in J. Michael Waller, "Soviet Policy in Middle America, 1919–1964: A Coherent Agenda Succeeds," unpublished study, December 1984.

2. Morris Rothenberg, "The Soviets and Central America," in *Central America: Anatomy of Conflict*, Robert S. Leiken, ed. (New York: Pergamon Press, 1984), pp. 141–142.

3. W. Bruce Weinrod, "Thirty Myths About Nicaragua," *The Heritage Lectures*: 54 (Washington: The Heritage Foundation), 1986, p. 2.

4. Marc Liebman, in *Armed Forces Journal* for July 1987, quoted in *Conservative Manifesto*, #81, September 1987, pp. 1–2. That same report notes that another flight plan regularly followed by Soviet Bear aircraft is down the west coast of Africa to refueling facilities in Angola. From there, they patrol the South Atlantic or around the Cape of Good Hope to cover sectors in the Indian Ocean, returning either via Angola or the Soviet base at Cam Ranh Bay in Vietnam. The four-engine turboprop planes have a range of more than 9,000 nautical miles. The report

notes that the Nicaraguan base would also enable those planes to fly from Nicaragua on a different mission, either transiting the Pacific Ocean across Micronesia, passing by U.S. bases in Guam and the Philippines before landing at Cam Ranh Bay, or down either coast of South America and then back to either Nicaragua or Cuba.

5. Morris Rothenberg, "The Soviets and South America," pp. 146–147. Rothenberg cites A. Glinken and P. Yakolev, "Latin America in the Global Strategy of Imperialism," *Morivaia Ekonomika i Mezh: dunarodnye Otnosheniia*, October 1982, p. 79.

6. Gary Lee, "Moscow Seeks Closer Latin Relations; Shevardnadze Begins Week-Long Tour of South America," *The Washington Post*, Sept. 27, 1987, p. A-26.

7. Cited by Joseph Cirincione and Leslie C. Hunter, in "Military Threats, Actual and Potential," *Central America: Anatomy of Conflict*, pp. 179–180.

8. Lionel Gomez, "Feet People," *Central America: Anatomy of Conflict*, op. cit., p. 219. He quotes from a Lou Cannon article in *The Washington Post*, "A Latin Axis Could Take Central America, Reagan Says," June 21, 1983, p. A1.

9. See Howard J. Wirada, "The Origins of the Crisis in Central America," *Rift and Revolution: The Central American Imbroglio*, Howard J. Wiarda, ed. (Washington: American Enterprise Institute for Public Policy Research, 1984), pp. 13–18.

10. V. I. Lenin, *Collected Works*, Vol. 24, quoted in *War and Peace: Soviet Russia Speaks*, Albert L. Weeks and William C. Bodie, eds. (New York: National Strategy Information Center, 1983), p. 32.

11. J. Michael Waller, "Soviet Policy in Middle America, 1919–1964: A Coherent Agenda Succeeds," unpublished study, December 1984, pp. 3–4.

12. *Ally Betrayed: Nicaragua*, Western Goals Foundation (Alexandria, Virginia, 1980), p. 6, in J. Michael Waller, *Consolidating the Revolution* (Washington: Council for Inter-American Security, 1986), p. 5.

13. John J. Tierney, Jr., *Somozas and Sandinistas: The U.S. and Nicaragua in the Twentieth Century* (Washington: Council for Inter-American Security, 1982), p. 22.

14. Thomas P. Anderson, *Matanza: El Salvador's Communist Revolt of 1932* (Lincoln, Nebraska: University of Nebraska Press, 1971), p. 25, in Waller, "Soviet Policy," p. 9.

15. Waller, pp. 9–10. The "three thousand pounds" figure was reported on December 22, 1931, by Major A. R. Harris, who is quoted by Anderson, p. 83; in Waller, "Soviet Policy," p. 10.

16. O. Rodriguez, "The Uprising in El Salvador," *Communist*, March 1932; in Waller, "Soviet Policy," p. 11.

17. Otto Kuusinen, "Report of the Commission for Work Among the Masses," from the 1926 Session of the Executive Committee for the Comintern, *Inprecor*, No. 28, p. 429; in Waller, *Consolidating*, p. 4.

18. Waller, "Soviet Policy," p. 16.

19. Daniel James, *Red Design for the Americas: Guatemalan Prelude* (New York: John Day, 1954), p. 72.

20. Waller, "Soviet Policy," p. 19

21. James, p. 202; see also pp. 69–70.

22. Ibid., p. 137.

23. L. Francis Bouchey and Alberto M. Piedra, *Guatemala: A Promise in Peril* (Washington: Council for Inter-American Security, 1980), pp. 16, 17.

24. Ronald M. Schneider, *Communism in Guatemala, 1944–1954* (New York: Praeger, 1958), pp. 274–275, in Waller, *Consolidating*, p. 7.

25. Bouchey and Piedra, *Guatemala,* pp. 19–20.

26. Bouchey and Piedra, pp. 19–20.

27. Carlos Franqui, *Family Portrait with Fidel*, trans. Alfred MacAdam (New York: Vintage, 1985), p. 159.

28. Barbara Walters, "An Interview with Fidel Castro," *Foreign Policy*, No. 28, Fall 1977, p. 32, in *The Soviet-Cuban Connection in Central America and the Caribbean*, p. 6, as reproduced in *Background Paper: Nicaragua's Military Build-Up and Support for Central American Subversion* (Washington, D.C.: U.S. Defense Department, 1984).

29. Rolondo Bonachea, "United States Policy Toward Cuba, 1959–1961," doctoral dissertation, Georgetown University, 1974, in *The Soviet-Cuban Connection in Central America and the Caribbean*, p. 4.

30. Broadcast on Madrid Domestic Service, January 5, 1984. Source: *Foreign Broadcast Information Service (FBIS)*, Latin America, January 9, 1984, p. Q4, in *The Soviet-Cuban Connection in Central America and the Caribbean*, p. 4.

31. Waller, "Soviet Policy," p. 24.

32. Joseph G. Whelan and Michael J. Dixon, *The Soviet Union in the Third World: Threat to World Peace?* (Washington: Pergamon-Brassey, 1986), p. 308. (Joseph G. Whelan is not related to James R. Whelan, co-author of this book).

33. From 1959-1979, the Russians supplied Castro with $16 billion in economic aid. In the three years following the triumph of the Sandinistas in Nicaragua, Soviet aid to Cuba was $14 billion. In an interesting essay arguing that Castro is now the tail that wags the Soviet dog in

western hemisphere tactical affairs, David Brooks says that the dramatic increase in aid to Cuba reflects grudging Kremlin recognition that Castro was right, and they were wrong: Violence is indispensable for the revolution to triumph in Latin America. David Brooks, "Latin America Is Not East of Here," *National Review*, March 14, 1986, p. 33.

34. Whelan and Dixon, p. 309. Figures on Cuba's armaments—as those for every aspect of life on what is, after all, an island shrouded in secrecy—vary widely. For example, Sen. D. Bennett Johnston, Jr., in a 1984 debate in Congress, put Cuba's armed forces at 153,000; armament at 250 aircraft and 850 heavy tanks; and defense spending of $1.3 billion. Debate on the Senate floor, Oct. 11, 1984, *Congressional Record - Senate*, p. 341. Two other researchers—drawing on *Military Balance, 1983-1984*, International Institute for Strategic Studies, London—give the same number for regular forces (153,000), but put reserves at 193,000 and the militia at 500,000. They also give 250 as the number of MIG-21 and MIG-23 fighters and 800 as the number of tanks, but put the number of Soviet military advisers at 2,400. Joseph Cirincione and Leslie C. Hunter, "Military Threats, Actual and Potential," *Central America: Anatomy of Conflict*, p. 173. Per capita figures are from *The World Almanac and Book of Facts, 1987* (New York: Pharos Books, 1986), p. 562 (1983 estimate).

35. *Background Notes: Cuba*, U.S. Department of State, August 1985, p. 7.

36. Three sources: ibid., p. 6; *The Challenge to Democracy in Central America*, U.S. Departments of State and Defense, June 1986, p. 8; *The Soviet-Cuban Connection in Central America*, p. 6.

37. *The Challenge to Democracy in Central America*, p. 10.

38. For example, the 1970 promise to service nuclear submarines in Cuban ports. See Christopher Whalen, "The Soviet Military Build-Up in Cuba," Heritage Foundation *Backgrounder* No. 189, June 11, 1982, p. 4.

39. Senator Johnston, op. cit. Johnston listed Afghanistan, Algeria, Angola, Benin, Cape Verde, Congo-Brazzaville, Ethiopia, Guinea, Guinea-Bissau, Iraq, Lesotho, Libya, Madagascar, Mozambique, Nicaragua, Nigeria, Sao Tome/Principe, Sierra Leone, Surinam, Syria, Tanzania, Uganda, Yemen, and Zambia. Cirincione and Hunter, "Military Threats," p. 175, give the number of Cuban troops serving abroad in 1983 as 40,000.

40. *Background Notes: Cuba*, pp. 5–6; and *The Soviet-Cuban Connection in Central America and the Caribbean*, p. 4.

41. For 1959–1984 per capita comparison, Senator Johnston, op. cit. Because Cuba—in common with many other Soviet bloc countries—does not provide statistical data to such standard source agencies as the World Bank, the International Monetary Fund, and the like, one must

apply special care in handling economic statistics. For pre-revolutionary Cuba, see, among other sources, Lowry Nelson, *Cuba: The Measure of Revolution* (Minneapolis: University of Minnesota Press, 1972), pp. 44–46. Lowry observes that in 1959, Cuba's average daily food consumption, per capita, was third in Latin America behind only agriculturally rich Argentina and Uruguay; Cuba already ranked third in literacy, and its steady growth gave it "probably the strongest middle class in Latin America" in relation to population. Disparities, problems there were; but the country was then on a sharp ascendant.

42. R. Bruce McColm, "Revolution's End" (an interview with Carlos Franqui), *The American Spectator*, Vol. 13, No. 5 (May 1980), p. 10.

43. Both quotations from Paul Hollander, "Political Tourism in Cuba and Nicaragua," *Society*, May–June 1986, pp. 28, 30. The writer of the letter is not named.

44. Armando Valladares, *Against All Hope: The Prison Memoirs of Armando Valladares*, trans. Andrew Hurley (New York: Alfred A. Knopf, 1986), p. 5.

45. Norman Kempster, "U.S. Curbs Cuban Migration, Trade," *The Los Angeles Times*, Aug. 23, 1986, p. 1.

46. Dan Williams, "Cuba Troubled by Political Shifts, Economic Hard Times," a Havana-datelined dispatch in *The Los Angeles Times*, Aug. 16, 1987, p. 8. Williams reported on an interview Castro had given a short time before to the French Communist Party newspaper, *L'Humanite*. In it, Castro said, "we are willing to let all those who want to leave the country do it." A few days later, taking Castro at his word, hundreds began gathering at the French Embassy to request visas. Several dozen were arrested, their heads shaved in jail, then released; the others were dispersed by police. Nonetheless, Williams said foreign observers believed Castro might be about to trigger another exodus such as the chaotic boat lift he set off in 1980 from the port city of Mariel, when 125,000 persons (many from the island's jail and lunatic asylums) swarmed to the United States.

47. McColm, "Revolution's End," p. 10.

48. James Reston, "Radical Latin Reds Open Havana Parley," *The New York Times*, Aug. 1, 1967, p. 9, in Waller, *Consolidating*, p. 9.

49. Jiri and Virginia Valenta, "Soviet Strategy and Policies in the Caribbean Basin," *Rift and Revolution: The Central American Imbroglio*, Howard J. Wirada, ed. (Washington: American Enterprise Institute for Public Policy Studies, 1984), p. 206.

50. Brooks in *National Review*, p. 33.

51. Whelan and Dixon, *The Soviet Union*, pp. 317–18.

52. Rothenberg, *Central America: Anatomy of Conflict*, op. cit., p. 145.

53. Whelan and Dixon, *The Soviet Union,* p. 316 (Castro's maneuvering); and Hollander, "Political Tourism," p. 32 (automobiles).

54. *The Economist,* "That Man in Havana," Sept. 26, 1987, p. 113. The reviews themselves, it should be noted, were remarkably uncritical of and sympathetic to Castro, reflecting a growing dichotomy between the level-headedness of the front of that magazine and the "leftism" of the back-of-the-book softer sections (such as "Books and Arts"), a distressingly familiar syndrome in publications.

55. Michael Wines and Ronald J. Ostrow, "U.S. Duped by Cuban Agents, Defector Says," *The Los Angeles Times,* Aug. 11, 1987. Azpillaga, described by one U.S. intelligence source as "a gold mine" of information, was the second senior official to defect to the U.S. in the space of a few months. In late May, Brig. Gen. Rafael del Pino Diaz, high-ranking Air Force official, flew to exile in Florida with his family in a light plane.

56. Jeane J. Kirkpatrick, "U.S. Security and Latin America," *Rift and Revolution,* p. 330.

57. Rothenberg, *Central America,* p. 133. Rothenberg cites I. M. Buylychev, *Nicaragua Today* (Moscow: Mezhdunarodnye Otnosheniia, 1983), p. 13. In Whelan and Dixon, 365.

58. In Whelan and Dixon, *The Soviet Union,* p. 365.

59. Robert S. Leiken, then a senior fellow at the Carnegie Endowment for International Peace, quoted in Whelan and Dixon, *The Soviet Union,* 258.

60. Fred M. Hechinger, "Latin Region Focus of Aid by East Bloc," *The New York Times,* Sept. 5, 1985, p. C10. Figure for Costa Ricans in Rothenberg, "The Soviets and Central America," op. cit., p. 145. Spending on the Fulbright program in Central America went from a low of under $500,000 in fiscal year 1984 to an all-time high of $18 million in fiscal year 1986.

61. Gregory Sandford, *The New JEWEL Movement: Grenada's Revolution* (Washington: Foreign Service Institute, U.S. Department of State, 1985), pp. 48, 30, 31.

62. "The People's Alliance: NJM's Reply," in Sandford, *The New JEWEL,* p. 31.

63. Jiri and Virginia Valenta, "Soviet Strategy," p. 220.

64. The Soviet-Cuban Connection in Central America and the Caribbean, p. 14.

65. Karen DeYoung, "U.S. vs. Cuba on Caribbean Isle of Grenada," *The Washington Post,* April 27, 1979, p. A27, in *Lessons of Grenada,* U.S. State Department, 1986, p. 4.

The Assault

66. Sandford, *The New JEWEL*, pp. 45–48.

67. Timothy Ashby, "The Grenada Rescue Mission Is Not Over," Heritage Foundation *Backgrounder* No. 380 (September 19, 1984), p. 2.

68. Sandford, *The New JEWEL*, pp. 91–92.

69. CBS-*New York Times* poll, cited in *Lessons of Grenada* (Department of State, 1986), p. 11. A poll taken three months later showed 75 percent of Grenadians in favor of making Grenada part of the United States (Ashby, "The Grenada Rescue Mission Is Not Over," p. 3).

70. *The New York Times*, editorial, October 21, 1983, p. A34, in *Lessons of Grenada*, p. 4.

71. Whelan and Dixon, *The Soviet Union*, p. 346.

72. Trevor N. Dupuy, Grace P. Hayes, John A. C. Andrews, *The Almanac of World Military Power*, 4th ed., by Gay Hammerman (San Rafael, CA: Presidio Press, 1980), p. 67 (Barbados); and Adrian J. English, *Armed Forces of Latin America: Their Histories, Development, Present Strength and Military Potential* (London: Jane's, 1984), pp. 420–21 (Trinidad-Tobago).

73. Department of State, *Grenada Documents: An Overview and Selection*, September 1984, pp. 1:19, 1:25, 5:5, 26:6.

74. *The Soviet-Cuban Connection in Central America and the Caribbean*, p. 13.

75. *Grenada Documents*, pp. 24:2.

76. Ashby, "The Grenada Rescue Mission Is Not Over," p. 6.

77. Quoted by Brooks, *National Review*, p. 32. As Brooks notes, Castro "exaggerates, as is his wont." Brooks then goes on to argue that the Soviet Union does not pose the most serious threat to U.S. interests in Latin America—"Cuba does." The basis for the argument is that Castro has persuaded the Soviets that he knows more about what works in the hemisphere than the Soviets do—his *via insurreccional* or *via armada* work, *via pacifica* has failed—and thus he is in charge. Brooks also argues in this article that Castro is considerably more independent of the Soviets than most are willing to imagine, and that if the U.S. is to deal effectively with the threat to our security in this hemisphere, we must go to the source of the problem, and the source is Cuba. The problem with that line of reasoning is that, however cantankerously independent and irksome Castro might be to the Soviets, he is dependent on them and cannot support and promote violence, subversion and terrorism without them. Whereas it may be true that the Salvadorans, Sandinistas and other guerrillas may not have been properly introduced in Moscow until Castro intervened, they all of them knew full well about Moscow, they knew full well where the real power and money came from, and, indeed, it would be Moscow's support—and not Castro's—which would enable them to become the revolutionary "successes" they would, once in power.

78. Ibid., p. 33.

79. Nikolai Leonov, "Nicaragua, experiencia de una revolucion victoriosa," *America Latina*, No. 3 (1980), p. 37, quoted by Robert Leiken, "Fantasies and Facts: The Soviet Union and Nicaragua," *Current History*, October 1984, p. 316.

80. Whelan and Dixon, *The Soviet Union*, p. 323.

81. "Cuba's Role as an Agent of Soviet-sponsored Subversion and Terrorism," an annotated map published in *West Watch* Vol. IX, No. 3 (April 1986), pp. 4–5, itemizes Cuba's subversive activities in sixty-one countries around the world, including thirty in the western hemisphere and twenty-three in Africa.

82. *Background Paper: Nicaragua's Military Build-Up and Support for Central American Subversion*, U.S. Department of Defense, July, 1984, p. 14.

2

The Way They Were*

THE five Central American countries—Costa Rica, El Salvador, Guatemala, Honduras and Nicaragua—have among them only 23.5 million people, which is considerably fewer than California's 26.4 million. In size, they are only 10 percent larger than California (170,000 square miles versus 156,300 for California), and the largest among them (Nicaragua, 57.1 thousand square miles) is not quite so large as the twenty-first U.S. state in size, Georgia.

Yet these five countries are, today, a powder keg threatening America's southern flank more seriously—and enduringly—than any menace ever before faced on that flank. Furthermore, this is a powder keg wedged between the vital Panama Canal to the south, and, to the north, Mexico's immense Campeche oil fields (at the northern point, only seven hundred and fifty miles removed from our Texas oil fields).

* (The material in chapters two, three, and four was adapted, with permission of the publisher, from *Catastrophe in the Caribbean: The Failure of America's Human Rights Policy in Central America*, Jameson Books, Ottawa, IL).

The keg is, for the most part, a product of the centuries—the imperfections of man compounded by the cruelties of nature.

The powder for the explosion has come, and continues to come, from ever-bolder Marxist revolutionaries, aided and abetted for many years by Soviet surrogate Fidel Castro, and more recently by the Sandinistas in Nicaragua.

The fuse, incredibly, was provided by the Carter administration, by a State Department which lurched in its policies between doctrinaire and outdated "leftism" and what Henry Kissinger described as "starting our own anti-American revolution."

The special tragedy of this new menace to American security—and the well-being of those twenty million Central Americans—is the contrast between the way they were before Jimmy Carter stumbled into the presidency without adequate knowledge, background, experience, or even sizable public support, and the shambles that those countries are today.

In 1977, as Jimmy Carter assumed the presidency, the five Central American countries were stable, prospering, progressive—and firmly allied to the United States.

In 1977, the Carter administration targeted one of them, El Salvador, for ostracism under its brand new "human rights" policy, and in 1978, it marked two more Central American countries for American wrath—Guatemala and Nicaragua.

The Carter administration did not, of course, cause Central America to disintegrate so rapidly, so ominously. But its policies, particularly in Nicaragua and El Salvador, were decisive catalysts. They fanned a flame that is now threatening to consume the surrounding area, licking away at one country after another.

Domingo Faustino Sarmiento, the distinguished Argentine statesman and educator of the past century once observed that "Central America has made a sovereign state of each village." Sarmiento exaggerated, but unruly factionalism did destroy the three federations actually forged during the last century binding all (at times; most, at others) of the five countries together. It is also true that rivalries—mainly among the caudillos who have mostly ruled these five countries—frequently saw neighbor pitted against neighbor.

A recent variation on that theme saw the Somozas in Nicaragua locked in long and implacable hostility toward Jose (Pepe) Figueres Ferrer, the father of Costa Rica's democracy. The Costa Ricans would later retaliate for Somocista-backed incursions against their government by allowing their territory to be used by the Sandinista guerrillas fighting Somoza (but not, later, by the freedom fighters opposing the Sandinista dictatorship).

Another deeply destructive rivalry was the 1969 "soccer war" between El Salvador and Honduras, a feud that nearly tore the booming Central American Common Market (CACM) asunder. That confrontation, long simmering and slow healing, was triggered not by personal or even ideological differences, but by a growing resentment in land-rich and underpopulated Honduras over a rising tide of illegal immigrants from land-poor and super-populated El Salvador.[1]

Still, the main trend in the seventies had been toward integration, a trend reflecting the inescapable reality that these five states are inextricably bound together by geography as well as by history and heritage. The main impetus came from the Common Market, founded in 1962, followed over the years by a multitude of accords that included a regional bank for funding area economic development. Common strategies were worked out in such areas as tourism, highways, and communications. Tariffs were progressively lowered. As regional trade steadily expanded, whole new industries sprang up, particularly in Costa Rica, El Salvador, and Guatemala.[2]

That trend toward integration halted in 1979. First came the Nicaraguan civil war and the renewed tension between Nicaragua and Costa Rica. Following the overthrow of

Anastasio Somoza Debayle on July 19, 1979, Nicaragua became an anemic trading partner, and because of cramping socialistic measures and reliance on nonregional credits to shore up its crippled economy, perforce turned to non-CACM suppliers. Next, on October 15, 1979, came the U.S.-supported coup in El Salvador, and the anarchy that ensued. But either of these events might have been a mere reverse were it not for the ideological war that has been unleashed in the region, dividing it more sharply—and perhaps more nearly irreparably—than at any time since the bloody and cataclysmic civil war (1826–31) during the first days of post-independence federation.

Against this backdrop, let us turn here and in the ensuing chapter to an inspection of each of those four claims—stable, prospering, progressive, firm allies—as they applied in 1977.

"Stable"

In Costa Rica elections every four years replaced coups as a way of political life in 1948. There was, in 1977, still no hint of the serious economic problems ahead, and Costa Rica had not yet been put on the Marxist hit list.

In El Salvador, elections had been held every five years beginning in 1962. There were, to be sure, irregularities and widespread claims of fraud, particularly in the 1972 and 1977 elections. But there were no violent revolutions or palace coups until the U.S.-supported (and, in large measure, U.S.-instigated) ouster of a constitutional president on October 15, 1979. He was replaced by a military-dominated regime, followed in short order by a new military-dominated junta, and more recently by an elected but eviscerated civilian government.

In Guatemala, elections had been held every four years since 1966 until a coup in 1982, and another in August 1983.

To the charge that Guatemala was ruled by a "military government," it is useful to observe that all three candidates, of all three parties—Right, Center, and Left—were drawn from the military in the elections. This reflects the reality that in Guatemala, as in much of Latin America, the military is the only organized, cohesive, and nationwide force in the land. An observation made by the distinguished political scientist Amos Perlmutter about Peru applies with equal force to Guatemala: "In the absence of stable patrimonial rule, the military became the major recruiting ground for the presidency."[3] Furthermore, inasmuch as these military figures have presided over thoroughly civilian governments, the pejorative term "military government" might as easily and aptly be applied to, say, the past U.S. governments of Eisenhower, Grant, Jackson, and Washington, among others.

In Honduras, the poorest and most violence-prone of the Central American countries, there were three coups during the 1970s. All were of the palace variety, and none affected the general calm of the country. (But then, two-thirds of Honduras's population is rural, and it is by now a commonplace of history—obvious, it would appear, to all but unread ideologues—that peasants neither start nor shape insurgencies, nor are they even notably responsive to the siren songs of revolution.) Doubtless spurred by the upheavals in neighboring lands and by three consecutive years of solid and impressive economic growth, Honduras's military overlords permitted elections in April 1980 to select a Constituent Assembly. The elections were so free that they were won, narrowly, by the opposition Liberal party. The Constituent Assembly, in turn, created the mechanisms for electing a president.

In Nicaragua, it is true that three consecutive Somozas ruled the country, directly or indirectly, from 1934 to 1979. But it is also true that the last of the Somozas returned to power in 1974 (after rewriting the constitution to enable him to do so) in elections observed by the Organization of American States (OAS) and adjudged clean and honest by most observers at that time. Those who charged that the elections were "unfair" did so because much of the opposition chose to abstain. But in this regard, it must be noted that (a) Somoza's "popularity," his ability to sweep any elections in that country at that time, could not be seriously disputed; (b) those elections were at least as "fair" as those in a number of countries with which the Carter administration maintained cordial relations—Mexico, for example, where the PRI has won *every* national election for the past fifty-nine years, because no serious opposition is permitted; (c) the absence of opposition in, say, the states of the U.S. Deep South did not (until recent years) stir heated tirades about the lack of democracy in the U.S.A. It is also important to remember that in 1981, Nicaraguans would have had a chance to elect a new president in a country by then certainly far more advanced economically and politically than most others in the Third World; instead, it is now an economic basket case and political corpse. As to the danger of civil war, in 1977, the Sandinistas, whose hard core never numbered more than three hundred, were a weak and scattered group. Their top leader, Carlos Fonseca Amador, was killed that year, and another top commander, Tomas Borge, was in jail.

Not a perfect panorama, of course. But there *was* stability, an atmosphere in which nations progress; without which, they cannot.

One other aspect of Central America's relative political stability bears noting, and that is the high degree of progress these countries had made (pre-Carter) in their political development. The Alliance for Progress, the most massive and concerted attack ever on Latin America's ills, made the development of democratic institutions its very first goal. When the Alliance began, in 1961, only one dictatorship survived on the entire South American continent. In Central America, three of the five countries were under democratic governments. The time was hailed as the "twilight of the tyrants." It would be a short-lived twilight.

Over the next eight years, no fewer than sixteen Latin governments fell in military coups. By the end of the decade, democratic government had collapsed in the biggest country (Brazil) and two of the most enlightened (Argentina and Uruguay). Democracy survived, in fact, in only three of the ten South American republics. In 1970, Chile—the toast of the Alliance, the country that had most closely adhered to the social-engineering prescriptions of the Alliance—would become the first free country in the world to elect a Marxist government, an event that would end three years later in the economic and political ruin of the country.

By contrast the record of the Central American countries was encouraging. In each, the elections, the political processes, the democratic institutions, were far from perfect. About *as* imperfect, say, as they were during the formative years of American democracy, when bosses ruled big cities and government power frequently was used to "repress" striking workers and others. The solution, it was generally held, was to improve our democracy, not discard it. Yet that is precisely what the Carter administration urged in Central America—the aborting of the evolutionary process leading to democratic development.

"Prospering"

The Central American countries did not move in lockstep on economic matters, any more than they did on political or social ones, and so outcomes were uneven. Two general observations do, however, apply: (1) The five were, until the mid-1960s, among the most backward countries in all of Latin America;[4] (2) they had, until recently, made faster progress in solving their economic problems than all but a few other Latin American countries, particularly in the years before Carter's ministrations. On two key indicators—percentage increase of domestic product and percentage increase of per capita income—four of the five Central American countries outpaced Latin America as a whole in 1976; all five exceeded the overall Latin American averages in 1977 (see table 1). (The purpose of this chapter is to show how the five countries were faring—politically, economically, socially—in 1977. Statistics reflecting their more recent realities are included as Appendix I, using, wherever possible, the same sources as those used for tables 1 through 11. In addition, more recent developments in all of those areas are discussed in detail in the individual country sections of chapter five, "Central America Today.")

Central America's solid growth gains can be seen even more concretely in table 2, which shows the gross domestic product for each of the five countries for the years 1974 through 1977, and those of Latin America as a whole for the same years.

Furthermore, Central America achieved its solid economic gains with less inflation[5] and less borrowing[6] than the rest of Latin America.

TABLE 1
Percentage Increases in Gross Domestic Product and
Per Capita Income, 1976 and 1977
(In 1970 U.S. Dollars)

	GDP		Per Capita	
	1976	1977	1976	1977
Costa Rica	4.3	6.9	1.8	4.4
El Salvador	4.7	5.5	1.7	2.4
Guatemala	7.6	8.5	4.4	5.3
Honduras	8.0	7.5	4.4	3.8
Nicaragua	5.2	5.5	1.8	2.1
Latin America	4.5	4.4	1.6	1.6

Source: *"Estudio Económico de América Latina,* 1977," Comisión Económica para América Latina, Naciones Unidas (Santiago, Chile, 1978), p. 15.

TABLE 2
Gross Domestic Product
(In Millions, 1976 Dollars)

	1974	1975	1976	1977	% Increase* 1977 over 1974
Costa Rica	1,924.8	1,965.3	2,073.7	2,234.6	21.2
El Salvador	2,243.4	2,368.2	2,461.5	2,589.4	15.4
Guatemala	4,672.3	4,763.4	5,115.3	5,542.5	18.6
Honduras	1,270.2	1,250.2	1,342.6	1,436.6	6.0
Nicaragua	1,729.9	1,767.9	1,866.6	1,980.8	14.5
Latin America	301,764.8	310,969.6	325,493.2	340,064.7	12.6

Source: *Economic and Social Progress in Latin America, 1978 Report,* Inter-American Development Bank (Washington, D.C., 1979), p. 420.
* Figures extrapolated from CDP figures.

A final word, before passing on to performance on social issues. In the latter half of the 1960s, it was a fashionable conceit that held that the countries with the fastest growth rates were actually widening the gap between rich and poor. (At that time, the country with the fastest growth rate in the hemisphere was Brazil; but Brazil, autocratic Brazil, was bounding ahead along a capitalist path under military rule, and not according to the doctrines of the social engineers, and so Brazil had to be "saved," which meant the military sent back to their barracks, statist economics resurrected. Less than two years of that democratic "enlightenment" has again reduced Brazil to a state of acute crisis.) The conceit gained special impetus early in the 1970s, when it was enshrined in the annual report of World Bank President Robert Strange McNamara. That conceit was punctured fairly decisively in an article in the September 1974 issue of *Finance and Development,* the quarterly published by the International Monetary Fund. The article, titled "Income Equality: Some Dimensions of the Problem," reported on a study done by the World Bank's Development Research Center and the Institute of

Development Studies at Sussex, England, and included the following observation: "The cross-section evidence does not support the view that a high rate of economic growth has an adverse effect upon relative equality. Quite the contrary, the rate of growth of GDP in our sample was positively related to the share of the lowest 40 percent, suggesting that the objectives of growth and equity may not be in conflict."

As the following section will demonstrate, rapid development was, in fact, bringing a better life to an ever-expanding number of inhabitants of Central America. Seeing that real record of achievement against the backdrop of an earlier ideological dogfight is relevant only because the Carter architects of American policy in Central America resurrected so many other hoary shibboleths from the dustbins of the sixties.

"Progressive"

Progressive is a word that has been expropriated by the Left, a buzzword reserved for those policies, programs, people, and regimes they approve of—no matter how destructive of life, limb, or "progress" they may in fact be. In applying this much-maligned word to the countries of Central America, we have something specific in mind for it—that it describe policies, programs, people, or even regimes that in fact brought better lives, political and material, to ever-expanding numbers of their inhabitants, at a pace far better and faster than that of most other developing nations. If they did so, we do not postulate them for canonization, or assert that they achieved the millennium, or even argue that they did the impossible—only that they were "progressive."

The record, we believe, supports the assertion that the countries of Central America were on a clearly progressive track before 1977. Since then, one way or the other, they have had to give far higher priority to the simple matter of survival.

Life itself is, of course, the most basic "human right." For those struggling to be born and stay alive, for those already alive who would like to live longer, the five Central American countries were answering the summons. By 1978, all five had added at least five years to the life expectancy of their inhabitants in the span of a single decade, doing better in this respect than all but one other of the nineteen Latin American countries. One of them, Nicaragua, compiled the best record among the nineteen in reducing infant mortality during that period, and all five were among the pacesetters of the region. The five were also among the leaders in reducing the death rates in their countries, as tables 3 and 4 demonstrate. Central America as a whole had traditionally lagged behind Latin America as a whole in literacy. During this same span, literacy rates in those countries were, however, boosted dramatically (see table 5).

These improvements came about because, from the very earliest days of the Alliance for Progress, the governments of Central America devoted a higher percentage of their gross national products and national budgets to education than did

TABLE 3

Pacesetters Among 19 Latin American Countries on Basis of Improvement in Key Health Indicators, from Mid- or Late-1960s to Mid- or Late-1970s (see details in Table 4)

Life Expectancy	Infant Mortality	Death Rates
1. Dominican Republic	1. NICARAGUA	1. Panama
2. GUATEMALA	2. Dominican Republic	2. Dominican Republic
3. Ecuador	3. COSTA RICA	3. COSTA RICA
4. EL SALVADOR	4. Chile	4. HONDURAS
5. HONDURAS	5. Panama	5. Paraguay
6. NICARAGUA,	6. Colombia	6. Peru
COSTA RICA	7. GUATEMALA	7. Chile
	8. HONDURAS	8. EL SALVADOR
		9. GUATEMALA
	12. EL SALVADOR	
		19. NICARAGUA

55

TABLE 4
Key Health Indicators

	Life Expectancy (number years at year of birth)			Infant Mortality (per 1,000 live births)			Death Rates (per 1,000 inhabitants)		
	Year[a]	Year[b]	Change in Years[c]	Year[a]	Year[b]	% Change[c]	Year[a]	Year[b]	% Change[c]
Argentina	1967 66.3	'75–'78 68.2	+1.9	1968 54.9	1970 60.1	– 9.4	1968 8.5	'75–80 8.8	– 3.5
Bolivia	1970 53.0	'70–75 48.2	–4.8	1968 89.0	'70–75 16.1	–89.8	1970 13.0	'70–75 18.0	–38.0
Brazil	1970 65.4	'75–80 63.4	–2.0	1970 85–95	1977 95–100	– 5.8	1970 9.1	'75–80 7.9	+13.1
Chile	1968 62.0	'75–80 64.4	+2.4	1968 78.7	1978 39.7	+49.5	1968 8.9	1978 6.8	+23.5
Colombia	1967 60.9	'75–80 63.4	+2.5	1967 78.3	1976 59.6	+23.8	1967 9.4	1976 7.4	+21.2
COSTA RICA	'65–70 66.8	'75–80 71.8	+5.0	1968 56.2	1977 27.8	+50.5	1968 6.5	1977 4.2	+35.3
Dominican Rep.	1969 52.0	1978 61.2	+9.2	1969 63.9	1978 29.5	+53.8	1969 7.0	1978 4.5	+35.7
Ecuador	1969 55.0	1978 62.1	+7.1	1969 86.1	1977 71.5	+16.9	1969 10.8	1975 10.7	+ 0.09
EL SALVADOR	1968 56.3	'75–80 62.2	+5.9	1969 63.8	1977 59.5	+ 6.7	1969 9.9	1977 7.8	+ 2.2

	Col 1	Col 2	Change	Col 4	Col 5	Change	Col 7	Col 8	Change
GUATEMALA	*1968* 48.8	*'75–'80* 57.8	+9	*1968* 93.8	*1977* 76.0	+18.9	*1968* 13.3	*1977* 10.8	+18.7
Haiti	*1969* 50.0	*'75–'80* 52.2	+2.2	*1969* 146.5	*1977* 141.1	+ 0.3	*1969* 16.9	*1977* 14.5	+14.2
HONDURAS	*'65–'70* 48.9	*1978* 54.1	+5.2	*1969* 34.0	*'78(p)* 28.0	+17.6	*1969* 8.5	*1978* 5.5	+35.2
Mexico	*1970* 63.0	*1978* 64.0	+1	*1969* 65.8	*1978* 56.0	+14.8	*1969* 9.2	*1978* 8.5	+ 7.6
NICARAGUA	*'65–'70* 50.2	*'75–'80* 55.2	+5	*1967* 52.4	*1976* 12.3	+76.5	*1967* 7.7	*'75–'80* 12.2	−58.4
Panama	*1968* 67.3	*'75–'80* 67.9	+0.6	*1969* 40.8	*1978* 24.8	+39.2	*1969* 7.3	*1978* 4.1	+43.8
Paraguay	*1968* 59.5	*'70–'75* 61.9	+2.4	*1968* 72.0	*1974* 84.2	−16.9	*1968* 11.0	*1978* 8.1	+26.3
Peru	*1968* 55.0	*1978* 57.2	+2.2	*1968* 105.6	*1978* 100.7	+ 4.6	*1968* 16.0	*1978* 11.8	+26.2
Uruguay	*1968* 68.4	*1978* 72.0	+3.6	*1967* 49.8	*1978* 48.6	+ 2.4	*1967* 9.2	*1978* 8.5	+ 7.6
Venezuela	*1969* 65.3	*'75–'80* 66.4	+1.1	*1969* 46.8	*1977* 43.0	+ 8.1	*1969* 6.7	*1977* 6.0	+10.4

Source: [a] *Socio-Economic Progress in Latin America; Social Progress Trust Fund, Tenth Annual Report, 1970*, Inter-American Development Bank (Washington, D.C., 1971), individual country reports.

[b] *Economic and Social Progress in Latin America, 1978 Report*, Inter-American Development Bank (Washington, D.C., 1979).

[c] Factors extrapolated from those reports.

57

TABLE 5
Comparative Literacy Rates

	(a)		(b)
Costa Rica	84.4% in 1965	and	89.8% in 1977
El Salvador	49.0% in 1961		59.5% in 1977
Guatemala	37.9% in 1964		45.4% in 1977
Honduras	47.3% in 1961		59.5% in 1978
Nicaragua	49.8% in 1963		53.6% in 1977

Source: [a] *Socio-Economic Progress in Latin America, Social Progress Trust Fund, Tenth Annual Report, 1970,* Inter-American Development Bank (Washington, D.C., 1971), pp. 177, 215, 226, 248, 287.

[b] *Economic and Social Progress in Latin America, 1978 Report,* Inter-American Development Bank (Washington, D.C., 1979), pp. 226, 257. 268, 300, 333.

most other Latin American countries. Tables 6 and 7 reflect those trends during the first decade of the Alliance.

That strong commitment to education continued through the 1970s. In 1977, two of the Central American countries—Costa Rica and El Salvador—ranked first and third in the share of their government's budget allocated to education; the lowest among them, Guatemala, continued, nonetheless, to place ahead of Argentina, Brazil, and Mexico in that category. In spending in still another key area of social development—public health—Honduras, by 1977, ranked second in all of Latin America, El Salvador fourth, and Guatemala seventh. Progressive Costa Rica, which has far fewer health problems to overcome than most Third World countries, placed fifteenth. Only Nicaragua lagged in this field (see table 8).

Moreover, there was strong and sustained progress in another important area, food—the amount produced, the amount consumed (see tables 9 and 10).

One other stereotype needs debunking; namely, that these countries traditionally had been ruled by militarists who, because of their "indifference" to social needs, drained their treasuries to acquire tanks and planes and other military toys. In fact, for the ten-year period 1968–77 the Central Ameri-

TABLE 6

Central Government Current Educational Expenditures as a Percent of Gross National Product, 1961–70
(1970 figures are provisional)

	1961	1962	1963	1964	1965	1966	1967	1968	1969	1970
Total*	1.6	1.8	1.8	2.0	2.1	2.1	2.3	2.2	2.3[a]	2.3[b]
Subtotal, C.A.*	2.3	2.3	2.2	2.3	2.5	2.7	2.8	2.8	2.9	3.2
Argentina	1.6	1.8	1.8	2.2	2.1	2.3	2.3	2.2	2.2	2.2
Bolivia	2.6	2.6	2.5	2.6	2.5	3.7	4.2	3.1	3.3	3.6
Brazil*	0.7	0.8	1.0	0.9	1.0	0.9	0.8	0.8	0.9	0.9
Chile	3.3	3.6	3.2	3.2	3.7	3.5	4.7	4.6	4.8	5.7
Colombia	1.4	1.8	1.6	1.7	1.8	1.5	1.4	1.9	1.9	2.2
COSTA RICA	3.6	4.3	3.8	4.0	4.4	4.8	4.9	4.7	5.5	5.6
Dominican Republic	1.9	1.5	2.5	2.5	2.1	2.8	2.7	2.6	2.9	3.2
Ecuador	2.3	2.5	2.6	2.6	2.7	2.5	2.5	2.7	NA	NA
EL SALVADOR*	2.8	2.6	2.6	2.6	2.7	2.9	2.8	2.9	3.0	3.6
GUATEMALA	1.9	1.6	1.5	1.6	1.8	1.8	1.9	1.8	1.9	2.0
HONDURAS	2.1	2.0	2.1	2.6	2.8	3.0	2.8	3.0	2.7	3.2
Mexico[c]	1.5	1.5	1.7	1.9	2.0	1.9	2.1	2.2	2.2	2.0
NICARAGUA	1.4	1.5	1.5	1.8	1.8	2.1	2.4	2.4	2.4	2.2
Panama	3.9	4.0	4.0	3.9	4.0	4.0	4.1	4.4	5.1	4.0
Paraguay	1.2	1.2	1.5	1.4	1.5	1.6	1.6	1.8	1.8	1.9
Peru	3.1	3.3	3.4	3.8	5.2	5.4	5.3	4.7	4.2	3.9
Uruguay	2.7	3.4	3.2	3.0	4.0	3.2	4.4	3.2	4.1	NA
Venezuela	2.5	2.5	2.4	2.5	2.6	2.8	3.1	3.1	3.3	3.6

Source: *Summary Economic and Social Indicators: 18 Latin American Countries, 1960–1970,* Office of Development Programs, Bureau for Latin America, Agency for International Development (Washington, D.C., April 1971), p. 63.

* All data for Brazil and El Salvador and figures for Nicaragua prior to 1965 refer to *all* central government education expenditures.

Notes: Symbol definitions are: E . . . Estimate, P . . . Preliminary, NA . . . Not Available.

Totals exclude countries shown as not available.

[a] Based on data which include AID estimates for Ecuador not shown separately.

[b] Based on data which include AID estimates for Ecuador and Uruguay not shown separately.

[c] Based on AID estimates.

TABLE 7

Central Government Current Educational Expenditures as a Percent of Total Expenditures
(1970 figures are provisional)

	1961	1962	1963	1964	1965	1966	1967	1968	1969	1970
Total	8.8	9.5	10.6	11.2	12.9	12.7	13.7	13.2	13.3[a]	13.9[b]
Subtotal, C.A.*	18.8	18.4	18.7	19.5	19.1	20.7	20.6	21.6	21.3	21.4
Argentina	16.4	14.0	12.2	18.9	17.8	18.7	23.1	13.6	16.7	20.7
Bolivia	16.4	14.0	12.2	18.9	17.8	18.7	23.1	13.6	16.7	20.7
Brazil	3.3	3.7	5.1	4.3	6.5	5.1	5.5	5.4	5.9	6.7
Chile	14.0	13.8	13.5	14.1	14.6	15.2	18.2	16.6	17.6	18.6
Colombia	11.7	15.3	15.2	17.4	17.1	14.5	13.7	16.5	15.7	18.0
COSTA RICA	21.1	23.1	22.0	22.7	21.8	26.1	26.1	26.7	29.0	29.0
Dominican Republic	9.1	7.1	13.2	12.8	10.0	15.2	14.8	15.1	15.7	17.5
Ecuador	11.2	12.7	13.5	13.1	12.8	12.8	12.6	12.5	NA	NA
EL SALVADOR	18.6	20.0	19.1	19.7	18.3	20.4	20.4	21.9	20.1	23.1
GUATEMALA	20.8	16.8	19.9	18.7	17.4	17.7	17.9	17.8	18.5	18.2
HONDURAS	16.5	15.8	16.2	21.7	23.2	23.9	22.3	23.0	17.2	19.4
Mexico[c]	12.4	12.0	13.3	14.0	16.3	15.3	17.7	17.0	16.9	16.4
NICARAGUA	13.4	13.5	13.3	14.4	15.4	16.0	16.8	18.9	19.6	14.8
Panama	22.0	24.8	24.6	26.7	28.4	26.1	25.7	29.6	24.1	19.9
Paraguay	12.3	11.8	14.8	14.5	11.9	11.3	10.2	10.5	10.2	11.1
Peru	21.3	22.0	22.0	20.8	27.2	28.7	27.1	25.6	24.0	21.1
Uruguay	14.0	17.1	17.5	17.0	25.0	21.5	28.5	25.2	27.7	NA
Venezuela	8.2	10.2	11.0	11.5	11.5	12.3	12.8	12.5	12.7	14.7

Source: *Summary Economic and Social Indicators: 18 Latin American Countries, 1960–1970*, Office of Development Programs, Bureau for Latin America, Agency for International Development (Washington, D.C., April 1971).

* See note for these three countries in Table 6.

Notes: Symbol definitions are: E . . . Estimate, P . . . Preliminary, NA . . . Not Available.

Totals exclude countries shown as not available.

[a] Based on data which include AID estimates for Ecuador not shown separately.

[b] Based on data which include AID estimates for Ecuador and Uruguay not shown separately.

[c] Based on AID estimates.

TABLE 8
Percentage of Total Central Government Expenditures, 1977

	Education	Public Health
Argentina	8.8	3.6
Bolivia	24.9	8.3
Brazil	7.9	2.8
Chile	17.8	7.0
Colombia	13.2	6.6
COSTA RICA	34.3	4.0
Dominican Republic	11.1	5.7
Ecuador	30.4	9.5
EL SALVADOR	22.4	9.6
GUATEMALA	10.7	7.1
Haiti	14.1	13.7
HONDURAS	15.2	10.2
Mexico	8.4	10.1
NICARAGUA	12.1	3.1
Panama	16.2	6.8
Paraguay	13.0	3.0
Peru	17.0	5.0
Uruguay	17.0	6.0
Venezuela	13.6	5.2

Source: *Economic and Social Progress in Latin America, 1978 Report,* Inter-American Development Bank (Washington, D.C., 1979).

TABLE 9
Indices of Per Capita Food Production
(1961–65 = 100)

	1975	1976	1977	1978	% Growth 1977–78
Costa Rica	139	134	133	138	3.8%
El Salvador	115	107	107	120	12.1
Guatemala	133	138	130	133	2.3
Honduras	73	87	85	89	4.7
Nicaragua	114	114	103	118	14.6
All of Latin America	110	112	111	112	0.9

Source: *Economic and Social Progress in Latin America, 1978 Report,* Inter-American Development Bank (Washington, D.C., 1979), p. 19.

TABLE 10
Apparent Daily Per Capita Consumption of Calories and Protein
(Based on minimum requirement estimated by FAO for each country.
Average minimum requirements for region as a whole,
2,320 calories per day).

	Energy (kilocalories)		
	1961	1971–73	% Change
Costa Rica	2,217	2,576	11.2%
El Salvador	1,880	1,916	1.9
Guatemala	1,929	2,155	11.7
Honduras	1,889	2,102	11.3
Nicaragua	2,140	2,467	15.3
Latin America	2,410	2,570	6.6

Source: *Economic and Social Progress in Latin America, 1978 Report,* Inter-American Development Bank (Washington: D.C., 1979), p. 139.

can countries were, with rare exceptions, below the average for Latin America as a whole in military expenditures as a percentage of gross national product. Rare too were the times when any one of them exceeded the levels of military spending of the rest of Latin America as expressed as a percentage of central government expenditures. Never did any of them come even close to the averages, in either category, for all developing countries (see table 11).

The remarkably low level of military spending contrasts sharply and revealingly with what happened in, for instance, El Salvador, when that country adopted the "reform" policies designed for and imposed upon it by the United States after President Romero's ouster. Those policies, plus the Carter administration-supported overthrow of El Salvador's constitutional government, plunged the country into a gruesome civil war, necessitating sharply increased military spending.

It is interesting, too, that El Salvador was one of the very first countries in the world ostracized by the Carter administration for "human rights" violations in 1977, with the result that El Salvador refused to accept further U.S. military aid.

TABLE 11

Military Expenditures as Percentage of Gross National Product (GNP) and as Percentage of Central Government Expenditures (CGE)

Years	All Developing Countries		All Latin America		Costa Rica[a]		El Salvador[b]		Guatemala[c]		Honduras[b]		Nicaragua	
	GNP	CGE	GNP	CGE	GNP	CGE	GNP	CGE	GNP	CGE	GNP	CGE	GNP	CGE
1968	6.1	42.0	1.8	14.3	0.0	0.0	1.3	9.8	1.0	9.6	1.1	7.9	1.5	11.3
1969	6.1	41.6	1.8	14.1	0.0	0.0	3.0	23.4	1.0	9.9	2.2	13.9	1.5	12.9
1970	6.1	42.3	1.9	14.7	0.0	0.0	1.0	9.1	1.6	15.4	1.0	5.9	1.6	12.1
1971	6.2	40.2	1.9	14.2	0.0	0.0	1.1	8.8	1.0	10.3	1.3	8.1	1.7	11.8
1972	6.2	38.8	1.7	12.8	0.0	0.0	1.3	9.7	1.1	10.1	1.6	10.0	1.5	10.0
1973	6.1	38.2	1.8	12.1	0.0	0.0	1.2	9.2	0.9	8.1	1.4	9.9	1.5	10.0
1974	5.8	36.1	1.8	11.9	0.0	0.0	1.2	9.3	0.9	8.4	1.3	8.1	1.5	8.1
1975	6.3	32.1	2.0	12.2	0.0	0.0	1.2	8.0	1.2	12.2	1.7	8.1	2.0	10.8
1976	6.2	31.4	1.6	9.6	0.0	0.0	1.0	6.2	1.2	9.2	1.8	8.1	2.0	11.8
1977	5.9	30.0	1.5	9.8	0.0	0.0	1.0	6.2	0.8	6.8	1.8	7.8	1.9	10.5

Source: "World Military Expenditures and Arms Transfers 1968–1977," U.S. Arms Control and Disarmament Agency, Publication 100 (Washington, D.C., October 1979), p. 27, 28, 39, 41, 44, 45.

[a] Costa Rica has no military establishment; internal security is the responsibility of a civil guard.

[b] The sharp increase in military spending in El Salvador and Honduras in 1969 and 1970 followed on the heels of their brief but bitter "soccer war."

[c] Exceptional military spending in Guatemala in 1970 and 1975 corresponded to a sharp increase in guerrilla activity, and the government's counter-insurgency measures to meet the threat.

63

TABLE 12
Central American Common Market: Intraregional Trade, 1966–69*
(millions of dollars)

	1966			1967			1968			1969		
	Exports	Imports	Balance	Exports	Imports	Balance	Exports	Imports	Balance	Exports	Imports	Balance
Costa Rica	25.8	23.2	2.6	31.0	34.2	− 3.2	37.6	49.5	−11.9	37.1	50.0	−12.9
El Salvador	57.8	52.0	5.8	74.9	54.5	20.4	84.8	65.7	19.1	74.5	60.1	14.4
Guatemala	55.1	33.8	21.3	65.6	41.8	23.8	77.9	49.4	28.5	86.1	55.7	30.4
Honduras	21.5	34.5	−13.0	23.5	40.7	−17.2	31.4	48.3	−16.9	23.4	44.0	−20.6
Nicaragua	14.9	31.6	−16.7	18.6	42.4	−23.8	27.4	46.2	−18.8	30.8	42.1	−11.3
Total	175.1	175.1	—	213.6	213.6	—	259.1	259.1	—	251.9	251.9	—

Source: Central America Monetary Council, Balance of Payments, 1969, San José, September 1970.
* The figures for exports are f.o.b. and those for imports are valued in country of origin.

TABLE 13
Central America: Intrazonal Trade, 1970–78
(millions of dollars)

	1970		1975		1976	1977	1978*		Annual growth rate (Percentage)			
	Value	% of CACM	Value	% of CACM	Value	Value	Value	% of CACM	1970–1975	1975–1978	1970–1978	1977–1978
Guatemala												
Exports to CACM (f.o.b.)	102.3	36	168.2	31	189.0	222.5	321.9	35	10.5	24.0	15.4	44.7
Imports from CACM (c.i.f.)	65.0	22	103.1	20	106.4	105.4	262.9	28	9.7	37.0	19.1	49.4
Balance	+ 37.3		+ 65.1		+ 82.6	+117.1	+ 59.0					
El Salvador												
Exports to CACM (f.o.b.)	73.8	26	141.8	27	176.1	215.5	235.8	26	14.0	18.5	15.6	9.4
Imports from CACM (c.i.f.)	60.6	20	136.9	26	170.4	210.3	247.4	26	17.7	22.0	19.2	17.6
Balance	+ 13.2		+ 4.9		+ 5.7	+ 5.2	− 11.6					
Honduras												
Exports to CACM (f.o.b.)	18.0	6	26.6	5	37.7	43.5	50.5	5	8.1	24.0	13.7	16.0
Imports from CACM (c.i.f.)	54.9	18	51.7	10	58.4	71.2	89.4	9	− 1.0	19.8	6.3	25.6
Balance	− 36.9		− 25.1		− 22.7	− 27.7	− 38.9					
Nicaragua												
Exports to CACM (f.o.b.)	46.1	16	92.6	17	117.8	134.0	139.7	15	14.9	14.7	14.9	4.3
Imports from CACM (c.i.f.)	50.1	17	112.7	22	140.3	165.5	146.8	16	17.6	9.2	14.4	−10.8
Balance	− 4.0		− 20.1		− 22.5	− 30.5	− 7.1					
Costa Rica												
Exports to CACM (f.o.b.)	46.1	16	107.2	20	130.7	174.4	176.6	19	18.4	18.1	18.3	1.3
Imports from CACM (c.i.f.)	68.7	23	114.7	22	135.6	168.0	201.4	21	10.8	21.0	14.4	19.9
Balance	− 22.6		− 7.5		− 4.9	+ 6.4	− 24.8					
Central America												
Exports to CACM (f.o.b.)	286.3	100	536.4	100	649.3	789.8	924.5	100	13.4	19.9	15.8	17.1
Imports from CACM (c.i.f.)	299.3	100	519.1	100	611.3	719.4	947.9	100	11.6	22.0	15.5	31.8

Source: SIECA.
* Estimated.

It was only when the Carter administration was able to put its "moral" policies into effect in that country, in 1980, after encouraging the overthrow of the legitimate government, that arms would begin once again to flow—and the dead, no longer human rights problems, fill the country's cemeteries.

As Kenneth W. Thompson, vice president of the Rockefeller Foundation, reminded us in a provocative article, "Moral Values and International Politics": "The wars of religion are an earlier example of absolutizing particularistic ends, and history attests that man is never so cruel and intractable as when he becomes a crusader for moral and religious goals."[7] Ask the frightened and despairing people of that broken and bleeding land that is now the battleground of a crusade and that was El Salvador.

The governments of Central America, emerging from their own feudal pasts, beset by problems not of their making (oil, natural disasters, subversion) as well as those of their own invention, did not re-create the Garden of Eden in the 1970s. But, contrary to the casual calumny that "they did not care" about the social needs of their population, they did care, and they did make decent progress in meeting those needs. It was at this point in time and progress that the United States lurched massively, clumsily, onto their small and crowded stage.

NOTES

1. Salvador's population density in 1977 was 512 per square mile; Honduras's only 74.9. To round out the Central America picture, Costa Rica's was 104.7, Guatemala's 152.9, Nicaragua's 45.8. *Information Please Almanac, 1978* (New York: Information Please Publishers, 1978), pp. 147–213.

2. The following two tables trace the growth of Common Market trade from 1966 through 1978. The first of them is from *Socio-Economic Progress in Latin America, Social Progress Trust Fund, Tenth Annual Report, 1970* (Washington, D.C.: Inter-American Development Bank, 1971), table 28, p. 36. The second is from *Economic and Social Progress in Latin America, 1978 Report* (ibid., 1979), table IV-6, p. 122.

3. Perlmutter speaks persuasively of the Latin American military as having abandoned, in the sixties, its earlier role—national defense and as an instrument of national foreign policy—in favor of a "new professionalism, which was concerned with internal security and national development." The groundwork was laid in the thirties when, with the Great Depression, fragile republican and civilian structures crumbled, "but the military were ready to reestablish order and to perform the daily routine of administration." In the years following, mass political parties failed to develop in most countries, and labor—a potential challenger for power—failed because of its notoriously poor organization, leaving it as "a supportive political force, not an independent one." He concludes, "The military's transformation from arbitrator to ruler in Latin America signified the change from liberal and fascist to mass praetorianism. The argument that the military either defends or represents classes in society (as seemed to be the case with the oligarchic liberal and fascist types) can no longer be accepted. In the mass praetorian phase, the military had three motivations—first, to head the modernization evolution; second, to institutionalize mass mobilization; and third, to prevent a Marxist or Castroite revolution, especially one within the military. The military also changed its role and instead of supporting the executive during the crises, it sought to dominate it"—Amos Perlmutter, *The Military and Politics in Modern Times* (New Haven: Yale University Press, 1977), especially pp. 167, 184, 192–93. Though the passage deals with Peru, another Perlmutter observation aptly fits the political reality of Guatemala: "In the absence of stable patrimonial rule, the military became the major recruiting ground for the presidency" (p.180).

4. In 1960, the per capita gross national products of the five Central American republics averaged $268 per year; for the eighteen Latin American countries as a whole, $387. In 1965, the figures were $300 and $434, respectively; in 1970, $333 and $496. Over the decade, the Central American countries showed only a 24.2 percent increase, or annual rate of 2.2 percent; Latin America as a whole, 28.2 percent. The same discrepancies occurred in such other areas as health care, housing starts, school enrollment, etc. *Summary Economic and Social Indicators, 18 Latin American Countries: 1960–1970* (Office of Development Programs, Bureau for Latin America, Agency for International Development, April 1971), p. 5.

5. In 1976, only seven Latin American countries were experiencing "mild" inflation (less than 5 percent), and three of them, Nicaragua, Costa

Rica, and Honduras, were in Central America. El Salvador and Guatemala that year belonged to the group experiencing "moderate" (between 5 and 15 percent) inflation. In 1977, Costa Rica was one of the only two Latin American countries with mild inflation—but the four other Central American countries remained in the "moderate" category. *Economic and Social Progress in Latin America, 1978 Report* (Washington, D.C.: Inter-American Development Bank, 1979), p. 15.

6. In 1976, Guatemala had the lowest ratio of external public debt to the value of its exports of goods and services (1.5 percent) in the Latin region, and one of the lowest such ratios in the world. El Salvador (with 4.2 percent) ranked third among all Latin nations. Costa Rica, with 9.4 percent; Honduras, with 6.3 percent; and Nicaragua, with 12.4 percent, were all below the overall average of 14.1 percent. Ibid., p. 463.

7. In *Political Science Quarterly* 88, no. 3 (September 1973), p. 369.

3

The Human Rights Tyranny: Firm Allies Spurned

THE United States has, of course, been an important element in Central American affairs for almost as long as those states have been independent. In fact, both El Salvador and Nicaragua, during the nineteenth century, actually petitioned to be admitted to the Union, and Nicaragua, as late as 1911, asked to be made a protectorate.

The United States first flexed its muscles in Central America in 1848, challenging growing British encroachment in the area. But it was not until 1903, with the creation of the new puppet state in Panama, and with it the right to build the Canal, that the United States took a strong, active hand in the affairs of the region.

The following year, 1904, President Theodore Roosevelt proclaimed the Roosevelt corollary of the Monroe Doctrine, under which the United States unilaterally declared its right to intervene in the case of danger from outside interference, or where internal order was threatened with collapse. The aim of that declaration was to protect the Panama Canal. Over the next quarter of a century, that corollary was invoked on several occasions to justify U.S. naval or land interventions in Central America. (Through this period, the various *de facto* governments of Central America continued to meddle in each other's affairs with an even greater regularity.) The last marine contingent was withdrawn from Nicaragua in January 1933, and U.S. interest in the area went with it. Caudillos seized power in four countries and settled in for long, iron reigns—Gen. Maximiliano Hernandez Martinez in El Salvador (1931–44); Gen. Tiburcio Carias Andino in Honduras (1933–49); Gen. Jorge Ubico in Guatemala (1931–44); and Gen. Anastasio Somoza in Nicaragua (1936–56). In Costa Rica, the old order continued to retain power in highly restricted elections (only 20 percent were eligible to vote, and only a handful actually did), but the fledgling Communist Party (founded in 1929) began to assert itself. In the 1934 elections, it won two seats in Congress, and gained considerable headway in organizing workers in the dominant banana industry.

Central America remained on the American "back-burner" until the 1951 rise to power in Guatemala of a fifty-one-year-old army colonel named Jacobo Arbenz (whose main rival had been murdered two years earlier in an assassination clearly linked to Arbenz). A Machiavellian maneuverer, Arbenz quickly embarked on a series of highhanded "reforms" in an increasingly authoritarian style: the press was muzzled; mobs were incited to seize lands; four Supreme Court justices who objected to the government's lawless handling of an agrarian-reform program were kicked off the court. He also worked closely with the country's increasingly bold Communist Party. The last straw came when Arbenz secretly ordered arms from behind the Iron Curtain to outfit a clandestine militia he was building up. On June 27, 1954, Arbenz was ousted in a virtually bloodless revolution in which the CIA played a supporting role.

Once again Central America receded into the American

background, although Costa Rica and El Salvador were singled out for exceptional Alliance for Progress funds and favor during the sixties. Throughout the period, the United States was chastised regularly for its earlier record of interventionism in the hemisphere; just as regularly, the United States vowed penance and a permanent policy of abstinence from those wicked ways. (Anyone who attended a major inter-American meeting during the sixties and seventies will recall the ritualistic rhetoric raising nonintervention and self-determination to the level of beatitudes.)

The United States was, of course, influenced by other factors in its systematic retreat from an active—activist, certainly—role in Central American (and hemisphere-wide) affairs, factors like Vietnam, civil rights, Watergate, etc. As a result, as Carter moved into 1600 Pennsylvania Avenue, the United States was, for the most part, a passive onlooker in the dramas of Central America. Curiously, for those who believe that human progress must be guided (by them, more often than not) if there is to be progress at all, it was a time of singular political, economic, and social progress in the region—without their "guidance."

Two literary allusions spring to mind in examining U.S. behavior since then. The first is from Lewis Carroll's *Through the Looking-Glass*. Those familiar with Carroll's whimsical tale will remember that once Alice wished her way into the Looking-Glass House, she entered a topsy-turvy world, where words were written backward, and where you approached the Red Queen by walking away from her, and where no matter how fast you ran, you never passed anything.

The other inevitable allusion is to George Orwell's decidedly unwhimsical tale *Nineteen Eighty-four* and particularly to "doublethink." Doublethink, Orwell explained, "means the power of holding two contradictory beliefs in one's mind simultaneously, and accepting both of them. The Party intellectual knows in which direction his memories

71

must be altered; he therefore knows that he is playing tricks with reality; but by the exercise of doublethink, he also satisfies himself that reality is not violated."[1]

U.S. policy in Central America, under Carter, was an admixture of Looking-Glass fantasy and Orwell's doublethink. The result was to forfeit Nicaragua to a totalitarian, Marxist, and antagonistic regime; in El Salvador, we embittered our natural friends and allied ourselves with a series of wobbly regimes of various hues; we hounded normally friendly Guatemala to the point of being perceived by many there, and particularly among the country's America-phile conservatives, as a dangerous menace. Costa Rica and Honduras have reluctantly, and warily, turned to the United States as the lesser of two evils, though the sniffily superior "Ticos" have never displayed strong allegiance to the United States in any case. The dependability of both of those countries, as friends and generally supportive allies, will be heavily influenced by the outcome of the desperate struggle for power going on in the entire area of Central America.

In 1977, the outlook was entirely different—the fourth and final claim about pre-Carter Central America.

"Firm Allies"

The attitudes of those five countries toward the United States in 1977 are reflected in the dryly objective summations appearing in the *Political Handbook of the World: 1977*:[2]

Costa Rica: "The country is a vigorous supporter of the inter-American system, and its relations with the U.S. have been especially cordial" (p. 87).

El Salvador: "El Salvador maintains cordial relations with the U.S., while refusing to enter into formal relations with Cuba or other communist countries" (p. 147).

Guatemala: "Relations with the U.S. in recent years have generally been cordial, and have resulted in valuable military and domestic assistance programs" (p. 155).

Honduras: "Relations with the U.S. are good" (p. 166).

Nicaragua: "The conservative and generally pro-U.S. outlook of the Somoza regime is reflected in a favorable attitude toward North American investment, and the strongly pro-Western anti-communist position in the UN, Organization of American States and other international bodies" (p. 285).

In 1976, there were no Soviet embassies in Central America.

In 1977, Costa Rica became the first to host one.

In 1979, Nicaragua became the second.

In 1976, there were no Cuban embassies in Central America.

In 1977, Costa Rica allowed a large consulate to be established there.

In 1979, Nicaragua welcomed a Cuban embassy.

There are, of course, those who would argue that the old regimes supported the United States because we "bribed" them with aid money, but history denies the calumny. Anastasio Somoza supported the United States, unwaveringly, because Somoza was an incurable Yankee-phile. Like his father before him, Somoza was educated in the United States, graduating from the true-blue United States Military Academy. In common with most of the graduates, he really believed in the manifest destiny of the United States as champion of the Western world and its values and as the bulwark against communism. Nor did he have to be "bought," having amassed a personal fortune he himself estimated at $100 million.

For the period 1962–75, the five countries of Central America received a total of $863.3 million in U.S. economic assistance.[3] During that same period, Alliance paradigm Chile ("paradigm," at least, in the fawning estimates of the factotums dispensing Alliance largess) collected $894.4 million in U.S. economic aid. This is especially notable because Chile's population, throughout most of this period, was less than half of the aggregate for Central America. Unlike the Central American countries—whose fealty the United States supposedly "bought" (and on the cheap, at that)—Chile repeatedly opposed the United States in international arenas during that period. Yet, the money kept gushing, all the same; and the Chileans responded by becoming the first people in the world to elect a Marxist (and thoroughly anti-U.S.) government in free and honest elections. The answer is clear: the United States did not "buy" the Central American countries. They stood by the United States, with almost stoic loyalty, *despite* the way we handled them.

There are those who might argue that the old regimes of Central America were doomed, anyway. Perhaps. But then the question becomes: did we hasten their doom?

The eminent theologian, and eminent liberal, Reinhold Niebuhr sounded a warning decades ago about the tendency of liberals to live in an idealized world of make-believe:

> The democratic idealists of practically all schools of thought have managed to remain remarkably oblivious to the obvious facts. Democratic theory therefore has not squared with the facts of history. This grave defect in democratic theory was comparatively innocuous in the heyday of the bourgeois period, when the youth and the power of democratic civilization surmounted all errors of judgement and confusions of mind. But in this latter day, when it has become important to save what is valuable in democratic life from the destruction of what is false in bourgeois civilization, it has also become necessary to distinguish what is false in democratic theory from what is true in democratic life.[4]

Squaring theory with the facts of history was not a defect from which Mr. Carter suffered. As his former chief speechwriter James Fallows has written, Mr. Carter brought to the presidency an innocence of historical perspective perhaps without parallel among our modern presidents. Fallows wrote that Carter approached every new international crisis as if it had no roots.[5]

It was in that spirit of unencumbered innocence that he mounted the podium at Notre Dame University on May 22, 1977, and revealed to the world the premises of his foreign policy.

"I have a quiet confidence in our own political system," Mr. Carter said. "Because we know that democracy works, we can reject the arguments of those rulers who deny human rights to their people. We are confident that democracy's example will be compelling, and so we seek to bring that example closer to those from whom in the past few years we have been separated and who are not yet convinced about the advantages of our kind of life."

(The political scientist Hans J. Morgenthau noted several years ago the "propensity [among self-proclaimed moralists in public affairs] for such moral and philosophical abstractions which has impeded the objective investigation of what other people want." He added, in the same essay,[6] his misgivings about those who imagine that "democracy is a kind of gadget which is capable of being installed in any political household, regardless of the qualifications and preferences of the inhabitants.")

"Being confident of our own future," Mr. Carter went on, "we are now free of that inordinate fear of communism which once led us to embrace any dictator who joined us in that fear."

Jeane Kirkpatrick has pointed out that, in formulating those views, Carter was unquestionably drawing heavily on the thinking of his national security adviser, Zbigniew Brzezinski. Brzezinski, she notes, had developed the basics of those ideas in his 1970 book, *Between Two Ages*:

The centerpiece of Brzezinski's analysis was the same theory of modernization that serves as the foundation of Carter administration foreign policy. According to that theory, the whole world is involved in a process of revolutionary change which will in the end render all societies modern in their technology; secular in their public attitudes; rational in their conduct of public affairs, and interdependent. This process of modernization will, it is understood, upset traditional patterns and create instabilities. In the long run, however, the modernization process is as beneficent as it is inexorable. Therefore, Americans should contribute to change instead of resisting it, tolerate any "superficial" affront to the national interest and understand that our true interest lies at the end of the rainbow where modernized nations live peaceably with one another.[7]

That paragraph epitomizes American policy in Central America during the Carter years. Nor is there another area of the world where this new moral imperialism was—or even could be—implanted with a greater vengeance than in this small region. Indeed, the ink was barely dry on Carter's speech when a legion of eager missionaries strode forth to save the first country from itself—tiny El Salvador. Nicaragua would follow soon afterward and Guatemala after that.

There were two good reasons why Central America made such a tempting target for salvation. The first of them concerns the mix of the American past there with the mentalities of those Carter recruits and the career diplomats who would, together, manage American policy in the region. Because of the record of American interventionism in Central America, there is, among many American Latinists, a widely held (and astonishingly uncritical) sense of guilt, reinforced by the crisis of "conscience" over the American role in Southeast Asia. These new crusaders brought to their tasks what Professor Peter Berger has called the deep conviction that "American power is one of the most vexing problems in the contemporary world, and [they] almost instinctively give the benefit of doubt to the enemies rather than the friends of the United States."[8] They would, for example, urge tolerance and rapprochement with Fidel Castro while at the same time urging unforgiving, relentless hostility toward the deeply anticommunist regimes of Argentina, Brazil, Chile, El Salvador, Nicaragua, and Uruguay.

The second reason has to do with the disdain of American policymakers for Latin American affairs. With the exceptions of Cuba and Panama, we have never developed anything resembling a sustained interest in any country in the region—the conduct of foreign policy in those latitudes is routinely left to middle-echelon bureaucrats who play out their power drama with far greater freedom than those charged with managing America's affairs in the "glamour" countries.

An example: one of the key people involved in the direction of American policy in the area was Robert Pastor, the Latin American specialist on Carter's National Security Council staff. Before joining the administration, Pastor had close ties to the far-left Transnational Institute of the Institute for Policy Studies (IPS), and was one of seven Latin specialists who authored a 1976 IPS study that contained the main outlines of what would later become the Carter administration's foreign policy in Latin America. It was, in its premises and its conclusions, vintage viewpoint for an extreme left-wing think-tank. What was novel was that these views would then become U.S. policy in the region. According to the IPS panel, communist or socialist governments in Cuba, Jamaica, and Guyana offer "a unique opportunity to establish a new pattern in U.S. foreign policy." In that vein, the United States should move to improve relations with Castro's Cuba (which the Carter administration did, almost immediately, by suspending U-2 flights, establishing quasi-embassies in Havana and Washington, and initiating other moves, all of which Castro reciprocated by stepping up the level of his military intervention in Africa and his subversive activities in Central America).

The report also called for early development and implementation of a Panama Canal treaty, and said the United States must "not intervene to shape governments and societies to our views and preferences," and thus should not "boycott and isolate . . . any country . . . because of political and economic differences. It means that our nation will not attempt to subvert foreign governments." (As we shall see in the later chapters on Nicaragua and El Salvador, and as reflected in U.S. behavior toward Guatemala, the authors, in expressing these moral precepts, had in mind restraint as to the governments with "political and economic differences" they approved of, but brooked no such patience with regimes they did not like.)

The report also foretold the most important single element of Carter's foreign policy in Latin America—"human rights." The United States, the IPS study said, must not continue to provide preferential aid treatment for countries that systematically violate the human rights of their citizens.

That IPS report revealed how morally bankrupt and hypocritical this policy would become from its very inception, damning anti-communist Chile for "human rights" offenses while urging close ties with a totalitarian regime of twenty years' standing, Castro's Cuba.

But the Carter administration "human rights policy" was never really a policy at all, but an ideological weapon wielded mainly against governments whose political philosophies were abhorrent to the New Leftists in the U.S. government. Even before Carter took office, Brady Tyson, who in 1972 distinguished himself as one of "the most militant, pro-Castro panelists" at a Washington conference on U.S.-Cuban relations, was quoted as predicting that human rights would be used to support revolutionary forces in the hemisphere. Pastor was quoted as making an identical prediction in 1977.[9]

Brady Tyson, a Latin specialist at the U.S. Mission to the United Nations, was a founding member of the North American Congress on Latin America (NACLA), whose basic ideological statement of May 1967 asked support from those "who not only favor revolutionary change in Latin America but also take a revolutionary position toward their own society."

That statement recalls an observation made by the columnist Stewart Alsop, in the early years of the seventies. "Yale," he wrote, "like every other major college, is graduating scores of bright young men who are practitioners of the politics of despair. These young men despise the American political and economic system." The Italian novelist Carlo Coccioli expressed it differently in 1980:

> Now it turns out that U.S. intellectuals and pseudointellectuals are even more neurotic than their colleagues abroad. Their neurosis sees the most abject self-criticism as an exquisite form of intelligence. In addition, there are politicians who like to think of themselves as intellectuals. Thus all the ingredients for American masochism are in place. . . . History records no people so self-critical. Nine of ten anti-Yankee themes heard around the world are hatched in the U.S. as Americans enjoy their delirium of self-persecution.[10]

The lack of faith verging on loathing of the American political and economic system and a sense of masochism bordering on neurosis about America's role in the earlier histories of these countries were combined in the Carter years with a messianic "morality," that in practice has turned out to be far more murderous and destructive than any "big stick" the United States ever wielded in the region. The Carter administration brought with it a conviction that the region needed, wanted, "revolutionary change" along socialist lines, in order to emerge, smiling into the modern world.

Henry Kissinger's words are worth recalling: We have been creating our own anti-American revolutions in Central America. The middle-echelon bureaucrats briefly mentioned (and others not mentioned for reasons of space) played a significant role in forming and managing our suicidal strategy. But however indifferent they were to the details of policy in the area, it was the men at the top—Carter, Brzezinski, Vance—who sanctioned the broad framework within which their largely invisible policy lieutenants operated: Carter, with his naive belief that communism no longer posed a danger, and equally naive belief that he could raise "human rights" to the level of a rigid policy; Brzezinski, who legitimized the predisposition of his lower-level colleagues to believe that "revolutionary change" was inevitable; and former Secretary of State Cyrus Vance, who, in a speech before the Foreign Policy Association of New York on September 27, 1979, echoed that theme when he said he hoped for friendly and close relations with the new Sandinista government in Nicaragua, even if its radical policies occasionally brought it into conflict with the United States. In the same speech, Vance said the United States supported similar "constructive change" in El Salvador, Guatemala, and Honduras "before ties between governments and people are strained to the point where a radical or a repressive solution forces out a moderate solution."[11]

Not twenty days later the world would discover just how eagerly we supported such "constructive change" when we succeeded in provoking the ouster of El Salvador's constitutional government. The themes Vance sounded in that speech would then harden into the Carter policy toward Nicaragua, El Salvador, Guatemala, and Honduras.

NOTES

1. George Orwell, *Nineteen Eighty-four* (New York: New American Library, Signet Classics, 1961), p. 178.

2. *Political Handbook of the World, 1977*, ed. Arthur S. Banks, et al. (New York: McGraw-Hill, 1977).

3. Compiled from individual country reports appearing in "U.S. Overseas Loans and Grants and Assistance from International Organizations; Obligations and Loan Authorizations, July 1, 1945–Sept. 30, 1978" (Office of Planning and Budgeting, Bureau for Program and Policy Coordination, Agency for International Development). The figures for Chile are taken from the same report. (We realize, of course,

that the Alliance, as such, had petered out by the early 1970s, but many of the same cadre of philosophies and strategies were continued by the same cadre of career technocrats—tempests at the pinnacle notwithstanding.)

4. In *The Children of Light and the Children of Darkness* (New York: Scribner's, 1960), p. 40.

5. James Fallows, "The Passionless Presidency," *Atlantic Monthly*, May 1979. Fallows wrote: "Through most of my last year at the White House, I kept asking myself, Why should a man as well-meaning and intelligent as Carter blithely forgo the lessons of experience and insist on rediscovering fire, the lever, the wheel? Why not temper the fresh view he brought with the practical knowledge of those who had passed this way before? Why, in a man whose language was peppered with 'bold' and 'competent' and 'superb,' was there so little passion to learn how to do the job?" Again: "The first clue to the solution of these questions was Carter's cast of mind: his view of problems as technical, not historical, his lack of curiosity about how the story turned out before.... When he said that, this time, tax reform was going to happen, it was not because he had carefully studied the tales of past failures and learned how to surmount them, but because he had ignored them so totally as to think that his approach had never been tried. In two years, the only historical allusions I heard Carter use with any frequency were Harry Truman's rise from the depths of the polls and the effect of Roosevelt's New Deal on the southern farm..." (p. 44).

6. Morgenthau, in *Control or Fate in Economic Affairs*, ed. Robert H. Connery and Eldon L. Jones (New York: Academy of Political Science, Columbia University, 1971), pp. 199–200.

7. "The Limits to 'Decency' in U.S. Foreign Policy," *The Washington Star*, November 18, 1979, p. 1-H. Professor Kirkpatrick was Leavey Professor of Political Science at Georgetown University.

8. "What Went Wrong and What Do We Do Now?" *The Washington Star*, February 10, 1980 (adapted from Peter Berger, "Indochina and the American Conscience," *Commentary*).

9. By Rowland Evans and Robert Novak, in their column in the *The Washington Post*, September 6, 1979.

10. Coccioli, as quoted in "Those Lovable, Self-Punishing Americans," *Latinview* (Coral Gables, FL: Opiniones Latinamericanas, 1980).

11. As quoted in *The New York Times* Information Bank digest of Vance's speech.

4

Tyranny's Allies

We will build a wall around Cuba, not a
wall of mortar or brick or barbed wire,
but a wall of dedicated men determined
to protect their own liberty and
sovereignty.

—John F. Kennedy
March 18, 1963

THAT was, for many years, American policy toward Fidel Castro—containment, Kennedy-style. The policy changed in 1977 under Carter, and Castro was quick to do his own wall-building, erecting a "wall" around that sea so long thought of as an American lake, the Caribbean.

On his side, the eastern rim, Castro forged a close friendship and ideological alliance with the very like-minded Michael Manley in Jamaica, and sponsored—reportedly, with men and munitions, as well as morally and with money—the revolution that brought to power a Marxist on the small island of Grenada.[1] Farther south, on the northeastern rim of the South American continent, Guyana—itself a neo-Marxist state—has close ties to Castro.

Thus, Castro had a foothold where he originally wanted to start, on the eastern side of the Caribbean, as well as on the west, in Central America. Under Carter, he had a completely unfettered hand, which was not hampered to any appreciable extent even when Red rumbles began to issue from Nicaragua.

But then, how could any of it have been otherwise? We had, after all, recovered from our "inordinate fear of communism." And what were socialist governments, if not "a unique opportunity to establish a new pattern in U.S. foreign policy?"

So it was that, when the Marxist Sandinistas shot their way to power in Nicaragua, Mr. Carter dismissed it as an isolated happenstance and cautioned Americans against worrying that such abrupt changes were "a result of secret, massive Cuban intervention."[2] Evidently he had not worried at all over an early warning in May 2, 1979, from the CIA in a "leaked" secret memo that Castro was on the march in Central America:

> The Castro regime apparently concluded by at least last fall that prospects for revolutionary upheaval in Central America over the next decade or so had markedly improved largely because of the weakened position of countries in Central America. As a result, Cuba has intensified its attempts to unify insurgent groups not only in Nicaragua—where Cuba has concentrated its efforts—but in Guatemala and El Salvador as well. While tailoring the extent of its support to the realities of the situation in each country, Cuba has stepped up its on-island training of guerrillas from each of these countries and—in the case of Nicaragua—has on at least two and probably three occasions supplied arms—for the first time in many years—to the Sandinista National Liberation Front. . . .

That memo was written three months before the fall of Somoza. That memo—detailing Cuba's stepped-up on-island training of guerrillas and renewed arms shipments after a hiatus of many years—was written at a time when the United States was supplying no arms to any of the three Cuban-targeted countries and, in the case of embattled Nicaragua, was blocking arms shipments from other countries still willing to help prevent a Marxist government from reaching power there.

Shortly after the fall of Somoza, *The Economist* took another look at Fidel Castro[4] and his aging "revolution," and had this to say: "Somehow, though, that impetuous figure shambling around in the fatigues of a war fought twenty years ago has blown cigar smoke into the eyes of a lot of people in the West. Until very recently, even many noncommunists looked on Cuba as an interesting experiment in Latin socialism. . . ." The *Washington Star* addressed the same phenomenon in an April 28, 1980, editorial, "The Lessons of Latin America." Noting that the Sandinistas were "settling into a no-compromise Cuban-style overhaul of Nicaraguan society," the *Star* said:

> One of the wonders of it all is that neither local idiosyncrasies nor profound cultural differences appear to matter. The process by which American-aided preemptive revolution, called "reform," helps Marxists gain complete power, the better to fight American "imperialism," seems to work the same way in Asia, Africa, the Middle East.
>
> A still greater wonder is that it can go forward in the midst of the most dramatic evidence that it bears bitter fruit [as witnessed by the] Cubans [who] by the tens of thousands—this hemisphere's version of the Southeast Asian boat people—risk their lives to get away from it. . . .
>
> When will the rest of the developing countries put two and two together? When will we?

For Castro, the subversion of two of the governments in Central America friendly to the United States was pure vengeance. In 1960, Guatemala allowed its territory to be used for a CIA-established training camp for the men who would later go ashore in the botched Bay of Pigs invasion. Nicaragua allowed its territory to be used as the staging area for the invasion itself. Not surprisingly, both countries were targeted by Castro for all-out subversion. With Washington's help, by late 1979, two friendly governments had fallen.

By early 1980, tentative noises began to emit even from the

dovish State Department. Myles Frechette, Cuban affairs director in the department, told the House Inter-American Affairs Subcommittee in mid-April that Castro, with Soviet backing, was casting about in the Caribbean and Central American waters to exploit "targets of opportunity" in Nicaragua, El Salvador, Jamaica, and Guyana.

A French official was less tentative. Paul Dijoud, the state secretary for French Overseas Departments and Territories, was quoted on March 13, 1980, as accusing Castro of fomenting unrest on the island of Martinique, supplying money and advice to independence groups on the island. "International communism is on the march in the Caribbean," Dijoud said, "and Cuba is the Central American staging post for Soviet action. France plans to halt this penetration together with the West and free nations."[5]

Before acquiring Cuba as a dutiful satellite, Moscow had to do its own dirty work in the Western Hemisphere. For the most part, that meant supporting the Moscow-loyal Communist Parties of Chile, Venezuela, Costa Rica, and other Latin countries, and extensive espionage operations from the only two embassies Russia then was allowed to operate in Latin America—Mexico City and Montevideo. There was one risky, overt—and backfiring—attempt at intervention. On May 15, 1954, the Swedish freighter *Alfhem* docked at Puerto Barrios, Guatemala, with two thousand tons in Czech (some reports say Polish) arms, to prop up the tottering pro-Soviet regime of Jacobo Arbenz; Arbenz was out six weeks later anyway, in a CIA-supported coup. (The CIA's involvement is regularly and routinely recalled as conclusive evidence of the United States' evil past in Latin America; Russia's decision to send two thousand tons in arms, through a satellite, is never even mentioned.)

Once Castro came to power, the Soviets were, for the most part, content to support him in his adventures, including his numerous, and feckless, guerrilla campaigns throughout Latin America. Eventually, the Soviets would clamp down even on those operations. Only recently, emboldened by the success of the Sandinistas in Nicaragua, have they displayed renewed interest in the tactics of the "armed struggle."[6]

Detente also put a damper on Soviet-inspired adventures in the hemisphere, though the Russians revived their taste for such adventures long before the Carter administration got around to noticing. A CIA report to Congress on February 6, 1980, recalled in the section "Soviet Use of International Front Organizations":

> At a meeting in February 1979 of World Peace Council (WPC) officials, a resolution was adopted to provide "uninterrupted support for the just struggle of the people of Chile, Guatemala, Uruguay, Haiti, Paraguay, El Salvador, Argentina and Brazil." Without resort to classified information, from this one may logically conclude that the named countries are the targets for Soviet subversion and national liberation struggles on a continuing basis. One may interpret "uninterrupted support" to the just struggle" to mean continuing financial and logistic support to insurrection movements.[7]

Once the "just struggle" of the Sandinistas ended with them in power, the Soviets, along with their Cuban puppets, moved with dispatch to capitalize. Totalitarian measures quickly strangled the arteries of freedom: the electoral process, the press, religion, labor, private enterprise—the gamut of life.

The media's bias, at the inception of Central America's agony, was well served by Amnesty International, which manifested its leanings, in one instance, in a report in 1979 in which it devoted twice as much space to human rights problems in the United States as it did to human rights problems in Cambodia (Kampuchea), and managed to do so without even alluding to the murder of that gentle land. Amnesty is an elitist organization that, its Nobel Peace Prize notwithstanding, persistently leans Left.[8] That focus is important in a Central American context because Amnesty, by relentlessly harping on human rights violations in Nicaragua, El Salvador, and Guatemala, succeeded in weakening these countries at home and isolating them abroad. The influence of Amnesty is important for two reasons: The press regularly and routinely trumpets its reports, most especially those dealing with right-wing countries; and Amnesty's grandiose reputation (based on the Nobel Prize) gives it added leverage with government agencies (such as Carter's State Department's Human Rights Division) and legislative committees around the world.

There is another group of institutionalized outsiders whose role in Central America bears noting—the churches, but mainly the Roman Catholic church. Like Amnesty, the churches, and church leaders, are routinely portrayed in press accounts as objective, dispassionate observers, concerned only with humane and humanitarian issues in government.

The fact is, however, that those who shape and enunciate policy for the large Protestant denominations and for the Roman Catholic church have, for a long time, brought anything but political neutrality to their pursuit of humanitarian goals. Overwhelmingly (there are exceptions, of course, though very few) these lay and clerical church leaders have sided in recent times with the Left—and, frequently, with the gunslinging Left—in developing countries, certainly in Central America.

In his book, *Arrogance of Power*, former U.S. Senator J. William Fulbright quotes a passage from a church publication that illustrates his own convictions about communism. Wrote Fulbright:

Communism, for all its distortions in practice and for all the crimes committed in its name, is a doctrine of social justice and a product of Western civilization, philosophically rooted in humanitarian protest against the injustices of nineteenth-century capitalism. In the words of the religious journal *Christianity and Crisis*: "What is at stake in the case of communism is different from what was at stake in the case of national socialism. Stalinism had many of the worst features of Hitlerism, but it proved to be a passing phase of Soviet communism. It showed itself more open-ended than we had supposed, capable of varying degrees of humanization if not democratization. It is not monolithic, nor is it permanent slavery; and, in its later phases, cooperative as well as competitive coexistence becomes politically and morally possible. . . ."[9]

That attitude would eventually evolve, in the pronouncements and behavior of such organizations as the World Council of Churches, the Quakers (American Friends Service Committee), and such large denominations as the Lutherans, Methodists, and Presbyterians, from one of passive optimism about the nature of communism to one of active support for revolutionary movements like that of the Sandinistas.

Nor has the passage of the years dampened the enthusiasm of mainstream church groups for the radical Left. Discussing plans for the 1987 session of Congress, the Rev. Jay Lintner, director of the Washington office of the 1.6-million member United Church of Christ, would say: "Central America will be the biggest issue, by far, and the key question is whether we could stop American funding of the *Contras*. Another big issue is South Africa."[10]

James L. Tyson, former research director for *Time-Life International* and author of *Target America*, authored a more recent study* documenting "the extensive support American church groups have provided to the Sandinista regime in Nicaragua, as well as to Cuban-supported insurgencies in El Salvador and elsewhere in Latin America." Among some of the highlights:

---

* James L. Tyson, *Prophets or Useful Idiots?: Church Organizations Attacking U.S. Central American Policy* (Washington: Council for the Defense of Freedom, 1987).

• On Nov. 14, 1982, the National Council of Churches claimed that there was no religious repression in Nicaragua, and that such reports were "part of a general trend in the U.S. to discredit the Nicaraguan government."

• Both the National Council of Churches and the U.S. Catholic Conference have contributed support to the far left Council on Hemispheric Affairs (more on COHA and other components of the "revolution lobby" in chapter eight). COHA is in the forefront of generating support for the Sandinistas and communist-supported guerrillas in El Salvador, and generating opposition to the *contras* in Nicaragua.

• The New York Presbyterian Peacemaking Program, in August 1985, distributed "Third World Sermon Notes" to clergymen which included quotations from Sandinista leader Tomas Borge. Allan C. Brownfeld, a writer with wide experience in international security affairs, described Borge as "the man in charge of Nicaragua's relations with the KGB, and the country's extensive prison system, where torture has been well documented." The Washington office of the Presbyterian Church (U.S.A.), active in promoting tours of Nicaragua, issued a report entitled "Our Nation Is Providing Support for the Powers of Death in Central America."

• In investigating the Puerto Rican Marxist terrorist organization, FALN, the FBI followed the trail to the Hispanic Affairs Commission of the Episcopal Church's central office in New York City. (The FALN has claimed responsibility for more than 120 bombings, including the attack on historic Fraunces Tavern in New York City, in which four persons were killed.) Although presiding Bishop John Allin cooperated with the investigation, the Commission's executive director and her secretary went to jail rather than tell what they knew about the whereabouts of Carlos Alberto Torres, a former commission member sought in connection with the bombings. With financial assistance from the National Council of Churches, the church paid the legal fees of the two defiant commission members and gave them $40,000 in church funds upon their release from prison.[11]

In the case of the Roman Catholic church, the watershed event in Latin America was the Bishops' Conference in Medellin, Colombia, in 1968, when the conference went on record as supporting "drastic change" in the hemisphere. Obviously, such a break with tradition had been long developing. Vatican II, from 1962 to 1965, emboldened radicals (mainly European Jesuits and Spanish exiles) already widely dispersed in the clergy, to move the church into ever more militant positions.

By 1972, several church groups were calling openly for formal alliances between Marxists and churchmen.[12] (It is a measure of the media's "honesty" in reporting events in Latin America that long after the about-face of the church had become unmistakable, news accounts would continue to invoke the testimony of churchmen as if they represented the "conservative" or "traditional" side of an issue.)

At the Puebla, Mexico, conference of Latin American bishops in January 1979, Pope John Paul II firmly rejected the "theology of liberation" adopted at Medellin, and pushed ever leftward in the years since. But by then, churchmen were already conspicuous in the front ranks of revolutionaries, and resistance to the papal initiative was strong.

"The Vatican," one priest-revolutionary in Nicaragua said, "is making a mistake in Latin America and Latin America will break the Vatican." The priest, Edgard Parrales, who made no secret of his own belief that a confrontation with Rome was overdue, spoke as the deputy director of the Sandinista government's Social Security Institute.

The Sandinistas would demonstrate vividly what they meant by "confrontation" when the Pope arrived in Managua on March 4, 1983, only to find himself harassed and ridiculed by Sandinista-organized mobs. (More on this incident, and later developments affecting the church in Nicaragua, in chapter 5.)

The pope, who had witnessed Marxism-Leninism first-hand in his native Poland, did not retreat. Instead, the Vatican began developing a counterpoint theology, "reconciliation theology." Joan Frawley Diamond, a contributing editor for *The National Catholic Register*, observed that, encouraged by the pope's exhortation in *Reconciliatio et Paenitentia* (Reconciliation and Penance), issued in 1984, and a more recent pair of documents on liberation theology issued by Cardinal Joseph Ratzinger of the Congregation for the Doctrine of the Faith, "key bishops and theologians have promoted Christian reconciliation, symbolized first by the Eucharist, as a means of healing societies divided by ideology, class and violence."

She quotes the Chilean theologian Fernando Moreno as explaining its basic thrust:

> A theology of reconciliation must deal with the same problems that are addressed by liberation theology—but not in the same way. We must adopt the perspective of the Gospel, which provides the doctrinal basis for an approach reflecting love and reconciliation. Confronting the problem of violence, for example, we cannot justify it as a means for resolving social conflicts. Rather, we must denounce violence. Many liberationists perceive social issues in the same way as Marxists. We do not share in their ideologization or mystification of our problems here. [13]

That attempt to re-direct the church's sense of mission has had no effect on the regime and its cadre of warrior-priests in Nicaragua, although it has had on the embattled and feisty traditional church itself. The fact is that nowhere in America, or the world, have Catholic clergymen emerged so clearly from the ideological shadows and taken positions of visible leadership in a Marxist regime as in the Nicaragua of the Sandinistas. Miguel D'Escoto, the foreign minister, is a Maryknoll priest. The minister of culture, Ernesto Cardenal, is a priest. (Both men were suspended from their priestly functions for defying a Vatican order to choose between their religious and secular offices.) Ernesto's brother, Fernando Cardenal, a Jesuit, is head of the country's literacy campaign (widely regarded as a campaign of unprecedented Marxist indoctrination of a nation's youth). Priests occupy high posts in the Ministry of Economic Planning and the Social Security Institute. Others are consultants. An American nun, Sister Mary Hartman, heads the Sandinista-run "human rights commission," a propaganda mouthpiece for the government designed to deflect attention from the independent human rights commission.

Others too have donned khakis. The Spanish priest Gaspar Garcia Laviana, parish priest in Tola, Department of Rivas, Nicaragua, not only donned a Sandinista uniform, but rose through the Sandinista ranks to become a commander. Father Garcia Laviana's "Leftist clericalism," one of those convenient code phrases, ended when he was killed in a clash with government troops in a tiny village of Rivas named—El Infierno (the Spanish word for hell).

Father Garcia Laviana was, in fact, following in the footsteps of many Latin American clergymen who alternated cassocks with khakis, the most celebrated forerunner of the current generation of Leftist revolutionaries being Camilo Torres, the Colombian priest killed in 1966 while leading a guerrilla band.

Church participation in radical politics in volatile El Salvador had been less widespread than in Nicaragua, but, because of the murder of Archbishop Oscar Arnulfo Romero in March 24, 1980, more spectacular. Archbishop Romero's political activism earned him a Vatican rebuke only a few weeks before his murder. He was also disdained by his fellow Salvadoran bishops, none of whom attended his funeral. The archbishop firmly opposed the U.S.-imposed junta. The junta, he said in a February 1980 letter to President Carter, "does not govern this country; rather, political power is in the hands of the unscrupulous military, who know only how to repress the people and favor the interests of the Salvadoran oligarchy." That was, in fact, the line taken by El Salvador's radical Left, which responded to the junta and its U.S.-promoted reforms by escalating its own war of terror and intimidation. The archbishop's analysis erred also in naming the "oligarchy" as masters of the military. The Right reacted with its own wave of violence to the junta and its "reforms," because the "reforms" were aimed mainly at robbing them of their land and financial wealth. Archbishop Romero, while repudiating military violence, nevertheless supported openly and often the "legitimate right to revolutionary violence."[14] None of this could or should, of course, excuse the vicious murder of an unarmed priest as he said Mass; it does, however, clarify that he had thrust himself into the center of a maelstrom of hatred and horror engulfing the country.

Seven years after the death of the archbishop, the Church in El Salvador, under the impetus of reconciliation theology, is a new and vital force in that country's embattled democracy. According to Ms. Desmond, moderate bishops and scholars argue that El Salvador in 1987 had changed for the better "because of the local Church's concerted effort to promote Christian principles, not political ideology, and dialogue, not confrontation." At a 1986 theological conference in Lima, Gregorio Rosa Chavez, San Salvador's auxiliary bishop, said that if El Salvador survived as a democracy, "it would further justify the bishops' advocacy of dialogue and their rejection of class struggle to achieve political freedom and economic justice."

Just as the El Salvador of 1987 is now the "flagship" of "reconciliation theology," neighboring Nicaragua remains the vanguard of the most radical brand of Marxist-overlaid liberation theology. Yet, as Ms. Frawley observes, the country is in such a shambles that even Gustavo Gutierrez, author of the seminal work, *A Theology of Liberation*, has "publicly distanced himself from the Sandinista vision of heaven."[15]

The alliance between the church and Marxism in Latin America was the result of a long process. Father Harvey (Pablo) Steele, a Canadian priest who had worked for twenty-five years in Latin America, summed up the sentiments of many, and particularly the legion of foreign priests and nuns in Latin America, when he told an interviewer in 1972: "I am convinced that the future of Latin America belongs to the Left."

Even the most basic of Christianity's documents, the Bible, has been subverted to Leftist political ends in one highly popular Roman Catholic edition called the Latin American Bible. One photograph of the Bible, for example, shows a crowded plaza in Havana, and a man holding a poster of Lenin with the inscription: "The Fatherland or Death." In the background, a man waves a Soviet flag. A huge billboard on the front of a building behind the crowd shows workers—one of them brandishing a submachine gun—holding up a banner that proclaims: "Long Live Our Socialist Revolution." Beneath the photograph is a message: "The faithful participate in political life and, under whatever type of regime, seek the kind of society which gives dignity to all."

As one writer put it several years ago, the church founded by the Prince of Peace has become "the subversive church."[16] Just as El Salvador and Nicaragua are, in the larger sense, the opposites in a contest between democracy and Marxism-Leninism, so, too, do the two countries offer side-by-side contrasts between a church of peace and one committed to conflict.

Such progress as the pope has achieved in rolling back a vision of Catholicism based on accommodation with an atheistic philosophy—Marxism-Leninism—it is clear, from the aggressive resistance he encountered during his September 1987 visit to the United States, that the U.S. church remains on a leftward course. (More on the role of the U.S. and local Catholic Church in Central America in chapters five and eight).

* * *

For many Central Americans, for many years, the "colossus of the North" referred not to the United States, but to Mexico.

Though mostly a passive spectator to the incandescent events in Central America, Mexico has consistently pursued a certain diplomacy: it will support the Left against the Right. Mexico, site of the first socialist revolution in the Americas, was, it should be remembered, the only member of the Organization of American States which refused to go along with the Venezuela-inspired boycott of Fidel Castro's regime and, later, the break in diplomatic relations with Castro.

So it was that, on May 20, 1979, President Jose Lopez Portillo of Mexico broke diplomatic relations with Somoza, while the battle for control of Nicaragua was still raging. Within days of Mexico's decision, two other countries, Panama and Grenada—both ruled by dictatorships—also invoked moral reasons for breaking with Somoza. These maneuvers cleared the way for the Sandinistas to declare a government-in-exile, quickly recognized by Costa Rica, Grenada, and Panama. This, in turn, gave the Sandinistas a legitimacy and leverage they had until then lacked, and was one of the decisive events in their final victory two months later.

More recently, Mexico has also proved a friendly haven for Guatemalan guerrillas, whose training camps house Cubans and Palestinians. A Nicaragua guerrilla, Ligdamis Gutierrez Espinosa, caught coming into El Salvador at the Guatemalan border in February 1982, said he trained at the Institute of Coahuila in Saltillo, near Monterrey, Mexico. (Of the forty trainees at the center, half were Salvadorans, six were Mexicans, and the rest Nicaraguans. The Mexican government hotly denied the charge; the Nicaraguan, it said, was an innocent university student on vacation.)[17]

The complex and crucial internal and external dimensions of Mexico's place on the larger stage of Middle America—the term geographers use to describe the seven countries lying between the Rio Grande and the dense jungles of the Darien Gap—are the subject of chapter 6 of this volume.

Two other non-Central American countries deserve brief mention. Panama supported the Sandinista uprising perhaps more intensively than any other country. The Sandinistas trained in Panama, and Panamanian planes ferried men and supplies to the Sandinista forward base camps in Costa Rica. Panamanian police and aviation advisers worked with the Sandinistas once they were in power.

The other country is Venezuela, long ambitious to exert a tutelary role throughout the Caribbean basin. Venezuela was a principal arms supplier to the Sandinistas and, with Mexico, a key factor in blocking OAS action against neighbors Costa Rica and Panama for their flagrant intervention in Nicaraguan affairs.

One other "outside" factor must be mentioned, because it has so persistently through the ages shattered man's best hopes and efforts. That "interloper" is nature.

Central America sits astride the so-called Circle of Fire of earthquake activity. In recent times there have been two earthquakes germane to this essay.

The first of them, one of the worst in Nicaragua's history, struck Managua shortly after midnight on December 23, 1972. More than six thousand persons were killed, twenty thousand injured, and three hundred thousand left homeless. The earthquake all but obliterated the capital city, destroying an estimated 90 percent of Managua's commercial establishments and 70 percent of the city's housing, and leaving sixty thousand jobless. Rebuilding costs were put at $772 million. (The U.S. earmarked some $200 million in emergency and reconstruction funds for Nicaragua, but not all of that money was actually delivered.)

Among the important aftershocks was the greed of Somoza, and some of the senior National Guard officers who hogged business opportunities arising from the reconstruction program. This brought Somoza into collision with the (until then) mostly docile business sector, which was far from blameless itself.

Yet another earthquake—actually a series of earthquakes—though less noted, was, according to *National Geographic* (June 1976), "one of the worst disasters ever to hit the Western Hemisphere," and ninety times more powerful than the one that destroyed Managua. The quakes wrenched a wide band across Guatemala in February 1976. Twenty-three thousand were killed, seventy-seven thousand injured, and one million left homeless. Damage was estimated at a billion dollars; yet, mainly because of Carter's "human rights" policy, precious little U.S. aid was forthcoming to ameliorate this catastrophic human suffering. The U.S. gave Guatemala loans and grants of all types in fiscal year 1977 of $27.5 million; $10.6 million in 1978; $40.2 million in 1979. (It should be remembered that Guatemala's population is nearly triple that of Nicaragua.)

On September 19, 1985, it was Mexico City's turn. That morning, a quake registering 8.1 ripped along a fault extending from the southwest coast inland, finally reaching the alluvial lake bed on which downtown Mexico City is built. More than 100 buildings collapsed, many more were damaged. Just as rescue workers were moving in, an aftershock the next day registering 7.5 created new havoc. Altogether, an estimated 20,000 persons died and rebuilding costs were put at $2 billion-plus. Foreign help—at first spurned—came pouring in, including a $300 million World Bank loan.

The following year, disaster would strike still another Central American capital—this time, violence-plagued San Salvador. The October quake, measuring 7.5 on the Richter scale, left an estimated 200,000 homeless and devastated the city center. An estimated 1,000 died.

Central America is also an area of intense volcanic activity.

There are thirty-four active volcanoes in the region. The region is also on the western fringe of the Caribbean hurricane basin. Roaring through the country's banana plantations and other coastal areas in 1974, Hurricane Fifi caused the economy of Honduras to "practically stagnate," in the phrase of the UN *Economic Survey of Latin America, 1976*. Agriculture, which generates approximately 30 percent of Honduras's gross domestic product and 75 percent of its export income, was so hard hit that, in contrast to steady growth in earlier years, it actually declined 8.6 percent in 1974 and 5.9 percent in 1975. Bananas, the top crop, suffered hardest: The value of banana exports declined 15.2 percent in 1974 and 22.5 percent in 1975. The country's overall gross domestic product, one of the fastest growing in Latin America during most of the seventies, dropped 0.8 percent in 1974 and barely crawled at 1.4 percent in 1975. (There was an impressive recovery in all of the above indicators in 1976.)[18]

In Central America, as in so many areas of this world, man proposes, God, with nature, disposes. Clearly, the very best efforts of nations and governments to solve their deep and agonizing problems are, in the end, vulnerable to the veto of forces well above and beyond those of man.

NOTES

1. The election of Edward Seaga in Jamaica on October 30, 1980, was a democratic victory that surprised both Cuba and the United States. The more recent events in Grenada—the bloody takeover of the country by Marxist General Hudson Austin, the assassination of Marxist Prime Minister Maurice Bishop, the imperiled one thousand American medical students, the call to the U.S. for help by six neighboring Caribbean nations, and President Reagan's intervention—have, of course, changed the scene. The ouster of the Cuban presence from Surinam is also significant in this respect. The open challenge to

Castro's rule in the region could not have taken place, it can safely be stated, had Carter still been at the helm of this country.

2. "It's a mistake," Mr. Carter said, "for Americans to assume or to claim that every time an evolutionary change takes place or even an abrupt change takes place in this hemisphere that somehow it's a result of secret, massive Cuban intervention. . . . We have good relationships with the new government. We hope to improve it." The Sandinistas had been in power less than one week. Quoted in Ray S. Cline, *World Power Trends and U.S. Foreign Policy for the 1980's* (Boulder, CO: Westview Press, 1980) pp. 161–62.

3. As quoted in a photostatic copy of the letter in the periodical *Spotlight*, March 3, 1980, p. 14. The distinguished British journalist Robert Moss had reported even earlier, August 31, 1979, on that CIA memo, in an article in *National Review* (p. 1076).

4. "Smoke in Whose Eyes?" *Economist*, April 12, 1980. Examples abound, of course, of Castro's failure to create anything other than a huge, impoverished, and totally dependent concentration camp.

5. Kincaid, in his column in *Washington Weekly*, April 8, 1980, cited a Reuters News Service dispatch of that date.

6. *Soviet World Outlook* reported on April 15, 1980, that "an upsurge of theoretical writings on the meaning of Nicaragua includes indications of a turnabout in Soviet assessments of Che Guevara's theories of armed struggle hitherto condemned by Moscow." *Soviet World Outlook*, Advanced International Studies Institute (Washington, D.C., in association with the University of Miami), "Increasing Focus on Central America," vol. 5, no. 4.

7. "CIA Study: Soviet Covert Action and Propaganda," presented to the Oversight Subcommittee, Permanent Select Committee on Intelligence of the House of Representatives, February 6, 1980, by the deputy director of operations of the CIA, p. IV-14. This important report—spelling out in book-length detail the CIA's analyses of how, why, and where the Russians carry on their $3.5 billion a year campaigns of propaganda and covert action—received scant press coverage. The same study (p. IV-13) reported that "a leader of the Mexican peace movement affiliated to the World Peace Council met recently with leaders of the North American Peace Movement in Los Angeles [and] agreed [among other things] to denounce the U.S. and especially CIA attempts to impede the Sandinistas in Nicaragua. . . ."

8. See, for example, Scoble and Wiseberg, "Human Rights and Amnesty International," in "The Annals of the American Academy of Political and Social Science: Interest Groups in International Perspective" (May 1974), Lancaster, PA. 17604; or, for a revealing critique of AI's Guatemala reporting, see L. Francis Bouchey and Alberto M. Piedra, *Gua-*

temala: A Promise in Peril (Washington: Council for Inter-American Security, 1980), pp. 65–73.

9. J. William Fulbright, *Arrogance of Power* (New York: Random House, 1966), p. 80.

10. Allan C. Brownfield, "How U.S. Church Groups Further Soviet Goals in Central America," in *Human Events*, June 6, 1987, p. 10.

11. Ibid., pp. 10–11.

12. For example, more than four hundred Catholic priests and laymen from all over Latin America gathered in Santiago, Chile, for an April 1972 conference to study the melding of Marxism and Christianity. An article in the Roman Catholic church publication *Maryknoll* that year (February 1972, vol. 66, no. 2) said a group of eighty Chilean priests saw the church as a "liberating stimulant for change," and that "Marxism and Christianity find common cause in a certain form of socialism which could open a new hope for man 'to become more fulfilled and at the same time more evangelical. . . .' " There were scores of such movements during that period, and an even greater number of statements on the compatibility of Marxism and the church.

13. Joan Frawley Desmond, "Liberation Through Reconciliation; Reconciliation Theology Has Made a Difference in El Salvador. It Has Yet to Be Tried In Nicaragua," in *Crisis*, July–August 1987, pp. 14–15.

14. The quote from the letter to President Carter is from a *Washington Post* story, "Clouds of Civil War Swirl over El Salvador," in the *Charlotte Observer*, March 26, 1980, p. 2-A. The "revolutionary violence" quote is from "Spreading Chaos in Central America," *U.S. News and World Report*, March 3, 1980, p. 26.

15. Ibid., pp. 14–15.

16. Father Steele was quoted in an article by Nathan Haverstock, "Is Foreign Clerical Force Menace to Latins?" *Evening Star and Daily News* (Washington, D.C.), September 30, 1972. Data on the Latin American Bible are from an Associated Press dispatch, "Controversy Spurs Sale of Latin American Bible," *Miami Herald*, November 26, 1976, p. 32-A. The "subversive church" quote is from a Copley News service article datelined Bogota, in *Times of the Americas* (Washington, D.C.), July 12, 1972.

17. "Nicaraguan Cited by Haig Finds Asylum," *The New York Times*, March 6, 1982. "Haig and Salvador Official Meet; Nicaraguan Is at Mexican Embassy," *The Washington Post*, March 6, 1982.

18. *Economic Survey of Latin America, 1976* (Santiago, Chile: Commission for Latin America, 1977), pp. 247–55.

5

Central America Today

> . . . *If we* [*the freedom fighters*]
> *disappear, the other Central American*
> *countries will not be able to stop the*
> *Sandinista efforts to expand into their*
> *nations. And every year after we lose or*
> *are out of the picture, United States*
> *economic and military aid to the region*
> *will double. . . .*
>> —Col. Enrique Bermudez,
>> commander of the Nicaraguan
>> Resistance Forces, reacting to
>> speculation about a cut-off of
>> U.S. military aid to freedom
>> fighters under the Arias "peace"
>> plan.[1]

ON January 14, 1984, the blue-ribbon commission headed by former Secretary of State Henry Kissinger recommended a five-year economic development plan for Central America. The total cost for four countries was pegged at $20.6 billion; with Nicaragua included, $24.6 billion. Of that total, $8 billion would come from the United States, the rest from other outside sources. Spending of that magnitude, the Commission found, would put the inhabitants of those countries—by 1990—right back where they were in 1979, before the Carter Administration set out to save them.[2] Those inhabitants, that is, who managed to live through the holocaust aided, abetted—and, as we have seen—in large measure made possible only because of what the United States did, what the United States refused to do. It is not, either, clear, how many would live to enjoy that standard of living in freedom, nor how well their permanently realigned societies could provide, alone, for themselves in the future.

The triumph of communism in Nicaragua has posed a serious and constant threat to all of Central America, a fact that is well recognized by the Central Americans themselves. Indeed, contrary to media-managed impressions in the United States, Europe, and elsewhere, Central Americans clearly understand that the danger comes not from the United States, but from the Soviet bloc and its puppets. For example, a Gallup poll in 1987 showed that: (1) three-fourths of all Central Americans view the Soviet Union as responsible for fomenting violence in the region; (2) from a low of 64 percent (Guatemala) to a high of 79 percent (Costa Rica), Central Americans believe the Sandinistas do not enjoy the support of the Nicaraguan people; are, in other words, a minority in their own land; (3) from a low of 46 percent (in El Salvador) to a high of 72 percent (in Costa Rica), Central Americans believe that the *contras* do enjoy the support of the majority of the Nicaraguan people (and even the Salvadorans, living in a war-ravaged country themselves, divided 46–20 on this question, the rest undecided); (4) two-thirds of Central Americans approve of U.S. military and humanitarian aid to the *contras*. In yet another survey, 80 percent of Costa Ricans said they have little or no confidence that the Sandinistas will comply with the peace plan drafted by their own president, Oscar Arias Sanchez.[3]

Morris Rothenberg, a specialist on Soviet affairs in the western hemisphere, has noted that the Soviets saw in the Sandinista triumph a demonstration of the possibility of anti-American revolutionary transformations in the "strategic rear" of the United States. He cites the Prague-based *World*

Marxist Review as affirming that the Nicaraguan triumph constituted "a further setback of imperialism that has, moreover, affected a most sensitive area traditionally regarded by imperialism as its most dependable 'hinterland.' " A Soviet diplomat—Vladimir Chernyshev, Moscow's ambassador to Brazil—was even blunter:

> The most important event has undoubtedly been the Sandinista victory in Nicaragua, and the way things are going, we will have another Cuba there.[5]

To explore the character of the communist threat and to see how well prepared the region is to deal with it, let us take a brief look at the five countries most immediately concerned—Nicaragua, El Salvador, Honduras, Guatemala, and Costa Rica.

NICARAGUA

In size and population, Nicaragua resembles the state of Iowa. With about 3.4 million people, it is the most sparsely populated country in Central America. One of the most important events in Nicaragua's recent history was its occupation by U.S. Marines almost continuously from 1912 to 1927. During that period American authorities ran the entire economic and political systems. The United States sought to establish democracy in Nicaragua, and in 1924 succeeded in organizing and supervising a fair and honest election—the fairest to date in the country's caudillo-ruled history.

The Marines left Nicaragua in 1925, optimistic about the prospects for a stable democracy, but a power grab by Emiliano Chamorro in 1926 sparked a civil war that triggered another U.S. intervention. It was after their return in 1926–27 that the Marines engaged the guerrilla forces of General Sandino, whose anti-American propaganda was so valuable to the Soviet Union.

Contrary to popular opinion, the United States did not "install" President Anastasio Somoza Garcia, the first of three Somozas to rule Nicaragua until the Sandinista takeover in 1979. The Marines withdrew in 1933, leaving Somoza in control of the Nicaraguan National Guard. He had Sandino murdered the next year, and seized power for himself in 1936.

Somoza, in turn, was assassinated in 1956. He was replaced by his son Luis Somoza Debayle, who retired in 1963. Luis's younger brother, Anastasio Somoza II, took over in 1967, beginning a twenty-two year tenure that was to become increasingly corrupt. What is often overlooked is that Somoza's rule was ratified in 1974, when he won re-election in balloting widely reported at the time as free, although, as in most Third World elections, there were numerous charges of irregularities.

The Sandinista National Liberation Front (FSLN) was founded in July of 1961 by Carlos Fonseca (a communist trained in the USSR and Cuba), Tomas Borge, and Silvio Mayorga. Given his own repudiation of communism, it is unlikely that General Sandino, whose name the Sandinistas appropriated, would have been sympathetic to their communist aims. Fidel Castro was sympathetic, however, so he provided the Sandinistas with training and funding from the start.[6] Castro advised them as early as March 1970 to downplay their Marxist ideology and to form a broad coalition with non-Marxists, the better to topple Somoza.[7]

In 1977, the FSLN launched an unsuccessful series of ambushes against the National Guard. By that time, the Sandinistas were led by the Ortega brothers, Daniel and Humberto; Carlos Fonseca had been killed and Tomas Borge was in jail for the murder of a policeman (having admitted, during his trial, his collaboration in sixty-one other murders).[8]

In January 1978, the murder of newspaper publisher Pedro Joaquin Chamorro of *La Prensa*, long one of Somoza's most vocal critics, coalesced opposition to Somoza as never before. (Chamorro's murder was a rallying cry of worldwide opposition to Somoza, who was repeatedly taunted for failing to find the murderer. Once in power, the Sandinistas made no serious effort to solve the crime, and little mention would again be made outside the country.) Later that year, the Sandinistas achieved a major terrorist success when Eden Pastora (*Comandante Cero*) boldly seized the National (legislative) Palace in Managua, taking 1,500 hostages. Somoza caved in to Sandinista demands, one of which was the release of Tomas Borge. The event catapulted the FSLN to the forefront of the anti-Somoza opposition.

Shortly after the Palace raid, the trickle of arms reaching the Sandinistas through Costa Rica became a heavy flow. The principal suppliers were Venezuela, Panama, and Cuba (the first, a left-wing democracy historically hostile to Somoza, the second two ruled by dictators, one pro-Soviet, the second a Soviet puppet). Nor was the stepped-up flow of arms an accident. In 1977, Fidel Castro assigned Armando Ulises Estrada, from the American Department of the Cuban Communist Party, to assemble a network for supplying weapons and logistical support to the Sandinistas. (He would remain on the job until the final Sandinista victory in 1979.)[9] Costa Rica provided base camps, while Panama, Cuba, and Venezuela contributed arms, training, supplies, and logistical support. When the Organization of American States contemplated taking action against this flagrant intervention, it was blocked by Venezuela and Mexico. Somoza had few friends.

President Jimmy Carter was not among them. The U.S. complicity in Somoza's ouster presents a sorry chapter in American diplomacy. Pulling the rug out from under Somoza was just part of Carter's naive human rights policy. While he sought to avoid a Sandinista takeover by replacing Somoza with a moderate government, key members of his administration appear to have been sympathetic to the FSLN, motivated more by Leftist ideology than by concern for either human rights or U.S. interests.[10]

As Somoza cracked down on increasing civil unrest and Sandinista-staged terrorism, abusing human rights in the process, the Carter administration cut back U.S. economic and military assistance, thereby signalling that Somoza stood alone. In February 1978, the State Department said that "the number of reported abuses and their severity have decreased markedly over the past year." Yet that month, U.S. Ambassador Mauricio Solaun advised the Nicaraguan president to make a public promise that he would leave office at the end of his term in 1981. Somoza complied on February 27.[11]

In September of 1978, the Carter administration suspended military aid to Nicaragua. Also in that month, the United States proposed the creation of a mediation team, to be sponsored by the Organization of American States (OAS), through which the U.S. could better influence negotiations between Somoza and his opposition. From that point on, the Carter administration played a key role in the course of events.

The U.S. representative on the three-nation mediation team was Special Envoy William Bowdler. According to journalist Shirley Christian—who won a Pulitzer Prize for her reporting on Nicaragua—Bowdler's assessment was that Somoza was a sick man who needed oxygen and that the United States controlled all the valves. On October 6, Bowdler told Somoza to resign.[12] About that time, the United States persuaded the International Monetary Fund to postpone a decision on a $20 million line of credit to which Nicaragua was entitled under IMF rules.

Seeking to bolster his credibility and legitimacy, Somoza proposed on November 6 that a plebiscite be conducted to test the relative strength of the various opposition groups, with the strongest group to be invited to join his government. Americans in Washington and Managua were divided on the plebiscite idea. Bowdler was against it, arguing that Somoza should be made to step down as soon as possible. Ambassador Solaun was less favorable toward an ultimatum. According to Christian, "Solaun thought the White House was too wrapped up in its own ideals to comprehend Nicaraguan reality. Gradually, however, the entire embassy staff, including Solaun, was cut out of the mediation process, and Bowdler and James Cheek, his deputy, handled virtually everything." It was decided to promote the plebiscite but to organize it so as to work against Somoza.[13]

On November 21, the OAS mediators issued a proposal for a plebiscite, to be supervised by the OAS, not to test the strength of Somoza's opposition but to determine whether he should stay or go. If Somoza won, the strongest opposition party would join his government; if he lost, he was out, to be replaced by a council of state and a three-man junta.

There were extensive negotiations over the terms of the plebiscite. The opposition insisted that Somoza and his family leave the country during the campaigning and voting. On November 30, Somoza accepted the plebiscite in principle but would not agree to leave the country. The negotiations stalled, and the mediators gave up on the idea in January 1979.

Excluded from the negotiations, Ambassador Solaun left Nicaragua in early 1979, soon to resign from the diplomatic service.

In March 1979, the three Sandinista factions, prodded by the Cubans, agreed to unite for the final offensive. The three —Prolonged Popular Struggle, Proletarian Tendency, and Third Force—named a nine-man directorate, which remains unchanged as the real government of Nicaragua to this day. A secret operations center was set up in San Jose, the Costa Rican capital, and the northwestern region of the country near the Nicaraguan border became the staging area for planes ferrying weapons from Cuba, Panama, and Venezuela. When that final offensive began, in June 1979, Cuban military advisers in radio contact with Havana were instrumental in training, arming and transporting the international brigades that joined the Sandinistas.[14]

Somoza's position rapidly deteriorated. In February, Carter formally ended the military aid that had already been suspended. Somoza turned to Israel for arms, but, in April, the U.S. pressured Israel to stop selling. On June 18, Lawrence Pezzullo, who had just replaced Solaun as U.S. Ambassador in Managua, met in Washington with Somoza's cousin, Luis Pallais, to ask for Somoza's resignation, demanding an answer by three P.M. the next day. Somoza offered conditional compliance. He wanted time to prepare an orderly succession to prevent a communist takeover.[15]

In a breach without precedent before or since of the two cardinal principals ostensibly underpinning the inter-American system—non-intervention and self-determination—the OAS, in an action fully orchestrated by the United States, joined the chorus on June 23, calling for Somoza's "definitive replacement." Interestingly, of the five Central American countries, only Costa Rica—locked in a blood feud with Somoza going back 25 years—would vote for that resolution. Indeed, despite heavy lobbying and arm-twisting, the United States was able to scrape up only the bare minimum of 17 votes needed to pass the resolution, an action tantamount to the overthrow of a government with which the U.S. was still formally allied. Nicaragua was also a country that had steadfastly supported the United States for years, and not infrequently in ways which were certain to arouse the wrath of Latin countries now clamoring for Somoza's scalp. That resolution bears closer inspection. Following a three-paragraph preamble that located the blame for the bloodletting in Nicaragua entirely with the legitimate government—and not with those who were trying to shoot their way into power—it then declared that "the solution of this serious problem belongs exclusively to the Nicaraguan people." The seventeen foreign ministers then proceeded to tell the Nicaraguan people what that solution should be:

1. Immediate and definitive replacement of the Somocista regime.

2. Installation in the Nicaraguan territory of a democratic government that involves in its constitution the representatives of the major groups opposed to the Somoza regime that reflect the free will of the people of Nicaragua.
3. Full guarantee of the Human Rights for all the Nicaraguan people without exceptions.
4. Carrying out free elections as early as possible that lead to the establishment of a true democratic government that will guarantee peace, freedom and justice.[16]

Once in power—power which it was never intended would belong exclusively to them, power they never had any intention of sharing—the Sandinistas would honor not a single one of those commitments. (In his tape-recorded conversations with Somoza during the final, crucial weeks of the regime—discussed in greater detail later in this chapter—U.S. Ambassador Pezzullo would repeatedly profess uncertainty as to the true character, composition and aims of the Sandinistas. Odd. The Sandinistas' 1977 strategy document said, quite specifically, that they would work with non-Marxist groups to oust Somoza, but

... we will prevent the dissenting bourgeoisie from assuming political leadership ... [and] maintain political hegemony among our forces during this tactical and temporary alliance. ...

The document calls capitalism an "archaic, dependent system," adding:

... once the People's Sandinista Revolution has achieved its purpose of ousting the dictatorship ... we will be able to develop along progressive Marxist-Leninist lines. We will be a party of iron, forged and tempered in the same process to enable us to fully organize and mobilize the masses. ... [17]

In this, the Sandinistas were as good as their word. Once in power, they moved swiftly, decisively, and often ruthlessly, to consolidate their own absolute control, crushing or reducing to impotence rival forces. It would take the OAS five years, and then only under the insistent prodding of a different kind of U.S. Ambassador, J. William Middendorf, to even take note of the Sandinistas' wholesale violations of the 14-point agreement they signed in conjunction with the OAS resolution.

Realizing he was finished, Somoza still struggled to spare his country a communist dictatorship. Acquiescing even to Ambassador Pezzullo's demand that he select a National Guard chief from among six names Washington had decided would be "acceptable," Somoza agreed to name Col. Federico Mejia. In so doing, he believed he had Pezzullo's pledge that the National Guard would be kept intact and merged with the Sandinista forces, thus providing some measure of safety for those Nicaraguans who had been loyal to him, as well as a cushion against a communist takeover. When Pezzullo gave him those guarantees, Somoza resigned,[18] with the understanding that he would be succeeded, at least temporarily, by Francisco Urcuyo, speaker of the lower house of the Nicaraguan Congress. According to Pezzullo, who did not speak to Urcuyo, an agreement was reached with Somoza that Urcuyo would immediately pass power to Archbishop (now Cardinal) Obando y Bravo, who would, in turn, hand it to a Sandinista-controlled junta.[19]

It was on the night of July 12 that Somoza summoned Urcuyo to his underground bunker to announce his impending resignation. According to Urcuyo, "Until that moment, I still believed I could count on the support of the U.S. government. I could never imagine the trap which the Pezzullo-Bowdler twosome on the one hand, and the Junta of Reconstruction [as the Sandinista government would be called] on the other, had woven together to bring, with blood, socialism to my country."[20]

On July 17, the Nicaraguan Congress was called into session, Somoza's resignation was read, and Urcuyo was elected president. Somoza then left for Miami. That night the National Guard ordered Managua evacuated: the Guard was running out of ammunition and the regime's military position was collapsing. In no small measure, that was a direct result of the effectiveness of the U.S. stranglehold over all arms shipments to Nicaragua. At midnight, Pezzullo advised the General Staff to surrender without any conditions or guarantees.

"Had Nicaragua been able to purchase arms and ammunition"—Somoza would write later—"we would have continued our fight against the aggressor forces alone. I am confident we could have defeated the enemy."[21]

Early the next morning, Pezzullo and his aides went to Urcuyo's residence and awakened him to demand that he surrender power to the archbishop, and ultimately to the junta. Urcuyo refused, saying he knew nothing of any deal made with Somoza and had no intention of transferring power to the Sandinistas.[22] With the disintegration of the National Guard, however, he had little choice. Some reports said he agreed to do so only after Somoza called him from Miami, telling him that Warren Christopher, number two man in the State Department, had warned him to tell Urcuyo that if he did not surrender power to the Sandinistas, Somoza would be handed over to them.[23]

Urcuyo contacted the president of Guatemala, who sent three planes to evacuate the new government, such as it was. At eight P.M. on July 18, 1979, Urcuyo and his staff flew into exile. The next day, Managua fell to the rebels.

In retrospect, I think of the two things I requested of the United States—only two. Repeatedly I asked for preservation of the Guardia Nacional, and a commitment from the United States that Nicaragua would not be turned over to the Communists. . . . The United States promised that the Guardia would be preserved, and the United States promised that the Marxists would not take over Nicaragua. . . . Every promise made to me, the government, and the people of Nicaragua was broken. . . . Out of these tapes comes the stark and frightening realization that the "word" of the United States no longer means anything. It's a certainty that other nations will act accordingly . . . .

—Anastasio Somoza, in *Nicaragua Betrayed*

Somoza might have added another broken promise. He had been promised he would be received in the United States as a Chief of State, enjoying the same protection of U.S. law as any other citizen. Within six hours, Warren Christopher, the number two man in the State Department, saying he was acting on President Carter's orders, told Somoza he was not welcome in the United States. On September 17, 1980, Somoza died in a barrage of machinegun and bazooka fire on a street in Asuncion, Paraguay, the third stop in his odyssey of exile.[24]

The civil war, which had cost Nicaragua ten thousand dead,[25] was finally over. The United States wasted no time in sending aid to the new Sandinista regime—nor in boasting of its role in overthrowing Somoza.[26] The Sandinistas, in turn, wasted no time in laying the foundations for a Cuban-style communist state. Even their program of government—"The Historic Program of the FSLN"—was based closely on Fidel Castro's "Manifesto No. 1 to the People of Cuba" of Aug. 8, 1955. (The FSLN document is included as Appendix # 2 because it reveals both the mendaciousness and cynicism of its authors—it is a litany of promises of freedoms and plenty that were never kept—but also of their searing hatred for the U.S., their unflinching devotion to Marxist-Leninist ideas.)

The Military Build-Up

The Sandinistas overthrew Somoza with a force of 5,000 men.[27] Since taking power, however, they have built the largest military force in Central America: 119,000 men, by most accounts.[28] Somoza's National Guard, by contrast, never numbered more than 15,000, even at the height of the war. Until mid-December 1987, it was believed that the goal of the Sandinista government was to expand its military to 250,000 men. Even at that level, it would be comparable, in terms of population, to the size of the U.S. military in World War II! But, deep into the process ostensibly designed to bring peace to Central America, a 34-year-old major, disillusioned with Marxism, defected to the United States and exploded a bombshell: Under secret accords signed with the Soviet Union, the Sandinistas were planning, over 15 years, to build a regular and reserve army numbering 600,000. Armament would include Soviet-supplied MiG21 jet fighters. Nor would that build-up be designed to deal with the *contras*, since the Sandinistas envsioned defeating them decisively in the period 1988–1990. In fact, the biggest part of the build-up—surpassing, in relative terms, even the Soviet-sponsored expansion of the Cuban military into the hemisphere's second largest armed force—would occur after 1990. And, it would be designed to ward off any invasion from the United States. Should such an invasion come, the Sandinistas would move to expand the conflict to other countries, including bombing neighboring Costa Rica. The source, Major Roger Miranda Bengoechea, knew whereof he spoke: for five years, he had headed the Sandinista Defense Ministry's secretariat. In that post, he participated in the most secret discussions and had access to the most sensitive secrets. When he defected on October 25, 1987, Defense Minister Humberto Ortega said Miranda's defection was "the most important betrayal" in the seven years of Sandinista rule.[29]

Even before that massive build-up, Nicaragua already had almost five times the number of military bases it had under Somoza, and it was in the process of building the longest airstrip in Central America, capable of handling any aircraft in the Soviet inventory.

113

The armed forces of the FSLN have at their disposal at least 150 Soviet T-55 main battle tanks and 300 other tanks (PT-76) and armored vehicles. (Somoza had only three battle tanks, ten tanks altogether; Nicaragua's neighbors, Honduras, El Salvador, and Costa Rica, today have among them fewer than thirty.)[30] Nicaragua already has several dozen Soviet HIND helicopters, a machine Ollie North has described as "the most devastating attack helicopter . . . the most sophisticated assault platform in the world today."[31] So far, the Soviets have spurned Sandinista requests for MiG fighter planes, but reports persist of the training of Nicaraguan pilots in Cuba—meaning that both the human resources and the physical facilities are in place to raise Nicaraguan military power from the regional to the strategic level. According to Major Miranda, the Sandinistas see delivery of those MiG21s—which he said the Soviets have promised Managua—as a test of whether the Russians are prepared to face down the United States and extend "an umbrella of protection" over the Sandinistas.[32]

While the Sandinistas like to claim that this enormous military build-up has been merely a defensive reaction to U.S. support for armed counterrevolutionaries, or *contras*, the facts do not bear this out. Soviet-bloc military deliveries to Nicaragua began in 1980, yet the Nicaraguan ambassador has admitted in a letter to *The Washington Post* that contra activity was insignificant as late as November of 1981, by which time the FSLN armed forces were already almost forty thousand.[33] Coincidentally, it was in that month that Ernesto Cardenal, Nicaragua's Minister of Culture, offered a more plausible explanation for the build-up. He predicted then that "there will be many Nicaraguas in the world, starting with the Americas."[34]

To help ensure the proliferation of Nicaraguas, the Soviet bloc has contributed more than two billion dollars in military aid—more than twice the total of U.S.military aid to the four front-line Central American states. Indeed: in only the first four months of 1987, the Soviets delivered to the Sandinistas more arms and equipment than the Nicaraguan resistance had received in the previous six years. It is also worth noting that the Soviets had dispatched specialized advisers and $560 million in military aid to Nicaragua by the end of 1983, *before* the *contras* had become a significant force.[35]

The Government of Reconstruction was only three weeks old when five Soviet generals arrived to advise the Sandinista Defense Ministry, according to Miguel Bolanos, a former officer with Sandinista State Security. They were followed by thousands of advisers, technicians, and specialists from the Soviet Union, East Germany, Bulgaria, Libya, North Vietnam, Czechoslovakia, North Korea, and the PLO.[36]

The Sandinistas were in power not three months when they established diplomatic relations with the USSR, and only eight months when Daniel Ortega would make his first pilgrimage to Moscow (he made his seventh trip there in early November 1987, for the 70th anniversary of the Bolshevik revolution). Although the Sandinistas had not yet achieved full-fledged "Socialist ally" status, Ortega was seated on that visit with the rulers of East Germany and Poland. As Soviet specialist Edward N. Luttwak observed, "the seating of Ortega conveys a very definite message: the Sandinista regime has been admitted to the very exclusive club of governments that the Soviet Union regards as *permanent*, organic allies" (emphasis Luttwak's).[37] Further: At mid-1987 the Sandinistas renewed party-to-party ties with the Soviet Communist Party for another five years.

Nicaraguan ties with Cuba are even closer. "The Cubans had everything planned before overthrowing Somoza, including how to handle eight, nine, ten thousand Nicaraguans in different areas going to school in Cuba," reports Bolanos.[38] In 1979, a Cuban "international brigade" fought side-by-side with the Sandinistas, providing them with five hundred tons of weapons and other supplies, while the first Cuban military advisers arrived on the very day the FSLN took power. Numerous accounts tell of secret meetings between Castro and top Sandinista leaders in the early days of their regime at the former Somoza seashore estate, *Montelimar*, at which Castro would make many of the key decisions for the new rulers.[39]

There are now between 7,500 and 8,000 Cuban advisers and technicians in Nicaragua, of whom 3,000 are military or security personnel, and the Sandinista army is staffed by Cuban officers down to the company and even the platoon levels.[40] Bolanos reports that many of the Cuban military personnel have posed as civilian teachers, and even the Cuban doctors in Nicaragua receive regular military training, according to one Nicaraguan witness.[41]

These Cubans are not merely advising the Nicaraguan government. Alvaro Baldizon, formerly a Chief Investigator for the Nicaraguan Ministry of the Interior, says that "the ones who give the orders are the Cubans. . . . Every program, every operation is always under the supervision of Cuban advisers."[42] This is corroborated by Alfonso Robelo, a former member of the Sandinista junta, who says that Nicaragua is an "occupied country . . . where no crucial decision is taken without the approval of the Cubans."[43] And Miguel Urroz Blanco, the former chief of Nicaragua's police for internal order, has said that "a suggestion made by the Cubans is an unbreakable order."[44]

According to defector Roger Miranda, Managua's military plans go first to Havana for review by Cuban deputy leader Raul Castro and the head of the Soviet military mission there before going on to Moscow for final approval. He said Cuba serves as a conduit for all Soviet weapons sent to Nicaragua, and the Soviets and Cubans must approve Sandinista shipments of arms to Central American guerrilla groups. Among the documents he brought with him when he defected was the secret five-year military plan for 1991 through 1995. Major Miranda said the earlier version of the second five-year plan, 1986 through 1990, had to be scrapped because *contra* successes in the field had depleted virtually all the arms and other military aid supplied free by the Soviets.[45]

Sandinista Ideology and the One-Party State

One lesson the Sandinistas learned from Fidel Castro was the importance of concealing their communist ideology so as not to precipitate any intervention from the United States. The FSLN established formal ties with the Communist Party of the Soviet Union in March of 1980, less than one year after seizing power. In June of 1981, Defense Minister Humberto Ortega announced to a gathering of Sandinista military officers that *Sandinismo* and Marxism-Leninism "are indissolubly united," and that "Marxism-Leninism is the scientific doctrine that guides our revolution."[46] This was demonstrated in 1983–84 at the 38th General Assembly of the United Nations, during which the Sandinista government voted with the Soviet-Cuban position 96 percent of the time. (They demonstrated their fealty from the very beginning, abstaining, for example, during a United Nations vote in January 1980 to condemn the Soviets for their invasion the month before of Afghanistan; by then, the Sandinistas had already established diplomatic relations with Poland, Romania, Yugoslavia, Hungary, Vietnam, East Germany and, of course, the Soviet Union and Cuba, as well as numerous trade and cultural agreements with those countries, Czechoslovakia, and Bulgaria.)

Once the Sandinistas could no longer conceal their communism, their fall-back argument, which was also learned from Castro, was that U.S. truculence had driven them into the arms of the Soviets. The fact is that Carlos Fonseca, the founder of the FSLN, identified his organization as far back as 1971 as "the successor of the Bolshevik October Revolution."[47] The Sandinista party anthem proclaims, "We shall fight against the Yankee, enemy of humanity." It has been used to indoctrinate all Nicaraguan school children since the Sandinistas came to power in July 1979. Two months after seizing power, as reconstruction aid was pouring in from the Carter administration, FSLN leaders were secretly referring to the United States as the "rabid enemy of all peoples."[48] And, as Shirley Christian notes, the Sandinista "propaganda organs were suddenly making the United States the main culprit for everything they found wrong with the world."[49]

The Sandinistas' "historic program" contains no fewer than 11 references to "Yankee" or "North American" transgressions, including the following:

> The Sandinista people's revolution will put an end to the use of the national territory as a base for Yankee aggression against other fraternal peoples and will put into practice militant solidarity with fraternal peoples fighting for their liberation.
>
> A. It will actively support the struggle of the peoples of Asia, Africa and Latin America against the new and old colonialism and against the common enemy: Yankee imperialism.
>
> B. It will support the struggle of the Black people and all the people of the United States for an authentic democracy and equal rights.
>
> C. It will support the struggle of all peoples against the establishment of Yankee military bases in foreign countries. . . .

The Sandinistas sought to conceal their totalitarian intentions by creating the appearance of a democratic, pluralistic society. In a secret three-day meeting held in September 1979, FSLN leaders explained to the party cadres that it was only because of "international opinion" that "political parties must be permitted to exist."[50] As opportunities arose, they said, non-Marxists must be stripped of authority.

One application of this strategy involved the Junta of National Reconstruction. This was a five-man body formed one month before Somoza's downfall and advertised as the future government of Nicaragua. Because the Sandinistas were then looking for international recognition, they arranged to have two prominent non-Marxists on the Junta. After the Sandinistas took charge, however, the Junta saw its authority gradually eclipsed by the National Directorate, an FSLN party organ consisting of nine *comandantes*, all dedicated communists.

At about the same time that the Junta of National Reconstruction was created, and for similar reasons, the Sandinistas announced plans for a Council of State, a thirty-three-member quasi-legislative body representing the broad spectrum of political, trade, and business groups opposed to Somoza. According to the proposal, a minority of the seats were to be allocated to the Sandinistas.

In October of 1979, the Sandinistas announced that the organization of the Council of State would be postponed until May 4, 1980. Then in April, less than two weeks before the Council was to convene, the Sandinistas decreed that it would be expanded to forty-seven seats and packed to ensure FSLN control. This sparked a protest by one of the Council's member organizations, the Superior Council of Private Enterprise (COSEP), which threatened to boycott the Council of State. FSLN *comandantes* Jaime Wheelock and Bayardo Arce, however, threatened to "break heads" if the private sector failed to come to terms, and American Ambassador Pezzullo helped persuade COSEP to cooperate.[51]

The packing of the Council of State prompted the Junta's two non-Marxist members, Violeta Chammoro and Alfonso Robelo, to resign. Robelo, a founder of the Nicaraguan Democratic Movement (MDN, which actually *was* democratic), had come to realize that his organization was being used "as a show to say that they still have pluralism," and to prove that "there was an internal opposition." Robelo said that because he refused to bow to the Sandinistas, "they bombed the MDN headquarters twice. There were some attempts to kill me."[52]

This Sandinista attitude toward pluralism was articulated with startling frankness by comandante Bayardo Arce in May 1984, when he spoke before the Nicaraguan Socialist Party. Unaware that he was being tape-recorded, Arce said,

> As part of that program [of national reconstruction] we spoke of bringing about revolutionary change based on three principles which made us presentable in the international context. . . . Those principles were non-alignment abroad, a mixed economy, and political pluralism. With those three elements we kept the international community from going along with American policy in Nicaragua.
>
> [Pluralism] is one factor that has been useful until now—to be able to say there are eleven parties here.
>
> We have a discussion pending with your political committee to work on three issues. . . . One, the idea of putting an end to all this artifice of pluralism . . . which has been useful thus far.

Arce noted that "our strategic allies tell us not to declare ourselves Marxist-Leninists," and he spoke of "building socialism with the dollars of capitalism."[53]

This strategy worked well for the Sandinistas. By 1982, their communist government had received $1.6 billion in Western aid. The United States provided more than $118 million in direct aid and endorsed over $220 million in Inter-American Development Bank credits. Although they welcomed the Yankee dollars, the Sandinistas rejected the U.S. offer of Peace Corps volunteers.

The maintenance of a one-party system requires widespread indoctrination. Hatred for "Yankees" is drummed into Nicaraguan school children, whose lessons in arithmetic are illustrated not by apples and oranges but by rifles and hand grenades (see figure 2). The Sandinistas' "literacy campaign," which purports to have made readers of the peasants, is actually indoctrination. This was admitted by its coordinator, Fernando Cardenal, who wrote, "We do not pretend to teach only how to read, write, and handle basic math; we also have

FIGURE 2

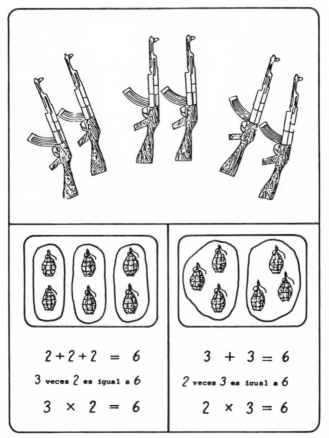

$$2 + 2 + 2 = 6$$

3 veces 2 es igual a 6

$$3 \times 2 = 6$$

$$3 + 3 = 6$$

2 veces 3 es igual a 6

$$2 \times 3 = 6$$

Grade-school arithmetic books use pictures of Soviet-made AK–47 rifles and hand grenades to teach children to count.

as key goals the consciousness raising and politicization of the illiterates."[54] And as Miguel Bolanos has revealed:

The literacy campaign was integrated into Security's plans. We took advantage of all these people who were going to areas outside of our network of informers to leave a network built by the time that they were finished. We moved a lot of Security men around the country along with the literacy workers. We had one conference with the Sandinista Youth—which contributed 60 percent of the literacy workers—on how to recruit informers.[55]

Indoctrination includes massive doses of Soviet propaganda. East Germany has sent 4.7 million Spanish-language school textbooks (that's nearly a dozen books for every primary, secondary and university student in the country). Especially talented students are shipped abroad for training. Since 1980, nearly 3,000 secondary, undergraduate and graduate students have been sent to Cuba. A new program was launched in 1986 to send 350 children between the ages of twelve and sixteen to Cuba for six years. They will not be allowed to return for visits or to see their parents until their indoctrination is complete.[56]

To deal with those who aren't amenable to indoctrination, the Sandinistas have devised a number of effective controls. One of the first steps they took was to place the army under FSLN party control. This was accomplished by a pair of decrees, one in August 1979 announcing that "the only armed force of the Republic" would bear the name "Popular Sandinista Army," and one a month later declaring that "Sandinista" was henceforth a trademark available only to the Sandinista party and such organizations as it may control.[57]

The regime also makes full use of the Sandinista Defense Committees, or block committees, which number around ten thousand.[58] Patterned after a Cuban model and run by Sandinista State Security, these committees encourage people to spy on friends, family, and neighbors. Comandante Tomas Borge refers to them as the "eyes and ears of the revolution."[59] Food is rationed in Nicaragua, and the block committees control the ration cards, which are withheld for failure to attend FSLN town meetings.

Another tactic of State Security is to organize mobs to attack people who are suspected of harboring doubts about *Sandinismo*. Borge calls these the *"turbas divinas,"* or "divine mobs." They are organized in all major cities in Nicaragua, according to Alvaro Baldizon (the former Interior Ministry investigator),[60] and they are especially valuable for their apparent spontaneity.

Turbas divinas were used during the 1984 election campaign to harass the handful of opposition candidates who bothered to participate. Writer-scholar Robert S. Leiken, until that time sympathetic to the Sandinistas, described the scene at an August 5 rally for presidential candidate Arturo Cruz, in Chinandega, a traditional bulwark of Sandinista strength:

> When Cruz began to speak, dozens of turbas armed with sticks, stones, and machetes surrounded the field. They came in on what appeared to be army trucks chanting "power to the people." They proceeded to break the windows and puncture the tires of demonstrators' cars. The police seemed to make no serious effort to restrain them. . . .

Leiken noted that the Sandinistas were able to get away with characterizing these demonstrations "their own way" because of the "almost complete absence of foreign and domestic press coverage . . ."[61]

Not even the "peace plan" curbed the zeal of the *turbas*:

> . . . within days of signing the Guatemala plan, Nicaraguan security forces using dogs and electric cattle prods broke up a peaceful demonstration of opposition groups and jailed the head of a human-rights commission and the president of the Nicaraguan bar association. . . .[62]

When all these techniques fail, the prisons are still available. In December 1985, ninety-three members of the Social Christian Party were in prison for their political views. Likewise, seventy members of the Independent Liberal Party were in prison as of February 1986. The value of a democratic façade was, nonetheless, appreciated by the Sandinistas when

FIGURE 3
Background of FDN Military Leaders:
Late 1985

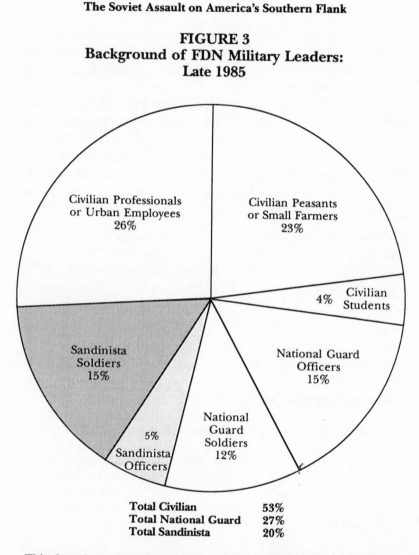

Total Civilian	53%
Total National Guard	27%
Total Sandinista	20%

This chart shows the background of leaders of the FDN, the largest of the resistance movements that have developed in reaction to the Sandinistas' betrayal of the 1979 revolution. Statistically, this chart is based on the top 153 command and staff positions. These are the headquarters positions, and the Regional and Task Force command positions.

they wrote to the Organization of American States in July of 1979 that upon taking power they intended "to convoke the Nicaraguans to the first free elections they will have in this century, so they can elect their municipal officials and a constituent assembly, and, later, the supreme authorities of the country."[63] It was more than five years before the promised elections were finally held, and they were anything but free. The FSLN controlled the press and the broadcast media. The independent newspaper, *La Prensa*, was required to submit all stories for prior censorship. The press was prevented from covering the Sandinistas' campaign opponents, who—as we have seen—were attacked by *turbas*, while the block committees kept watch over their neighbors. Observers were not allowed to certify the number of votes cast at each polling station.[64]

Just how brazen the Sandinistas could be was revealed by their reaction to a rally held September 27, 1987, by members of what is thought to be the largest political party operating inside Nicaragua, the Social Christian Party. En route home from that rally, 18 party members were hauled off a bus and forcibly drafted into the Sandinista army. They were later released—after President Reagan publicized the incident in a speech before the Organization of American States.[65]

Not surprisingly, Comandante Arce described elections as a "nuisance" in the aforementioned 1984 speech to the Nicaraguan Socialist Party. "Of course," he said, "if we did not have the war situation imposed on us by the United States, the electoral problem would be totally out of place in terms of its usefulness."[66] Comandante Humberto Ortega told an audience of teenagers that demands for elections were part of a counterrevolutionary threat. "Keep in mind," he said, "that [ours] are elections to advance revolutionary power, not to raffle off power." When he asked the crowd whether they approved of the FSLN's use of power, they shouted *Si!*

"Then," he responded, "this is a vote, a popular election. This is Sandinista Democracy."[67]

On November 4, 1984, Nicaragua "elected" Comandante Daniel Ortega to serve as president.

On January 9, 1987, the Sandinistas promulgated their new Constitution to replace the 1974 Constitution that they had abolished one day after taking power. They waited only three hours before announcing that the following rights guaranteed in that Constitution would be suspended:

- Right of personal freedom, personal security, and *habeas corpus*;
- Right to be presumed innocent until proven guilty;
- Right to trial and appeal;
- Freedom of movement;
- Freedom from arbitrary interference in personal life, family, home, and correspondence;
- Freedom of information;
- Freedom of expression;
- Right of peaceful assembly;
- Freedom of association;
- Right to organize unions;
- Right to strike.[68]

No wonder that one so closely identified with the Sandinistas from the very beginning, one of such conspicuous Leftist views, as Arturo J. Cruz, would write in 1983:

"Nicaragua's Revolution, in my judgment, is in danger of dying in its infancy."[69]

The Press

Another one of the promises the Sandinistas made to the OAS in June 1979 was that "a special guarantee shall be granted to the freedom of issuing information and the publishing of information . . . [and] all laws that repress freedom of information shall be abolished."[70] Upon taking power, however, they immediately seized all television stations and most radio stations. Government censorship began in January 1980 and increased with decrees in August and September that banned news pertaining to domestic security or the economy. More than thirty news programs were forced off the air.[71]

The Catholic Church's newsletter was banned and its radio station shut down. The Permanent Commission for Human Rights, which had published daily reports of human rights abuses under Somoza, had its director driven into exile.

When the Sandinistas seized power, four independent newspapers were publishing in Nicaragua. Once in power, only one independent newspaper—*La Prensa*—was tolerated. It had opposed Somoza and supported the revolution, but because it was not willing to refrain from criticizing the Sandinista dictators, its personnel were attacked by *turbas* and imprisoned, their homes vandalized and families threatened. *La Prensa*'s editor, Pedro Joaquin Chamorro, Jr., was driven into exile in 1984 by threats on his life. In 1986, after numerous previously imposed suspensions, the paper was closed down completely.

La Prensa was allowed to reopen on October 1, 1987, in line with Sandinista pledges to liberalize their regime as required by the vaguely worded Guatemala "peace plan." How long it will survive in freedom might be gauged by the fact that the paper was given enough newsprint to print a 12-page edition for two months. It might also be gauged from a warning sounded by President Ortega when the ink was barely dry on the paper's first editions. At a New York press conference following a United Nations address, Ortega, on October 7, 1987, said *La Prensa* could be closed again if it "starts to defend the Reagan policy" of funding the *contras*. The meaning of such a warning would not be lost on *La Prensa*'s embattled editors: You will be allowed to be "free" only so long as you are not too "free."[72] When *La Prensa* reopened, only five reporters and four photographers were on hand, a fraction of the normal news staff. Editor Jaime Chamorro explained that "all our reporters are outside the country and we haven't been able to persuade them to come back." (Among the missing: Editor Pedro Joaquin Chamorro, son of the slain editor-publisher and the man who had become most identified with the paper's independent style. Thoroughly disillusioned with the Sandinistas, he had gone into full-fledged opposition as a member of the Resistance directorate.) Also permitted to reopen under the peace plan: the Roman Catholic's *Radio Catolica* station. But, it was not permitted to broadcast news, and when a West German foundation donated a portable transmitter to bolster the station's weak and sputtering signal, it was held up in customs for several days, and finally reported "lost."

Significantly, none of the other twelve independent radio stations that had operated before the revolution was allowed to reopen. Nor was there the slightest intimation that television, privately operated in pre-Sandinista days, would ever again be independent. Nor was *Iglesia*, the Catholic Church's widely read newsletter, allowed to reappear (meaning the Archbishop's sermons, customarily reprinted in it, would remain mainly hidden from public view.)[73]

COSEP, the private sector coordinating group, has indicated it would like to put a private television station on the air, and others talk about opening a second independent newspaper.[74] Assuming the necessary resources would become available to finance these ventures, the Sandinista reaction would provide a real test of whether they are truly practicing "*glasnost*"—or mere tokenism.

To go beyond such tokenism, the Sandinistas would need to abandon the essence of their philosophy about the proper role of the media. As explained by Comandante Luis Carrion, "Revolutionary journalism means doing and saying all that and only that which will promote the people's victory."[75]

In that, the Sandinistas have found ample echo in the

reports of most Managua-based foreign correspondents. As Leiken wrote:

> The Sandinista *engano* [deceit] has been most successful among the resident foreign press. Journalists familiar with the atrocities of the right-wing tyrannies of Central America wish to believe, quite understandably, that the Sandinistas present an alternative. In today's Nicaragua, it is easy to confuse desire with reality. The resident press also frequently merges with the larger population of "internationalists," a term which embraces all those foreigners expressing solidarity with the Sandinistas, from Bulgarian and Cuban *apparatchiks* to idealistic North Americans and West Europeans. It is the general feeling among Nicaraguans that the foreign press in Managua strongly sympathizes with the government, and that is is dangerous to speak openly with them. . . .[76]

Human Rights

The first month they were in power, the Sandinistas issued the Public Order Law, a vaguely worded decree used to prosecute political opponents. This was followed by a series of increasingly repressive "emergency" decrees in 1981, 1982, and 1985. Even those who try conscientiously to obey all these laws may be apprehended in the course of a mass arrest—as many as 5,300 civilians were arrested in 1986 alone, according to one account. And if a suspect manages to evade capture, the Sandinistas are not above holding his family hostage pending his surrender.[77]

Public Order Law cases are tried by the special Popular Anti-Somoza Tribunals created in 1983. The defendant receives no legal counsel and faces a 99 percent likelihood of conviction.[78] Political prisoners incarcerated under such kangaroo court procedures number between 3,500 and 6,500, according to the International League for Human Rights. Tomas Borge has admitted to holding 5,000 political prisoners, and some estimates put the number at 7,000, although one human rights investigator has placed the figure at 11,000 to 13,000. Antonio Farach, a former member of the Nicaraguan diplomatic service, has claimed there were 15,000 political prisoners in 1984.[79] That would be equivalent to over a million political prisoners in the United States.

As one observer would put it: "Suffice it to say, the Sandinistas have built four new prisons."[80]

Nicaraguan prisons bear a striking resemblance to their Cuban models. Many cells leave no room to lie down; prisoners are often denied food and water. Torture is commonplace and is frequently used to extract false confessions. Sofonias Cisneros, head of the Nicaraguan Christian Parent-Teacher Association, reports being brutalized by State Security Director Lenin Cerna himself.[81]

Torture is not limited to the prisons. A physician who visited several refugee camps treated many victims who had been abused by the Sandinista military. He saw some people whose backs were scarred from whippings and others whose eyes were scarred by sand or pepper. He found many people with severed tendons—in the hand, the wrist, or behind the knee.[82] For captured counterrevolutionaries, the Sandinistas have a treatment known as the "vest cut": the prisoner is taken to the nearest village, where his arms and legs are cut off and he is left to bleed to death.

Again, there is scant reason for optimism that the "peace plan" will rescue more than a handful of those prisoners. The plan calls for the pardoning of all prisoners jailed on political charges. By early October—one month before the "plan" was to become fully effective—the Sandinistas "mobilized its Mothers of Heroes and Martyrs, a network of thousands of women whose relatives died fighting Somoza's National Guard of the U.S. backed-rebels."[83] The purpose: to "persuade" the same government orchestrating the "protests" to reject blanket pardons. When, finally, the first prisoners were released—nearly three weeks after the deadline—only 985 were freed, and they were pardoned, not amnestied as the peace plan required. Furthermore, only a handful were from a list approved the previous March by the rubber-stamp National Assembly. As for the remaining political prisoners, including at least 2,000 National Guardsmen whose only adjudicated crime was to have served as soldiers in their country's army, the Sandinistas said a general amnesty would not be granted until an international monitoring commission finds that the U.S. and other Central American countries have ended all aid to the *contras*.[84]

Despite massive evidence of systematic official cruelty, one of the Sandinistas' most assiduous apologists in the U.S. Senate—Claiborne Pell (D.-RI)—has described the *contras* as "terrorists" for fighting against such a regime. And, he has used a definition which not only would seem to locate the Managua government in the same civilized category as, say, Switzerland or Australia, but rule out taking up arms, under any circumstances, against any government, no matter how cruel, how corrupt, how barbarian. "To my mind," Pell said on the floor of the Senate in the fall of 1984, "the *contras* really are terrorists. The definition of terrorism is the changing of the policy of government through violence and murder and the like. This is exactly what the *contras* are seeking to do now in Nicaragua."[85] (By that "definition," of course, other terrorists were the Hungarian freedom fighters, the Zionists who fought for a Jewish homeland, the French underground in World War II, George Washington and his *contras* who used "violence and murder and the like" against the legitimate government of King George III—or, for that matter, the Sandinistas themselves who practiced rampant violence, murder and the like in order to reach power, the ultimate in "changing the policy of government.")

Nicaragua likes to brag that it has eliminated the death penalty. In fact, thousands of Somoza guardsmen who surrendered during the final days of the war were executed by the Sandinistas. The Nicaraguan Commission of Jurists estimated that over 8,600 people were executed by the Sandinistas for political reasons by December 1982.[86]

When Tomas Borge's Interior Ministry began to receive frequent complaints of human rights abuses from the Inter-American Commission on Human Rights, he formed a Special Investigations Commission to look into them. The Chief Investigator for the new commission was Alvaro Baldizon, who later fled Nicaragua. Baldizon reports that 90 percent of the charges investigated by his commission proved to be true, but that the reports he filed were used to concoct cover stories for the guilty parties.[87] He has documented numerous political murders and summary executions, and even the mass execution of peasants. These are not the crimes of renegade soldiers, for Baldizon revealed the existence of a secret order authorizing the use of "special measures," i.e., summary executions, subject to the approval of Borge and his first Vice-Minister, Luis Carrion. In deference to public opinion abroad, special measures were to be applied only to people whose detention was not widely known. According to Baldizon, Borge has authorized more summary executions than he can remember.[88]

The Indians

Nicaragua had 165,000 Miskito, Sumo, and Rama Indians living in the forests and along the rivers in the large wilderness region along the East Coast. Traditionally farmers and fishermen, they led a relatively isolated tribal existence for hundreds of years. Their circumstances were changed somewhat by the Somozas, who sought to exploit the natural resources of the region for export, relying on the Indians to supply the wage labor. Still, while the Indians did not enjoy many of the benefits of this development, they retained effective control over most of their communal lands and resources. As one Indian woman put it, "Somoza was bad but he just took the money. We had our land to live from and to pass on to our children. And we could work anywhere."[89]

Because of dissatisfaction with Somoza's policies, some of the Indian leaders gave moral support to the Sandinista revolution, changing the name of their organization (Alliance for Progress of the Miskitos and Sumos) to MISURASATA, which stood for Miskito-Sumo-Rama-Sandinista. The trust they placed in the FSLN was soon to be betrayed.

Immediately upon taking power, the Sandinistas began expropriating Indian lands to create state-run farms. They replaced the Indians' Moravian and other Protestant school-teachers with Cubans. Protests followed, and the Sandinistas reacted brutally. Large-scale arrests began in September 1979—less than three months after Somoza's defeat—and a prominent Indian leader, Lester Athas, was executed.[90]

Tensions grew as the new dictators sought to impose communism through local block committees and other communist "mass organizations." In February 1981, a union leader was murdered in the coastal town of Puerto Cabezas, and thirty-three MISURASATA leaders were arrested. On December 22, the Sandinistas arrested eighty Miskitos, and executed thirty-five of them, dumping their bodies in a mass grave. The next day, two Indian communities were bombarded by FSLN aircraft.[91]

To prevent the development of an organized resistance movement, the Sandinistas decided to begin a mass evacuation of the northeastern border areas. In January 1982, ten thousand to twelve thousand Indians were forced at gunpoint to march many miles to crowded internment camps. Many who resisted were tortured or murdered. To discourage them from attempting to return, their property was confiscated and their homes burned. *Time* magazine reported in March that forty-two Miskito villages had been firebombed (and forty-nine churches destroyed).[92]

The persecution continued. Two hundred and fifty Miskitos were executed in 1982, another 150 the next year.[93] By

1985, sixteen thousand Indians were being held in relocation camps, where they were forced to work on collective farms. Many were released later that year, but attacks on Indian villages have continued, and refugees have reported that FSLN soldiers disguised as Red Cross personnel have visited the reinhabited border villages to gather intelligence. The number of Nicaraguan Indian refugees in Honduras reached about thirty-six thousand in 1986, which is nearly a third of the population of Miskito, Sumo, and Rama Indians who lived in Nicaragua when the FSLN came to power.[94]

Miskito Indian leader Stedman Fagoth has reported that during his incarceration in a Sandinista prison in 1981, he was visited by Interior Minister Borge, who vowed that "Sandinismo would be established on the Atlantic Coast, even if every single Miskito Indian had to be eliminated."[95] Borge's sincerity is borne out by the testimony of Russell Means, an American Indian spokesman who visited the Miskitos: "I have seen the mass graves."[96]

Labor

The Sandinistas acted very quickly to create a puppet labor union, the Sandinista Confederation of Labor (CST), which was soon to be affiliated with the World Federation of Trade Unions (a Soviet front). While seeking to coerce all workers to join the official union, they have permitted the independent Nicaraguan Confederation of Labor (CTN) and Confederation of Trade Union Unity (CUS) to continue to exist for the sake of appearances.

To undermine the independent unions, the dictators have prohibited private employers from paying wages or bonuses higher than those paid by the state, and strikes were banned in September 1981 by a State of Economic and Social Emergency. The State of National Emergency of March 1982 went further, banning trade union demonstrations and public meetings. Beyond that, union leaders have been repeatedly harassed, arrested, threatened, tortured, and attacked by the *turbas*, and union property has been vandalized and looted.

The CTN headquarters were shot up by the FSLN as early as December 1979. Two years later, a CUS representative was denied permission to attend a training course presented in Turin, Italy, by the International Confederation of Free Trade Unions, though the government's CST representative was cleared. In May 1985, a Sandinista mob attacked a CUS-sponsored vocational training center. The private bar association has been denied the right to incur debts, maintain a post office box, own vehicles or real estate, or hire employees.[97]

Since 1983, about five hundred CTN members, including all seven directors, have been temporarily imprisoned, while CUS reports three hundred have been jailed.[98] Others have been forced to leave the country.

Economy

Since 1979 the economy of Nicaragua has gone the way of all communist economies—down.

In 1977, the year before the Sandinistas' final offensive brought chaos to the country, Nicaragua's gross domestic product grew by 5.5 percent—well above the average for Latin America as a whole. In 1985, the last year for which reliable figures are available as of this writing, Nicaragua's gross domestic product *declined* by 4.1 percent, and preliminary figures for 1986 showed that it continued to slide that year, the third straight year of decline.[99]

With the printing presses working overtime to churn out money—the device incompetent governments always resort to to literally "paper" over their blunders—*The Washington Post* would report that money was, in a very real sense, going out of style. (For Nicaraguans old enough to remember just ten years back, this is particularly galling since they grew up accustomed to a currency traditionally on a par with the dollar; although tourists are required on arrival to exchange 60 of their dollars at an official rate of 70 cordobas to the dollar, the real going rate is a preposterous 6,200 to the dollar.) Since virtually nothing else does work in Nicaragua except those printing presses, even Big Brother, the Soviets, are getting testy about the squandering of their handouts. Enrique Bolanos, president of the Superior Council of Private Enterprise, would remark acidly: "Economically, we are now down to the level of Haiti."[100]

By confiscating land and factories, the Sandinista government has come to control 20 percent of Nicaragua's agriculture and 40 percent of its industry. (Only about two dozen of the 168 U.S. businesses operating in Nicaragua when the Sandinistas came to power remained by late 1987, and most of them were down to caretaker levels. About 30 American companies were confiscated between 1979 and 1985. The biggest surviving U.S. operation: an oil refinery owned by Esso Standard Oil Ltd., an affiliate of Exxon, which refines about 10,000 barrels of Soviet-supplied oil per day. It is the only refinery in the country.)[101]

The government regulates all wages and most prices, monopolizes export trade, and while roughly half of the economy remains nominally "private," in reality the private sector lives completely at the mercy of the state. Almost all agricultural products must be sold to the government, which then distributes them to retailers through the Nicaraguan Basic Foods Enterprise (ENABAS). This allows the FSLN to keep private vendors in line.

The state's share of the gross national product rose from 15 percent in 1978 to 40 percent in 1984.[102] Meanwhile, according to the UN and other official sources, real wages have fallen every single year since the Sandinistas took power: by almost 13 percent in 1982 and by more than 25 percent in 1983, 5.1 percent in 1984 and 14.3 percent in 1985.[103] Beef exports have fallen by over 85 percent since the last Somoza years, and to make matters worse, one cattleman—obviously at great risk to himself—felt so enraged that he went public with a charge that the Sandinistas were rustling cattle for sale to neighboring Honduras.[104]

Inflation, according to one experienced observer, was raging at an out-of-control one thousand percent by the fall of 1987.[105] Food is rationed, but that hasn't eliminated shortages of meat, chicken, bread, butter, beans, eggs, and rice. In one Managua supermarket in February 1984, there was no bread, flour, or milk to be found. Yet ironically, it was necessary on one occasion to destroy twenty thousand pounds of meat because government officials had bought the wrong kind of packaging.[106]

The country would face a serious debt crisis—except that the Sandinistas refuse to pay their debts. The official 1987 economic plan says Nicaragua will make debt payments only when these payments will release credits and financing larger than the service payment itself. Few bankers are willing to take the Sandinistas up on that "offer" and so the foreign debt stands at $6.7 billion and holding—despite massive Soviet-bloc giveaways.[107]

As David Reed, a writer experienced in Latin American affairs puts it:

Nicaragua's economy is in ruins, due partly to the guerrilla war but mostly to socialist mismanagement. Rather than lose money by selling crops to the government, farmers grow only enough for their own use or divert crops to a booming black market. The Sandinistas have printed so much money that the largest bank note in circulation, 1000 *cordobas*, was worth just 17 cents on the free market when I was there. The average salary equaled about $7.50 per month. When the Sandinistas took over from Somoza, a thousand *cordobas* was worth $100 and real income was more than eight times what it is now.[108]

The economic shortages have hurt health care as well. The Lenin Fonseca Hospital has had to function without an X-ray machine, and the Manolo Morales Hospital without adhesive tape or gauze bandages. In the first quarter of 1986, the Velez Paiz Hospital received only about a third of the supplies it ordered from the Central Supplies Office.[109]

Low wages have made for a labor shortage, requiring state farms to conscript workers. One article that was censored from *La Prensa* in 1985 began, "There is a great deal of unrest among the state employees who were notified of their 'voluntary' mobilization for coffee picking, and who will presumably leave for the northern mountains and the central zone on 26 November."[110]

The Sandinistas like to blame their economic woes on the U.S. boycott and on the guerrilla war being waged by the anticommunist resistance forces. The U.S. boycott, however, did not begin until May of 1985, and as foreign affairs specialist Robert Leiken has noted, "the economic situation had been worsening since the end of 1981 before the war with the rebels became a major factor and after the U.S. and other Western governments contributed $1.6 billion to aid the Nicaraguan government."

An International Monetary Fund study done in December 1981—well before the *contra* presence became a reality—noted that real wages in Nicaragua had already fallen 71 percent in the first two full years the Sandinistas were in power. Leiken adds:

> One of the most depressing aspects of our trip was to hear from so many that their lives are worse today than they were at the time of Somoza. Before the revolution Nicaraguans ate well by Central American standards. Thanks to the country's fertile soil and its small population, even poor Nicaraguans were accustomed to beef and chicken. Now consumer goods available to the masses in other Central American countries are no longer obtainable. Barefoot children are hardly uncommon in the region, but I had never seen so many completely naked. As we encountered them, their distended stomachs displaying the telltale signs of malnutrition, Nicaraguans

would bitterly recall the government slogan: "Los ninos son los mimados de la revolucion." (Children are the spoiled ones of the revolution.)

Leiken was writing after his sixth (and longest) visit to Nicaragua since the revolution. He wrote as "one who has sympathized with the Sandinistas." He wrote as one who, on each succeeding trip, "drains my initial reservoir of sympathy for the Sandinistas." He wrote as one who has testified in Congress against aid to the *contras*.

He wrote now: "This visit convinced me that the situation is far worse than I had thought, and disabused me of some of the remaining myths about the Sandinista revolution."[111]

Morton Kondracke, a self-described "moderate-liberal," would write after a visit to Managua three years later:

A visitor finds no joy in Managua, a city of dirt, broken pavement, uncertain water supplies and electric power, and wooden shacks. Honduras used to be poorer than Nicaragua, and El Salvador also was hit with a ruinous earthquake. Yet there is music and life in those countries. Managua is desperate and sad. . . .[112]

A final note on the economy: just how utterly dependent the Sandinistas had become on Soviet hand-outs was driven home dramatically in August 1987 when the Russians, reacting to Gorbachev's efforts to woo consumer support at home, cut oil shipments to the Sandinistas. The Soviets, since 1985, had supplied virtually all of Nicaragua's oil. In 1986, that came to 4.6 million barrels. For 1987, the Soviets provided only 2.2 million barrels and told the Sandinistas to get the rest from other Eastern bloc nations. In September 1987, Gorbachev relented partially, by pledging 730,000 more barrels—but the pledge was tied to a demand that Ortega attend the revolution's anniversary celebrations which coincided with a crucial moment in the peace plan. Under strong pressure from the Soviets, the Nicaraguan government responded by doubling the price of gasoline and tightening rationing (to 17 gallons a month, down from 19 gallons a month). Then, en route back from Moscow in November, Ortega tried to persuade his hard-pressed allies, the Mexicans, to resume their oil shipments suspended in 1985. The Mexicans told him they would not until the Sandinistas paid the $500 million they already owed.

The Soviets had demonstrated their restiveness about hand-outs to the Sandinistas earlier in the year (though no such reluctance in providing war material). During a March visit, Soviet official Boris Yeltsin (then one of Gorbachev's top confidantes, later ousted as Moscow party chief) told the Sandinistas Moscow expected repayment of part of the estimated $2 billion debt. Although Nicaragua was already selling only 8 percent of its exports for hard currency, the Soviets demanded even further increases in exports to the East bloc countries—worsening that hard currency crisis. In 1986, Nicaragua exported 12 percent of its goods to the Soviet bloc; in 1987, that figure jumped to 40 percent. But, with a $520 million trade deficit in 1987, and an economy almost totally dependent on Moscow's hand-outs, the Sandinistas had no choice but to comply.[113]

Religion

Lenin, a Sandinista guiding light, once wrote that "the fight against religion must not be limited nor reduced to abstract ideological preaching. This struggle must be linked up with the concrete practical class movement; its aim must be to eliminate the social roots of religion."[114] Not surprisingly, then, in September 1979 the Sandinistas spoke of the need to "neutralize" the traditional church.[115] In the case of some Protestant denominations, this meant seizing churches to force their pastors to support the party line; for many Moravians on the Atlantic Coast, it meant execution.

The FSLN, which enjoys close ties with the PLO, has also been quite vindictive with the small Jewish population of Nicaragua, whose places of worship have been dubbed "Synagogues of Satan." In 1978, the Sandinistas firebombed Managua's only synagogue, which they later confiscated, along with many Jewish-owned businesses. Many Jews received threatening phone calls encouraging them to leave the country. Few remain today.[116]

The Catholic Church, however, presents larger problems for the communists, for 85 percent of Nicaraguans are Catholic, and many are very devout. Led by Cardinal Miguel Obando y Bravo, most Nicaraguan Catholics are unwilling to worship the state. As a result, the Sandinistas have not been able to ride roughshod over the Catholic Church. In need of a fall-back strategy, they have turned to "liberation theology," which serves their purposes very well.

As the new regime eagerly encouraged the development of a radical "popular church," liberation theologians from abroad flocked to Nicaragua to see and assist the new experiment. The great majority of Nicaraguan Catholics, both clergy and laity, have been loyal to the pope, but the liberationists have been influential beyond their numbers. The government supports a number of organizations that promote its chosen church, and, according to Cardinal Obando, they "have abundant resources. They have exclusive access to the State communications networks." Conversely, the cardinal was required to submit even his sermons to censors 24 hours before he could deliver them.[117]

In March 1980, the liberationists issued a document leaving no doubt about their loyalties. They declared that "the only way to love God . . . is by contributing to the advancement of this revolutionary process. . . . Only then shall we be loving our brothers. . . . Therefore, we say that to be a Christian is to be a revolutionary."[118]

Journalist Shirley Christian attended mass at a "popular church" where the interior decor featured "life-size murals that glorified the Sandinista Front and its war against the National Guard." A poster on the door showed a U.S. military helicopter "hovering over a peaceful peasant scene . . . carrying the caption: HEROD SEARCHES FOR THE CHILD TO KILL HIM."[119]

The "popular church" provides a convenient screen behind which the communists can carry on their attack against the legitimate church. As Arturo Cruz, himself a former high official of the regime has written, "the Popular Church, sponsored by the Sandinistas in order to mortify the traditional Church, is more fiction than reality . . ."[120] Just a few months after toppling Somoza, the Sandinistas prepared a secret document to circulate among local cadres, instructing them in how to deal with the approaching Christmas celebration. The celebration of Christmas, it said, was to be oriented specifically toward children and was to be given

> a different, fundamentally political content. . . . It is thanks to the Sandinista Revolution that our children can now celebrate Christmas in liberty and grow up in a country that assures them their future and their happiness. This is the central thinking of the celebration.
>
> This does not mean to reinforce a tradition, particularly a religious one, but, by contrast, to interpret the subjective reality of our people today; so as, in the process, to transform it. To confront a tradition of more than 1,979 years in a direct manner . . . would carry us into political conflicts and we would lose influence among our people.

The document concluded that it would be unwise to try to "totally eradicate" the Christmas tradition during the Sandinistas' first year in power.[121]

Since then the assault on the church has been constant. The Sandinistas have forced Catholic schools to adopt Marxist textbooks. The regime has ridiculed members of the clergy through the state-controlled media and has organized mobs to vandalize church property and attack priests. The laity have been threatened for their participation in church activities, and some have been forced to sign false documents attacking the clergy, while priests have been harassed and threatened by State Security agents.[122] Cardinal Obando, thanked by the Sandinistas in 1980 for his active stand against Somoza's abuses, has since been denounced by them as a *Somocista* for his resistance to the FSLN tyranny.

In October 1983, Sandinista mobs attacked twenty churches in the Managua area, interrupting services and breaking windows. Nicaraguan bishop Monsignor Pedro A. Vega reports being physically attacked twice and having his home vandalized. Former FSLN counter-intelligence officer Miguel Bolanos has told of attempts by State Security (DGSE) to infiltrate the clergy of a number of churches.[123]

In 1982, a plan was devised by Interior Minister Borge and DGSE Chief Lenin Cerna to implicate a priest in a phony sex scandal. Father Bismarck Carballo, the director of Catholic radio and spokesman for the archbishop, was contacted by a female agent of the Interior Ministry, who requested spiritual counseling. After a series of meetings, she invited him to her home. Shortly after he arrived, a DGSE agent burst in, struck him on the head, and forced him to undress. Then other DGSE agents rushed in dressed as police and took Carballo prisoner. They paraded the naked priest outdoors before a jeering mob that included conveniently present news cameramen. Sandinista media published and televised the pictures.[124]

When Pope John Paul II spoke in Managua in 1983, he was interrupted by a mob of hecklers provided, according to Miguel Bolanos, by the government. Bolanos added that security agents used microphones connected to the pope's public address system to harass him.[125] When he was finished, according to a State Department report, the comandantes stood on the platform with clenched fists raised while the Sandinista anthem was played and the loudspeakers repeated the chant, "National Directorate—Give your orders!"[126]

"There are," Cruz would write later, "no words to describe the shabby treatment of the Pope."[127]

Many of the Sandinistas' offenses remain largely ignored by religious groups in the United States, although some Catholic leaders have reacted recently to the continued persecution of the church in Nicaragua. In the summer of 1986, when Nicaragua expelled Bishop Vega from the country and barred Monsignor Carballo from returning to Nicaragua after a trip abroad, Father Daniel F. Hoye, general secretary of the U.S. Conference of Catholic Bishops responded, "The bishops of the United States stand in solidarity with Cardinal Obando and his colleagues in the church in Nicaragua." The Conference's president, Bishop James Malone, spoke of a "new [sic] and dangerous repressive policy" in Nicaragua.[128]

Such criticism seems to have caught the attention of President Ortega. In December 1985, Cardinal Obando and the bishops of the Episcopal Conference of Nicaragua wrote Ortega to protest "the continual appearance of new conflicts and the lack of fulfillment of those goals presumably previously agreed upon but which have lent themselves to 'unilateral interpretations.' " They noted that "on three separate occasions we have directed ourselves to you in writing without having obtained even an acknowledgement of the receipt of our requests."[129] In August of 1986, however, just after the American expression of solidarity, Ortega called upon the Catholic Church to participate in a "dialogue" with his regime. "The road to an understanding," he said with unintended irony, "has not been made easy."[130]

Monsignor Carballo finally was able to return at the end of September 1987 in order to reopen the Catholic Radio Station, one of the first crumbs from the table of the Guatemalan peace accords.

It was more than three decades ago that one of the top

personages in the Yugoslav Communist Party, Marshal Tito's long-time associate, Milovan Djilas, would stun a naive world with his revelations about the privileges of those who claimed to speak in the name of the common man but who, in reality, lived and behaved like a new ruling royalty.

Those familiar with the privileges of the elite in Moscow learned to expect such behavior (Salvador Allende in Chile was yet another case in point). Many never learned, and so they might profess surprise—indignant denial, even—at learning that the Sandinistas, self-annointed saviors of the common man, fit the sordid pattern all too well.

Again, from Leiken, a self-professed sympathizer of the Sandinistas, until the weight of evidence would crush his illusions:

FIGURE 4
Should the United States Provide Assistance to the Resistance Forces in Nicaragua?

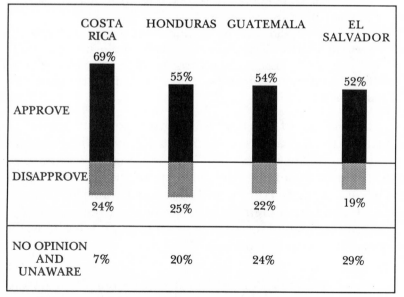

	COSTA RICA	HONDURAS	GUATEMALA	EL SALVADOR
APPROVE	69%	55%	54%	52%
DISAPPROVE	24%	25%	22%	19%
NO OPINION AND UNAWARE	7%	20%	24%	29%

According to a 1985 Gallup International survey, U.S. support for the democratic resistance is overwhelmingly endorsed by Central Americans.

145

The life-styles of the new rich contrast vividly with that of the rest of the country and with official rhetoric. A Sandinista *nomenklatura* has emerged. Party members shop at hard-currency stores, dine at luxury restaurants restricted to party officials, and vacation in the mansions of the Somoza dynasty, labeled "protocol houses." Vans pull up daily at government and party offices, to deliver ham, lobster, and other delicacies unavailable elsewhere. In a private state dining room, I ate a sumptuous meal with a *comandante* at a long table, attended by five servants. . . .

Intellectuals and former officials claim that decadence is endemic in upper government and party echelons. A former Sandinista diplomat recounted tales of high jinks and extravagance by Sandinista officials on foreign junkets, and women state employees complained of the same sexual harassment and blackmail that is common elsewhere in Central America.

The swinging Sandinista leadership cynically presents an image of revolutionary asceticism to the outside world while being addicted to the very vices that it routinely denounces in "degenerate bourgeois society."

The widespread corruption from the lowest to the highest levels of government makes it hard for Nicaraguans to accept the notion that their problems originate from abroad, or that they should endure further sacrifices "to confront the imperialist enemy. . . ."[131]

That image of corruption was given powerful reinforcement by the revelations of Major Roger Miranda following his defection in late October 1987. He reported on a numbered Swiss bank account (#58946) set up for the personal use of Defense Minister Humberto Ortega containing $1,494,596. He also said other high-ranking Sandinistas drew on funds of dummy companies set up in Panama to buy luxury items for themselves and their families.[132]

The "revolution" was not yet five years old when Arturo Cruz, himself once a key figure of the revolution, said: "After 45 months of Sandinista rule, the nation is in a calamitous state. The people are divided by hatred and resentment; the economy is in a shambles and war rages. . . ."[133]

In the three years since he wrote those lines, the tentacles of calamity have only extended and tightened their grip on a country coaxed, cajoled and coerced into that calamity by a nation which once believed, with John Stuart Mill, that there is something worse than war—and that is having nothing worth fighting for. That nation was the United States of America.

EL SALVADOR

About the size of Massachusetts, El Salvador is located on the Pacific side of Central America. It has land borders with Guatemala and Honduras, while Nicaragua lies just a few miles away across the Gulf of Fonseca. The economy is primarily agricultural, with coffee constituting more than 50 percent of total exports.

The most important of El Salvador's vital statistics is its population. With just under five million people, this little country has one of the highest population densities in the world, exceeding even India's. This is especially critical in view of the country's dependence on agriculture. A Mexican diplomat was asked, a few years ago, what his country would be like if it had El Salvador's population density. "A basket case," he said. "A Bangladesh."[134]

In 1931, a year before Farabundo Marti's communist uprising was brutally crushed, power was seized by General Maximiliano Hernandez Martinez, and from that time until 1980 all but one of the country's presidents were army officers, usually installed in rigged elections. One such was General Carlos Humberto Romero, who won the presidency in 1977. About forty people were killed in clashes between security forces and demonstrators protesting his election.

Without excusing the brutalities committed by government forces, it must be noted that their overreaction occurred within an atmosphere of insurrection and terrorism. This surge of violence came on top of what was already one of the world's highest homicide rates. Romero's government responded with a Law for the Defense and Guarantee of Public Order, which permitted the arrest of any person committing acts "contrary to the national interest."

This measure proved practically ineffective, but it did raise the hackles of the human rights lobby in the United States. Concerned about U.S. pressure, the Romero regime replaced that tough law in early 1979 with another aimed specifically at terrorist acts. The government also strengthened the capabilities of the police and military.

These steps brought the government no closer to solving the terrorist problem than before. In the view then of Risks International, an authoritative private organization monitoring terrorism for private clients,

the Salvadoran government does not now possess the capability to counter activity by the three major terrorist groups in-country.

In contrast to ineffective and untrained police and military units, terrorists associated with the three main groups in-country have demonstrated an ability to operate—at will—anywhere in El Salvador. Well organized, disciplined, and possessing an excellent intelligence collection apparatus as well as quantities of automatic weapons, they have proved more than a match for government forces.

Facing a very serious problem in both quantitative and qualitative terms, the government of El Salvador must cope with three major terrorist organizations which are extremely skilled, highly sophisticated and totally dedicated to the achievement of a Marxist revolution in that nation. With an estimated 2,500 members, the three groups are backed by financing allegedly in excess of $45 million.[135]

Foreign businessmen were the most frequent targets of the terrorists. Their goals: discourage foreign investment, and collect large kidnaping ransoms to fund continued terrorism. The terrorists succeeded in eliminating twenty-five thousand jobs and increasing their war chest, by mid-1980, to $60 million.[136]

Clearly, the terrorists presented El Salvador with a serious problem. It must be remembered, however, that their violent crimes against foreign businessmen did not directly threaten the lives of ordinary Salvadorans. While these ordinary citizens had to contend with a relatively violent society, by no means did they face chaos.

One indication of this was the healthy state of the economy. Under Romero, El Salvador was riding the crest of a wave of economic progress. According to a State Department report,

> between 1960 and 1979, economic growth [in El Salvador] was so high that, despite rapid population growth, real per capita income rose by roughly 50 percent.
>
> The manufacturing and service sectors both expanded and were beginning to relieve some of the pressure on the land. Agriculture and mining actually fell from more than 30 percent of national production in 1960 to some 25 percent in 1979.[137]

In 1977, El Salvador's production of basic foods increased by 38 percent, and between 1976 and 1979, the minimum wage in agriculture increased by 37 percent. Workers in seasonal crops saw wage increases of 77 percent.[138]

One of the complaints most often raised against the Salvadoran economy in the late 1970s was its uneven distribution of income. Thus we are told that in 1977, for example, the top 5 percent of El Salvador's earners received 24 percent of the national income while the lowest 20 percent received only 5.7 percent of the income, according to figures from the Economic and Social Council of the Organization of American States. Yet these figures are less lopsided than the corresponding averages for all of Latin America, where the top five percent received 32.7 percent of the income, while the bottom 20 percent got only 3.7 percent of the economic pie. Even more interesting: the figures for the United States are not much different.[139]

Another positive aspect of Salvadoran society under Romero is the fact that in 1979 the government devoted a greater portion of its budget (34 percent) to education and health than all but one other Latin American country (Costa Rica). Beyond this, Romero sought to forestall U.S. criticisms by implementing a series of reforms, including new labor and election laws, a five-year rural development program, and improved rural housing.[140]

Still, Romero's admittedly corrupt regime was targeted by Washington's human rights lobby. Frank J. Devine, who served as U.S. Ambassador to El Salvador from 1977 to 1980, has written of the human rights campaign:

> To understand the all-pervasive influence of this factor, it is important to recognize the size and power of the human rights lobby, which today exists and functions to defend the persecuted and to promote the cause of justice, as it defines these concepts.
>
> In the lexicon of today's El Salvador, repression has also come to be applied to every law enforcement action. The arrest of a person apprehended in an act of violence, the dislodgement of strikers illegally occupying a seized industrial plant, the recovery for owners of a rural property taken over by hostile peasants, all of these are immediately and publicly denounced by the Opposition, by the extremists of the Left, and often by the Catholic Church, as acts of repression.[141]

Ambassador Devine notes that the human rights activists within the Carter administration had begun to focus on El Salvador by 1977, and that "they completely outmaneuvered their opponents in dealing with members of Congress and their staffs. They were accused of engaging in skillful character assassination of those whom they saw as being unhelpfully loyal to interests of the United States Government other than the cause of human rights." In reference to their unethical tactics, Devine contends that "it was impossible to run a coherent foreign policy under these conditions."[142]

Coherent or not, the foreign policy of human rights carried on, as the United States attempted to coerce its neighbors to Washington's vision of reform. Many Latin American nations, according to Devine, "asked what right the United States had to constitute itself as judge and jury. . . . They protested that we were unilaterally redefining 'intervention' in such a way as to exclude any action we might take in the name of human rights. Some came to view our efforts more as zealotry than diplomacy."[143]

If the Carter administration was blind to the danger, El Salvador wasn't. Vice President Julio Astacio pointed out to Ambassador Devine (as paraphrased by Devine) that "reforms touch the very heart and structure of a society . . . and therefore must be accomplished in a way, and at a pace, that society can bear. Otherwise violence and disaster may result. . . . For outsiders, in the name of human rights, to attempt to force this pace is unrealistic and can be very dangerous."[144]

Washington's Solution

On October 15, 1979, Romero was ousted in a bloodless military coup. The officers behind the coup fit the State Department's image of "reform," and the junta they set up incorporated representatives of a number of political parties (including the Left) and the private sector as well as the military. The State Department, seeing the junta members as "centrists and moderate," said it was "encouraged," and within a few days the United States had rented ten rooms in the El Salvador Sheraton and installed a team of advisers.[145]

In a matter of weeks, the junta fell apart as the extreme

Left (State's "centrists") withdrew to join the guerrillas. What took its place in January 1980 was a new five-member junta, which this time included the Christian Democratic Party, led by Jose Napoleon Duarte who had been denied the presidency in 1972 by an illegitimate, army-supervised vote count.

The new junta was almost as incohesive as its predecessor, but it managed to survive. It proceeded with its plans for political, economic, and social reform, and eventually succeeded in establishing democracy in El Salvador, for which it deserves no little credit. Yet it is reasonable to ask whether democracy could have been established by some other, less costly course; for the economic "reforms" carried out in the 1980s destroyed the economy, and tore the social fabric to shreds. Violence erupted on all sides—on the Left, the Right, and within the military—with politically motivated violent deaths reaching eight hundred a month during the junta's first year.[146] Only four months after the October revolution, Risks International was to describe El Salvador as "bordering on civil war."[147]

To make sure that the "reforms" were carried out satisfactorily, Carter relieved ambassador Frank Devine, sending Robert E. White to replace him. At his confirmation hearings in February 1980, White described himself as a supporter of the "passionate Left."[148] According to journalist Virginia Prewett, (the late) Senator Jacob Javits said to White:

> while theoretically you may be an ambassador and buried in the bureaucracy, you are a proconsul so far as we are concerned. You are going to go down there and work as an ambassador. If you do only that, the United States will not be well served. You really have to be an activist and take a chance with your career. . . . I believe you are going to get a strong backing from this committee. You are a "proconsul," not just an ambassador in this matter.[149]

Prewett reports that (the late) Committee Chairman Frank Church, sympathetic to Leftist causes and ideas throughout his career, endorsed those words on behalf of the committee. White took these instructions seriously, for on the day he was confirmed he said, "It is the judgment of the U.S. government that no Salvadoran government can stay in power unless it embarks on a broad spectrum of reforms."[150] Through White and other "advisers," the U.S. took it upon itself to decide what those reforms must be.

The centerpiece of the junta's program would be land reform. It was felt that too few people owned the farmland in El Salvador, so it must be seized and redistributed. (In the United States, the world's leader in agriculture, the trend for forty years had been toward larger and larger farms.) In densely populated El Salvador, efficiency of production would be subordinated to land distribution.

So on March 4, 1980, the country's top 180 agronomists and agricultural bureaucrats were summoned to a meeting in San Salvador. While the hotel where they met was surrounded by government troops for their "safety," they were told the details of the plan they were supposed to help implement. It involved three phases. Under Phase I, all farms larger than 1,235 acres were to be seized and converted into cooperatives. Phase III gave renters and sharecroppers title to the land they worked. Phase II, which was not put into effect until December 1983, required farmers to sell any land in excess of 605 acres.

The dispossessed were "compensated" with government bonds that quickly lost their value as El Salvador's money deteriorated. Because the peasants lacked the technical and administrative skills to manage the new, large co-ops, the government ended up running them—a practice adopted earlier by the Soviet Union, where it has produced sixty-six years of "bad weather."[151] A member of a co-op cannot sell his share, and any investment he makes in the enterprise must be abandoned if he ever leaves the co-op. As for the recipients of small plots, they had better enjoy farming, because in order to receive title to "their" new land, they must live on it and farm it for thirty years. Thus none of the "beneficiaries" of land reform acquired collateral against which to raise credit.[152]

On March 5, troops began to comb the countryside, confiscating the large farms at gunpoint. According to Virginia Prewett:

> Everything was seized. All the crops in the fields and in the barns. All the seed, all the farm tractors and other machinery essential to extensive, modern farming. All the trucks, jeeps, small planes, gasoline and machinery-repair tools. All the equipment for cultivating, harvesting and processing coffee. The sugar mills; all the schools and employees' houses on the farms. All the owners' homes, with all their contents. "I can't even get my children's letters from a drawer at my farm," one owner said later.

Many were left with only the clothes they wore.[153]

It is incredible that White and Company could not have foreseen the violent reaction that such a policy would inevitably produce. Subsequent State Department reports on the subject attempt to dodge responsibility by using anesthetizing double-talk. "The extreme right saw the [land] reforms as a threat to their interests," says one report. Another notes that "delays in payment [to the original owner] have motivated some former landowners to evict the new beneficiaries." Another, written in April 1983—before the details of Phase II were final—mentioned that some private farmers had proposed a "free market" land reform for Phase II, whereby they would be permitted to sell their "excess" land rather than forfeit it. The report concluded that "such an approach might engender less hostility than Phases I and III." Might?[154]

By 1985, more than 23 percent of El Salvador's total farmland had been transferred to the state.

That, however, was not the end of the reforms. On March 7, 1980, the junta nationalized the banks and savings and loan associations. Clearly, the Carter administration was determined to have socialism in El Salvador on a scale that U.S. voters would never tolerate at home. In April, there was an article in *The Washington Post* entitled "New Diplomacy Tested by U.S. in El Salvador." Staff writer Michael Getler wrote that "the tiny, violence-torn Republic of El Salvador has become the testing-ground for an unorthodox brand of last-minute U.S. diplomacy." He referred to

> intense U.S. pressure on the military members of the junta to broaden its political base, carry out truly revolutionary land ownership and banking reforms, and stop the killing being done in the countryside by elements of its armed forces in the name of reform.
>
> This plan has put the United States in the unusual position of advocating overturning a wealthy landowning class.[155]

Members of Carter's State Department later told Alan Riding of *The New York Times* that since change is inevitable, "U.S. interests are best served by 'stealing' Cuba's cause and promoting change."[156]

Not everyone in El Salvador liked Cuba's cause, however. In May, a group of women staged a protest at the U.S. embassy residence in El Salvador. On the gate they painted a message to Ambassador White: "Communist, Go Home!"[157]

The Deluge

The sweeping land and banking "reforms" directly attacked the most essential prerequisite of a healthy economy: individual property rights. The social turmoil and economic collapse that attended the changes were enormous. Coffee production, after increasing by about 50 percent between 1975 and 1980, fell nearly 25 percent by 1985; an Inter-American Development Bank report ascribed production problems "mainly to lack of investment to rehabilitate coffee plantations and to combat borers and rust which attacked coffee-growing regions." The same report added: "The situation of cotton is even bleaker. The area planted has decreased to less than a third of what it was in 1979 . . ."[158] Sugar production dropped 30 percent in 1984 from 1979 levels. Between 1979 and 1982, gross domestic product (GDP), which had climbed steadily for twenty years, dropped by about 25 percent in real terms. Preliminary estimates for 1986 pegged GDP at still about ten percent below 1980 levels. Exports fell by 20 percent by 1982, and their continued slide put them, by 1986, fully 33 percent below 1980 levels. GDP per capita steadily declined from its 1978 peak and, by 1984, had fallen to 1970 levels. Unemployment rose from 3.6 percent in 1978 to 34 percent in 1985. These declines occurred despite an outpouring of U.S. assistance without precedent: in 1987, U.S. foreign aid to El Salvador amounted to $609 million, exceeding that country's own $582 million contribution to its budget, the first time that had ever before happened in the entire history of the U.S. foreign aid program anywhere in the world. (It, of course, goes without saying that no other country in the region received more U.S. aid: $2.3 billion since 1979. El Salvador's public debt continued its precipitous climb, from $3 billion in 1978 to just under $40 billion in 1986.)[159]

Of course, this economic disaster cannot be entirely attributed to the junta's socialist reforms. In common with all developing countries, El Salvador was hit hard by the oil price increases of 1979–80, as well as by worldwide high interest rates, and by communist-sponsored domestic sabotage. In addition, the country suffered a severe earthquake in October 1976. Measuring 7.5 on the Richter scale, it devastated San Salvador's city center, killed 1,000 and left 200,000 homeless.

The State Department rightly points out that political violence "has triggered large-scale capital flight, reduced public and private investment, interfered with production and exports, and generated fear and uncertainty in the private sector."[160] What the Department fails to mention is that all these ills are also caused by the wholesale destruction of private property rights.

The State Department also overlooks what part its "reforms" might have played in encouraging the political violence. As noted above, violence increased dramatically in 1980—the year of "reform." In addition to the predictable efforts of landowners to defend their property and, later, to avenge their losses, there was a great rise in Leftist insurgency. The State Department explained this by saying that "the extreme left knew that agrarian and other reforms would do much to remove the grievances and hatred upon which their 'class struggle' depended."[161] It is equally plausible, however, that the guerrillas saw the junta's illegitimacy and instability as a golden opportunity, and that the disruption caused by the reforms played into their hands.

In any case, the guerrillas' fortunes changed rapidly after the coup of October 1979. In December, Castro brought the leaders of three competing communist guerrilla factions to Havana, where he persuaded them to coordinate their efforts. In April 1980, three small non-communist political parties joined with the Marxist guerrillas to form a political organization called the Democratic Revolutionary Front (FDR). This provided the "broad coalition," the democratic facade advocated by Castro that had proved so useful to the New JEWEL Movement in Grenada and the Sandinistas in Nicaragua.

In May, the three guerrilla organizations brought together by Castro met again in Havana, where they were joined by a fourth group. Responding to Castro's promises of aid in exchange for their unification, they agreed to form the Unified Revolutionary Directorate (DRU).[162] By the end of the year, a fifth terrorist organization had joined them to form the Farabundo Marti National Liberation Front (FMLN) as the military counterpart of the FDR, both of which were placed under the direction of the DRU. The democratic elements of the FDR had no voice in the DRU, which was the governing body for the unified guerrilla movement.

International communist support for the Salvadoran guerrillas predated even the Sandinista triumph in Nicaragua. By July 1979, two hundred of the Salvadoran rebels had already been trained in Cuba. Another nine hundred trained there the next year.[163] In April 1980, according to a State Department report:

Salvadoran guerrilla leaders met in the Hungarian embassy in Mexico City with representatives of Cuba, the USSR, Bulgaria, East Germany, Poland, and Vietnam. In June and July 1980, the Salvadoran communist leaders went to Moscow and then with Soviet endorsement visited East Germany, Bulgaria, Vietnam, and Ethiopia—all of which promised them military and other support. The commitment of weapons was estimated at about 100 tons.

The Cuban/Soviet bloc military supply operation used western weapons (some from Vietnam) for "cover" and covertly shipped some 200 tons of weapons through Cuba and Nicaragua to arm the Salvadoran guerrillas for their intense but unsuccessful "final offensive" in January 1981.[164]

The "western weapons" used for "cover" included about a thousand American M-16 rifles captured by North Vietnam at the end of the Vietnam War. The advantage of these weapons was that the Salvadoran guerrillas could claim to have captured them from the U.S.-supplied Salvadoran armed forces, and indeed the guerrillas were under orders to deny the true source of the weapons.[165]

In October of 1980, representatives of the communist parties of Central America, Mexico, and Panama met in Havana and agreed to form a commission to oversee the provision of material assistance to the guerrillas in El Salvador.[166] Nicaragua provided the location for the guerrillas' command and communications facilities as well as several training camps. Arms from Cuba and elsewhere were channeled through Nicaragua. From there, they were sent to El Salvador by air, by land (through Honduras), and by boat (across the Gulf of Fonseca). This well-established fact has been vehemently denied by Nicaragua and by American Leftists, notwithstanding its repeated confirmation by former guerrillas.[167] On November 1, 1980, the DRU logistics coordinator in Managua was able to inform the guerrillas' general staff that 120 tons of military equipment were in Nicaragua awaiting shipment to El Salvador, while another 300–400 tons were expected to be on their way by mid-month.[168]

The extent of Cuban involvement in FMLN affairs is suggested by Adin Ingles Alvarado, a guerrilla officer who defected in 1985. He described preparations in Cuba for a special mission:

> I was one of the 28 men being trained in Cuba to carry out this operation against the [Salvadoran] Fourth Brigade. We even had combat exercises using a mock-up of the garrison.... Besides the training, they gave us all the material to use against the Fourth Brigade. The explosives, ammunition, and machine guns were sent from Cuba. Nicaragua was only the conduit or staging point.[169]

Eventually Cuban control became so complete as to demoralize some of the Salvadoran rebels. One guerrilla defector complained of the "subjection of the FMLN to the tactical and strategic control of the Cubans and Sandinistas."[170] "All commanders from the rank of platoon upwards have graduated in the Soviet Union or Cuba," reported another.[171] Former guerrilla commander Alejandro Montenegro has said, "I was very demoralized . . . especially because the Cubans were already deeply involved and were practically directing the five FMLN commanders"; and on another occasion, "All the acts of violence that take place at a national level are ordered by Cubans or Nicaraguans."[172]

In 1980, however, there was no sign of disaffection as the guerrillas prepared for their "final offensive." Late that year,

Sandino Airport in Managua was closed to traffic from ten P.M. to four A.M. for several weeks, as Cuban cargo planes ferried arms, ammunition, and supplies to Nicaragua for use in El Salvador.[173] On January 10, 1981, the rebels launched their attack, hitting targets throughout the country. The operation was deliberately timed to overwhelm the Salvadoran military before Ronald Reagan took office as the new U.S. president.[174] The guerrillas captured a number of radio stations, overran a National Guard post, burned buses, and shot down two helicopters. The success they envisioned and confidently predicted depended on a popular uprising, which never materialized.

The final offensive was a total defeat for the rebels, but by no means did it put them out of business. As arms continued to pour in from Cuba and Nicaragua, the guerrillas gained in strength. In 1982, they had six thousand fighters, supported by five thousand to ten thousand part-time activists, many of whom would become combatants as weapons were made available.[175] They began to operate in larger units, with more sophisticated weapons and equipment, and during 1983, put the Salvadoran army on the defensive. Considerable U.S. training and aid, as well as a major reorganization of the army (to weed out the many incompetents), were required to turn the tide.

Although the Soviets have denied vehemently a direct role in arming the FMLN, their ties to the guerrillas are much older than those they maintain with the Sandinistas. This is because of their close relationship with the dominant force in the umbrella organizations of the strongly pro-Moscow Salvadoran Communist Party. Soviet attitudes towards the struggle in El Salvador have waxed and waned according to a combination of events in the country, their evaluation of U.S. commitment, and their own internal commotions. A postmortem on the "final offensive" was that it was premature, launched in a panicky reaction to Ronald Reagan's election.[176]

The tide did turn in 1984, but the communists have remained active, adopting a strategy of sabotage aimed at the nation's economic assets. Roads, bridges, buses, trains, utilities, and agricultural processing facilities became the usual targets. More than a hundred water facilities have been damaged, more than a fifth of the country's bridges have been destroyed, and much of the country's rolling stock rendered useless. From February 1981 to November 1982, the guerrillas caused more than five thousand interruptions in electrical power—almost eight a day. The State Department estimates the total economic damage at close to $1 billion.[177]

The human costs have been very high as well. The guerrillas have acknowledged killing six thousand people in the first year of the rebellion alone.[178] The victims have often included civilians. El Salvador's Human Rights Commission reported on an attack on the Salvadoran city of Berlin in February 1983:

> The FMLN-FDR indiscriminately attacked the population of that city, causing fires, looting government offices, stores and private residences, and causing, with its continuous shelling, the exodus of thousands of people, including children, elderly people and women.... At no time could the city of Berlin represent a military or strategic objective, since there were only 43 members of the armed forces ... in the city.... They caused the deaths of at least 12 defenseless civilians.[179]

Roger Reed, then of the Council for Inter-American Security, described an attack on Suchitoto, a township of twenty thousand people: "The rebels took control of the main highway, cutting off Suchitoto from the capital, blew up several high-tension towers, and destroyed the water lines and prevented their repair. There was no drinking water or electricity for twelve days."[180]

As the war dragged on the communists lost what popular support they had enjoyed. "It is evident that after three years of civil war, the guerrilla movement is now alone. . . . They are a guerrilla army fighting alone," said ex-guerrilla Montenegro in March 1983.[181] By 1984, they were kidnaping young men for conscription into their armed forces. According to Salvadoran estimates, there were fifteen thousand such "recruits" in a nine-day period in March of that year.[182] Needless to say, this practice has not improved their popularity or significantly strengthened their military position.

A Congressional Research Service study, released late in 1982, would assert:

> The success of the insurgents in El Salvador has not been matched by political victories. It is not popular support that sustains the insurgents . . . this insurgency depends for its lifeblood—arms, ammunition, financing, logistics—upon outside assistance from Nicaragua and Cuba. . . .[183]

The Advent of Democracy

In early 1979, Ambassador Devine had been instructed to push President Romero for elections the following May. Romero doubted whether his opposition would be willing to risk elections that might reveal its weakness. That turned out to be precisely the case, at least as far as the Marxists were concerned. According to Devine, "the LP-28 [28th of February Popular Leagues] sent back word that the time was not appropriate for talks with the Yankee embassy," while "the BPR [Popular Revolutionary Bloc] told us explicitly to go to hell!"[184]

The junta of 1980, however, went ahead and chose March 28, 1982 as the date for the election of a constituent assembly to write a new constitution. Political violence was still all too common in El Salvador, but the junta did everything it could to ensure the safety of all participants.

The Marxists knew their popularity was low. The Christian Democrats took a poll that showed only 12 percent support for the rebels. As Archbishop Arturo Rivera y Damas had pointed out a year earlier, the guerrillas "have made violence and loyalty to Marxism their watchword, and because of that the majority have turned their backs on them."[185] So once again, the communists scoffed at elections. They announced a boycott, claiming that their candidates' lives would be at risk in open campaigning. In fact, it was the guerrillas who contributed most to the danger.

As the elections approached, Castro's arms shipments to the communist guerrillas increased substantially. In Costa Rica, authorities discovered a cache containing over 150 weapons awaiting shipment to the FMLN. According to a captured terrorist, the weapons were "for the elections."[186]

The FMLN threatened to kill not only participating candidates, but anyone who voted. "Vote in the morning, die in the afternoon," was the rebel slogan. They distributed posters saying, "Those who vote, we will kill,"[187] and they announced that "by participating in the elections you are helping the genocidal plan of imperialism."[188]

Despite all this, six political parties fielded candidates, and they campaigned actively for four months. The rebels, meantime, prepared coordinated attacks across the nation on election day.

In the early morning of March 28, the assault on democracy was launched. In groups of up to five hundred they attacked the polling places. "But still the people came," wrote *Time* magazine,

by hundreds, thousands, and hundreds of thousands—defying the guerrillas' threats and claims on their allegiance. Under a sweltering sun in the San Salvador suburb of Mejicanos, voters stood in a half-mile queue while a firefight raged six blocks away. When the action moved closer, the people dropped to the ground until it passed, keeping their places in line. In another northern suburb, San Antonio Abad, voters hid in their homes until the end of the skirmish that left twelve rebels and three soldiers dead. When the fighting stopped about 8:30 A.M., the people had to step over the bodies and rivulets of blood in the dusty streets to vote. But vote they did.

One woman proclaimed, "They can kill my family, they can kill my neighbors if we vote. But they cannot kill us all."[189] One and a half million Salvadorans voted that day—80 percent of the eligible electorate—in a crushing defeat for the communists. More than two hundred international observers and seven hundred members of the international press were there, and the verdict was virtually unanimous: The elections were free and fair. *The Washington Post* editorialized on March 30:

> One understands now why the guerrillas were so eager to destroy, and the political opposition to denounce, the elections in El Salvador. They seem to have sensed that the people would choose to take the way offered by the government to express their pent-up longing and have done with the war and reconstruct the country. . . . The process seemed fair. The voters came out despite death threats. . . . The insurgents were hurt badly by the elections.[190]

A constituent assembly of sixty members was elected. No party won an absolute majority, so a multi-party Government of National Unity was formed. Alvaro Magana was chosen by the assembly to serve as provisional president.

The assembly then proceeded to write a constitution aimed at providing stronger legislative and judicial branches than El Salvador had hitherto enjoyed. The new constitution, which took effect in December 1983, called for further elections. Eight political parties participated in the presidential election of March 1984, but none of the candidates received a majority, so a runoff was held in May.

Then, as in the March elections, the contest was between a charismatic leader of the Right, Major Roberto D'Aubuisson, and the socialist-minded Jose Napoleon Duarte. The State Department threw its weight massively behind Duarte, while

D'Aubuisson was the target of an international smear campaign portraying him as a death squad assassin. To make the point even more explicit, Washington told Salvadorans that should D'Aubuisson win, the United States would be forced to re-think its policy toward El Salvador—a clear signal that the life-support system of U.S. economic and military aid might end.

Even so, Duarte won with only 54 percent of the vote. He began his five-year term in June as El Salvador's first honestly elected president in fifty years. Duarte's Christian Democratic Party also won control of the assembly in March 1985, as nine parties took part in legislative and municipal elections. By then, the main opposition party, D'Aubuisson's Republican Nationalist Alliance (ARENA), was divided, and D'Aubuisson had yielded the leadership to a Georgetown University-educated businessman named Alfredo Cristiani.

In all three elections held since 1982, the Salvadoran army has remained politically neutral; in all three, the Marxist guerrillas have attacked and harassed the voters. And in every case, the voters have turned out in droves—never less than 75 percent of the eligible electorate.[191]

With better training, the Salvadoran Army has become more professional in recent years, more respectful of human rights, and better able to cope with the guerrilla threat. Political violence has declined dramatically since mid-1984, except for guerrilla-sponsored urban terrorism, which has increased. In response to this development, the government has placed some restrictions on constitutional rights, but groups sympathetic to the guerrillas have been free to advertise, march, demonstrate, and publicly criticize the government.[192]

Diminished by casualties and desertions, the FMLN has largely been defeated in the field.[193] Increasingly sophisticated weapons have continued to flow in from Cuba and Nicaragua, however, and the communists have now taken their violence to the cities. President Duarte initiated a dialogue with the guerrillas in 1984, holding two meetings that year, failing in an attempt to meet again in 1986, again in the aftermath of the 1987 "peace" plan. (The process drew warm praise from the State Department. Reacting to the 1984 talks, State professed to see dialogue between a democratic government and an insurgency—made possible only through the support of two governments of questionable legality themselves, Cuba and Nicaragua—as holding out prospects "for the peaceful resolution of critical issues and, hopefully, for the eventual reincorporation of the insurgents through electoral process.")[194]

In July 1986, the guerrillas announced a six-point peace plan that called for bringing them into the government. The government's position was that they must first lay down their arms and win a place for themselves through popular support demonstrated at the polls.

In May 1987, the guerrillas submitted an 18-point plan for "humanizing" the war. In it, they offered to stop using mines and economic sabotage if the government would stop using artillery and aerial attack. No sooner had the Arias "peace pact" been signed in Guatemala City in August 1987 than Duarte announced new talks with the guerrillas, which opened October 4 in the Salvadoran capital. The rebels responded to the call for talks as they had in the past: by stepping up violence in order to strengthen their hand at the bargaining table. At mid-August, three policemen were shot to death and three others wounded in apparent guerrilla attacks, four unidentified men were shot to death in the western province of Sonsonate, and a National University professor was shot to death by an unknown assailant. On October 29, 1987, the FMLN high command announced it was breaking off truce talks with the Duarte government and renewing a military offensive. A week later, the rebels ignored a cease-fire which Duarte compelled a reluctant army to respect unilaterally. (In justifying its position, the FMLN linked the decision to the murder of Herbert Araya, head of a pro-guerrilla human rights organization. Rightist "death squads" were blamed for the killing, as they had been for the 1980 murder of Archbishop Romero, though that killing, like this one, clearly benefited the Left more than it did the Right. Duarte promptly offered a $10,000 reward for information leading to the arrest of Araya's killers, and appointed an investigating commission. A similar commission named to investigate the archbishop's murder failed to turn up a suspect. As these lines were being written, Duarte made a flamboyant claim that he had uncovered "proof" that D'Aubuisson was the "intellectual author" of the Romero murder. The key witness, Amado Antonio Garay, 37, who allegedly drove the getaway car the day of the March 24, 1980, murder, disappeared immediately after Duarte's dramatic announcement, into "protective custody" in an unnamed "neighboring country." D'Aubuisson's ARENA party called the accusations "calumnies and insults" and accused Duarte of "politicizing the Romero case" to camouflage the "moral decomposition of his party" and the "corruption and ineptitude" of his government. Even *The Washington Post* noted that "the disclosure of Garay's testimony struck many observers here as politically motivated."[195]

Duarte played a key role in engineering the Guatemala City agreement, the Arias peace plan. He would later tell an interviewer than it was his proposal—that all actions anticipated under the plan should go into effect simultaneously, on November 7, 90 days after its signing—that broke the impasse blocking agreement. The practical effect of that "compromise" was that whereas aid to the *contras* would have to end automatically on that day, it would be enough for the Sandinistas to *claim* they had made the required moves toward democratization.

Although, in common with other Christian Democrat leaders in Latin America, Duarte finds rapprochement with the Left far easier to accept than with the Right, he had previously resisted such "peace" accords. But, under strong prodding from Washington and facing elections for the national Legislative Assembly in May 1988, and presidential elections the following May, Duarte apparently gambled that he might succeed in getting the guerrillas off his back and restore his sagging popularity. His anxieties have been heightened by the appearance of new vigor in the ARENA party since D'Aubuisson stepped aside to make way for the 39-year-old Cristiani.

While Duarte was busy lobbying for the peace plan, Cristiani told an interviewer that the president was putting himself out on a perhaps untenable limb.

"The problem," Cristiani said, "is that he [Duarte] really doesn't have the representation of the majority of the Salvadoran people" in the negotiations. Cristiani also alluded to a point increasingly rankling the country's military leaders, that Duarte's concessions strengthen the guerrillas at the minimum by giving them time to regroup and reorganize, and could surrender to them what they have never been able to win on the field of battle: a power-sharing role.

On November 13, 1987, Cristiani's judgment was echoed when all eight opposition parties withdrew from a panel formed to implement the "peace" plan—a further rude blow to Duarte's image-building campaign. In fact, about the only support he did get came from the hard Left. The political leadership of the FMLN returned to El Salvador late in November, announcing plans to contest the March 1988 municipal and legislative elections. Their return produced at least a temporary split with the armed faction, and was interpreted as both a boon to Duarte and a blow to the violent wing since it would weaken their case before U.S., European and Latin American supporters for their continued resort to arms.[196]

There is one important battle the Salvadoran guerrillas have won: the U.S. (and European) media. In a spectacular display of moral myopia, the media routinely treat guerrillas trying to shoot their way into power against a democratic government (El Salvador) the same as they do a guerrilla force opposing an unelected, totalitarian regime which broke every important promise it ever made, including many made to those who have taken up arms against it. Both the Salvadoran government and the *contras*, routinely are, in press reports, "U.S. (or CIA)-backed." The Salvadoran guerrillas and the Sandinistas themselves are seldom (ever?) Soviet (or Cuban)-backed, but rather simply "Leftist."[197]

GUATEMALA

Guatemala is the most populous country in Central America; more than half of its 8.2 million people are descendants of the Maya Indians. It also has the broadest economic base in Central America, with a gross domestic product (in 1985) of just under $10 billion. Since their brush with communism under Jacobo Arbenz, the Guatemalan people have tended to be strongly anti-communist, prompting *Forbes* magazine to refer to the country in 1982 as the "free enterprise linchpin of the floundering Central American Common Market."[198]

With the ouster of Arbenz in 1954, the military became the ruling class in Guatemala. From then until the 1980s, the presidency was in the hands of military men (with one exception), who were generally elected. Though the elections during this period have been widely regarded as fraudulent, they did not produce a static, one-party rule, for there was genuine competition among various coalitions. It must be understood that these military men ruled in a civilian sense. As foreign affairs specialists L. Francis Bouchey and Alberto M. Piedra wrote in 1980:

> Three of Guatemala's last four presidents have been retired generals, but it is hardly accurate to characterize the government as a "military regime," especially when one realizes that in underdeveloped countries the Army is by far the largest insti-

tution for training public administrators and accounts for the largest pool of personnel experienced in public affairs. It must be remembered that the Army is the most important avenue for upward professional and social mobility for the poor and less advantaged, and it also functions as a public works, community service agency as well as a military machine.[199]

This is the political/military tradition that brought General Fernando Romeo Lucas Garcia to the presidency in July 1978.

Lucas was elected as a Centrist (it was the Right that complained of election fraud). His government was corrupt, but was hardly an instrument of the land barons. In 1980, for example, more than 64 percent of the budget was devoted to a variety of social programs, and there was an incredible 186 percent increase in the minimum wage for all farmhands. This did not mean, however, that he could satisfy the Carter administration, for President Lucas had a human rights problem.

Communist guerrilla forces have operated in Guatemala since 1961. Guatemala's Revolutionary Armed Forces was, in fact, one of Fidel Castro's first pawns in his campaign to bring his brand of communism to the hemisphere. During the government of Colonel Carlos Arana Osorio (1970–1974), the guerrillas were all but annihilated. In the late 1970s, guerrilla activity revived, in the form of both urban and rural terrorism. That, in turn, provoked reactions from right-wing vigilante groups. President Carter's response, in 1977, was to end U.S. military assistance to Guatemala. During President Lucas's tenure, Washington kept up the pressure, notwithstanding a State Department report that in 1979 the human rights violations "remained lower than in the decade prior to 1978."[200]

To Guatemalans attempting to deal with the terrorism and violence, such interference seemed unwarranted. In a March 1980 speech to the American Chamber of Commerce, Mario

Ribas Montes, the managing editor of Guatemala City's daily afternoon paper *El Imparcial*, told of Guatemalans who were headed for Washington to present a "plea for mercy that our country should not be pushed over the brink.... We Guatemalans can resist Communist subversion as it has been manifested before, but not as it presents itself of late, with a powerful ally which performs an important part of its work for it."[201] In August, Mario Ribas Montes was gunned down by three armed motorcyclists while sitting in his car at a busy intersection. That summer, President Carter recalled his ambassador to Guatemala, Frank Ortiz, for being too soft on the Lucas government.

If Jimmy Carter failed to see Guatemala's vulnerability, it was not lost on the international community of Leftist revolutionaries. At a December 1979 strategy meeting in Costa Rica, the leaders of several Leftist rebel groups identified Guatemala and El Salvador as the principal targets for 1980.[202] With the help of the Sandinistas, Castro persuaded Guatemala's four major revolutionary organizations to meet in Managua in 1980, and a merger was later announced at a press conference in Havana. The new umbrella organization was called the Guatemalan National Revolutionary Union (URNG), with a directorate known as the General Revolutionary Command. This was, of course, a replay of the formula Castro had already used in El Salvador and Nicaragua. The four are the Guerrilla Army of the Poor (EGP), the Organization of the Armed People (ORPA), the Rebel Armed Forces (FAR), all Marxist-Leninist groups—and the communist Guatemalan Workers Party (PGT).

The merger was not entirely successful—the four groups were reluctant to work together—but it did bring about an escalation of the violence. (By 1987, the PGT was said to have pulled out of the formal alliance, but was still willing to work with the other groups[203]—a familiar stance of the communists vis-a-vis other "revolutionaries" in the early stages of rebellion.) The guerrillas attacked electrical facilities, bridges, buses, post offices, and telephone offices. In the countryside, they used Indian hostages to shield themselves against army attacks. In May 1980, three policemen were machine-gunned to death in their car, and a police commando squad was ambushed. The EGP claimed responsibility. The murder of army officers by terrorists using machine guns, even in public streets, became commonplace.

Vigilante activities increased as well, fueled by the inability of the police and the courts to deal with the problem effectively. Bouchey and Piedra made this observation:

> Judges trying terrorists have been frequent targets of threats against themselves and their families. A judge is not eager to find against a terrorist when he knows the terrorist's comrades will retaliate against him or his children. Police understandably have little confidence in court proceedings in such cases. Thus, the vigilantes have represented a "solution" for both police and judges, a solution more palatable to a frontier mentality than to academic observers.[204]

This is the context in which James Cheek, Deputy Assistant Secretary of State for Inter-American Affairs, visited Guatemala in April 1980 and reportedly said, "The price of U.S. friendship is a series of reforms considered important by the U.S. State Department."[205]

Meanwhile, Cuba and Nicaragua proceeded to increase their support for the guerrillas, providing arms and training. In April and July of 1981, Guatemalan security forces discovered large caches of guerrilla weapons at safehouses in Guatemala City. Some of the arms were American-made and could be traced to Vietnam.

Thanks to this outside support, the terrorist violence continued to mount. In December 1981, Maximiliano Sosa Zecena, a bodyguard for the U.S. ambassador was ambushed and killed. A few days later, Mario Dary, the rector of the National University was shot. Roberto Giron Lemus, the publisher of a Guatemala City newspaper, was machine-gunned to death in early 1982. The EGP claimed responsibility for killing eighty-six people in a single month.

In February 1982, the guerrillas launched an offensive, prompting Mexico to become concerned about the security of its southern oil fields. The Mexican army was put on a state of alert and a week later had begun to form a four thousand-man quick-reaction force. The purpose, according to one official, was "to defend the country's southern border and lucrative oil fields against a possible spillover of Central America's turbulent guerrilla wars."[206]

Despite guerrilla efforts at disruption, elections were held in Guatemala on March 7, 1982. The winner was General Anibal Guevara, but the process had been openly fraudulent. The reaction came on March 23, when troops commanded by junior officers surrounded the National Palace. The officers approached retired Brigadier General Efrain Jose Rios Montt, who had been cheated out of the presidency by election fraud in 1974. He agreed to lead a three-man junta. A political anomaly, Rios Montt was a born-again Christian running a nation firmly rooted in Catholic culture. Many were alienated by his compulsive proselytizing, but he had considerable administrative skills.

The new junta abrogated the 1965 constitution, dissolved the congress, and suspended elections. Rios Montt became president when the two other members of the junta resigned in June, and on July 1 his government imposed a state of siege. Civil liberties were restricted, and special courts were created to function under the executive branch. This attracted much criticism inside and outside the country, but the new president said that political freedom would return once order had been restored. As it turned out, he meant it.

Rios Montt managed to clean up government corruption and virtually eliminate the death squads. To deal with the insurgency, Rios Montt devised a plan that combined military and civic elements. Known as the "rifles and beans" program, it borrowed the strategy that had worked in the 1960s for Colonel Arana. It provided the Indians in the highlands with food, medicine, and economic assistance to encourage their loyalty, and supplied them with weapons for self-defense. Civil defense patrols were organized to guard roads, villages and crops and to alert the army to suspicious activities. The program was a dramatic success. A UN report said of the civil defense patrols, "The security they provide, particularly to remote communities, enables the population to continue living in their traditional villages, whereas the army could not possibly provide such protection."[207]

The guerrillas were offered amnesty. Some surrendered; the others were forced to retreat to Mexico, their supply lines largely broken.

Rios Montt made plans for the return of democracy. The state of siege was lifted in March 1983, and constituent assembly elections were scheduled for July of the following year. There were some senior army officers, however, who were impatient to be rid of Rios Montt. They liked neither the way he mixed religion with politics, nor his foreign policy of non-alignment, but they were especially concerned about his disruption of the military hierarchy through the appointment of junior officers to senior civilian positions. On August 5, 1983, the president said in an interview that he would turn over power to an elected successor in 1985 "unless they get rid of me before then."[208] Three days later, he was ousted by the Defense Minister, General Oscar Humberto Mejia Victores.

The new head of state restored all constitutional rights and abolished the special courts. He branded the Sandinista government a threat to the continent and acted at once to form a closer military relationship with El Salvador. Mejia then followed his predecessor's schedule for elections. On July 1, 1984, a record number of Guatemalans went to the polls to choose a constituent assembly in what international observers have judged to be a free and fair election. To the surprise of Guatemala's critics, the military remained neutral.

A presidential election was held in the fall of 1985, and on January 14, 1986, Vinicio Cerezo, a moderate liberal representing the Christian Democrats, became Guatemala's first elected civilian president in twenty years. In addition to the security question, he faced considerable economic and social problems. In June of 1986, he announced a new economic program. Preliminary figures indicate the program has yet to take hold: Guatemala's Gross National Product (GNP) declined by one percent in 1985, and remained stagnant in 1986, but an Inter-American Development Bank Report said there were grounds for cautious optimism. Guatemala had a low level of inflation, an increase in non-traditional exports, and exchange stability. Against those: continuing depressed prices for coffee (which accounts for 47 percent of the country's exports), continued decline in cotton output (due to high costs of production), and a low level of foreign investment (still only one-half the highs reached in the late 1970s).[209]

Contrary to the policy of his predecessors, Cerezo has actively sought rapprochement with the Sandinistas, and—although the guerrilla forces have been considerably weakened—agreed to talks with the Guatemalan National Revolutionary Union. (By one account, the guerrilla forces by the fall of 1987 had dwindled to 2,000, down from a high of 10,000—although another authoritative source, citing U.S. intelligence services and Guatemalan military officers, estimates fewer than 1,000 remain in the guerrilla ranks.)[210] The GNRU had sought such talks since 1982, occasionally publishing paid advertisements in local newspapers to state its positions, including an open letter addressed to Central American presidents during their August 6–7, 1987, summit. According to a source cited by *The Washington Post*, the rebels did not intend to demand power-sharing in these talks—which opened October 7 in Madrid—but rather would seek "economic and political reforms." At all odds, those talks lasted two days, "went nowhere," and two weeks later the guerrillas announced stepped-up operations and the army resumed counter-insurgency operations in Quiche Province.[211]

Though a cease-fire would prove to be short-lived (it was to last so long as the talks did), it stirred inevitable resentment among army officers. They also pointed out that full-fledged democracy had now been restored to the country, so there was no reason to accord guerrillas special privileges and status not granted voters and others who participate in the open political process. Partly to mollify such critics, Cerezo was careful to describe the talks not as negotiations, but "contacts."

Still, the Guatemalan delegation to the Madrid "contacts" was high-level: Roberto Valle, first president of the Congress, flanked by four military officers. Heading the guerrilla organization was Rodrigo Asturias, whose father, Miguel Angel Asturias, won a Nobel Prize for literature. The younger Asturias heads the Organization of Armed People.

HONDURAS

Honduras, for the first time in almost sixty years, would, in January 1986, inaugurate an elected civilian president to replace an elected civilian president. Whether this will prove to be an anomaly or the beginning of a democratic tradition is hard to predict. Soon after his inauguration, President Jose Azcona Hoyo stitched together a National Patriotic Accord between his 46 Liberal Party deputies and the 63 National Party deputies who had backed his opponent, strengthening his hand in both the legislature and in the courts.

Honduras has been slipping in and out of nominal democracy for more than thirty years. During that time, there have been five coups, sometimes for the ostensible purpose of replacing one democracy with another. The pattern of military coup, leading to the election of a constituent assembly, leading to a new constitution, leading to an elected president (leading to another coup), has almost become the standard procedure.

Until 1972, the cycle seemed to require eight or nine years. Then the pattern was disrupted by three coups and two consecutive military governments. The last coup was in 1978, when the armed forces installed a three-man junta headed by General Policarpo Paz Garcia. In 1980, the return to democracy was begun. The November 1981 presidential election was won by the Liberal Party candidate, Roberto Suazo Cordoba, a civilian, who took office the next January. Later, according to *The Wall Street Journal*, Suazo "was toying with the idea of extending his term" but was dissuaded by the United States.[212] Elections were held on schedule and, in January 1986, Jose Azcona Hoyo became president.

Politically, Hondurans have been more fortunate than some of their neighbors in Central America. Their government is tolerant of dissent and respectful of human rights. The press is virtually unrestricted. Hondurans don't have to contend with a landed oligarchy, nor with the turmoil of land reform (which was carried out years ago). Their labor unions are the strongest in the region.

Still, Honduras is the least developed country in Central America, and the third poorest in all of Latin America (although Nicaragua, under the Sandinistas, is rapidly closing that "gap").[213] According to journalist Roger Lowenstein, "Roughly half the population is illiterate, and there isn't a single well-paved road leading off the highway that connects the two major cities."[214] The agricultural economy, dominated by bananas and coffee, enjoyed strong economic growth in the late 1970s but has been hit hard in the eighties by rising oil prices, a declining demand for exports, and a scarcity of capital, the last stemming in large part from the security threat posed by Nicaragua. Unemployment has been as high as 45 percent. To make a bad situation worse, in 1983 70 percent of the banana crop was destroyed by hurricanes.

But, from 1984 through 1986, the country's economy showed plodding but steady growth. Growth (three percent in 1986) was not strong enough to maintain per capita income levels (still slightly below where they were in 1980), nor to create sufficient jobs to absorb the huge number of youths entering the job market each year. But growth was propelled largely by new flows of private investment, signalling investor confidence in the economy which, if continued, could bear important fruit.[215]

Honduras shares five hundred miles of border with Nicaragua to the south, with Guatemala and El Salvador to the west. This makes Honduras a major land route for the supply lines of Central American terrorism and gives the country a strategic importance.

This importance is appreciated by the Soviets, Cubans, and Nicaraguans, and, inevitably, by the United States. The Soviets and their Nicaraguan and Cuban allies turned their attention to Honduras just as soon as the Sandinistas were installed in Managua. This is affirmed by Miguel Bolanos, the Sandinista State Security officer who defected in 1983. He told *The Washington Post*:

When I was an assistant to Cuadra [Joaquin Cuadra, Vice Minister of Defense of the Nicaraguan Government and Chief of the General Staff of the Sandinista Army] in 1979, a month after the triumph, I was able to witness five or six Soviet generals that were his advisors. They looked at a map of Nicaragua and Honduras. The map outlined symbols of men and airplanes and where they were. Also outlined were the Sandinista forces and the number of people necessary to become a force. From that time on we began to study how to use confrontations with Honduras. We looked at the real possibilities. . . . The plan was to beat Honduras.[216]

Yet Honduras was not the first target on the list, and Castro realized the importance of Honduras as a conduit for arms from Nicaragua to El Salvador and Guatemala. So, in 1981 he offered Honduras a deal. In exchange for Honduran neutrality, Castro would spare Honduras from the terrorist violence he was orchestrating against the other two countries. The Hondurans were not to be taken in, and continued to do what they could to slow down the arms traffic. Trucks carrying arms and ammunition to guerrillas in El Salvador and Guatemala were intercepted by Honduran authorities in January and April of 1981.

The year the Sandinistas came to power, some Honduran terrorists formed the Morazanist Front for the Liberation of Honduras (FMLH) as part of the "increasing regionalization of the Central American conflict," according to one of its leaders.[217] The role of the Sandinistas in this regionalization included the creation of another Honduran terrorist organization, the Honduran Front for Popular Liberation (FHLP). The FHLP was formed in Nicaragua at the instigation of high-level Sandinistas; its headquarters was in Managua, and its members were trained in Nicaragua and Cuba. All this was revealed by documents captured at an FHLP safehouse in Tegucigalpa, the capital of Honduras. Also captured were classroom notes from a one-year training course held in Cuba in 1980. Captured FHLP members say they were funded by the Nicaraguan government.[218]

Sandinista complicity became public in March 1981, when members of a third Honduran terrorist group, the Cinchoneros, hijacked a Honduran airliner bound for the U.S. and diverted it to Managua. They threatened to blow up the plane and its passengers unless Honduras agreed to release ten Salvadoran FMLN terrorists who had been captured smuggling arms to El Salvador. The Sandinistas refused to allow Honduran government officials to use the airport's radio control tower to communicate with the hijackers, nor did they permit a commando raid on the plane. The Hondurans were ultimately forced to give in, and the imprisoned terrorists were flown to Cuba.

Further attempts to gain the release of captured guerrillas included the hijacking of another plane by the Popular Revolutionary Forces (FPR) in April 1982 and a September attack by the Cinchoneros on the Chamber of Commerce in San Pedro Sula (Honduras's second largest city), in which 110 hostages were taken. In both cases the terrorists had to settle for safe passage to Cuba, where they were quite welcome.

That same year, a number of terrorist attacks were carried out in Honduras by the Salvadoran ERP guerrillas. These included the sabotage of Tegucigalpa's main electrical power station and the bombing of the Honduran offices of IBM and Air Florida.

What is most striking about all this activity is its international origins. Directed by Castro, the saboteurs and murderers who make up this regional network of terror demonstrate their absolute cynicism when they trumpet the cause of "national liberation."

By 1983, Castro had decided it was time for the Honduran guerrilla factions to unite. So, in March, he brought them together under the National Unity Directorate of the Revolutionary Movement of Honduras. The FMLH, the Cinchoneros, and the Central American Workers Revolutionary Party (PRTC) issued a joint statement announcing their war against Honduras, and according to subsequent defectors, 250 Hondurans were recruited for guerrilla training in Nicaragua.[219]

The first major operation against Honduras occurred a few months later. Hondurans recruited in 1981 first trained in Cuba and then joined Sandinista army units in Nicaragua to gain battle experience against the Nicaraguan resistance. Armed and equipped in Nicaragua, ninety-six of these guerrillas entered Honduras in July 1983 to set up base camps intended to be reinforced and expanded later for operations in four provinces. Nicaragua promised to keep them supplied by air.[220]

They were doomed from the start, however, by defections that resulted in the timely notification of Honduran authorities. Many defectors reported that they had never intended to become guerrillas but had been duped, in 1981, into going to Nicaragua for what they were told would be agricultural and mechanical schooling. Once there, they were sent to Cuba for nine months of Marxist-Leninist indoctrination and training in guerrilla tactics. Those who failed to cooperate were punished. Some who attempted to desert after the group returned to Nicaragua were imprisoned by Sandinista security,[221] and some who were not captured by the Hondurans after they crossed the border were later found dead, apparently starved (so much for their popular support).

A similar attempt at infiltration was made one year later, though with a smaller force. Again, the guerrillas were trained in Nicaragua and Cuba. Again they were stopped by the Honduran army.[222]

In April 1985, seven Nicaraguans were arrested in Honduras trying to deliver arms to the Cinchoneros. This time the group included a member of Sandinista State Security.[223]

In response to all this, Honduras has allowed its territory to become the principal staging area for the Nicaraguan resistance forces, the *contras*—as Costa Rica had allowed its territory to be used, a decade before, by the Sandinistas in their war against Somoza. The Sandinistas have claimed that this makes them the victims of foreign aggression, but the Hondurans justify their position on defensive grounds. The Sandinistas, with the Soviets, were plotting the destruction of Honduras long before the *contras* existed. They were training Honduran guerrillas before the resistance was active or had the backing of any government. Nicaragua was openly collaborating with the Cinchoneros hijackers a full year before the resistance carried out any significant operations.

The Sandinistas were in power only three days, in fact, before they would stage their first raid on Honduran territory, the first of what have been described as "hundreds" of such

181

incursions.[224] In 1985, they shot down a Honduran helicopter inside Honduras, killing all eight men aboard.[225]

The Honduran armed forces are no match for the Nicaraguan army. With fewer than twenty thousand active-duty military and reserves, the Hondurans are outnumbered six to one. Against the Sandinistas' arsenal of the most advanced Soviet main battle tanks, HIND attack helicopters, and other sophisticated weaponry—not to speak of raw numbers—Honduras' military machine is primitive. The one exception is its air force, still one of the best in the region, stocked with Korean War vintage F-86E Sabres, and French Super Mysteres. But, to counter those sixteen Honduran fighters and fourteen tactical support aircraft, the Sandinistas have 130 anti-aircraft guns and 800 surface-to-air missiles.[226]

To deal with the threat of the Nicaraguan military build-up, Honduras has had to rely on the support of the United States. In 1983, the two countries began a series of joint military maneuvers that at various times have involved at least nineteen U.S. warships and about twenty-four thousand U.S. troops. The United States has improved Honduran airstrips and increased Honduran radar capability. About a thousand U.S. troops remain stationed in Honduras.

The early months of the Arias peace process created considerable confusion about the future of the U.S. military presence in Honduras. When 6,000 Sandinista troops staged two days of maneuvers close to the Honduran border, that confusion ended. Foreign Minister Carlos Lopez Contreras announced that his government will continue to allow U.S. troops to conduct training exercises in Honduras. U.S. troops would be asked to leave, he said, when the Sandinistas expel all Cuban and Soviet military advisers from Nicaragua. For the present, he said, U.S. forces were needed to "compensate for the military disequilibrium that has been produced in Central America in recent years"—a reference, of course, to the Soviet and Cuban build-up of Sandinista military power.[227]

While the Honduran government values U.S. cooperation in containing the Sandinistas, it is also apprehensive about the long-term reliability of U.S. support. As foreign affairs analyst Bruce McColm explained in 1983 to the National Committee to Restore Internal Security, "Psychologically, the Honduran military is very sensitive to the issue of being the lead man for the United States, only to discover that we led them out on a limb and cut them off . . . because they know that the Cubans wouldn't hesitate in getting involved in such a conflict, while the United States would."[228]

Recently, the Hondurans have tried to bargain for a stronger commitment from the United States, and with good reason. President Suazo Cordoba said shortly before he left office, "I think ideological subversion will be on the rise. We in Honduras know from where it will come."[229]

In a May 1986 visit to Washington, President Azcona said his country would accept U.S. aid to support the 15,000 to 20,000 *contras* and other Nicaraguan refugees on Honduran territory, but he added that Honduras would "not be used as a launching platform for attacks against any neighboring state." (That is, nonetheless, precisely what has been happening and continued to happen through the August 1987 peace talks.) U.S. military and economic aid to the country has also continued to flow: a total, 1980–1985, of some $100 million (one third the total given the country over the preceding 18 years).

If there was confusion about the U.S. military presence, there was even greater confusion as the peace process got underway about *contras* on Honduran soil. Nicaragua insisted they had to be expelled. Honduras countered that this should happen only when Nicaragua was in full compliance with terms of the August accord. Finally, the Hondurans said they would disarm any *contras* found on their territory, and reiterated an earlier offer of direct bilateral talks with the Sandinistas to demilitarize the Honduran-Nicaraguan border. They also offered Honduras as the site for any direct talks between the Sandinistas and the Reagan administration.[230]

* * *

In addition to the *contras* and their families, there are, of course, the thousands of other refugees who have fled oppression in Nicaragua. The United Nations High Commission for Refugees, in 1985, was providing assistance to 19,093 Nicaraguan refugees inside Honduras.[231]

Whatever the ultimate outcome of the August "peace process," Honduras is certain to be profoundly affected—more profoundly, perhaps, than any other country in the region.

COSTA RICA

Costa Rica is an anomaly in Central America. To start with, it is the region's oldest and institutionally strongest democracy. There have been only a few lapses in its democratic tradition since the country's first free elections in 1899. Costa Ricans, or "Ticos," as they like to call themselves, have enjoyed open, fair elections every four years since 1950. During that period, the presidency was retained by the party in power only twice. One of those occasions was February 1986, when Oscar Arias was elected to succeed President Luis Alberto Monge, both of the National Liberation Party, an affiliate of the Socialist International.

Unlike other countries in Central America, Costa Rica has a largely homogeneous population. Its citizens are overwhelmingly of European descent, predominantly Spanish. The indigenous Indians were so decimated by the Conquest that today there are 20 percent fewer Indians in Costa Rica than there were when the Spanish first settled in 1522.

Also setting Costa Rica apart is the fact that it has become Central America's version of the modern liberal welfare state. According to *The Wall Street Journal*, "Its array of health care, education, pension and other benefits has lifted Costa Rica above the misery common to Central America. Infant mortality, for instance, is 19 per 1,000 live births, compared to 87 per 1,000 in Honduras."[232]

The Costa Rican labor movement has strong ties to the AFL-CIO, though communists have managed to infiltrate and control some unions. While this has led to some violent strikes, Costa Rica was virtually free of violence or terrorism until 1981. The generally agreeable conditions in Costa Rica have made it attractive to Americans as a retirement home.

Finally, Costa Rica has no army. The military was abolished by the constitution of 1949. Since 1979, however, the military build-up in neighboring Nicaragua has given Costa Rica good reason to be concerned about its lack of defense forces. Domestic order is maintained by eight thousand Civil and Rural Guards, but they have no tanks, artillery, or other heavy weapons. In fact, until 1984, they were using World War II vintage rifles and had just one .50-caliber machine gun to repel air attacks.[233] For defense, therefore, Costa Rica relies on the Organization of American States, the Inter-American Reciprocal Assistance Treaty, and the United States, which has a considerable interest in the preservation of Costa Rican democracy.

With a welfare economy and a state monopoly on banking, Costa Rica has long been hooked on government spending. For years, this was supported by a growth economy based on coffee, banana, and sugar exports, and, beginning in the mid-1970s—ever heavier borrowing. By 1986, that debt had become so onerous—at $4.2 billion—that Costa Rica appealed to its commercial bank creditors for a 25-year rescheduling of $1.4 billion of it at below-market interest rates. The banks refused, and Costa Rica began token debt service payments.[234]

The severe economic crunch hit in the early 1980s. Coffee prices plunged as oil import costs more than doubled. Even heavier borrowing ensued, and, as interest rates rose, Costa Rica claimed the unenviable distinction of being one of the world leaders in foreign debt per capita. An additional factor that puts a strain on finances is the presence in Costa Rica of two hundred thousand refugees from Nicaragua, El Salvador, and Guatemala—a 7 percent increase in Costa Rica's population.[235]

The economic crisis was such that in 1982, real gross domestic product (GDP) actually fell by 8.8 percent. Yet in 1984, the GDP shot up again by 8 percent and living standards were on the rise. The reason? U.S. aid, says *The Wall Street Journal*'s Roger Lowenstein. U.S. economic assistance has increased dramatically since the Sandinistas moved in next door, with the result that by 1985 Costa Rica received more U.S. aid per capita than any nation except Israel. Lowenstein quotes Roberto de la Ossa, the Executive Director of the Central American Institute for International Affairs: "Our best industry is Sandinistas."[236]

That remark notwithstanding, Costa Rica's new president, Oscar Arias Sanchez, elected on February 2, 1986, actively pursued a policy of detente with the Sandinistas, culminating with his role as the principal architect and advocate of the Guatemala City peace accords. Arias, a Leftist who defeated the strongly anti-communist candidate Rafael Angel Calderon Fournier, was no sooner in office than he pledged that Costa Rican territory would not be used as a base for *contras*.

That stance contrasts sharply, of course, with Costa Rica's position in the mid-1970s when that country played a major role in putting the Sandinistas in power, an extension, in large measure, of a long-standing feud with the Somozas. (Costa Rica had actually aided an assassination attempt against the first Somoza in 1954.)[237] In 1978, when it appeared that Somoza might be in trouble, Costa Rica broke off relations with his government and expropriated Somoza's landholdings in the Costa Rican province of Guanacaste. Starting in early 1979, Costa Rica allowed the Sandinista guerrillas to use its territory for their base camps. Arms from Venezuela and Panama flowed openly through Costa Rica to the Sandinistas.

A few Costa Rican pilots and government officials also secretly collaborated with Castro to deliver Cuban arms (twenty-one plane-loads). The operations were "secret"— though by 1978, a widely-reported open secret—because of Costa Rican fastidiousness about being seen as an accomplice of a dictator. The Costa Rican legislature professed to be unaware of the Castro connection, but then-president Rodrigo Carazo not only knew, he was a prime mover in those operations.[238] The smuggling ring continued even after the Sandinista triumph, shipping arms to the Salvadoran guerrillas until the government put a stop to it in 1981. Many of the arms remain in terrorist hands in Costa Rica.

Sandinista gratitude was predictable. Terrorism erupted in Costa Rica in 1981. In March, a vehicle carrying three U.S. embassy guards and a Costa Rican driver was attacked. In June, three policemen and a taxi driver were killed. Both incidents were traced to an offshoot of the People's Revolutionary Movement, whose leader had close ties to Cuba and Nicaragua. In January 1982, two Salvadorans were apprehended in an attempt to kidnap a Salvadoran businessman in San Jose. One admitted he had been trained in Nicaragua. In July, three Nicaraguan embassy officials were expelled from Costa Rica for their involvement in the bombing of the San Jose office of the Honduran National airline. In November, members of a Costa Rican communist organization killed a Japanese businessman in a botched kidnaping. Also in 1982, Nicaragua provided safe haven for the Salvadoran terrorists who kidnaped a San Jose resident for ransom. The Sandinistas have even kidnaped a Nicaraguan from the Costa Rican embassy in Managua, where he had sought asylum.[239]

Meanwhile, the Soviets were busy promoting labor strife in Costa Rica. For such activities, the Monge administration asked Moscow to cut its embassy staff by almost 75 percent in

1982. As President Monge said the next year, "In forty years of Somocismo we never had the threat that we have in four years of Sandinismo."[240]

Sandinista hostilities against Costa Rica have not been limited to terrorism, but include frequent violations of Costa Rican territory by the Nicaraguan military. In June of 1984, the Sandinistas attacked the Costa Rican town of Jocote, forcing residents to flee. And in May of the following year, Nicaraguan soldiers ambushed a Costa Rican Civil Guard patrol inside Costa Rica, killing two guardsmen and injuring eleven.[241]

Such incidents have generated debates within the Costa Rican government over the question of defenses. Some have advocated upgrading the security forces and participating in U.S. training exercises. So far, however, force improvements have been very modest, and the government has maintained formal neutrality in the regional conflict by avoiding too close an association with the United States. President Arias has said, "We object to Soviet and Cuban aid to rebels in the region; however, we also object to military aid from the United States [N.B.: *military*] to countries in the area."[242]

Many argue that that's the kind of thing a Central American president has to say. Not all Costa Ricans agree. An editorial in *La Prensa Libre*, one of Costa Rica's leading newspapers, offered a reaction to the president's position: "We do not share his openly anti-U.S. attitude."[243]

Nor did all Costa Ricans buy their president's peace plan. An editorial in *La Nacion*, the country's largest daily, put it plainly:

> Everything points to the conclusion that the title on the peace plan was one more exercise of Sandinista cynicism.
> Hitler also signed a "peace" with Chamberlain in Munich, Stalin agreed to the democracy of Eastern Europe with Roosevelt, and the heirs of Ho Chi Minh [agreed to] the independence of South Vietnam with Nixon. Why would the promises of [Nicaraguan leaders] Ortega, Borge and company be

more credible than those of their colleagues of totalitarian dogma?[244]

NOTES

1. In an interview with Michael R. Caputo on Aug. 24, 1987, "*Contra Leader Discusses Arias Peace Plan*," in *Human Events*, Sept. 5, 1987, p. 3.

2. "Back where they were" is a highly-relative term, referring in this case only to per capita income. Source: "Summary of the Report of the National Bipartisan Commission on Central America," Appendix 1, in *Central America in Crisis, Washington Institute Task Force Report* (Washington: The Washington Institute for Values in Public Policy, revised 1984 edition), pp. 241-244. Interestingly, Robert A. Pastor—who as National Security Council specialist on Latin America during the Carter years had so much to do with crafting the policies so instrumental in producing the debacle—co-authored a paper at the same time proposing that the U.S. contribute $10 billion to a Central American Marshall Plan over a five-year period. In common with so many other "progressive" thinkers who walk blithely away from the wreckage produced by their nostrums, Pastor accepts no responsibility for the ruin the region would become, citing instead, global economic factors and internal rising expectations—none of which are, of course, unique to Central America. Yet the fact remains: Central America pre-Carter/Pastor was doing well, very well, vis-a-vis other developing countries; since then, very poorly. Richard E. Feinberg and Robert A. Pastor, "Far From Hopeless: An Economic Program for Post-War Central America," in Robert S. Leiken, ed., *Central America: Anatomy of Conflict* (New York: Pergamon Press, 1984), pp. 193–217, particularly pp. 198–202 (Causes of the Current Crisis) and p. 210.

3. A summary of that survey, conducted by the Costa Rica affiliate of Gallup International and conducted in Guatemala, El Salvador, Honduras, and Costa Rica (surveys are forbidden in Nicaragua), is in "Contras Score Military Gains Inside Nicaragua," Heritage Foundation Executive Memorandum #174, by Policy Analyst Jorge Salaverry, Aug. 31, 1987. Further details of that survey are in *National Review*, Aug. 14, 1987, p. 18; and in Morton Kondracke, "Who Wants Peace (And The Price To Be Paid)," in *The New Republic*, Sept. 28, 1987, p. 19. These 1987 results echo those of a 1985 Gallup poll in *The Challenge to Democracy in Central America*, U.S. Departments of State and Defense, June 1986, p. 58. Nicaragua was identified as a military threat by the majority of the citizens in Costa Rica, Honduras, El Salvador, and Guatemala.

4. Morris Rothenberg, "The Soviets and Central America," in Leiken, ed., *Central America: Anatomy of Conflict*, p. 133. Rothenberg cites Alvaro Ramirez, "Nicaragua: From armed struggle to construction," in *World Marxist Review*, No. 1, January 1980, p. 52.

5. David Brooks, "Latin America Is Not East of Here," *National Review*, March 14, 1986, p. 33.

6. John J. Tierney, Jr., *Somozas and Sandinistas: The U.S. and Nicaragua in the Twentieth Century* (Washington: Council for Inter-American Security, 1982), p. 52; and *Violence and Oppression in Nicaragua*, hearing before the Task Force on Central America of the Republican Study Committee, U.S. House of Representatives, June 1984 (Washington: American Conservative Union), p. 28.

7. Allan C. Brownfeld and J. Michael Waller, *The Revolution Lobby* (Washington: Council for Inter-American Security, 1985), p. 74.

8. Ibid., p. 75.

9. "Political Conflict and Violence," *Central America in Crisis: Washington Institute Task Force Report*, Marcelo Alonso, Task Force Chairman (Washington: The Washington Institute for Values in Public Policy, revised 1984 edition), p. 167 (hereafter *Central America in Crisis*).

10. See James R. Whelan and Patricia B. Bozell, *Catastrophe in the Caribbean: The Failure of America's Human Rights Policy in Central America* (Ottawa, IL: Jameson Books, 1984), p. 48, regarding Assistant Secretary of State William Bowdler and his deputy, John A. Bushnell; and Brownfeld and Waller, *The Revolution Lobby*, pp. 82–83, regarding Assistant Secretary of State for Human Rights Patricia Derian and her deputy Marc Schneider.

11. Brownfeld and Waller, *The Revolution Lobby*, p. 75 (State Department finding); and Shirley Christian, *Nicaragua: Revolution in the Family* (New York: Vintage Books, 1986), p. 59 (Solaun advice).

12. Christian, *Nicaragua* p. 85; and Brownfeld and Waller, *The Revolution Lobby*, p. 75.

13. Christian, *Nicaragua* pp. 88–91.

14. "Political Conflict and Violence," *Central America in Crisis*, p. 167.

15. Ibid., 119–120.

16. Anastasio Somoza, as told to Jack Cox, *Nicaragua Betrayed* (Boston: Western Islands Publishers, 1980), pp. 264–265. The book would be invaluable if only as an otherwise ignored chronicle of the systematic betrayal and crushing of a regime that had not only demonstrated its responsiveness to pressure for change, up to and including surrendering that power in honest elections; but which, by the standards of

human rights monitoring organizations such as New York's Freedom House was among the second tier of the world's developing nations in terms of political rights and civil liberties. The book has, however, yet another value: the verbatim transcript (pp. 333–381) of tape-recorded conversations between Somoza and U.S. Ambassador Lawrence Pezzullo during the days of final crisis, in late June and July of 1979. It is doubtful that any American diplomat in modern times has ever behaved more imperiously toward a sitting head of state—certainly not one of the Left. For some reason, however, that was not, characterized either as "arrogance of power" to borrow from the title of a book which became fashionable as a denunciation of U.S. antagonism toward left-wing regimes in the sixties); nor was it condemned as meddling or intervention in the affairs of another country.

17. Cited by Kondracke in *The New Republic*, op. cit., p. 18.

18. Ibid., pp. 382–383. At an earlier meeting, Pezzullo told Somoza the choice of top commanders was entirely up to him, "he can leave and make whatever decision he wants about the Army" (p. 373); On July 15, Pezzullo reneged on the earlier deal, saying Somoza had to choose from a Washington-drafted slate of six candidates (p. 383). Pezzullo also gave Somoza repeated assurances that the United States wanted the National Guard to survive, that it would survive; for example, on June 29: ". . . because this structure will hold the Guardia will survive, not in the same form, but it will survive" (p. 363); or this, on June 28: ". . . your Liberal Party will survive, your Guardia will survive—under a different name, probably, but the elements of that Guardia [will] stay there . . ." (p. 356.) Within a few weeks of their taking power, the Sandinistas had jailed some eight thousand Guardsmen, executed hundreds, and disbanded the organization. The State Department made no protest of any kind whatever.

19. Christian, *Nicaragua* pp. 128–132, 136.

20. Whelan and Bozell, *Catastrophe,* p. 50.

21. Somoza and Cox, *Nicaragua Betrayed,* p. 266.

22. Christian, *Nicaragua,* p. 132. Urcuyo said later that he did not believe a deal was ever made.

23. "Political Conflict and Violence," in *Central America in Crisis,* pp. 168–169. Somoza himself does not mention this in his own book.

24. Somoza and Cox, *Nicaragua Betrayed,* pp. 380. Somoza, a West Point graduate, responded to a 1961 U.S. SOS to allow his territory to be used for Bay of Pigs air raids against Castro's Cuba. In 1965, his country was one of two in Latin America to respond to the US appeal for support in averting a left-wing takeover of the Dominican Republic. He was so thoroughly Americanized, in fact, that he preferred speaking English to his native Spanish. As to the third broken prom-

ise: Somoza was ready to quit in late June, after the OAS resolution; Pezzullo repeatedly asked him to hang on until "arrangements" could be completed. (He would later rue that willingness to serve U.S. purposes; if he had left in late June, the Guard would have been intact, U.S. bargaining leverage would have been gone, and the outcome might have been different.) When those made-in-Washington arrangements were ready, Pezzullo assured Somoza that he would enjoy "all the protections of the law. Same as any other citizen. No difference" (p. 374). Somoza: "Mr. Warren Christopher, on direct orders from President Carter, advised me that I would not be welcome in the United States. This was less than six hours after I had arrived in Miami, Florida, on July 17, 1979. It was also less than twenty-four hours after I had, in accordance with an agreement reached with Ambassador Lawrence Pezzullo in Managua, resigned as President and Chief of the Army of Nicaragua. Ambassador Pezzullo had told me that I would be welcomed in the United States as a Chief of State and that he was speaking for President Carter." (p. 401). From Miami, Somoza and his family moved to the Bahamas; under U.S. pressure, they would later leave there for Paraguay.

25. Christian, *Nicaragua,* p. 137. Higher estimates are often seen, but Christian argues persuasively that they cannot be correct; the Sandinistas have inflated the count considerably.

26. Somoza, for example, quotes a United Press International dispatch dated June 22, 1979: "The U.S. aim in Nicaragua since last fall has been to oust Anastasio Somoza—and 'we did it,' says the U.S. Ambassador Lawrence Pezzullo; and another, an Agence France Presse dispatch dated Aug. 13: " 'The Jimmy Carter Administration actively participated in the overthrow of the Somoza government,' states former U.S. Secretary of State Henry Kissinger." Somoza and Cox, *Nicaragua Betrayed,* pp. 420–421.

27. *The Soviet-Cuban Connection in Central America and the Caribbean,* U.S. Departments of State and Defense, March 1985, p. 21.

28. For example, "The Freshening Winds of War," *Time,* August 11, 1986, p. 26. The figure represents about 75,000 active duty forces and 44,000 reserves and militia. More recent estimates of reservists put their number at 60,000 or more; see, for example, "Why We Must Act To Help Nicaragua," by Sen. Jesse Helms (R.-NC), in *Conservative Digest,* Sept. 1987, p. 93.

29. William Branigin, "Nicaragua Describes Major Arms Buildup," a Managua-datelined story in *The Washington Post,* Dec. 13, 1987, p. 1. Learning that Miranda, who had already provided the CIA with numerous briefings as well as documents he brought with him, was by then talking to reporters in Washington, Defense Minister Ortega

decided to upstage him, announcing the build-up plans in Managua. Predictably, his brother, President Daniel Ortega, the next day attempted to soft-pedal those statements, claiming that Humberto was talking only about army proposals which the government had not yet accepted.

30. *The Military Balance, 1986–87* (London: International Institute for Strategic Studies, 1986); and (for Somoza's tanks) John Keegan, *World Armies* (New York: Facts-on-File, 1979), p. 511, and Rep. Jack Davis (R-IL), "A New Freedom Fighter and Strategy," #117 in The Heritage Lectures, given April 30, 1987, at The Heritage Foundation, Washington, D.C. Figures for T-55 and PT-76 tanks and armored vehicles from the testimony of Lt. Col. Oliver L. North before the Select Committee of the House and Senate, July 14, 1987, as recorded in *Taking the Stand: The Testimony of Lieutenant Colonel Oliver L. North* (New York: Pocket Books, 1987), p. 677 (referred to hereafter as *Taking the Stand*).

31. Both the "by the dozens" quote and the descriptions are in *Taking the Stand*, pp. 277 and 678.

32. Joseph G. Whelan and Michael J. Dixon, *The Soviet Union in the Third World: A Threat to World Peace?* (Washington: Pergamon-Brassey, 1986), pp. 314–15. (Joseph G. Whelan is not related to James R. Whelan, author of this book.) Miranda told reporters in Washington that the Soviets had promised a squadron of the planes, more important by far to the Sandinistas for their symbolic value than as a needed element in their already-awesome arsenal. Judith Havemann, "U.S. Calls Managua Buildup 'Direct Threat' to Neighbors," *The Washington Post*, Dec. 14, 1987, p. A-32.

33. *The Soviet-Cuban Connection*, p. 25 (1980 deliveries). *The Challenge to Democracy in Central America*, U.S. Departments of State and Defense, June 1986, p. 20 ("forty thousand"). Ambassador Carlos Tunnermann wrote in *The Washington Post*, March 30, 1986, that prior to November 1981 "there were only a few hundred ex-GN soldiers staging sporadic raids on farms along the border. Their principal occupations were cattle-rustling and extortion."

34. "Habra Muchas Nicaraguas en el Mundo, Empezando por America," *Diario las Americas* (Miami), Novemeber 8, 1980, in Whelan and Bozell, *Catastrophe*, p. 55.

35. The two billion figure is from *West Watch*, July 1987, p. 5: "Soviet Military Aid to Nicaragua Hits $2 billion." The publication gives as its source the U.S. Department of Defense. The first four months comparison is from Rep. Jack Davis, "A New Freedom Fighter Aid Strategy," op. cit. The comparison with U.S. military aid to all other Central American countries is from *The Economist*, Aug. 15, 1987, p. 33. Sen. Helms writes that in 1986 alone, Soviet military shipments to

Nicaragua were valued at $600 million, and that since 1981, they have received 79,000 tons of Soviet military equipment (Senator Jesse Helms, "Why We Must Act To Help Nicaragua," *Conservative Digest*, September 1987, p. 93).

36. Brownfeld and Waller, *The Revolution Lobby*, pp. 79, 81.

37. Edward N. Luttwak, "A Member of Moscow's Exclusive Club," op-ed column in *The Washington Post*, Nov. 22, 1987, p. C-7. Luttwak added: "While Americans continue to argue over the sincerity of the Sandinista acceptance of the Arias peace plan, it seems that in Moscow the question is regarded as settled. Leninist governments can make all sorts of tactical accommodations, but they must retain an unchallenged monopoly of power. If there were any suspicion that the Sandinistas might actually allow the democratization required by the Arias peace plan, creating the possibility of a peaceful change of governments by free elections, Ortega would not have been seated where he was." Luttwak holds the Arleigh A. Burke Chair in Strategy at the Center for Strategic and International Studies, Georgetown University, Washington.

38. *Violence and Oppression in Nicaragua*, p. 43.

39. Among those, Brooks, "Latin America Is Not East of Here," p. 33.

40. Whelan and Bozell, *Catastrophe*, p. 53 (international brigade); and *Turmoil in Central America*, A Special Report by the United States Senate Republican Policy Committee (Golden, CO: Independence Institute, March 1986), p. 27 (Cuban advisers) Sen. Helms puts the number of Cubans in Nicaragua at 65,000 (op. cit., p. 93).

41. *"Revolution Beyond Our Borders": Sandinista Intervention in Central America*, U.S. Department of State, September 1985, p. 4 (Bolanos); and Glenn Garvin, "In Nicaragua, Cubans Turn Up Everywhere," *The Washington Times*, July 17, 1986, p. 8A.

42. *Turmoil in Central America*, op. cit., p. 53.

43. Brownfeld and Waller, *The Revolution Lobby*, p. 81.

44. Whelan and Bozell, *Catastrophe*, p. 54.

45. Joe Pichirallo and Terri Shaw, "Top Defector Disillusioned By Marxism," *The Washington Post*, Dec. 13, 1987, p. 1.

46. Christian, *Nicaragua* pp. 172, 222.

47. *Background Paper: Nicaragua's Military Build-Up and Support for Central American Subversion*, U.S. Departments of State and Defense, July 1984, pp. 5–6.

48. W. Bruce Weinrod, "Thirty Myths About Nicaragua," *The Heritage Lectures*, No. 54 (Washington: The Heritage Foundation), 1986, p. 24.

49. Christian, *Nicaragua* p. 164.

50. Whelan and Bozell, *Catastrophe* p. 62.

51. Jose Francisco Cardenal, briefly vice-president of the Council, as quoted in Whelan and Bozell, *Catastrophe* p. 63 ("break heads"); and Christian, *Nicaragua* p. 182 (Pezzullo).

52. Whelan and Bozell, *Catastrophe*, pp. 63–64.

53. Arce speech published as *Commandante Bayardo Arce's Secret Speech before the Nicaraguan Socialist Party (PSN)*, U.S. Department of State, March 1985, pp. 4, 5, 7.

54. Humberto Belli, *Breaking Faith* (Westchester, IL: Crossway Books, 1985), p. 102.

55. *Violence and Oppression in Nicaragua*, p. 46.

56. Helms, op. cit., p. 95.

57. *West Watch* (Washington: Council for Inter-American Security), April 1986, p. 6.

58. Congressional testimony of Dr. Jack Wheeler of the Freedom Research Foundation (Malibu, California), in *Violence and Oppression in Nicaragua*, p. 20.

59. *Turmoil in Central America*, p. 54.

60. *Inside the Sandinista Regime: A Special Investigator's Perspective*, U.S. Department of State, February 1986, p. 18.

61. Robert S. Leiken, "Nicaragua's Untold Stories," in *The New Republic*, Oct. 8, 1987, as reprinted in a special June 15, 1987, edition of *The Congressional Record*, pp. HR 4811–4812.

62. "Should the Sandinistas Be Trusted? And does it matter," in *Newsweek*, Aug. 31, 1978, p. 28. The two officials—Lino Hernandez, president of the only independent human rights commission, and bar association president Alberto Saborio—were released a month later as a sop to the "peace process." There is an official "human rights commission," headed by an American nun, Sister Mary Hartman. Kondracke quotes her as justifying mob violence against dissenters by saying it is directed "only at people who support the United States" (op. cit., p. 18).

63. Letter from the Sandinista leadership to the Organization of American States, quoted in Christian, *Nicaragua*, p. 128.

64. Ibid., p. 348; *Selected Articles Censored from La Prensa*, U.S. Department of State, June 1986, p. 2: and *Turmoil in Central America*, p. 43.

65. Julia Preston, "Opposition Group Leaves Meeting With Sandinistas," Managua-datelined story in *The Washington Post*, Oct. 9, 1987.

"Reagan Says Arias Plan Insufficient; President Tells OAS Soviet, Cuban Forces Must Leave Nicaragua," *The Washington Post*, Oct. 8, 1987, p. 1-A.

66. Arce speech, loc. cit., p. 4.

67. Christian, *Nicaragua*, pp. 197–98.

68. Helms, op. cit., p. 95.

69. Arturo J. Cruz, "Nicaragua's Imperiled Revolution," *Foreign Affairs*, Summer 1983, as reproduced in special edition of *Congressional Record*, op. cit., p. H-4616. Cruz was the Sandinistas' first Central Bank president, then agreed to serve on the bogus Junta for a year before becoming Nicaragua's ambassador to the United States, resigning in disillusionment in 1981. Cruz was the leading opposition candidate for president in the 1984 elections. He is well-connected within the Socialist International network in Europe and Latin America and has strong ties to self-styled "progressive" groups and individuals in the U.S.

70. *Selected Articles Censored from La Prensa*, p. 1.

71. Glenn Garvin, "Nicaragua Throws a Party, but Not Everybody's Going," *The Washington Times*, July 14, 1986, p. 10A.

72. Michael J. Berlin, "Ortega Attacks Reagan, but Urges Talks; Nicaraguan Suggests Opposition Paper Could Be Closed Again," *The Washington Post*, Oct. 9, 1987, p. 1-A. Later, when the original deadline for implementation of the peace plan came and went, Ortega reaffirmed that *La Prensa* would be "free" only within Sandinista-defined limits. During a television discussion with several Nicaraguan journalists, including *La Prensa* news editor Cristiana Chamorro, Ortega suddenly confronted her with a question: does the newspaper support the Reagan administration's plans to ask for $270 million in new funding for the *contras*? When Ms. Chamorro surprised him by saying the paper did not, Ortega said: "If that is *La Prensa*'s position, then you will not be affected by any restrictive measures we might take if the U.S. Congress approves the $270 million . . ." (Apparently, neither Ortega nor anyone else on the program bothered to mention that the Reagan administration had said it would seek the new funding only if the Sandinistas failed to comply with the peace plan.) In the doublespeak of so much of major media reporting, Ortega's "concession" was termed "assurances." Julia Preston, "La Prensa Receives Assurances," Managua-datelined dispatch in *The Washington Post*, Nov. 19, 1987, p. A-44.

73. Julia Preston, "La Prensa Goes to Print," *The Washington Post*, Managua-datelined dispatch Oct. 2, 1987, pp. A-15 and A-19. Curiously, there was no mention of the plight of the other media in Nicaragua in a largely gushing letter written to the influential journal

of the American newspaper industry by the chairman of the Freedom of the Press Committee of the Inter-American Press Association: "La Prensa reopens, but doubts remain," letter from Wilbur G. Landrey, given news story display in *Editor & Publisher*, Oct. 17, 1987, pp. 5, 41. Nor, for that matter, was there in Ms. Preston's story, nor in any of the other major media stories reporting on "progress" under the peace plan reviewed by the authors in the two months following the signing.

74. Kondracke, op. cit., p. 19.

75. Whelan and Bozell, *Catastrophe*, p. 60.

76. Leiken, "Nicaragua's Untitled Stories," *The New Republic*.

77. Senator Helms, p. 95 (for mass arrests); *Selected Articles Censored from La Prensa*, p. 34 (families held hostage).

78. Nina H. Shea, "Human Rights in Nicaragua," *The New Republic*, Sept. 1, 1986, p. 21; and *Turmoil in Central America*, p. 46.

79. "Sandinistas Called Guilty of Rampant Rights Violations," *The Washington Times*, July 15, 1986 (ILHR estimate); public statement by investigator Wesley Smith, March 13, 1986 (11,000–13,000); *Violence and Oppression in Nicaragua*, p. 53 (Farach estimate).

80. Shea, "Human Rights in Nicaragua," *New Republic*, p. 21. The 5,000–7,000 figures from Representative Davis, p. 3, as well as the four new prisons quote. 1986 figures from Helms, p. 95.

81. Shea, "Human Rights," p. 22.

82. Congressional testimony of Dr. Othniel Seiden, in *Violence and Oppression in Nicaragua*, pp. 59, 68.

83. Julia Preston, "Nicaraguans Debate Prisoner Release: Sandinistas Describe Some Inmates As 'Genocidal Murderers,' " *The Washington Post*, Oct. 4, 1987, p. A-32. 'Genocidal Murderers' is a term the Sandinistas invented to justify the jailing of all National Guardsmen they were able to capture—a novel depiction of soldiers who fought in defense of a legal government. Over the years, the Sandinistas released an estimated 5,000 Guardsmen, but as of October 1987, it was estimated they were still holding around 2,200. Ms. Preston cites in her dispatch, as an example of how recklessly sentence was pronounced, the case of Roger Antonio Corea. Corea, sentenced in 1980 to 11 years' imprisonment, was a 19-year-old hospital security guard, who deserted from the Guard in 1977, was recaptured and served time in a stockade during the revolution for trying to desert again. It is a measure of the hypocrisy of international "human rights" organizations that no cry has ever been raised on behalf not only of cases such as this, but against the larger abuse of the arbitrary imprisonment of all soldiers as "war criminals."

84. Julia Preston, "Nicaragua Frees 985 Prisoners," Tipitapa, Nicaragua-datelined story in *The Washington Post*, Nov. 23, 1987.

85. Special edition of *The Congressional Record*, op. cit., p. H-4845, covering Senate debate Oct. 11, 1984.

86. *Turmoil in Central America*, p. 15. On December 21, 1979, five months after the fall of Somoza, President Carter's State Department estimated that the Sandinistas had already executed four hundred people. (Brownfeld and Waller, p. 79.)

87. *Inside the Sandinista Regime: A Special Investigator's Perspective*, p. 4.

88. Peter Samuel, "Defector Describes 'Bloody,' 'Corrupt' Regime," *Human Events*, October 12, 1985, p. 12.

89. *Violence and Oppression in Nicaragua*, p. 75.

90. *Dispossessed: The Miskito Indians in Sandinista Nicaragua*, U.S. Department of State, June 1986, p. 3.

91. Ibid.

92. Ibid., pp. 1, 3; and *Time*, March 1, 1982, p. 22, in *Violence and Oppression in Nicaragua*, p. 19.

93. *Dispossessed*, p. 4; and interview with Alvaro Baldizon by journalist Peter Crane, September 30, 1985, p. 3.

94. *Dispossessed*, pp. 5, 6, 8.

95. Written statement of Steadman Fagoth, Washington press conference, February 23, 1982, in Whelan and Bozell, *Catastrophe*, p. 57.

96. M. Stanton Evans, "Who Are the Contras?" *Human Events*, June 28, 1985, p. 7.

97. *Turmoil in Central America*, pp. 56, 58; Whelan and Bozell, *Catastrophe*, p. 65; and Glenn Garvin, "Sandinistas Boost Crowds for Rallies with Job Threats," *The Washington Times*, July 15, 1986, p. 8A.

98. Shea, "Human Rights," p. 22.

99. Source for 1977, *Estudio Economico de America Latina, 1977*, Comision Economica para America Latina, United Nations (Santiago, Chile, 1978), p. 15; source for 1985, *Economic and Social Progress in Latin America, 1986 Report* (Washington: Inter-American Development Bank, 1987), p. 323 (referred to hereafter as *Economic and Social Progress-1986*); source for 1986, *Progreso Economico y Social en America Latina: Informe 1987* (Washington: Inter-American Development Bank, 1987), pp. 368–369 (referred to hereafter as *Progreso Economico y Social 1987*).

100. William Branigin, "Inflation Leaps, Output Falls in Nicaragua; Eco-

nomic Crisis Said to Be Factor in Flexibility on Peace Pact," Managua-datelined story in *The Washington Post*, Aug. 18, 1987, p. A-1. Inevitably, the *Post* would offer this explanation: "The economic effects of the U.S.-financed rebellion against the Sandinista government have combined with poor management, runaway inflation, declining exports and a number of other factors to bring the Nicaraguan economy to the brink of ruin, Nicaraguan and foreign analysts say." Of course, war takes a toll, but the insinuation here is that one ought never take up arms against tyranny because it might do damage to tyranny's economy. (And note: it is the U.S.-financed rebellion, but not the Soviet-financed tyranny.) But with that glib half-truth, Branigin: (a) omits the offset of huge Soviet bloc credits, including their provisioning of virtually the entire war effort; (b) fails to take note that the rot and ruin of the Nicaraguan economy set in within the first months of Sandinista "governance."

101. An Exxon spokesman was quoted as saying that the 24-year-old refinery would keep running "as long as it is economically feasible and as long as the U.S. government and the Nicaraguan government want us to stay." Other U.S. companies still in the country: IBM, Xerox Corp., American Standard Inc., Chevron Corp., H.B. Fuller Co., General Mills Inc., Hercules Inc., Intercontinental Hotels Corp., Kem Manufacturing Co., Inc., Nabisco Brands Inc., Texaco Inc., and United Brands Co. From Sally Jacobsen, *The Associated Press*, "U.S. Firms Hang On in Nicaragua; Number Dwindles From 168 Before Revolution to Two Dozen," a Managua-datelined story in *The Washington Post*, Oct. 11, 1987, p. K-2.

102. *"Revolution Beyond Our Borders,"* p. 44.

103. Brownfeld, "How Nicaragua Fell to Communism," *Human Events*, May 31, 1986, p. 13; source for 1984 and 1985 figures, *Progreso Economico y Social 1987*, p. 368.

104. Glenn Garvin, "Marxist Economy Leaves Plenty of Nothing in Nicaragua," *The Washington Times*, July 16, 1986, p. 8A (beef); and Branigin, op. cit., p. A-11 (rustling).

105. Kondracke, op. cit, p. 18 (inflation). The 1986 IADB report, op. cit., put inflation for 1985 at 219 percent. Branigin (op. cit., p. A-1) also reports that inflation is running at an estimated 700 to 1,000 percent in 1987. There is nothing to resemble this in all of Latin America—except for Argentina, which—ever since the advent of another "Populist" dictator, Juan Domingo Peron—has managed the unenviable feat of turning that silk purse of an economy into a sow's ear.

106. Garvin, "Nicaragua Throws a Party," p. 10A; Brownfeld, "How

Nicaragua Fell," p. 13; and Garvin, "Marxist Economy Leaves Plenty of Nothing," p. 8A.

107. Branigin, op. cit., p. A-11. He quotes the U.S. Embassy as estimating the size of the foreign debt. He also notes that since the revolution, the Sandinistas have received a total of $9.8 billion in credits—which works out to roughly $3,300 for every man, woman and child in the country, or the equivalent of roughly four full years' income at the present per capita levels.

108. David Reed, "High Stakes in Nicaragua," *Reader's Digest*, Sept. 1987, p. 75. As the preceding paragraphs demonstrate, the money is even more worthless in August 1987 than when Reed was there, a few months earlier. The exchange rate was 100 cordobas to one dollar in the war year of 1979; but, for most of the Somoza years prior to that, the cordoba was at par with the dollar. As to money supply: it zoomed from an annual growth rate of just over 20 percent in 1980 to 180 percent in 1985. Source, *Economic and Social Progress 1986*, p. 320. Indeed, if one looks at the eight graphs of key economic indicators on those two facing pages (320–321), the only rising lines are the wrong ones (inflation, external debt, etc.), and those showing declines also are the wrong ones (balance of payments, gross domestic product, etc.).

109. *Voice of Nicaragua*, No. 6 (July 1986), pp. 3, 5, 6.

110. *Selected Articles Censored from La Prensa*, p. 26.

111. The first citation is quoted in Weinrod, pp. 25–26. The second (and longer) quotation, and "he wrote" passages are from Leiken, "Nicaragua's Untold Stories," as reproduced in special *Congressional Record*, op. cit., p. H-4810.

112. Kondracke, op. cit., p. 18. He might have added that El Salvador has also been hit by civil war very nearly as bloody but even more protracted than that suffered by Nicaragua.

113. "Price of Gasoline Doubled As Managua Faces Supply Cut," *The Washington Post*, Aug. 31, 1987, p. A-23. Branigin, op. cit., p. A-11, reported that the Sandinistas would need about 750,000 metric tons of oil and oil products for 1987, but Moscow said it would ship only 630,000 metric tons. Of that, only 305,000 metric tons would come from the Soviet Union itself, the rest requisitioned from reportedly-grumbling East Bloc countries. Venezuela and Mexico, which had flamboyantly announced an opulent program of subsidized oil to the Sandinistas when they came to power, both quietly ended their shipments when the Sandinistas failed to pay even the cut-rate costs (and, of course, when economic crunches hit both of those oil-glutted

countries). Data on bid to Mexico from Branigin, "Ortega: Costa Rica Harbors *Contras*," Mexico City dispatch in *The Washington Post*, Nov. 17, 1987, p. A 22. Later data on Soviet oil and debt demands from Julia Preston, "Ortega Goes to Moscow Amid Economic Crisis," Managua dispatch in *The Washington Post*, Nov. 1, 1987, p. A 37.

114. V.I. Lenin, *Religion*, Little Lenin Library (New York), Vol. 7, p. 14, in Raymond S. Sleeper, ed., *A Lexicon of Marxist-Leninist Semantics* (Alexandria, Virginia: Western Goals, 1983), p. 233.

115. *Attack on the Church: Persecution of the Catholic Church in Nicaragua*, U.S. Department of State, July 1986, p. 9.

116. *In Their Own Words: Testimony of Nicaraguan Exiles*, U.S. Department of State, March 1986, p. 11 (synagogue); and Brownfeld, "How Nicaragua Fell," p. 14 (phone calls).

117. *Voice of Nicaragua*, No. 5 (May 1986), p. 2. Sermon censorship cited by Sen. David Boren (D-Okla.) on the floor of the Senate, Oct. 11, 1984 (cf., special *Congressional Record*, op. cit., p. H-4848).

118. Brownfeld, "How Nicaragua Fell," p. 13.

119. Christian, *Nicaragua*, p. 263.

120. Arturo J. Cruz, op. cit., p. H-4618.

121. Christian, *Nicaragua*, p. 249.

122. Letter from the Nicaraguan bishops to President Daniel Ortega, December 6, 1985; quoted in a communique from Cardinal Obando y Bravo to Secretary-General of the United Nations, Javier Perez de Cuellar, reprinted in *Policy Forum*, Vol. III, No. 3 (March 1986), newsletter of the National Forum Foundation, Washington, D.C.

123. *Violence and Oppression in Nicaragua*, p. 42.

124. *Inside the Sandinista Regime: A Special Investigator's Perspective*, p. 19.

125. Congressional testimony by Bolanos, *Violence and Oppression in Nicaragua*, p. 36.

126. *Attack on the Church*, pp. 12–13.

127. Cruz, op., cit., p. H-4618.

128. "Abrams Rips Potential Filibuster," *Human Events*, July 26, 1986, p. 3.

129. Letter from the Nicaraguan bishops to President Ortega, loc. cit.

130. Quotation from "Ortega Seeks to Mend Relations With Church," *The Washington Post*, August 9, 1986, p. A 18. On September 27, 1986, Cardinal Obando agreed to resume talks with the government. One high-ranking church official, however, confessed privately that the church entertained little hope for a major breakthrough; he noted a

history of negotiations designed by the Sandinistas to placate public opinion (Edward Cody, "Ortega Meets With Prelate," *Washington Post*, September 28, 1986, pp. A 27–28).

131. Leiken, "Nicaragua's Untold Stories," op. cit., p. H-4810.

132. Pitchirallo and Shaw, op. cit., p. A-49. When *The Washington Post* tracked down two of the three Panamaniam companies Miranda mentioned, Sandinista President Daniel Ortega said the actual purpose of those companies was to enable his people to evade the U.S. boycott and buy automobiles and needed spare parts.

133. Cruz, op. cit., p. H-4619.

134. Whelan and Bozell, *Catastrophe*, p. 70.

135. *Executive Risk Assessment, Terrorist Incident Chronology*, January 1980 (Alexandria, VA: Risks International), in Whelan and Bozell, *Catastrophe*, pp. 71–72.

136. Whelan and Bozell, *Catastrophe*, pp. 71–72.

137. "El Salvador: Revolution or Reform?" Current Policy No. 546, U.S. Department of State, February 1984, p. 2.

138. Virginia Prewett, *Washington's Instant Socialism in El Salvador* (Washington: Council for Inter-American Security, 1981), p. 30.

139. Ibid., pp. 29–30.

140. Whelan and Bozell, *Catastrophe*, p. 74.

141. Frank J. Devine, *El Salvador: Embassy Under Attack* (New York Vantage Press, 1981), pp. 45, 115.

142. Ibid., p. 46. Devine reports being told by one high-ranking officer that "in his entire career he had never been the object of so much vilification, viciousness, and underhanded attacks as he had suffered in his present position" (p. 46).

143. Ibid., p. 44.

144. Ibid., p. 114.

145. Whelan and Bozell, *Catastrophe*, pp. 74–75, 77.

146. "El Salvador: Revolution or Reform?" p. 2.

147. *Executive Risk Assessment, Terrorist Incident Chronology*, February 1980, p. 4, in Whelan and Bozell, *Catastrophe*, p. 73.

148. Whelan and Bozell, *Catastrophe*, p. 75. White supported the Left so passionately that later, representing a private Leftist think tank, he gave misleading congressional testimony accusing one of the major political parties in El Salvador of operating death squads directed by

Salvadoran exiles in Miami. It was later revealed that his source had received $50,000 from the think tank for providing the "information."

149. Prewett, *Washington's Instant Socialism,* p. 30.

150. Whelan and Bozell, *Catastrophe,* p. 74.

151. The problem of a lack of qualified managers has been acknowledged by the State Department in a backhanded sort of way. "El Salvador's Land Reform," a State Department *Gist* report dated April 1983 states, "A major problem with Phase I is the unwieldy nature of the large cooperative farms. El Salvador's big cooperatives barely cover their production costs, and they owe more than $300 million in land mortgage payments.... An effort to improve the management of Phase I cooperatives is underway with AID support. Farm managers and accountants are being trained."

152. The problems posed by the lack of private ownership have been so frustrating to some peasants that several coops have petitioned the government, unsuccessfully, to return the land to its former owners (Claudia Rosett, "Economic Paralysis in El Salvador," *Policy Review,* Fall 1984, p. 45).

153. Prewett, *Washington's Instant Socialism,* pp. 1–2.

154. *The Challenge to Democracy,* p. 47; "El Salvador: Revolution or Reform?" p. 6; and "El Salvador's Land Reform," U.S. State Department *Gist* report, April 1983, p. 2.

155. Michael Getler, "New Diplomacy Tested by U.S. in El Salvador," *The Washington Post,* April 17, 1980, in Prewett, op. cit., p. 5.

156. Alan Riding, "U.S. Loses Ground in Central America and Backs Changes in Bid to Recoup," *The New York Times,* July 9, 1980, in Prewett, op. cit., p. 4.

157. Prewett, op. cit., p. 9.

158. *Economic and Social Progress in Latin America, 1986 Report* (Washington: Inter-American Development Bank, 1986), p. 269. The same report notes that despite the dramatic drop in production, higher prices and sale of stocks kept the value of coffee earnings about at 1984 levels; sale of unsold stocks also pushed cotton exports 322 percent higher than 1984.

159. Data on 1987 aid exceeding local budgetary funding from a report "Bankrolling Failure: United States Policy in El Salvador and the Urgent Need for Reform," by Sen. Mark Hatfield (R-Ore) and Reps. Jim Leach (R-Iowa) and George Miller (D-Calif.), cited by Stephen S. Rosenfeld, "An Even Tougher Case: El Salvador," *The Washington Post,*

Nov. 20, 1987, p. A-19. Predictably, given the liberal bent of the study's authors (and Rosenfeld), they draw precisely the wrong conclusions: that what is needed is *more* of the reform medicine that has already left a once-prospering, pre-"reform" economy in an utter shambles. Balance of the data from: *Progreso Economico y Social en America Latina: Informe 1987* (Washington: Inter-American Development Bank), pp. 450, 452, 305. (The Spanish edition of the report was released first, hence the use here of that 1987 version.) The $2.3 billion figure is for the period 1979 through 1986, and is taken from *Encyclopaedia Britannica: 1987 Book of the Year* (London: Encyclopaedia Britannica, Inc., 1987), p. 547 (hereafter *Britannica 1987 Year Book*).

160. *Background Notes: El Salvador*, U.S. Department of State, February 1985, p. 6.

161. *The Challenge to Democracy*, p. 47.

162. Roger Reed, *El Salvador and the Crisis in Central America* (Washington: Council for Inter-American Security, 1984), p. 13.

163. *Background Paper: Nicaragua's Military Build-Up*, p. 15; and *"Revolution Beyond Our Borders,"* p. 9.

164. *Background Paper: Central America*, U.S. Departments of State and Defense, May 1983, p. 6, in Whelan and Bozell, *Catastrophe*, pp. 80–81.

165. This was confirmed by former guerrilla commander, Alejandro Montenegro. See *Background Paper: Nicaragua's Military Build-Up*, pp. 18–19. Most of the M-16s subsequently taken from the Salvadoran guerrillas could be traced by their serial numbers to Vietnam (*"Revolution Beyond Our Borders,"* p. 46).

166. *"Revolution Beyond Our Borders,"* p. 7.

167. Former guerrilla leader Alejandro Montenegro has reported that units under his command in 1981–82 received nearly all of their arms from Nicaragua in monthly shipments (*Background Paper: Nicaragua's Military Build-Up*, pp. 18–19). For more information, see *"Revolution Beyond Our Borders"* and *The Challenge to Democracy*.

168. *"Revolution Beyond Our Borders,"* p. 7.

169. *The Challenge to Democracy*, p. 13.

170. Napoleon Romero, quoted in *The Challenge to Democracy*, p. 51.

171. Julian Ignacio Otero, a prisoner-defector and former chief of logistics and Finance for the FPL, one of the five groups that constitute the FMLN, quoted in Prewett, *Washington's Instant Socialism*, p. 21.

172. Whelan and Bozell, *Catastrophe*, p. 81.

173. *The Challenge to Democracy*, p. 49.

174. An FMLN radio station boasted that Reagan would come into office too late to prevent a guerrilla victory (*"Revolution Beyond Our Borders,"* p. 21).

175. Whelan and Bozell, *Catastrophe,* pp. 81–82. The State Department report "El Salvador: Revolution or Reform?" dated February 1984, notes that "an estimated 9,000–11,000 guerrillas are now actively engaged in the field against the Salvadoran Armed Forces. Over recent months, through continued training and access to arms, the Salvadoran guerrillas have managed to provide formerly noncombatant personnel with equipment for combat. While this has increased the number of people with arms, it is not a reflection of increased popular support, and the overall number of people involved in the guerrilla movement itself has not really grown" (p. 6).

176. Morris Rothenberg quotes Kremlin press spokesman Leonid Zamiatin as responding during the 26th Soviet Party Congress in 1981 to State Department charges: "The Soviet Union does not provide El Salvador with arms. It never has. It never will." Rothenberg also is the source for the waxing-waning observation. He quotes N.S. Leonov, "Salvadoran Drama," in *Latinskaia Amerika,* Aug. 1981, p. 14, on the premature quality of the "final offensive." Rothenberg, pp. 137–138.

177. *"Revolution Beyond Our Borders,"* p. 10; and (for the $1 billion estimate) *Background Notes: El Salvador,* p. 5.

178. Alexander M. Haig Jr., *Caveat* (New York: Macmillan, 1984), p. 117.

179. Quoted in Reed, *El Salvador,* p. 30.

180. Ibid., p. 31.

181. *FBIS: Latin America,* March 16, 1983, p. P4, in Reed, *El Salvador,* p. 39.

182. *Background Notes: El Salvador,* p. 5.

183. Special *Congressional Record, op. cit., p. H-4606.*

184. Devine, *Embassy Under Attack,* pp. 128–29.

185. Whelan and Bozell, *Catastrophe,* pp. 83 (poll), and 88 (Arturo Rivera y Damas).

186. *"Revolution Beyond Our Borders,"* pp. 10–11.

187. Thomas A. Sancton, "Voting for Peace and Democracy," *Time,* April 12, 1982, p. 38; and Steven Strasser, "Salvador Tries the Ballot," *Newsweek,* February 22, 1982, p. 35; both in Reed, op. cit., p. 32.

188. Whelan and Bozell, *Catastrophe,* p. 84.

189. Sancton, in Reed, *El Salvador,* pp. 32–33.

190. Quoted in *The Challenge to Democracy,* p. 50.

191. "Sustaining a Consistent Policy in Central America: One Year After the National Bipartisan Commission Report," U.S. Department of State, April 1985, p. 7.

192. A State Department estimate of April 1986 puts FMLN strength at five to seven thousand (*The Situation in El Salvador*, U.S. Department of State, April 1, 1986, p. 5).

193. John M. Goshko, "U.S. Cites Progress in Salvadoran Rights," *The Washington Post*, Dec. 25, 1984, p. A-28. The story reported on the State Department's quarterly report to Congress justifying continued U.S. aid to El Salvador.

194. *The Washington Post*, Nov. 7, 1987, p. A-16. The story reported that less than twenty-four hours after the unilateral cease-fire was ordered, the guerrillas announced that "the order for combat is given," killed four soldiers in one ambush and blew up at least ten primary power transmission lines and four secondary lines in Chalatenango Province. When the rebels continued to fight, the Salvadoran armed forces finally were allowed to resume operations on Nov. 20. Charges against D'Aubuisson from Branigin, two stories in *The Washington Post*: "Duarte Says Romero Case Solved," and "Salvadorans Act in Case Of Prelate," both datelined San Salvador, Nov. 24 and Nov. 25, 1987, respectively, pp. A-15, A-14. The charges against D'Aubuisson had been investigated once before and dismissed for lack of evidence.

195. Duarte's role in the Guatemala City agreement, and reference to his sagging popularity from Julia Preston, "Duarte Pledges To Fight Pessimism Toward Pact," San Salvador-datelined dispatch in *The Washington Post*, Aug. 23, 1987, p. A 21. Reference to Cristiani in Deroy Murdock, "ARENA: Strong Second Party Emerging in El Salvador," *Human Events*, Aug. 22, 1987, p. 10; "Opposition Parties Quit Salvadoran Peace Panel," UPI story in *The Washington Post*, Nov. 14, 1987, p. A-23. The story quoted Cristiani as saying the parties reacted to "the irresponsible and unilateral way [the] government has sought to comply with the agreement." (Although the *Post* gave prominent display to virtually every stage of the "peace" plan process, a reader would have needed to search hard for this tiny, two-paragraph item under a small headline.)

196. Two examples, among many which could be presented: From the previously cited Aug. 23 Julia Preston story in *The Washington Post*: "Duarte's U.S.-backed government, and Nicaragua, where the United States supported rebels trying to oust the leftist Sandinista government." Or this, from the Marjorie Miller story in the Aug. 16, *Los Angeles Times*: "In the short term, the accord favors Duarte over the guerrillas, just as it favors Nicaraguan President Daniel Ortega over the *contras* fighting to oust the Sandinista government in Managua. The plan calls for international recognition of the Nicaraguan and

Salvadoran governments and does not require either to hold early elections or to draw up a new constitution." Yet another egregious example was offered by *Washington Post* editorial writer Stephen S. Rosenfeld, who managed to construct an entire op-ed article around the proposition that El Salvador—not Nicaragua—was the real peace plan problem. Why? Because Nicaragua had experienced its revolution—not perfect, perhaps, but revolution all the same—while El Salvador had not. Not only does this line of "reasoning" raise revolution to an unheard-of standing in the polemics of politics, but Rosenfeld added the insult of paying only token lip service to the reality that El Salvador is a democracy, Nicaragua a totalitarian stooge of the Soviet Union. Rosenfeld, "An Even Tougher Case: El Salvador," op. cit.

197. Allan Dodds Frank, "Guatemala: The Ultimate Price," *Forbes*, May 10, 1982, p. 109, quoted by Virginia Polk in "The New Guatemala Deserves U.S. Support," Heritage Foundation *Backgrounder* No. 435 (May 22, 1985), p. 4.

198. L. Francis Bouchey and Alberto M. Piedra, *Guatemala: A Promise in Peril* (Washington: Council for Inter-American Security, 1980), p. 24.

199. U.S. State Department report submitted to the House Committee on Foreign Affairs and the Senate Committee on Foreign Relations, February 4, 1980, quoted in Whelan and Bozell, *Catastrophe*, p. 96.

200. Bouchey and Piedra, *Guatemala*, p. 85.

201. Ibid., p. 83.

202. William Branigin, "Guatemala, Guerrilla Alliance Announce Cease-Fire, Peace Negotiations," a Mexico City-datelined story in *The Washington Post*, Oct. 3, 1987, p. A-24.

203. Ibid., p. 60.

204. Ibid., p. 87.

205. Polk, "The New Guatemala," p. 5.

206. UN Report on the Situation of Human Rights in Guatemala, quoted in Polk, op. cit., p. 8.

207. Ibid., p. 100.

208. *Progreso Economico y Social en America Latina, Informe 1987*, pp. 307, 318.

209. Edward Cody, "Guatemalan Government, Rebels Meet Formally for First Time," *The Washington Post*, Oct. 7, 1987, p. A-49. Madrid was chosen because of guerrilla claims that they feared for their lives were they to meet in the Guatemalan capital. The Spanish government of Socialist Felipe Gonzalez was a willing host, but remained on the

sidelines during the talks. The 1,000 estimate is from J. Michael Waller, "Guatemala's Marxist Guerrillas Nearly Defeated," a report from Guatemala City in *West Watch*, October 1987, pp. 1 and 6.

210. Branigan, op. cit. The "went nowhere" quote is from *The Economist*, "Central America's peace train runs out of steam," Oct. 24, 1987, p. 49. *The Washington Post* called the renewed combat "the most intense fighting in at least six months" (Julia Preston, "On Eve of Peace Pact Deadline, Central American Fighting Intensifies," Managua-datelined story in *The Washington Post*, Nov. 5, 1987).

211. Roger Lowenstein, "Hondurans Finally Face Up to the Facts: They Depend on Bananas and U.S. Aid," *The Wall Street Journal*, September 17, 1985, p. 32.

212. Honduras' per capita income in 1986, according to preliminary estimates was $780 (compared to $342 for Haiti, and $714 for Guyana, another country which has followed a Socialist path to ruin; that country's per capita income is lower now than it was in 1960). As for Nicaragua: in 1980, it stood at $1,025, but by 1986, was down even further from pre-Sandinista levels, to $862. Source: *Progreso Economico y Social en America Latina: Informe 1987*, p. 450.

213. Lowenstein, "Honduras," op. cit.

214. *Progreso Economico y Social 1987*, pp. 340–341.

215. Quoted in *Background Paper: Nicaragua's Military Build-Up*, p. 26. Bolanos told the Council for Inter-American Security that the Soviet generals "had plans to provoke Honduras and start a war" (Brownfeld and Waller, op. cit., p. 79).

216. *"Revolution Beyond Our Borders,"* p. 14.

217. Ibid.

218. *Background Paper: Nicaragua's Military Build-Up*, p. 28.

219. Ibid., p. 27.

220. Roger Reed, *El Salvador and the Crisis in Central America* (Washington: Council for Inter-American Security, 1984), p. 3; and *Background Paper: Nicaragua's Military Build-Up*, p. 27.

221. *"Revolution Beyond Our Borders,"* p. 15.

222. Ibid.

223. Ibid.

224. Timothy Ashby, "Honduras' Role in U.S. Policy for Central America," Heritage Foundation *Backgrounder* No. 412, February 28, 1985, p. 7.

225. Ibid., p. 6.

226. Wilson Ring, "Honduras Seeks Accord With Nicaragua on Maneuvers," *The Washington Post*, Nov. 22, 1987, p. A-26.

227. Quoted in Whelan and Bozell, *Catastrophe*, p. 105.

228. *FBIS: Latin America*, Foreign Broadcast Information Service, January 22, 1986, pp. 11–12, in *The Challenge to Democracy*, p. 62.

229. Ring, "Honduras Seeks Accord."

230. Special *Congressional Record*, op. cit., p. H-4845

231. Roger Lowenstein, "Costa Ricans Cheerfully Absorb U.S. Aid Sent as Immunization Against Nicaragua," *Wall Street Journal*, September 19, 1985, p. 36. While Costa Rica's infant mortality rate of 19 per thousand is low for the region, it is noteworthy that pre-Sandinista Nicaragua enjoyed an even lower rate: 12.3 per thousand, in 1976. See table 4, in chapter 2.

232. Virginia Polk, "Why Costa Rica Needs U.S. Help," Heritage Foundation *Backgrounder* No. 371 (August 2, 1984), p. 1.

233. In 1970, Costa Rica's foreign debt stood at $229 million; by 1975, it had leaped to $731 million, more than doubling again by 1978 to $1.6 billion. The binge has continued uninterrupted ever since. When the banks declined Costa Rica's proposal, interest payments were resumed in the fourth quarter at a token level of $5 million per month (about one-sixth the amount due). Had Costa Rica met its debt obligations, those payments would have gobbled up 48 percent of total export earnings; as it is, debt service claimed a staggering 29 percent (*Progreso Economico y Social 1987*, pp. 490 and 283).

234. *Background Notes: Costa Rica*, U.S. Department of State, May 1986, p. 4.

235. "Costa Ricans," op. cit., p. 36.

236. Polk, "Why Costa Rica Needs U.S. Help," p. 3.

237. *"Revolution Beyond Our Borders,"* pp. 16–17. A special commission of the Costa Rican Legislative Assembly reported in May 1981 that both President Rodrigo Carrazo and his security minister, Juan Jose Echeverria, connived in those "secret" arms shipments to the Sandinistas. See "Political Conflict and Violence," in *Central America in Crisis*, p. 187, among numerous other sources for that assertion of "connivance."

238. Ibid., pp. 17–18; *Background Paper: Nicaragua's Military Build-Up*, p. 32; and *Sustaining a Consistent Policy in Central America: One Year After the National Bipartisan Commission Report*, U.S. Department of State Special Report No. 124, April 1985, p. 8.

239. Georgie Anne Geyer, "Taking the Sandinistas at Their Word," *The*

Wall Street Journal, August 23, 1985, p. 15, in *"Revolution Beyond Our Borders,"* p. 16.

240. J. Polk, "Why Costa Rica Needs U.S. Help," p. 7 (Jocote); and *Background Notes: Costa Rica*, p. 4 (ambush).

241. *West Watch*, May 1986, p. 4.

242. Ibid.

243. As quoted in *Human Events*, Sept. 19, 1987, "Wright Says Sandinistas Acting in 'Good Faith,'" p. 3.

Townspeople of Grenville, Grenada, welcome the arrival of U.S. marines. A CBS-*New York Times* poll found 91 percent approval of the U.S. intervention. (*Photo credit: U.S. Navy*)

This family is typical of many thousands of Nicaraguan refugees living in Honduras without government assistance. (*Photo credit: Steve Johnson*)

Seen in a Honduran refugee camp during a March 1985 fact-finding mission: L. Francis Bouchey, President of the Council for Inter-American Security; Congressman Vin Weber (R-MN); Teresa, a Nicaraguan refugee (with arm in sling); her mother and sister; and Congressman Robert Dornan (R-CA). Teresa was injured when the Sandinistas attacked a private home in which she was attending a prayer meeting with her family. Her brother was killed in the attack.

Members of the Nicaraguan resistance at a *contra* training camp. The State Department reports that 90 percent of the resistance soldiers are between 18 and 22—too young to have served in Somoza's National Guard.

These *contra* recruits are still wearing the uniforms of the Sandinista militia, from which they had recently defected as a unit. (*Photo credit: J. Michael Waller*)

6

Mexico: The Smoldering Volcano

PORFIRIO DIAZ, who ruled Mexico for thirty years, is credited with the saying: "Poor Mexico, so far from God, and so close to the United States." At the risk of trivializing a very dangerous state of affairs, that saying, three-quarters of a century after it was first uttered, really ought now to read: "Poor United States, whatever our distance from God, so close to Mexico." For Mexico is, today, a smoldering volcano whose eruption would wreak havoc in this country.

Moscow targeted Mexico for penetration soon after the Bolshevik revolution had succeeded in consolidating its power in the Soviet Union. Communist success in establishing a menacing presence in Mexico—menacing now for Mexico, as well as for the United States—has usually been aided and abetted by the combination of romantic leftism and pathological anti-Americanism of Mexico's elites.

So long as Mexico would remain relatively stable, the United States could afford to shrug off that state of affairs. Although you are not yet seeing it in the pages of your newspapers or on your television screens to the extent the situation warrants—for reasons rooted both in the nature of news and in the ideological prejudices of the major media—the fact is that the very stability and safety of the United States itself is at greater risk now from our southern flank than ever before in our history.

In his new and extremely important book, *Mexico: Chaos on our Doorstep*, Sol Sanders puts it starkly: The PRI (Partido Revolucionario Institucional), which has ruled Mexico for nearly sixty-five years, "is dying. To clouds of incompetence, corruption, and venality that have hung over the regime has now been added the critical ingredient for any form of governance, indecision—that fatal hallmark of bankrupt government . . ."

"To predict the exact scenario of a breakdown of Mexican society would be foolhardy," Sanders tells us, in another passage.[1] But one thing is beyond dispute: Should that breakdown occur, the United States would suffer the consequences of the devastating fall-out. Although eschewing conclusions, *The Economist*, in a characteristically thorough and probing special 1987 supplement on Mexico, describes the PRI as "a party that had lost confidence in its ability to maintain public order and industrial discipline" and calls this "the central fact of modern Mexican politics."[2]

Writes Sanders, an experienced international observer and careful reporter: "Should the U.S. one day face any of a variety of possibilities—destabilization in Mexico, chaos on the border, a flood of refugees, armed infiltration—it would demand an immediate reordering of military priorities of a magnitude not seen since Pearl Harbor."[3]

Another source has estimated that it would take a quarter of a million troops to protect our 1,933 mile border with Mexico should a Soviet-satellite communist regime seize power there, and that is one-third of the total size of our present army. Just to secure the border against a floodtide of refugees would take four army divisions.[4]

From Riches to Rags

A few years ago, it was fashionable to speak of Mexico as "the Saudi Arabia of the Americas." While it would be a gross exaggeration to say that Mexico had managed to lift its burgeoning population out of poverty, it would not be an exaggeration to say that the country's rulers believed they then held in their hands an Aladdin's Lamp that would enable them to do that. That Aladdin's lamp was oil. But well before the oil boom, which began in the mid-1970s, Mexico seemed well on the way to realizing the promise of its immense natural wealth.

With an unaccustomed dash of hyperbole, *The Economist* wrote:

> Some 20 years ago Mexico had the most successful economy and society of any country where Iberian languages are spoken. It had had 40 years of political stability, with little in the way of political violence and less of military coups. Its political culture was not exactly democratic by the lights of North America or Northern Europe, but it was at least not particularly repressive. It was, and had been for four decades, culturally irrepressible. Its economy, in one of the great success stories of the post-1945 world, had grown by around 6% a year. The country was growing richer and more confident in its relations with the world outside. . . .[5]

All of that would change under the weight of demagoguery, and specifically of populist rhetoric, and the economic policies it would spawn (protectionism, import substitution, hostility to foreign investment, an expanding role for the state in the economy). The result: "Despite the appearance of an economy gathering strength up until the end of the 1970s, there is a remarkable consensus among Mexican businessmen and commentators that the rot had set in at least ten years earlier."

To economic error would be added a blunder that shook to the very foundations the PRI's image and sense of legitimacy: the massacre in Mexico City on October 2, 1968, of at least 300 persons in the capital's Tlatelolco Plaza during a peaceful demonstration on the eve of the Olympic games. Until then, the PRI confidently presented itself as not only the expression of national aspirations, but as a repository sufficiently copious to accommodate all shades of opinion, all significant differences.

In the aftermath, President Luis Echeverria, who governed from 1970 to 1976, would accelerate the headlong rush into statism—and ruin. As a consequence of his policies, a country that had known neither inflation nor devaluation of its currency experienced both; the current account deficit tripled, from $1 billion in 1970 to $3 billion in 1976. The government resorted increasingly to borrowing. During Echevarria's last year in office, fearing that Mexico might default on its external public debt—then a relatively modest $27 billion—the U.S. joined with the International Monetary Fund (IMF) and World Bank in what later became a dismaying pattern of debt-rescheduling and an avalanche of new loans.

Massive oil discoveries intervened to postpone what might have been a moment of fiscal and policy truth. Instead, flushed with the country's new-found oil wealth, the new president, Jose Lopez Portillo, went on a twin spending-and-borrowing binge. The government bureaucracy ballooned from 600,000 to 1.5 million employees in fewer than five years, and in just three years (1978–1981), the federal budget tripled in size. Foreign banks (mainly American), and international institutions (heavily funded by the U.S.) rushed to proffer loans that ultimately would make Mexico the second most heavily mortgaged debtor nation in the so-called developing world.

The bottom fell out when oil prices began their steep slide in 1982. At that point, the Reagan administration stepped in with a second massive bail-out—but by that time, Mexico's external debt stood at more than $80 billion. Lopez Portillo—a former finance minister who seemed to promise fiscal responsibility when he assumed the presidency—responded to the new crisis by blaming the private sector and nationalizing the banks. By mid-1986, debt payments were eating up 18 percent of the gross domestic product (in the U.S., as debt-burdened as we are, the figure is about half of that). In order to meet the demands of the banks and the International Monetary Fund, the government was forced to resort to severe austerity measures.

A *Washington Post* correspondent put it this way: "By piling up such outside financing, Mexico until recently had largely shielded its eighty million inhabitants, particularly the poor among them, from the full impact of their economic situation."[6] With belt-tightening, the shield dropped and sharp price increases were pushed through for everything from tortillas, a staple of the Mexican diet, to subway fares. However necessary these measures, they hit hard a population that was already poor and getting poorer. Mexican per capita income declined from $2,734 in 1980 to $2,407 in 1986 and was only one-seventh that of the United States. This is not at all an irrelevance in the case of Mexico, given that country's cheek-by-jowl proximity to the gringo cornucopia. Mexico was also already waging a losing battle against what appeared to be runaway inflation. According to the *Post*, workers have lost about 40 percent of their purchasing power since 1980. Inflation, galloping at more than 100 percent a year in official calculations during 1986, was expected to reach 150 percent by the end of 1987. To make matters worse, estimates of Mexico's unemployed and under-employed range as high as 45 percent, and of those who are working, close to 40 percent are employed in one of the world's most incompetent agricultural systems, on state-run farms created by "revolutionary" ideology.[7]

The money has run out, in more ways than one, as we shall see in a moment. The question now is whether time is also running out on a government trapped in the straitjacket of a failed and tragically flawed ideology, tottering between fiscal ruin on one side and a popular explosion on the other.

Even such a quick sketch of the agony of Mexico would be incomplete were two other elements not included.

The first of them concerns the population itself. In 1930, Mexico had just under 17 million inhabitants. By 1960, that number had reached 36 million; a decade later, it had grown by nearly half as much, topping 50 million. The current estimate is 80 million, and by the turn of the century, Mexico is expected to have at least 109 million.[8] The 1981–1986 population growth rate (2.9 percent) far exceeds that of any of the big "rich" countries, and among the poor ones, puts Mexico in a class with some of the very poor ones (the Philippines, Nigeria, Pakistan). Obviously, only a strong country with a sturdy, solidly expanding economy can hope to create jobs fast enough to absorb all of those new people coming onto the job market. For Mexico, that means creating one million jobs per year. In 1981, more Mexicans were caught and turned back by the U.S. Immigration and Naturalization Service (866,000) than the number of new jobs created that year inside Mexico (731,000).[9] Sooner or later, those jobless and desperate people are going to batter down someone's door in search of work.

The second element that needs mentioning is a relatively new threat to Mexico's internal security: a communist guerrilla force operating in the jungles mantling the 1,500-mile southern border. Given the fact that Mexico's army is both weak and small (100,000 men, smaller than the armed forces of Nicaragua, a country with one-fortieth of Mexico's population), policymakers are beginning to express real anxiety about their ability to contain those rogue forces, particularly because they operate in close proximity to Mexico's rich Campeche oil fields.

Together We Stand

Like it or not, the United States and Mexico are inextricably bound together. Until now, that is an embrace Mexico found mostly unwelcome and unwanted. Increasingly, as Mexico forces itself into American awareness, the discomfiture will be on the American side, as well. Yet the consequences of a Mexican collapse would be, for the United States, too awful to contemplate. For the Mexicans, there really is nowhere else they can look for meaningful salvation—assuming, that is, that it remains within the power of any country to rescue Mexico from its own past.

To begin with, there is the inescapable fact of that frontier—a 1,933 mile sieve, really. As one after another of the promises of the "revolution" proved hollow, Mexicans sought escape from hopelessness in their own bulging capital (it has mushroomed at the rate of 30 percent per year for the past ten years, and now has a population of around eighteen million). But, they also swarmed northward, to now-teeming border cities (Juarez's metropolitan population is now put at four million, and there are two-million-plus in Tijuana, which because of an "emergency" which has lasted ten years, relies on San Diego to process nearly 40 percent of its raw sewage.)[10]

Next, there are economic realities. Mexico is the second largest exporter of oil to the U.S. from the developing nations (having relinquished the top spot to Venezuela in 1987). Americans have an estimated $7 billion invested in Mexico. Although there has been a steady decline in trade between the two countries, Mexico still sells in excess of 65 percent of its exports to the United States, buys about an equal amount from this country, and is, in fact, the U.S.'s third trading partner (behind only Canada and Japan). Then there are the immigrants, the legal ones, the illegal ones, who work so many of our farms and factories, staff our restaurants and hotels. And, finally, there are Hispanics of Mexican origin: 10.3 million, according to the latest census figures. Overwhelmingly, these Mexican-Americans, though not yet a powerful political force, retain strong ties to their ancestral land and culture. And, a University of California study estimates that, by 2030, 40 percent of California's population will be of Hispanic origin (compared with about 20 percent in 1980)—and that group will come overwhelmingly (80 percent) from Mexico.[11]

Dark Horizons

Our problems with Mexico divide into roughly three categories: (1) security; (2) illegal immigrants; (3) crime.

Security: Ever since reopening its embassy in Mexico City in 1942, the Soviet Union has used it as a control center for subversion not only in Mexico, but also throughout Latin America—and to reinforce measures directed at the U.S. For many years, until the 1960s, there were only two Soviet embassies south of the Rio Grande, in Mexico and Uruguay. Until 1977, indeed, there were no Soviet embassies in all of Central America.

According to author Sanders, the Soviet embassy in Mexico City today houses the largest contingent of KGB secret police outside the Soviet bloc. As 1986 ended, that number was reliably put at ninety diplomats, forty-two trade and commercial officers and eighty wives employed in the mission. (Cuba, twenty-five times smaller than the U.S.S.R., maintained at the same time what amounted to an even more gargantuan staff: thirty-two diplomats, twelve trade and commercial officers, and twenty working wives.) Former CIA analyst Harry Rositzke, echoing a generalized judgment that many of those KGB operatives are there to handle U.S. affairs, says "Mexico, not Canada, is the principal base for third-country operations against the United States."[12] That such activity does go on there was specifically confirmed when it was learned that spies Christopher Boyce and Andrew Dalton Lee, who in 1984 were convicted of selling the Soviets plans for a secret CIA satellite system used to communicate with agents in dangerous areas, worked through the Soviet embassy in Mexico City.

Of equal concern to intelligence analysts is the extent to which the Soviets are infiltrating agents into the U.S. among the illegal aliens crossing our frontiers at the rate of nearly three thousand per day. A number of such cases have been documented. *Mexico 2000: A Look at the Problems and Potential of Modern Mexico*, a major study of that country published in 1980, contains this: "Reports of cooperation between militant Chicano groups in the United States and Mexican terrorists of the Liga Comunista del 23 de Septiembre abound. Documents seized in Ciudad Juarez late in 1978 indicated that the Communist League of September 23 was trying to recruit Chicanos for an uprising in the states of Nayarit, Durango, Chihuahua, Sinaloa, Sonora and Baja California. Other Mexican groups of chauvinistic inclinations propose using radical Chicanos and illegal immigrants as a potential Fifth Column for reconquering the U.S. Southwest."[13] In a 1979 meeting with then-President Lopez Portillo of Mexico, Cuban dictator Fidel Castro said of that tactic: "Cuba supports . . . the legitimate demand of the Mexicans who emigrate—fruit of the bitter and inevitable mutilation of the national territory and underdevelopment imposed by . . . the arrogance and domination of the United States."[14] Castro was also quoted as saying: "The Yankees cannot even begin to imagine the capabilities that we have in their country."[15]

In July 1987, the Border Patrol was put on alert following intelligence that suspected Islamic Jihad terrorists—a 10 person "hit" team—were planning to cross the border to assassinate an American law enforcement official. That report underscored a sharp increase in the arrests of non-

Mexicans crossing the border. While most were from Central America, a great many others were not: people of 76 nationalities were caught crossing the border illegally in 1986.[16]

West Watch, the incisive publication of the Council for Inter-American Security, spotlighted the same problem in an article headlined: "U.S.-Mexico Border: Gateway for Terrorists." *West Watch* reported on the hunt for three Libyan terrorists in the Mexican border state of Chihuahua (opposite Texas and New Mexico). Interpol agents had learned that they had planned to enter the U.S. through Ciudad Juarez.[17]

Illegals: Though support for it has increased over the past year or two, the Border Patrol remains a step-child of official Washington—probably because official Washington continues to mainly ignore the developing crisis. Until a recent and dramatic build-up, only four hundred officers—fewer than the number of police guarding the U.S. Capitol—had been assigned to securing that 1,933 mile border, much of it desolate, barren and rugged. (By late 1987, the number of agents stood at 2,934.) Not surprisingly, a great number of illegal aliens make it through to safe haven in this country, in no small measure cloaked by a church-backed Sanctuary Movement which is in itself illegal. Conservative guesstimates put at 1.5 million the number who manage to slip into the U.S. illegally each year.

How effective the new immigration legislation will be in curbing illegal immigration remains to be seen. But, again, what does not remain in doubt is the effect of any upheaval in Mexico. Communist takeovers and revolutionary violence have, again and again, caused millions to flee their homelands. Given the desperate plight of Mexicans already, it is inevitable that literally millions would flock across our virtually defenseless borders should collapse—or communism—come to Mexico. And, even if we had the troops to deploy, what on earth would we order them to do—shoot unarmed men, women and children?

Even allowing for payment of taxes by many "illegals," a 1983 study estimated that each one million illegals already were costing U.S. taxpayers $982 million.[18] With courts increasingly holding that illegal or not, immigrants are entitled to educational and social services, that cost quotient can only go up. Indeed, facing "a flood of immigrant children," the Los Angeles city school board voted in October 1987 to put all of its schools on a year-round schedule, making it the largest year-round school district in the country.[19]

There is an important footnote to the current problem. Among some intellectuals on both sides of the border, the argument is made that, because part of the western United States were wrested from Mexico, these lands "belong" to Mexicans at least as much as to Americans, and thus the border must be "open." Though the present volume is not the place to review the events which led up to the sixteen-month Mexican-American War of 1846–1848, it is useful to recall that, in the words of one historian, the lands "wrested" away were "provinces it [Mexico] could not develop and apparently could never use." He referred to the fact that Mexico City was not only largely indifferent to the northern provinces (including Texas, New Mexico, Arizona, and California), but had never succeeded in persuading more than a handful of Mexicans to settle in those Indian-infested territories. At the same time that "Anglos" continued their relentless push westward, settling in those areas in wave after wave. That same historian also makes the point that the Treaty of Guadalupe Hidalgo that ended the war "took territories that were only nominally Mexican for what at the time was a realistic price; the income of usable resources of Mexico was not reduced; only a few Mexican citizens in these territories were affected, and the defeated nation was not required to pay the usual indemnities. The terms were not harsh."[20]

Yet, in international as well as in personal relations, it is not enough for a position to be correct or even right for it to prevail, so we are likely to hear the "ownership" issue pressed more stridently in the future.

Crime: The crime problem comes in two parts. The first part concerns illegal aliens themselves—as anyone who has seen the movie "Border," starring Charles Bronson, will remember vividly. The second involves drugs.

Smuggling aliens across our border has become a big business, and like any other large-scale criminal activity, it not only involves breaking the law, but breeds other crime, as well. This "trade" generates huge profits—"coyotes" charge aliens as much as $1,000 to smuggle them across the border, and, although not all illegal aliens use the services of coyotes to cross, the number who do runs to the tens of thousands. Typically, the coyotes not only get a "customer" across the border, but arrange to place him in a waiting job—usually of the "sweat-shop" variety—in a distant city. Although the money those hard-working people send back home gives an important boost to the Mexican economy, and in some cases is the decisive factor in the survival of small villages, the profits from the smuggling operations flow to criminal hands which re-direct some of them to still other criminal activities.

Of all the criminal activities along the border —prostitution, gambling, smuggling of goods—none rivals drugs in magnitude nor ominousness. Sanders reports that in 1975, at the peak of the heroin epidemic in the United States, 87 percent of the heroin consumed in the United States originated in Mexico.[21] More recent estimates are that one-third of the heroin sold in the U.S. comes in from Mexico, as well as 32 percent of marijuana imports. Despite widespread corruption among Mexican officials, Mexicans bridle at U.S. accusations that they are "indifferent" to the drug problem, pointing out that they have lost as many as 400 soldiers and agents to drug operatives. They also point out that the U.S. appetite for drugs means that they have to commit one-

222

quarter of their meager armed forces to combating the trade in their country.[22]

It is into what Sanders describes as "this atmosphere of fear and violence" that more than 150 religious congregations across the U.S. have waded with the so-called Sanctuary Movement aimed at thwarting U.S. immigration policy. Leaders of the movement are largely animated by an ideological conviction that immigrants from Central America are victims of U.S. policies of "aggression" in the region, and thus entitled to "sanctuary." Debating "sanctuary" is not germane to this book. What is pertinent is that—as Sanders puts it— "the growing defiance of the law is creating a belt of vigorous criminal activity along the Mexico border."[23]

For those who see the world in simplistic terms, turmoil along our southern border is easily explained: The rich U.S. has "exploited" and "bullied" poor Mexico. Yet, as historian T. R. Fehrenbach points out, it is instructive to contrast the situation along our southern border with the one along our much longer (5,525-mile) and even less defended Canadian border. "Vastly more United States capital and enterprise entered Canada and brought the Canadian economy inevitably into the North American (U.S.) orbit without making Canada in any way a United States political satellite, and there were not reprisals or interventions against Canada because Canada was a stable society where businessmen, investments, or foreign-owned property were never threatened by disorder, nor were foreigners molested without proper recompense. There were no troops on the Canadian border because there was never the remotest need for any. . . ."[24]

The International Dimension

As true as it is that Mexico's governing and intellectual elites view the world through Leftist-skewed lenses, it is truer yet that Mexico harbors an attitude hovering between distrust and disgust toward the United States. (One example: a 1986 poll of 550 Mexicans found that 59 percent view the United States as an "enemy country," only 31 percent "a friendly country.")[25] That mind-set has not escaped the attention of enemies of the United States, who have been quick to exploit it as far back as the First World War.

In a fascinating article entitled "Mexico: The Achilles' Heel of NATO," J. Michael Waller resurrects a forgotten episode of history that ultimately became known as the "Zimmermann Telegram," and was the proximate cause of the U.S. declaration of war against Germany in 1917.[26]

As early as the late 1800s, Kaiser Wilhelm of Germany had tried to purchase Baja California so as to establish a naval base there and project Germany's naval power into the Pacific. Later, agents of the Kaiser ingratiated themselves with Mexican revolutionaries to the extent that Pancho Villa said he would help the Germans in World War I because that would facilitate Mexican recovery of its lost northern territories.

In the famous telegram, German Foreign Minister Arthur Zimmermann instructed his ambassador in Mexico City to pursue an alliance with Mexico in the event that efforts to keep the U.S. neutral should fail. Included among the terms: "That we shall make war together and together make peace. We shall give general financial support and it is understood that Mexico is to reconquer the lost territory of New Mexico, Texas and Arizona." When President Woodrow Wilson published the intercepted and decoded document on March 1, 1917, Zimmermann not only admitted it was authentic but said he had also tried to persuade Mexican President Venustiano Carranza to expand the alliance to include Japan. Though there was strong pro-German sentiment in Mexico—and even stronger anti-American sentiment—Carranza prudently rejected the deal.

The new communist rulers of Russia lost no time in mak-

ing their move in Mexico. In 1919, Lenin dispatched Mikhail
Borodin to set up a Communist Party which, in turn, organized other communist cells throughout the hemisphere.

The ruling PRI party has never, itself, been controlled by
communists but the PRI has always been heavily infiltrated by
communists and usually tolerant-to-benign in its attitude
toward Moscow. The exceptions have been few, such as in
1930 when the Russians clumsily encouraged the local communist party to launch a coup against the government. Mexico quickly crushed the revolt, expelled the two Soviet agents
who helped hatch the plot and broke relations with Moscow, a
hiatus that would last until 1942.[27]

But Mexico has been even warmer in its embrace of Fidel
Castro. The first significant funding for Castro's revolution
came from the then aging, ex-president Lazaro Cardenas of
Mexico. The Mexican Communist Party supported Castro
beginning in 1955, three years before the Cuban communists
threw in with him, on the very eve of his final triumph. When,
in 1962, the Organization of American States voted to expel
Castro's Cuba because of his subversive onslaughts against
other hemisphere nations, only Mexico—supposed citadel of
non-interventionism in hemisphere affairs—refused to go
along. Alone among OAS members, Mexico never did break
with Castro. In 1972, President Luis Echeverria—who, more
than any other chief executive until then, steered Mexico's
foreign policy onto an activist, leftward path—built a huge
embassy for Castro.

As if to thumb their noses at Uncle Sam, the Mexicans, in
1983, granted Cuba a $55 million credit, only a few weeks
after U.S. creditors, pressured by official Washington, had
agreed to re-schedule Mexico's $90 billion foreign debt.
Interestingly, that credit to the Cubans came only days after
they had been discovered delivering explosives to a group
they believed were Mexican communists. That incident
raised questions about the sturdiness of one of the pillars of

Mexican foreign policy: that cozying up to Castro (and international communism) would insulate the country against communist subversion at home.

Such policies do not spring primarily from pragmatic considerations alone. As indicated earlier, communists and Marxists have always been close to the pinnacle of power in the PRI. Echeverria, for example, relied on three Marxists as key advisers: Horacio Labastido Munoz, Jesus Reyes Heroles, and Porcidio Munoz Ledo. Labastido later went on to join two other self-proclaimed Marxists in creating the Commission for National Ideology, which recommends policy and, in the words of a Heritage Foundation study, "is usually closely tied to the President and his cabinet."

Mexico's current foreign minister, Bernardo Sepulveda, emerged from the extreme Left of Mexican politics. In 1980, he was treasurer of the Vicente Lombardo Toledano Center for Philosophical, Political and Social Studies, named for a communist labor leader prominent in the 1930s, and an organization described by the conservative Mexico City group Desarrollo Humano Integral as "part of Mexico's pro-Soviet left." Sepulveda's predecessor as foreign minister is married to a woman widely rumored in Mexico to be a former code clerk at the Soviet embassy in Cairo, and their son is an avowed communist.

Mexico's enchantment with regimes of the Left is not only old, it also verges, on occasion, on fanaticism. Until a few years ago, Mexico was the only country in the world to recognize the "government" of the Spanish Republic, the left-wing losers in a war that ended in 1939.

Mexico and Central America

Marvin Alisky, who teaches political science at Arizona State University and who is a close and astute observer of Mexican affairs, has noted that the United States and Mexico seem to have similar hopes for Central America: economic stability and political growth.

The emphasis belongs on the word "seem." For, as a Heritage Foundation analyst would write, in a generally benign interpretation of Mexican foreign policy, there are three elements in it that bring it into conflict with U.S. policy in Central America. To fail to understand that—and far too many in Washington and among America's "intelligentsia" do—is to mis-read altogether Mexico's role and intentions as regards the region. (For example, in 1981, one hundred U.S. congressmen petitioned the State Department to consider a Mexican-French initiative which endorsed the Salvadoran guerrilla movement as a legitimate political group, even though, as Heritage's analyst Esther Wilson Hannon points out, "this initiative had been condemned almost universally by the rest of the Latin American states.")[28] A few years later, the number two man in the Mexican government, Home Secretary Manuel Bartlett Diaz, heading a delegation to Moscow, was quoted as telling his Kremlin hosts: "Mexico and the Soviet Union coincide in their policies toward Central America."[29]

That, is, in fact, the nub of the problem. Since Mexico, together with the rest of Latin America, remains largely shrouded in the darkness of disinterest, public as well as official, appearances deceive all too easily. The side with the best rhetoric has a much better chance of prevailing where facts, the indispensable stuff of understanding, lie neglected or hidden. Few Americans are aware, for example, that when Central Americans spoke of the "the colossus of the North," they were, for many generations, more often than not referring to Mexico—not to the United States.

To return to those three differences. First, Mexico seeks to limit U.S. influence in the region, viewing a U.S. presence as "imperialistic" and threatening to Mexican sovereignty. Second, Mexico's own revolutionary ideology has reinforced the Mexican predilection to support other, usually leftist, revolutionary causes. Third, the "protection-buying" syndrome, discussed earlier.

These differences are as much understood throughout Latin America as they are little understood in the U.S. Equally well understood in Latin America, as it is little understood in the U.S., is that Mexico has never been perceived in the region as a regional leader. This is not, of course, to insinuate that Mexico is without influence in the region, or that all Mexican initiatives are cold-shouldered. That was particularly so when Mexico was, a few years ago, in the position of being able to dispense petro-dollar largesse. But it is to say that to oppose Mexico is not necessarily—or even usually—the same as opposing Latin America, or Central America.

Indeed, Mexico's ideological obstinacy served to severely discredit that country vis-a-vis both Nicaragua and El Salvador. In the case of Nicaragua—to quote again from the Heritage Foundation analysis[30]—"Mexico continues to tell Western European and American audiences that good will and economic assistance will allow Nicaragua to become an independent, nonmilitaristic power in the region"—despite the fact that this was tried and failed. That "the U.S. and Western European countries gave over $2 billion in credits and economic assistance to the Sandinistas in their first years of power, from 1979 to 1981, seems to make no difference to Mexico." Nor do the Mexicans apparently choose to take note of the obvious fact that—to quote again from the Heritage study—"ideology and not external pressures impels the government of Nicaragua to choose a Soviet-allied, Marxist-Leninist path." Notes Heritage: "President Miguel de la Madrid (the current president) continues to defend vigorously the unelected government of Nicaragua, though the rest of the region has ceased doing so."[31]

Again alone among the democratic states of the region, Mexico continued to shelter and support the Salvadoran guerrilla movement and urge negotiations with it long after the Salvadoran people, massively and in defiance of guerrilla threats, went to the polls twice in 1984 to elect a president. The hypocrisy of a country which loudly trumpets its democratic character and commitment to the twin principles of self-determination and non-intervention and yet which refused to distance itself from a ruthless guerrilla war against an elected government has not been lost on Latin Americans. There is, however, an element of irony in all of this: as *The Economist* observed in its 1987 in-depth special supplement on Mexico, "it is a matter of debate whether Mexico ever had a tenth of the influence with the Sandinistas between 1979 and 1982 that it claimed. Central Americans are nearly as cynical about Mexico's foreign policy as North Americans."[32]

In all of this, the Mexican government has been shielded by a press that—while technically free—hews, for the most part, to official doctrine. As Professor Alisky notes, in an article replete with specific examples: "Mexican media and government officials invariably describe the Marxist Sandinistas as 'progressive' or 'liberal' and the Communist guerrillas of El Salvador as 'democratic' or 'leftist.' If these Mexican politicians and journalists had been alive in 1912 when the Titanic struck an iceberg, they would have asserted that a luxury liner had stopped to take on ice."[33]

The Road Ahead

The best that can be said is that it is a road fraught with peril. But there are hopeful signs.

As long ago as 1962, a rise of left-wing activity in Mexico caused a capital flight of 1.5 billion pesos (approximately $125 million, a huge sum for the time). In the aftermath, the inner clique chose as president the most conservative and pro-U.S. member of the cabinet, Gustavo Diaz Ordaz—a decision largely influenced by the need to repair the damage done by excessive "Leftism."[34]

Three added incentives exist for course-correction now. One of them is corruption, for so many years said to be "the glue that holds Mexico together." In recent years, it has raged out of control, even by Mexican standards. According to Alan Riding of *The New York Times*, former President Luis Echeverria—who used the presidency as a bully pulpit for attacking "capitalists" and "imperialists" the world over—is believed to have stolen between $300 million and $1 billion during his term in office. That would, however, pale in comparison with the "achievement" of his successor. Former president Jose Lopez Portillo (1976–1982) is believed to have looted the national treasury of as much as $3.5 billion before leaving office. "Whatever the actual sum," wrote author Sol Sanders, "Lopez Portillo fled the country with an enormous fortune. Mexico had experienced nothing like it since Cortes and the conquistadores had melted down the golden religious treasure of the Aztecs to carry it off to Spain."[35] Though his successor, Miguel de la Madrid, came into office vowing to punish wrong-doers and stamp out corruption, little effective action has been taken. Still, there is now an acute awareness in Mexico City that, while punish-or-perish won't work (rewarding the party faithful is still vital to the party's stranglehold on power), restraint is the alternative to fiscal ruin.

The second is the debt crisis, which, as external pressure (the IMF, the banks) has increased, has strengthened the hand of moderates in the de la Madrid government. The government says it is now committed to shedding some of the more than 1,155 state-owned corporations ("parastatals"), many of them acquired during the rush to socialism that began under Echeverria in 1970. Mexico recently announced its decision to join the General Agreement on Tariffs and Trade, implicitly repudiating in so doing a failed, forty-year-old policy of import substitution (building up and subsidizing inefficient local industries to produce what might have been imported far more cheaply from abroad). Though the severely restrictive foreign investment law of the Echeverria regime remains on the books, Mexican officials now are saying foreign investment is welcome, and the Echeverria rules will be applied "pragmatically" (principally the one limiting foreigners to a maximum 49 percent ownership). In an August 1986 interview with *West Watch*, Gerald J. Van Heuven, vice-president of the United States-Mexico Chamber of Commerce, said the combination of these moves should "send a message" to foreign investors: "that the 'rules of the game' are changing and that it is now more desirable to invest in Mexico."[36] But as 1987 moved to a close, the jury was still out on how well the programs were working, how earnestly they were being applied. Against the pragmatic imperatives, there is a permanent "pull of populism." The PRI's orthodoxy holds that the state should never surrender "rectorship" of the economy. Heritage Foundation researcher Melanie Tammen, in a paper on the failure of bailouts of the Mexican economy, argued that "a government that has subjected its populace to cuts in consumer subsidies, drastically increased taxes, and a real wage cut of 50 percent between 1983 and 1985 without a mass revolt, surely can survive the divestiture of the bulk of its inefficient state-run enterprises and substantial cuts in its bloated bureaucracy."[37]

The third incentive is political. In July of 1983, the PRI suffered the worst electoral defeat of its history, losing in the states of Chihuahua and Durango to candidates of the National Action Party (PAN), a conservative Catholic nationalist party formed in 1939. When PAN candidates again won in seven of thirty-eight municipal elections in Coahuila, in December of 1984, PRI operatives refused to recognize the results, triggering riots that left two dead and eighty injured, and the town hall of Piedras Negras burned and destroyed. The PAN candidate had to flee across the Rio Grande to Eagle Pass, Texas.

PRI support fell to an all-time low in congressional and

gubernatorial elections on July 7, 1985—elections marred by widespread charges of ballot-stuffing and other irregularities. Although the PRI won all seven state governorships and 289 of the 300 Chamber of Deputies seats at stake, turnout was light (50 percent), and the PRI polled only 65 percent of the vote, 16 percent voting for PAN. So blatant was the fraud in those elections that Juan Molinar of the National University was commissioned to do a study. His "dispassionate" study turned up "devastating" evidence of wholesale fraud.[38]

Though the PRI's lock on power remains strong, the warning signs of mounting public disenchantment with sixty years of one-party rule have registered with the leadership.

These trends have been accelerated by a growing gulf between the rapidly industrializing northern states and the poorer south. (Just five major industrial groups headquartered in the northern city of Monterrey produce about $48 billion a year in goods and services—roughly 25 percent of Mexico's GNP—and the ten northern states, though mostly arid and sparsely-populated—produce 65 percent of Mexico's agricultural exports.)[39] Wrote *The Economist*:

"It is among these northerners, proud, close to the United States, conscious of North American concepts of democracy, hard-working and entrepreneurial, that the legitimacy of Mexico's political system is crumbling. In Mexico City, this is troubling and not only because the northern political movement challenges the hegemony of the PRI. Equally worrying is any regional factionalism. . . ."[40]

Taken together, these three factors could lead to a shift away from the corrupt and socialist policies that have kept Mexico a nation as rich in resources as it is poor in reality.

Furthermore, the country will get a new president in 1988, and given the awesome power of the Mexican presidency, a chance for yet a new beginning. That president (barring an act of God) will be Carlos Salinas de Gortari, a 39-year-old Harvard-educated economist who has served as the Budget Director and chief architect of the country's new and potentially-promising economic program. (Elections for that six-year term will be held on July 6, 1988, but PRI President Jorge de la Vega Dominguez knew whereof he spoke when, on October 3, 1987, he presented Salinas to a press conference with the remark: "You will be the next president of Mexico."[41] In 58 years, the PRI has never lost—never permitted itself to lose, to be more accurate—an election for president, governor or senator.).

Salinas enjoys the respect of the international banking community (but, then, so too did another technocrat: Lopez Portillo). And, indeed, Mexico's stock market, already booming through 1987, broke its own records in the first hour of trading the day following Salinas' selection. Following "Black Monday"—the worldwide stock market debacle in October 1987—the Mexican market fell farther (60 percent) and harder (grossly over-extended brokerage houses later needed a $600 million bailout to survive) than any other.

At his inauguration in December 1988, Salinas would, at 40, be the youngest president in four decades.

By contrast with euphoria in financial circles, his selection so rankled a dissident, radical left-wing faction of the PRI that it announced it would run its own candidate: Cuahtemoc Cardenas, son of the former (and radical) president Lazaro Cardenas. The party leadership reacted by expelling Cardenas and dismissing his political base as "microscopic." Although he could cut into the party's leftist and union support, Cardenas' candidacy was not viewed as a major threat to Salinas.[42]

As to what Mr. Salinas' ultimate selection means, Jorge Castaneda, an oft-quoted and respected Mexican commentator would offer an observation:

"The power of the president is so mysterious that it is futile to try and anticipate what a man will do before he gets it."[43]

Two external factors—and an internal reality—offer some hope of averting a Mexican cataclysm.

The internal reality is that Mexico is a rich country—rich in the resourcefulness of its people and rich in natural resources. The potential for national redemption is there. To quote from a Heritage Foundation study:

> Mexico's . . . citizens through the years have contributed significantly to the worlds of art, literature, and international business. . . . Mexicans, moreover, have demonstrated a remarkable capability for resilience and private initiative, as demonstrated by their stunning response to the 1985 Mexico City earthquake. In contrast to many other developing countries, Mexico is rich in natural resources and industrial capacity. The nation's estimated oil deposits of 49 billion barrels make it the world's fourth largest in terms of petroleum production and fifth in terms of reserves. Mexico also ranks seventh in the world in natural gas reserves, has proven coal deposits of 643 million metric tons (compared to 490 billion metric tons in the U.S.), and is one of the world's largest silver producers. The country also contains important deposits of copper, zinc, lead, fluorspar, and iron ore. . . .
>
> Mexico ranks tenth in the world in terms of gross domestic product originating from manufacturing and alone accounts for more than 10 percent of the developing world's total manufacturing output. In absolute terms, the value of Mexico's industrial output is twice that of South Korea and more than five times that of Israel.[44]

The first of the external factors is that Washington is, little by little, beginning to push Mexico to a place of priority on the national agenda. The Justice Department, for example, is said to have drafted a secret plan for containing a refugee avalanche should that occur, a move which, at least, would reflect an awareness for reactive thinking.[45]

The second is that Japan appears to be taking an increasing interest in Mexico. By 1983, Japanese investment in Mexico amounted to $1.2 billion, and was second only to the U.S. in its volume of trade with Mexico. Japanese banks also rank second to the U.S. in the volume of their loans to Mexico. The

Japanese, eager to ease their dependence on Mideast oil, have a lively interest in Mexican oil. Free of the emotional baggage of past ideological antagonisms, Japan is well-positioned to nudge Mexico along a free-market path that would include relaxing present restrictions on foreign investment in the country.

Pragmatism does not always win out over ideology, no matter how clear the case, how great the need. Mexico is, itself, living proof of this. Nor is danger always sufficient to provoke body politics or policymakers to defuse a crisis before it explodes; the world's behavior during Hitler's rise, and more recently, in the face of Soviet expansionism, give ample evidence of that.

It has been said that, for international communism, Nicaragua and El Salvador and Guatemala are only a prelude, dominos on the way to the real prize—Mexico. For many, even those schooled in hemisphere affairs, the notion of a Soviet-satellite state arising in Mexico has seemed preposterous.

Yet, unless pragmatism and caring do intervene, what once seemed preposterous may yet prove simply calamitous.

NOTES

1. Sol Sanders, *"Mexico: Chaos on Our Doorstep* (Lanham, Md., Madison Books, 1986), pp. 1, 99.

2. Michael Elliott, "The shadow of the past," *The Economist: A Survey of Mexico*, Sept. 5, 1987, p. 3.

3. Sanders, *Mexico*, p. 189.

4. J. Michael Waller, "Mexico: The Achilles Heel of NATO," *West Watch* (Washington: Council for Inter-American Security), April 1986, p. 8.

5. *The Economist*, op. cit., pp. 3–4. Although all three were beginning to

show the fissures created by years of welfare state economics and populist politics, Argentina, Chile, and Uruguay, in the late 1960s, were arguably at least as "successful" in the post-war era as was Mexico. So, for that matter, was pre-Castro Cuba. Balance also requires injecting at this point that the Mexican government did not need to be repressive. Coming to power as it did at the end of two decades of bloodshed that claimed as many as one million lives, it then proceeded to seize control of all of the levers of power and avenues of opportunity in the society. As to Mexico's riches, Elliott points out that, in 1800, on the threshold of its own independence (twenty years later), Mexico's exports were about equal in value to those of the newly independent United States (though per capita output was only 44 percent that of the United States and total output only about half that of the U.S.).

6. Edward Cody, "Strings Tightening on Mexican Economy," *The Washington Post*, September 1, 1986, p. A-1.

7. Source for per capita income: *Progreso Economico Y Social en America Latina: Informe 1987* (Washington: Inter-American Development Bank, 1987), (hereafter *Progreso Economico y Social 1987*); Fe de Erratas for Table I-1, "Producto interno per capita y su cambio, por paises, 1970, 1980, 1986," p. 2. In fairness, it should be pointed out that per capita income declined in 22 of the 25 countries south of the border in the same period (1980–1986), though Mexico's rate (9 percent) was significantly higher than the average (5.7 percent) for Latin America as a whole; inflation estimate from Cody, op. cit.; the actual figure for 1986 was 105.7 percent (*Progreso Economico y Social 1987*, p. 359; unemployment data, Cody, op cit.; the 1980 estimate of those employed in agriculture was 37.8 percent—again, considerably higher than the average for all of Latin America that year (32.4 percent), cf., *Progreso Economico y Social 1987*, p. 98.

8. *1986 Britannica Book of the Year* (Chicago: Encyclopaedia Britannica, 1986), p. 829.

9. Sanders, *Mexico*, p. 158. Estimate of number of persons coming on the job market each year from Timothy F. Ashby, "For Mexico's Ailing Economy, Time Runs Short," Heritage Foundation Backgrounder paper, June 4, 1987, p. 3. The most important of the positive signs: gradual rise in oil prices; the government had projected a price of $12 a barrel, and with prices by the fall of 1987 in the high teens, that would give Mexico an oil windfall estimated at $2 billion for the year (each dollar increase puts another half billion dollars in Mexico's treasury); secondly, capital flight has been reversed, at least temporarily: attracted by high interest rates and a booming stock market, about $1.6 billion (of the $30 to $50 billion Mexican nationals have stashed abroad) was repatriated, an equal amount expected to flow back in 1987; the country's reserves, at mid-year 1987, hit an all-time high ($13

billion), an important element in inducing international bankers to re-schedule the debt and pledge $14.4 billion in new credits. Sources: *The Economist*, op. cit., pp. 9–10; Ashby, p. 9.

10. Sanders, *Mexico*, p. 147.

11. Cited in *The Economist*, op. cit., p. 20.

12. "Soviet KGB Meddles in Canada and Mexico," *West Watch*, December 1984–January 1985, p. 3.

13. *Mexico 2000: A Look at the Problems and Potential of Modern Mexico*, anthology published by the Council for Inter-American Security, Washington, D.C., 1980, pp. 61–62.

14. Ibid., p. 62.

15. "Soviet KGB Meddles in Canada and Mexico."

16. Williams Branigin, "Patrol Alerted Along Border With Mexico; Islamic 'Hit Squad' Report Cited," *The Washington Post*, July 26, 1987, p. A-21.

17. "U.S.-Mexico Border: Gateway for Terrorists," *West Watch*, May 1986, p. 8.

18. "Illegal Immigration: Cost to U.S. Taxpayers," *West Watch*, November–December 1983, pp. 1, 3.

19. Jay Matthews, "L.A. Schools to Run Year-Round; Response to Influx of Immigrant Children Symbolizes Growing Crisis," in *The Washington Post*, Oct. 14, 1987, p. A-3. The year-round plan is to go into effect in July 1989. Overcrowding is not, however, a factor in the predominantly Anglo neighborhoods of the city's San Ferando Valley, prompting some parents and community leaders there to threaten to pull their schools out of the Los Angeles system.

20. T. R. Fehrenback, *Fire and Blood: A History of Mexico* (New York: Macmillan Publishing Company, 1973), pp. 376, 401. Sanders also points out that at the time of the U.S. annexation, fewer than a hundred thousand persons inhabited the lands between Louisiana and San Francisco—and most of them were Indians, p. 154 (*Mexico*).

21. Sanders, *Mexico*, p. 167.

22. *The Economist*, op. cit., pp. 19–20.

23. Sanders, *Mexico*, op. cit., p. 166.

24. Fehrenbach, *Fire and Blood*, pp. 473–474.

25. The poll was conducted in August 1986 by the Mexico City daily *Excelsior*, and reported in the October–November 1986 issue of *West Watch*, p. 4. As *West Watch* observed, *Excelsior* is not only Mexico's largest

newspaper, but "is considered a mouthpiece for that country's ruling Institutional Party of the Revolution." The survey was conducted by a left-of-center firm called Grupo Con Ciencia.

26. Waller, "Mexico: The Achilles Heel of NATO."

27. J. Michael Waller, "Soviet Policy in Middle America, 1919–1964: A Coherent Agenda Succeeds," unpublished study, December 1984, p. 8.

28. Esther Wilson Hannon, policy analyst, "Why Mexico's Foreign Policy Still Irritates the U.S.," Heritage Foundation *Backgrounder* No. 383 (September 26, 1984), p. 4.

29. "Mexico and Contadora," *West Watch*, June–July 1985, p. 6. *West Watch* attributed the quote to an unnamed Mexico newspaper. Interestingly, too, *The Economist* describes Mr. Bartlett as "virulently anticommunist," adding: "It is likely that the only good thing he thinks has ever come out of Cuba is its cigars . . ." op. cit., p. 18.

30. Hannon, "Why Mexico's Foreign Policy," p. 3.

31. Ibid., p. 5.

32. Michael Elliott, "The Shadow of the Past: A Survey of Mexico," *The Economist*, Sept. 5, 1987, p. 20. And those years (1979–1982) were ones in which Mexico was pumping subsidized oil into the floundering Nicaraguan economy.

33. Marvin Alisky, "Revolutionary Mystique: Central America's Big Brother," *National Review*, June 28, 1985, p. 29.

34. Fehrenbach, *Fire and Blood*, p. 630.

35. Riding is cited by Ashby, op. cit., p. 4. He also notes that Jorge Diaz Serrano, a federal senator and director general of PEMEX, the government oil monopoly, was accused of embezzling $34 million. Top labor leaders, particularly of what *The Economist* described as the "corrupt, ruthless and venal oil workers union," have been implicated in thievery of comparable proportions. The Lopez Portillo data is from Sanders, *Mexico*, p. 48.

36. "Mexico Moves to Salvage Its Economy," *West Watch*, August 1986, p. 3.

37. *The Economist*, op. cit., pp. 10–11. That publication reports that, on paper, at least, "privatization" (a term the Mexicans will not, for "political reasons," use) is moving ahead swiftly: of those 1,155 entities in which the state had investment at the beginning of the de la Madrid government, only 500 remain. But, as the magazine points out, the statistics conceal a good deal of paper-shuffling (consolidating various enterprises, counting ones in which the government's share was small to begin with, etc.), and "the big fish" (the huge energy industry, the state-run airline, the biggest banks) remain in government hands.

Mexico: The Smoldering Volcano

Ashby, in his Heritage Foundation study, refers to "the pretense of divesting parastatal(s)," and gives as one example of caricatures of the process the sale in February 1987 of 34 percent of the stock of two major banks. "Most of these shares, however, were sold beforehand at bargain prices to insiders and supporters of the ruling ... PRI." (Ashby attributes the quote to *The New York Times*, February 23, 1987. As to GATT, *The Economist* reports Mexico plunged in with enthusiasm, while keeping its "patrimonial" (oil, gas, etc.) and infrastructure industries outside this opening of its markets to the outside world. Melanie Tammen, "Deja Vue of Policy Failure: The New $14 Billion Mexican Debt Bailout," *Heritage Foundation* Backgrounder #588, June 25, 1987, p. 11. Tammen adds that debtor governments, such as Mexico's, "will modify their policies only if continued pursuit of these policies leads to economic breakdown threatening the ruling parties and elites. If Mexico and similar countries are rescued, they will continue their suicidal policies."

38. *The Economist*, op. cit., pp. 15–16.

39. Paula R. Wisgerhof, "Mexico's Many Faces," *The Heritage Foundation Backgrounder* #581, May 19, 1987, p. 2.

40. *The Economist*, op. cit., p. 14.

41. William A. Orme, Jr., "Mexico Taps Economist for Presidency; Budget Director Has Guided Reconstruction; Victory Expected," Mexico City-datelined story in *The Washington Post*, Oct. 5, 1987, P. 1-A. While Mr. Salinas may yet bring a new sense of realism to the conduct of Mexico's fiscal—and foreign—policies, the method of his selection bodes ill for hope of a true reform of the political system. In August 1987, the PRI, in a much ballyhooed move, claimed to be "opening" the system to broader participation by announcing a slate of six candidates, and then parading them before the party's leadership to offer what amounted to "campaign" speeches. A story in *The Los Angeles Times* ("Mexico Ruling Party Picks 6 Candidates; PRI Breaks With Tradition, Planning Forums For Contenders," Aug. 15, 1987, Part I, p. 3) reflects, in its hyperbole, the mania of major media for wanting to give leftist Mexico the fullest possible benefit of the doubt. The first paragraph of that story described the move as "a sharp break from tradition." A measure of the genius of many political scientists is contained in the same story, which quotes Samuel del Villar, "one of Mexico's leading political scientists," as saying: " 'The move is significant because it eliminates the possibilities of surprises.' " Except as a charade, a break it was, a sharp break it was not; nor did it, in the slightest, eliminate surprises. Mr. Salinas was, in none of the speculation we have been able to uncover, given more than a slim chance of being selected. That a man *The Post* (Orme, op. cit., p. A-18) would describe as "relatively unpopular among party regulars" would be selected only underscores how intact

239

remains the old system of the *"destapado"* (or uncovered one), or *"dedazo"* (putting the finger on) whereby the outgoing president "uncovers" or "fingers" the man who will be the new president.

42. Stock market reaction from "Mexico's Anointed Heir," in *The Economist*, Oct. 10, 1987, p. 46. Cardenas candidacy from William Branigin, "Mexican Challenges Ruling Party; Dissident To Run for President," a Mexico City-datelined dispatch in *The Washington Post*, Oct. 17, 1987, p. A-19.

43. *The Economist*, op. cit., p. 17. In advance of the selection, he offered another: history indicates that there is little sense in trying to predict who the next president will be in advance of the *dedazo*.

44. Timothy F. Ashby, The Heritage Foundation, p. 2. Ashby cites as the source for the GDP output comparisons, James H. Street, "Mexico's Development Crisis," in *Current History*, March 1987, p. 101.

45. Sanders, *Mexico*, p. 192.

7

The Fight for Peace—The War on Honor

There is a chance it [the peace plan] will bring a sort of democracy to Nicaragua. The greater chance is for a muddy compromise that will leave the Sandinista regime in power, mostly unchanged and unopposed. . . .

> —The Economist, commenting on the Arias peace plan, Sept. 5, 1987

What if this Communist regime acts like every other Communist regime throughout history and does not allow internationally supervised free elections—what will President Arias ask the free world to do? I still don't know.

> —President Oscar Arias of Costa Rica, responding to a question concerning probable Sandinista non-compliance with the plan he authored, one month after its signing.[1]

FOR one week those who witnessed it are not likely to forget, a once-obscure Marine Corps officer of modest, field grade rank captured the imagination of the American people. On July 7th, the day he would first testify, *The Washington Post* headlined its story: "Lacking Old Luster, North Returns to Testify. Disclosures of His 'Dark Side' Weaken Credibility of Affair's Most Intriguing Affair."

Whatever luster Oliver L. North, Lt. Col., USMC, may have lacked when he walked into the Senate Caucus Room on that muggy morning, he lacked none of it when he would, on Tuesday afternoon, July 14, finally step down as a witness before the Select Committee of the House and Senate investigating the Iran-*contra* affair. An experienced commentator would write of the drama that would open on that July day, a drama which would rivet millions of Americans to their television sets watching gavel-to-gavel live coverage:

"Then the miracle happened—a reputation was resurrected and a superstar was born."[2]

But it was more than merely the resurrection of a reputation and the birth of a superstar. It was the resurrection of hope that Central America could be saved from communist tyranny, the birth of new opportunities for the Reagan Administration to recover the initiative from those who believed that the issue was not security, nor freedom, but peace—peace at any price.

Those hopes would evaporate in a swamp of indecision and political blunders, the grotesqueries of an enfeebled and aimless administration in the ghastly twilight of its eight-year rule.

Going into North's testimony, American support for the Nicaraguan resistance, the *contras* as their enemies had named them, never climbed much above the mid-30s in public opinion polls. Immediately after Colonel North's electrifying testimony, a *Los Angeles Times* national poll showed voters evenly divided, roughly as many supporting aid to the resistance as now opposed it.

"With the testimony of Col. North, the *contra* cause, the anti-Communist cause, has been given one of its great victories of the decade." Such was the verdict of Patrick J.

Buchanan, until only a few months before the combative Director of Communications for the White House. Buchanan added that North "had left the [Select] committee 'a smoking ruin,'" but that continued success "requires of the White House more of the mindset of Ollie North."[3] (It is one of the awful ironies by now so much built into the way Washington works that it cost slightly more to *investigate* Iran-*contra*—just under $4 million—than was actually diverted to the *contras*— $3.5 million—to carry their fight against the communist enemy.)[4]

That "mindset" had long since disappeared from the senior circles of the Reagan Administration. Instead of the offensive Buchanan (and many others) urged, Ronald Reagan allowed himself to be led into a "peace" plan trap he himself realized was "fatally flawed." Instead of capitalizing on the momentum North had given it, the high command at the White House went to pains to distance itself from North.

Thus, by mid-August, yet another—and perhaps decisive—battle for the minds and hearts of the American people had been lost. The same *Los Angeles Times* national poll showed 48 percent of voters now opposed aid to the freedom fighters, only 34 percent supporting it.[5]

There will be further discussion of official and unofficial Washington's role in the developing calamity in the next chapter. For the present, two sets of headlines suffice to reflect the disarray afflicting the White House:

"Reagan May Seek Interim Aid for Contras"—Aug. 14, 1987

"White House Retracts Hints on Contra Aid"—Aug. 15, 1987

"Reagan, in Reversal, To Back Arias Plan; OAS Speech to Reflect Conciliatory Approach"—Oct. 7, 1987

"Reagan Says Arias Plan Insufficient; President Tells OAS Soviet, Cuban Forces Must Leave Nicaragua"—Oct. 8, 1987[6]

The White House march into the swamp of indecision had

actually begun long before. For months, Washington was rife with reports that Michael Deaver, former deputy chief of staff at the White House and a long-time confidante of First Lady Nancy Reagan had, together with the First Lady, concluded that the correct course for the final years of the Reagan presidency was to position the president as an apostle of peace. The ultimate payoff: a Nobel Peace Prize, and a place of honor in a pantheon of heroes. Admission to that mystical pantheon has, for many years, been very much dominated, around the world, by "progressives." It has, for many years, been equally clear that these "progressives" place a much higher premium on peace than they do on such other values as liberty, freedom or human dignity. (The White House would sharply and bitterly deny the Nobel-at-any-price rumors when they seemed to surface at mid-October 1987 in a campaign speech made by presidential candidate Pat Robertson; by contrast, advance press reports of a book written by Deaver and scheduled for 1988 publication, strongly reinforced the validity of the reports.)[7]

In the aftermath of the December 1987 Washington Summit with Soviet General Secretary Mikhail Gorbachev, there is a good chance that Ronald Reagan will, indeed, win that Nobel Peace Prize, or, more likely, share one with Gorbachev. Of the sixteen Americans to win (or share) the Peace Prize since its creation in 1901, few, however, would be widely remembered today as architects of anything resembling real peace. The last American individual to win the prize (share it, actually), was Henry Kissinger, for his role in negotiating the end of the Vietnam war. But Kissinger was uneasy about the validity of the award even as it was announced, because he knew that without the ability to enforce the peace agreement, it was little more than a scrap of paper. His apprehensions were confirmed, all too soon: the fighting did not stop, and within two years, not only Vietnam, but Cambodia and Laos had fallen to communist enslavement. Within six months of receiving the prize, Kissinger returned it to the Nobel Committee.[8]

Virtually no one believes Ronald Reagan was guided in his talks with Mikhail Gorbachev by motives other than a sincere desire for peace. Yet, it is equally clear that in those talks, ringing rhetoric about supporting the freedom fighters notwithstanding, Reagan devoted no more than 15 seconds to the subject of the massive Soviet military support to the Sandinistas. The only discussions of Nicaragua were both not only inconclusive but so cryptic that White House insiders later couldn't agree on what actually had been said. (The Soviets later had no qualms about clearing up the confusion: the notion that Gorbachev might have offered to cut off his Sandinista comrades was, Moscow said, "at odds with reality.")

The president's reticence to press Gorbachev on the subject during many hours of summit conversations is all the more baffling because of what he must have known going into the talks. On October 25, 1987, Major Roger Miranda Bengoechea, for five years the head of the secretariat of the Sandinista Defense Ministry and thus privy to the innermost secrets of the regime, defected to the United States. In extensive "debriefing" sessions with the CIA, Miranda provided not only chapter-and-verse detail, but numerous documents revealing the existence of secret protocols between the Soviets and the Sandinistas to build Nicaragua into an armed fortress state on a staggering scale without precedent in the history of Latin America. Yet, during a stroll in the Rose Garden, and again at a brief exchange at lunch, the president not only made no recorded mention of the startling intelligence, he also declined to press Gorbachev either to clarify the general secretrary's vague remarks on the subject of future Soviet arming of the Sandinistas. One senior aide described Reagan, instead, as "antsy" at the time about progress on follow-up arms negotiations.[9]

* * *

What is beyond dispute is that an unmistakable course correction occurred in the Reagan White House following the ouster, early in 1987, of White House Chief of Staff Donald Regan, National Security Adviser Admiral John Poindexter, Colonel North and others in the wake of the Iran-Contra disclosures. By early May of 1987, *The New York Times* would report that the administration would mute its calls for military aid to the freedom fighters. The *Times* described the new direction as a "repositioning" which would place greater emphasis on diplomacy. "Under the new approach, the officials said, Mr. Reagan will stress that his goal is a diplomatic solution," the *Times* reported. With more than a touch of smugness, a liberal senator, Dale Bumpers (D-Ark.)—never a friend of the Nicaraguan freedom fighters—would write: "First, Frank Carlucci and Howard Baker Jr., his national security adviser and chief of staff, respectively, are pragmatists who see Nicaragua as a quagmire, that the president should get out of." ("Pragmatist," is, of course, the code word liberals use to describe people on the other side whose views are not so terribly different from their own.)[10]

Thus it was that the first fateful step would be taken on July 22 when Tom Loeffler, a former congressman from Texas and then the White House lobbyist on aid for the Nicaraguan resistance, would meet with fellow Texan Jim Wright, the new Speaker of the House of Representatives.

"You know, Mr. Speaker," Loeffler was quoted as saying, "one of the things that's a new revelation to me is all this talk about a diplomatic track. The President is sincere about the diplomatic track."

The report continues: "Wright perked up. 'Is the President really sincere?' he asked, sounding both pompous and oily. Loeffler's answer was yes. 'Tom,' said Wright, 'you show me there is sincerity, and I'd like to pursue it.' "[11]

What would ensue over the following weeks—almost in oblivious ignorance of the public opinion turn-around produced by Ollie North—was a tragedy of errors compounded by crass political miscalculations. The biggest one: that Wright, who had always opposed aid to the freedom fighters, could be "tricked" into joining forces with the White House.

On August 3, a draft written almost entirely by Wright was shown to the president. It called for specific moves toward genuine democracy in Nicaragua, while Sandinista-Contra talks went forward for a cease-fire to go into effect September 30, the date U.S. aid to the resistance would expire. Learning of it at that eleventh hour, Defense Secretary Caspar Weinberger raised strenuous objections, particularly because among the glaring loopholes in Wright's plan was failure to curb the massive Cuban-Soviet military aid and presence in Nicaragua. His objections led to a White House paper containing 21 points reflecting its interpretation of the plan. (Domestic policy adviser Gary Bauer, one of the few surviving conservatives around the president, also objected that under the plan, the president agreed to say nothing on the issue while cease-fire talks were going on—but there was no such restraint on Congress.)

The leaders of the Nicaraguan resistance, in Washington at the time, weren't shown the plan until August 4, the day before was announced. On August 6, Nicaraguan President Daniel Ortega demanded direct negotiations on the plan between Managua and Washington. Secretary of State George Shultz said no, there must be multilateral talks. (On August 7, charging that the White House's 21 points were not part of the deal, Wright repudiated the plan. Press reports, nonetheless, continued to refer for weeks after to alleged commitments binding on the Administration under the Wright-Reagan plan as though it still existed.)

Meanwhile, 1,800 miles southeast of Washington, the foreign ministers of the five Central American nations had been meeting July 30 and 31 in Tegucigalpa, the capital of Honduras. Before them was a regional peace plan presented to them by their colleagues in the so-called *Contadora* group— Colombia, Mexico, Panama and Venezuela. That document was, in turn, a modification of a peace proposal originally put forward by Costa Rican President Arias in February—the one Reagan had called fatally flawed because it would cut off support for the *contras* before the goals of internal "reconciliation" and democratization had been met by Managua. By July 31, the ministers had modified it to require national reconciliation talks within 30 days of the signing with "all unarmed political opposition groups and with those who are willing to give up the armed struggle." That would seem to compel the Sandinistas to do what they had said repeatedly they would never do: meet with the *contras*.

With agreement on an eleven-point plan, the ministers then moved on to Guatemala City for a summit meeting of the five Central American presidents. That meeting, which began August 5 with intense debate, was given a sudden—and dramatic—impetus by Secretary Schultz' endorsement of multilateral talks.

On August 7, the five presidents announced agreement on the revised Arias plan. Ironically—as we have seen in chapter 5—the crucial compromise was put forward by the man whose country risks the greatest loss under the plan: Jose Napoleon Duarte, president of El Salvador. Going into the night of August 6, Duarte said that on each point the vote was four to one—the four other Central American presidents on one side, Nicaragua's Ortega on the other. Then, Duarte—who had balked at the plan previously—offered that key compromise: that all of the main provisions would go into effect at the same time, on November 7, or 90 days after signing. That meant that the Sandinistas would be free to make the internal changes required—or not make them, since the plan makes no provision for sanctions or penalties of any kind—without the military threat from the *contras*. The advantage to the Sandinistas was obvious: so long as a "peace" process was allegedly underway, there was no chance that the U.S. Congress would provide any new monies for the *contras*—

and September 30 was the cut-off date for previously-authorized funding. Thus, the Sandinistas could gamble that with a few token gestures, they could buy time for themselves while the only force capable of forcing a true political opening in Nicaragua was left to twist in the wind, forgotten and unfunded. It was a gamble the Sandinistas would win—easily.

Why did Duarte switch?

A *Washington Post* reporter would write: "Only last month Duarte, in his fourth year as president, was avoiding reporters. His popularity was at a low ebb, polls showed. His U.S. backed Christian Democratic government was under attack as corrupt and bureaucratic, and the leftist guerrillas were showing new muscle . . ."

The Los Angeles Times, noting that Duarte faced legislative elections in May 1988 and presidential elections a year later, headlined its story: "Duarte Gets Needed Boost From Regional Peace Plan."[12]

Among the plan's major features:

- political talks between governments and their *un*armed opponents;
- a return to full electoral democracy in each country. (The only country which did not then enjoy full electoral democracy was Nicaragua. By acceding to the clause, the four democratically-elected presidents fell into a semantic trap, knowingly or not: equating their democratic governments with the totalitarian government of Nicaragua. Besides, the Sandinistas made it plain straightaway that they had no intention of advancing the date for elections not scheduled in their country until 1990. As a further demonstration of their cynicism, Nicaraguan President Ortega told an audience just a month after signing the pact that Nicaragua didn't need reforms, because his country already was democratic.)[13]
- cut-off of foreign aid to guerrilla forces. (Although nominally this is supposed to mean that the Sandinistas, and

Cubans, will stop supporting the Salvadoran guerrillas, the practical effect—and the only part, indeed, which seemed to interest not only the Sandinistas but international onlookers—was that the United States would abandon, cold turkey, its *contra* allies. The plan imposes no restraints on foreign aid to sitting governments, which means that the biggest suppliers of military aid in the region, the Soviet Union and Cuba, went right on arming their Nicaraguan satellite—on a stepped-up basis, at that. Of course, it also meant the United States could go right on arming the Salvadorans. Although the distinction is usually ignored in press commentary, it will not be here: the Soviets supply the Sandinistas in order to enable them to consolidate their totalitarian grip on government. The United States supplies arms to the Salvadorans in order to enable a democratic government to defend itself against communist attack aimed at seizing power forcibly;

- a ban on the use of any nation's territory by guerrillas of another nation. The practical effect, again, is to get the *contras* out of Honduras. History has shown how easy it is to enforce compliance with agreements in open societies (Honduras, for example), how virtually impossible it is in closed police states (Nicaragua, for example);[14]
- a region-wide cease fire;
- a general amnesty for all political prisoners, including anti-government combatants who agree to lay down their arms;
- creation of a new Central American parliament, beginning in 1988. (Though no one had any notion what it would do or what its powers might be, except that it would be patterned vaguely after the European Parliament, a largely-ceremonial and immensely-expensive entity. Interestingly, no provision was made, either, for paying for the new parliament.)

It was a plan hatched in haste, as long on grandiose promises as it was short on the means to achieve them, mired from its very inception in the quicksand of cynicism on all sides, the triumph of guile and gullibility and gall over reason and righteousness. Predictably, the United Nations hailed it; less predictably, the Nobel Peace Prize committee made a shambles of its own rules and even of its sense of decorum in awarding its Peace Prize to President Arias. In so doing, the committee joined in the worldwide delirium of "progressive" hosannas to a peace which had not happened, and if it did, would leave tyranny untouched, and silence the guns only of those fighting for freedom.

Writing in the Fall 1987 issue of *Foreign Affairs*, Susan Kaufman Purcell observed that "peace in Central America will depend on the resolution of a number of significant ambiguities in the revised Arias plan. . . ."[15] She understated the problem.

The "plan" was not even three months old, indeed, when the rot of sly temporizing would seep in. "Give peace a chance," came the cry when it was realized that freedom had, under this plan, died still-born amid empty gestures and farcical posturing.

But, then, how could it have been otherwise, when President Arias, the principal author, admitted he didn't expect that the only true villains of the piece—the Sandinistas—would really comply anyway (and, besides, he had his own fish to fry: Arias hoped, in vain, as it would turn out, to stem the tide of refugees fleeing into his land).

To make matters worse, there was considerable evidence that—to quote a *Washington Post* analyst—"at the very end of the road that Oscar Arias wants the hemisphere to go down as an alternative to American military intervention in Nicaragua lies, crazily enough, American military intervention in Nicaragua. . . ." Describing it as "a very long shot," Stephen S. Rosenfeld added: "But he [Arias] has stated in at least a few quarters that if the Sandinistas finally do not comply with the commitments they have undertaken in the Central American peace plan, then he will consider invoking the hemisphere's basic security charter, the Rio Treaty, and asking for American intervention. . . ."[16]

Duarte, the man of the great compromise, looked to this dramatic moment on history's stage to shore up his sagging political fortunes. It would then be oh-so-little noticed when Duarte would himself be the first to jettison the very essence of that great compromise: "simultaneousness," the proposition that both democracy and peace would arrive on the same date, November 7. (The deadline was later amended to read November 5; the plan was drafted in such haste that no one bothered to consult a calendar before announcing that 90 days from August 7, date of the signing, would arrive on November 7.)

November 5 came and went with precious little in the way of moves toward an authentic democracy in Nicaragua, and even less in the way of peace in the region. In all three countries with insurgencies—Nicaragua, El Salvador and Guatemala—the shooting wars only escalated. But military aid to the *contras* had ended, as a pusilanimous and doddering Administration allowed itself to be maneuvered into quietly shelving its plans to ask for $270 million in new *contra* aid. Instead, the Administration agreed to postpone that request until at least after the first of the year, caving in still later on a bid to obtain $30 million needed to keep the contras a viable fighting force at least through February 1988. Congress, meanwhile, moved to assure the certain death of the freedom fighters: on December 9, 1987, the House voted 215–200 to ban the administration even from seeking military aid from other nations. Ironically, that vote came amid the euphoria of the Reagan-Gorbachev summit, when the subject of massive Soviet military supplies to the Sandinistas was barely mentioned.[17] And, the administration's about-face on fighting for even meager military support for the *contras* came just as reports in even the liberal media would grudgingly acknowledge freedom fighter successes.[18]

* * *

With the November deadline less than a month away, seeing that nothing of real consequence was happening, November 5th no longer seemed important to Duarte—nor to anyone else. *The Washington Post* reported:

> As the plan evolved, its Nov. 5 deadline went from being the last day to comply with the accord to being the first. . . .[19]

Instead, Central Americans—and official Washington—began talking about January 5 as the date for measuring progress on democracy. The part that would remain unchanged was the death sentence for the *contras*; no more aid for them, came the argument on all sides, let's give peace a chance. (Although the plan did not require it, Duarte suggested no such similar cut-off of the vastly-greater American military aid to his country, in order to "give peace a chance.")

Guatemala's Cerezo—like Duarte and Arias, a Christian Democrat "progressive"—could scarcely lag behind in such a sanctimonious exercise. Accordingly, he bought into the charade that the handful of guerrillas moping about in his country were the moral or military equivalent of the *contras*, so as to reinforce the hoax that a democracy under siege is really the same as a dictatorship under siege. (Duarte had, of course, bought into that same lie. But in his case, there might at least be the justification that the bloodletting was of such magnitude that, no matter who was right or who was wrong, he should grasp at the straw that the Sandinistas might actually cut their umbilical to the Salvadoran guerrillas in return for getting their own way at home.) Azcona, the Honduran president, tried at first to put up a stern front, but outflanked, marooned—and, most of all, nervously eyeing an undependable but indispensable support system called the United States—he, too, eventually caved in.

Indeed, how to blame any of them when the key, the real key, was not in their hands at all. On the one side, they faced in their midst a military juggernaut supported unflinchingly by the Cuban-Soviet axis, forces which had shown time and time again that they had the will and the resolve to see a fight through to the finish. On the other side, an ally which not only clearly had lost the cohesiveness, the will, to "pay any price, bear any burden, meet any hardship, support any friend, oppose any foe, to assure the survival and success of liberty," but which, since John F. Kennedy had uttered those words, had, in fact, abandoned one friend after another when the going got too tough. If the one nation capable of making the crucial difference could no longer be counted on, then how to blame those who, alone, could never hope to prevail?

Nor was the blame in Washington limited to the White House. Congress, which from the very beginning showed it had neither stomach nor vision for the struggle, would first hog-tie Ronald Reagan in December 1982. That was the date the Congress passed the first of what ultimately become five "Boland" amendments, named for Rep. Edward P. Boland (D-MA). That one prohibited giving military hardware or advice to the *contras* "for the purpose of overthrowing the government of Nicaragua." The next one, in November 1983, limited aid to $24 million. Boland 3, in October 1984, would become the centerpiece of the charges against Ollie North and his confederates at the National Security Council and elsewhere in the government: no government funds could be spent on behalf of the Nicaraguan resistance by the CIA, the Pentagon, or agencies involved in intelligence agencies. Boland 4, passed in August 1985, ladled out a measly $27 million in "humanitarian" aid. Boland 5, in November 1985, authorized what former Assistant Defense Secretary Richard Perle would describe as "Praise the Lord and pass the communications:" the U.S. could share intelligence data with the *contras* and supply communications support—but no military assistance.

The result of these measures, Perle observed, was to create "tin-cup diplomacy"—the United States panhandling countries such as Brunei to keep the resistance alive. (Ultimately, of course, it would lead to the diversion of funds from the sale of military hardware to the Iranians in order to raise funds for the *contras*, the central theme of the celebrated joint committee hearings.)

Viewing this grotesque spectacle, Patrick Buchanan wrote: "If the letter of the Boland Amendment was not violated [by Ollie North and Poindexter], its 'spirit' merited contempt. For the Boland Amendment was rooted in malice; it was a calculated, cold-blooded congressional act to abandon to their communist enemies thousands of Nicaraguan patriots who had taken up arms, at the urging of the United States, to expel Moscow's Quislings from Central America. . . ."[20]

By 1985, even state governors were inserting themselves into foreign policy decisions. That year, California's George Deukmejian, a Republican, refused to allow 450 California National Guardsmen to take part in combat training in Honduras. Next, the governor of Maine nixed training for his Guardsmen in Panama. When, in 1986, Rep. G.V. (Sonny) Montgomery (D-MS) added a rider to an appropriations bill stripping governors of the right to veto an overseas Guard assignment on policy grounds, Gov. Rudy Perpich (D-FL) refused to allow units of the Minnesota Air Guard fly to Honduras and, joined by ten other governors, went to court, arguing that the amendment violated the separation of powers. A federal judge overruled him, and the states appealed.[21]

The first deadline under the Arias plan was easily met: a meeting, within 30 days of signing, of the five foreign ministers with their counterparts from the four Contadora countries, plus four Latin American "support" nations to agree on verification procedures. Verification was to be the business of "national reconciliation committees" within each country (that one was easy, because in the one country where it mattered—Nicaragua—it was doubtful the committee would have any real power anyway) and, more importantly, of an international commission. That commission was to be made up of the 13 foreign ministers who met in Caracas August 22, 1987, plus the secretaries-general (or their representatives) of the United Nations and the Organization of American States. It would be nearly two months later, with only three weeks remaining until what was supposed to be the moment of truth, the November 5 deadline, that it would be noticed there was no commission because there was no money to set up one.[22] Into that breach would rush the United Nations which, though financially strapped itself, dispatched a team to Central America to discuss mechanisms for monitoring the shooting wars—but not for monitoring progress on democratization. Nor, of course, was a U.N. team the same thing as the "international commission" envisioned in the plan.[23]

That November 5 was, as indicated, to have been the crucial one: no compliance, no plan. But, as that deadline neared with little in the way of concrete results, both Duarte and Azcona, visiting Washington, began waffling, placing greater emphasis on the most distant deadline: January 5. Later, that, too, was pushed back, to January 16th, when the five presidents were to meet anew, this time in Costa Rica, to evaluate the findings of the international commission by then belatedly on the job. The presidents would then determine whether the agreement was working. (Yet another "deadline" had come and gone without anyone taking particular notice of it: The commission was to render its first report 120 days after signing, or the first week of December. But with Washington aglow with Summit fever—the Reagan-Gorbachev missile talks—there was no outcry.)[24]

Once the August agreement had been signed, Ortega stopped in Managua long enough to brief his comrades, then headed immediately for Havana and a meeting with his Cuban patron, Fidel Castro, ostensibly to seek the Cuban dictator's "support" for the agreement.

As indicated at the outset of this chapter, the plan's principal author, Oscar Arias, did not really expect the Sandinistas would comply.

"The purpose of my initiative is to give the Sandinistas a chance, to get rid of the excuse that they won't advance toward democracy because of the *contras*." Though he didn't know what might be done if the Sandinistas failed to comply, he was clear about something else, aid to the one force which could compel the Sandinistas to negotiate, the freedom fighters.

"I would never be in favor of that," he said.[25]

Yet, though skeptical of Sandinista compliance, Arias never could bring himself to condemn the much vaster avalanche of Soviet arms into the only truly bellicose and menacing nation in the region—neighboring Nicaragua.

On October 13, 1987, the Norwegian Nobel Committee announced that the 1987 Nobel Peace Prize would go to Oscar Arias Sanchez, for his "outstanding contribution to the possible return of stability and peace to a region long torn by strife and civil war." The statement hailed him as "a strong spokesman for democratic ideals, with freedom and equality for all." It was later learned that the 46-year-old Arias had not even figured on a short list of finalists for the prize, and that he had received only one nomination, and that one after the February 1 deadline. (Arias was nominated by Swedish legislator Bjorn Molin; virtually all of the other 93 nominees—individuals and organizations—were supported by dozens of nominations and letters of support.) Explaining the committee's surprise decision, chairman Egil Aarvik said: "We are not operating the committee in a vacuum. We have windows on the world. We read newspapers and watch television."[26]

Informed of the award, House Majority Whip Tony Coelho (D-CA) said the prize spelled the end of aid to the freedom fighters.

"This kills it; it's dead," Coelho said.

President Reagan—making a belated bid to rally support for the resistance—plainly got the same message. He, at first, limited himself to a dry: "I congratulate him." Rep. Jack Kemp (R-N.Y.), one of the strongest battlers for freedom fighter aid was less circumspect: "They [the Nobel committee] ought to save the peace prize until they see what happens in the future." But then Kemp was less circumspect from the beginning; on August 13, he urged Reagan to junk his plan and disregard the Arias plan because it is "not a path to peace but, I'm afraid, to appeasement." He said the president ought to fight for $270 million in new funding for the *contras*.[27]

If—as *The Washington Post* reported early in September 1987—the Administration seemed to be losing its grip on the Nicaraguan situation, it lost its footing, as well, in a series of events in November. The wily Nicaraguan President Daniel Ortega cut short his pilgrimage to Moscow (for the celebration of the 70th anniversary of the Russian Revolution) and flew into Washington one week after peace and democratic openings were supposed to have already happened. There, he sprung his trap, in a November 12 meeting with *Washington Post* editors: he proposed indirect cease-fire talks with the *contras* that would involve Speaker Jim Wright and Cardinal Miguel Obando y Bravo. The next day Wright—who had only a week before declined such a role, and the cardinal, who had agreed only to come to Washington to hear Ortega out—were corralled by Ortega. Ortega presented them with an 11-point peace proposal of his own, the effect of which was to cloud even further the already-foggy Arias plan. The nub of Ortega's plan: a month-long cease fire to begin December 5th. During that time, the *contras* would have to go to one of three zones with a total area of 10,000 square kilometers (6,200 square miles). All U.S. aid would have to cease; the now-surrounded resistance would receive clothing, food and medical supplies from a mutually agreed-upon neutral agency. Those *contras* who agreed then to lay down their arms would be given amnesty and allowed to participate in the political process. Talks on the plan would have to be held in Washington—not Managua (nor, as Ortega would insist afterward, anywhere in Central America, either). "Mr. Ortega," *contra* spokesman Bosco Matamoros said, "wants us to surrender on the Washington stage; we want a serious dialogue in Nicaragua." Later, when the freedom fighters finally got a chance to present their own cease-fire proposals, the Sandinistas rejected them out of hand.[28]

At the same moment Ortega was unveiling his peace plan in Washington, the Sandinistas launched what was described as a major offensive against the now-weakened *contras* inside Nicaragua. The offensive reflected Ortega's statement before leaving for Washington that the Sandinistas would deal with the resistance "with billy clubs and bullets." *The Washington Post* reported that "western observers said the Sandinistas seem to be pursuing a strategy of trying to dismantle the rebels through a combination of peace initiatives designed to choke off their U.S. aid lifeline, an amnesty program aimed at whittling down their numbers and battlefield actions to deplete their supplies. Specifically, the offensive is seen as an effort to get the *contras* to use as much of their ammunition and supplies as possible while U.S. military aid to them is suspended."[29]

The administration at first reacted angrily, branding the Ortega-Wright talks "unbelievable melodrama" and an "exercise in guerrilla theater" that dealt "a serious setback" to the peace process. Susan Kaufman Purcell, director of the Latin American Project at the Council on Foreign Relations (generally leftish on most international issues) was blunter:

> Until House Speaker Jim Wright decided to play an active role in the cease-fire negotiations between the Sandinistas and the *contras*, the Sandinistas had been on the defensive, which had forced them to make important concessions.

Now, thanks to the behavior of the speaker, the focus of attention has shifted from the conflict inside Nicaragua to the conflict within the U.S. government. The result may well be the destruction of the *contras*, the undermining of the Central American peace plan and the eventual consolidation of the Sandinista dictatorship in Nicaragua. . . .[30]

Wright lamely defended his role as a surrogate Secretary of State by saying he did not need permission to talk with "friends from other countries." He also hoisted the Administration on its own petard: He had not, he said, forced himself into the peace process, but been invited in by the administration, back in June. The next day, after an acrimonious meeting at the White House at which President Reagan reportedly berated Wright, the administration caved in: Secretary of State Shultz and Wright appeared at a joint press conference where they said the bickering involved misunderstandings over tactics and had been patched up. Both Shultz and Wright urged Cardinal Obando—wary about being used as a mere cat's paw, without real power to influence the talks—to accept the mediation role.[31] The Cardinal reluctantly accepted, and flew off to San Jose, Costa Rica to receive the *contra* peace proposals. (*Contra* leaders, a few days earlier, were again turned back when they attempted to fly into Managua to present their proposals there.)[32]

For Ortega and the Sandinistas, his Washington gambit was a smashing triumph. The Sandinistas were already under heavy pressure from the other four Central American presidents to bargain with the *contras*. Their own mis-managed economy was not only under increasing strain, but they were being pressured by the Soviet patrons to put their fiscal house in order. Further, the *contras* were showing greater strength in the countryside, aided by a population ever more embittered toward their communist rulers. In one series of dazzling maneuvers, Ortega succeeded in deflecting attention away from the Sandinistas and carrying the battle to the one place where it mattered most: Washington. In November of 1987, as in the past, in a Washington of a liberal-dominated Congress already willing to suspend all disbelief as to the sincerity of the intentions of a communist regime, in a Washington of a gutted administration, grand-standing succeeded even more than it had in the past. The deeds of a dictatorship were no longer on trial; on trial were the deeds of the U.S. and the other democracies involved.

While El Salvador's democratically elected legislative assembly was voting to grant amnesty so generous that left-wing groups protested it would cover even common criminals, the Sandinistas continued to make a mockery of that requirement of the peace process as well. Well past the agreement's deadline, they freed 985 of the 7,000–10,000 political prisoners in jail. Only a handful of those freed were from the ranks of former National Guard soldiers held since 1979, many without trial, their only crime that of having served as soldiers in their country's army. Nor were those released amnestied, only paroled—which meant they retained their criminal records. Full amnesty—like lifting of the five-year-old state of emergency—would take effect, the Sandinistas said, only when the international verification commission had certified that the *contras* were receiving no aid from either Honduras or the United States. Once again, there were no protests from the signers, from official Washington, even though the Arias plan required full and unconditional amnesty for all political prisoners, except those convicted of heinous crimes. The Sandinistas also made it plain that state security prisons, where they held an estimated 1,500 or more prisoners, were off limits to human rights groups and verification commissions, and that those inmates would not even be considered for release.[33]

That same Sandinista strategy of continuing to talk while yielding little of real consequence had paid off handsomely for them during the prolonged and inconclusive Contadora "peace" process. It was working again.

The Sandinistas could afford to hang tough. In fact, there were at least three good reasons why they knew they had little to fear from the "peace process":

(1) Even if permitted to operate in an atmosphere of genuine freedom, the political opposition inside Nicaragua was badly fragmented: 15 parties, including 11 legally-registered. So badly-divided among themselves they were that they could not even agree on a single candidate to represent the opposition on the four-member National Reconciliation Commission theoretically supervising the cease-fire and democratization processes. As a result, Ortega was able to name his own choice, Mauricio Diaz Davila, a 37-year-old law school dropout who headed a small left-wing splinter group which broke away from the Social Christian Party. Diaz, a lifelong politician, joined two Sandinistas on the commission, headed by an authentic independent: Miguel Cardinal Obando y Bravo.

Political dialogue—against a backdrop of continuing official harassment—broke down at the very first meeting, October 8, when the government refused to seat more than four opposition representatives (the opposition wanted to seat 14).[34] Nor was this the first such failure; two previous attempts at political dialogue since October 1984 also ended in failure. By mid-December 1987, political dialogue collapsed in the rubble of hollow words, when it became clear to the entire political opposition that the Sandinistas had no intention of allowing anything vaguely resembling genuine democracy to operate in the country.[35]

(2) Much more importantly, the Sandinistas kept a firm grip on the real mechanisms of power, the armed forces and state security, the bureaucracy. (Referring to such "reforms," one of the nine Sandinista comandantes earlier had said: "We repeat until we are exhausted that the political, economic and

social system of Nicaragua is not a subject for discussion and negotiation.")[36]

(3) Time is against their only serious rival for power—the *contras*. The Reagan Administration was able to wheedle no more than $6.7 million in non-lethal sustenance money to tide the *contras* over after the September 30 funding cut-off. The top *contra* military leader, Col. Enrique Bermudez, was asked point-blank in the wake of the peace plan signing how long his men could survive without renewed U.S. aid.

"Let's say," he said, "a couple of months."

(Late in October 1987, the leadership of the Nicaraguan Resistance, as the combined civilian-military command was now called, was reported meeting secretly in Miami to discuss a phased-out withdrawal of the 12,000 men deployed on Nicaraguan soil. However, in late November, yet another report claimed that stepped-up air drops had provided the resistance with munitions and provisions sufficient to keep them in the field and able to fight "well into" 1988. That report seemed to fly in the face of the administration's half-hearted attempt to squeeze $30 million in provisional aid which it said was needed to sustain the *contras* as a viable fighting force through February 1988. For reference purposes, it is useful to observe that it cost more than $30 million to respond to the takeover late in 1987 of the Atlanta federal penitentiary. Even more to the point: by late 1987, Soviet arms shipments to the Sandinistas amounted to $30 million every two weeks.

As though to echo that, the top Democrat in the House—Speaker Jim Wright—said a few days later that he had seen "signs of good faith" from the Sandinistas, but not from the Reagan Administration.[37]

Still later, in the wake of published reports of Sandinista-Soviet plans to put 600,000 Nicaraguans under arms—one in every five men, women and children in the country—a spokesman for the speaker brushed off the reports. "I'm sure the people eager to continue the war will find (Miranda) useful," the aide was quoted as saying. "But I don't think it will have any significant impact." The same report said "Democratic aides said that the Soviet role in Nicaragua is already well known, and it is not surprising that the Sandinistas want a greater Soviet military commitment." Still other Democrats in Congress reacted to this spectacular display of Sandinista-Soviet contempt for the "peace process" by saying that the solution was for Ronald Reagan to negotiate directly with the Sandinistas.[38]

Those "signs of good faith" which Speaker Wright purported to see were not detected by the people involved—the ones lucky enough to be able to vote with their feet. Two months into the "peace process," the flood of Nicaraguan refugees streaming across Nicaragua's southern border into Costa Rica reached a record peak. The irony, as a *Washington Post* reporter wrote, was that "the exodus came as President Oscar Arias, who recently won the Nobel Peace Prize, is busily promoting a regional peace plan that he wrote in part to lessen the flow of Nicaraguan exiles into Costa Rica." Ordinary Nicaraguans would demonstrate vividly in yet another way how much confidence they had in the "peace process." Late in November, rumors spread that the U.S. would celebrate Thanksgiving by handing out hundreds of visas to enter the U.S. More than 2,000 persons lined up at the Embassy in Managua before dawn before learning, dejectedly, that the reports were untrue. Said one woman, refusing to budge: "Maybe God will soften their [American] hearts, and they will give us a Thanksgiving gift."[39]

Ronald Reagan said repeatedly during the fall of 1987, as he had so often in the past, that he would "never abandon" the freedom fighters. His deeds did not reflect his words—even before the summit. It would be early October before the president revealed his thoughts on the Arias peace plan and aid for the *contras*. His words were ringing: The peace plan, he said, was "a positive movement . . . a step in the right direction." But, he added, it "does not address U.S. security concerns in the region because it does not require the departure of Soviet-bloc and Cuban troops from Nicaragua." The president said he intended to ask Congress for $270 million in aid over 18 months for the *contras*—but that the money could be converted to humanitarian purposes if true democratic reforms were undertaken in Nicaragua and the *contras* were "allowed to contest power politically without retribution."

"We cannot forget," the president told the Organization of American States meeting, "that there already exists a negotiated settlement with the Sandinistas that predates the Guatemala plan—the settlement of 1979, in which this organization, in an unprecedented action, removed recognition from a sitting government, the government of Anastasio Somoza, and helped bring the Sandinistas to power. As part of that settlement, the Sandinistas agreed to implement genuine democracy with free elections and full civil liberties. . . .

"We know now that the Sandinistas never intended to carry out those promises. Just a few months later, the Sandinistas met in secret and drafted what has come to be known as 'The 72-hour Document,' in which they spelled out their plans for building another Cuba in Nicaragua. . . .

"The Sandinistas must learn that democracy doesn't mean allowing a rally to take place and then arresting those who take part—it means hundreds of such rallies, free from harassment, either by the secret police or by what the Sandinistas call the 'divine mobs.' Democracy doesn't mean opening one newspaper and one radio station—but opening them all. Democracy doesn't mean releasing a few political prisoners—but all 10,000 of them, some of whom have been imprisoned as long as eight years. Democracy doesn't mean selectively granting temporary freedoms in order to placate world opinion—but permanent, across-the-board human rights, guaranteed by a constitution and protected by the checks and balances of democratic government. . . .

"Ultimately—and this is the most important lesson of all—democracy means returning power to the hands of the people. . . ."

The same day the president spoke—in a move calculated to upstage him—the U.N. General Assembly expressed by acclamation its "firmest support" for the peace agreement signed two months before.[40]

Speaking before the General Assembly the next day, Ortega launched what one newspaper described as "a scathing attack on Reagan," blaming the president "personally" for what Ortega claimed were 40,000 killed or wounded in the Nicaraguan fighting. In that same speech, he warned that *La Prensa*, the one and only opposition newspaper which had been allowed to reappear only a few days before, could be closed if it "starts to defend the Reagan policy" of aid to the resistance. He also made it plain the Sandinistas had no intention of granting amnesties to what he claimed were 2,000 still-imprisoned former National Guardsmen and 2,000 captured rebels—as called for in the peace plan. He also repeated a press conference statement made the day before: the November 5 deadline did apply in one area: "It is," he said, "simply a fact that if aid continues to flow to the *contras*—even if it is aid already in the pipeline—it would violate the agreement, which says specifically there should be a total cessation of outside aid. If on November 7 [sic], the president of the United States does not declare an end to all direct or indirect *contra* assistance, then we would be under no obligation because there would be none of the simultaneity that the United States says is crucial to effective implementation of a peace agreement. . . ."[41]

* * *

Ortega might have saved his wrath. As *The Washington Post* reported a week later: "Reagan and his senior advisers. . . . reacted to the Central American plan with a confusion that tilted increasingly toward hostility. But [Speaker Jim] Wright moved into the void and became the broker who blessed the agreement. He encouraged the Central Americans to go forward. . . . and pointed the way for Congress to push *contra* aid into the background with the argument that the peace process first should be given a chance to succeed. While that was happening, the administration has shown an inability to get a grip on the situation and put its imprint on the unfolding process. Instead, it consistently has sent mixed signals. . . ."

The echoes of the president's stirring speech before the OAS had barely subsided when the administration quietly retreated again, saying it would delay its request for more *contra* aid until "sometime around Thanksgiving."[42] By mid-November, all but token *contra* aid was on indefinite hold.

Alfredo Cesar, who gave up a prestigious and lucrative job as the president of Nicaragua's Central Bank, breaking with his former comrades, the Sandinistas, to join the resistance, directed an eloquent public appeal at that same time:

"The United States should provide the resistance with non-lethal aid for the next 18 months to prevent the Sandinistas from dragging their feet . . . Lethal aid should be provided if the Sandinistas do not comply with the accord by November 7—including a cease-fire negotiated between them and the resistance, as defined by the president of Costa Rica.

"I believe this is a real chance for peace with democracy. The Nicaraguan resistance has made its contribution by forcing the Sandinistas to sign the Central American peace plan. Now it is up to the United States to prevent another betrayal of the Nicaraguan people's aspirations. History will judge who gave peace a real chance. . . ."[43]

* * *

On January 20, 1981, Ronald Reagan became President of the United States. The serious policy issues that immediately confronted the new administration included a weak economy and continuing Soviet occupation of Afghanistan. Yet no problem was more urgent than the grim situation in Central America. Nicaragua was pursuing its massive military build-up and assisting the spread of terrorism throughout the region, with the result that the total strength of the armed Left in El Salvador, Honduras, Guatemala, and Costa Rica had grown from about 1,450 in 1978 to almost 8,000.[44] In El Salvador, the FMLN rebels had launched their "final offensive" just ten days earlier, prompting President Carter to offer to resupply the embattled government with ammunition, the first such aid since 1977.

The offensive was beginning to slow down when Reagan took his oath of office. There was, however, no reason to believe that the war was over—Nicaragua and Cuba could be expected to continue the arms supply.

By January 1981, the Carter administration could no longer ignore its own intelligence reports.[45] Those reports revealed that arms shipments from Nicaragua to El Salvador had sharply increased during the months and weeks preceding the final offensive. The Nicaraguan government provided planes and pilots for many shipments; additional loads travelled by land and sea. On the day the offensive was launched, the Sandinista *Radio Managua* broadcast: "A few hours after the FMLN General Command ordered a final offensive to defeat the regime established by the military-Christian Democratic junta, the first victories in combat waged by *our* forces began being reported."[46]

The fighting in El Salvador represented just one manifestation of a larger war that was international not only in origin but in objective. "The foreign policy of the Sandinista People's Revolution is based . . . on the principle of revolutionary internationalism." Thus went the official party line, as articulated at a secret Sandinista party gathering in September 1979. Said one Salvadoran guerrilla commander, "This is not just a Salvadoran revolution. . . . After we triumph here we will go to Guatemala and offer our proletarian brothers the benefit of our experience. . . . Eventually we will fight in Mexico."[47] Sandinista Interior Minister Tomas Borge, the last surviving founder of the FSLN, was asked in a 1983 interview, "Then will you respond to the general thrust of [U.N. Ambassador Jeane Kirkpatrick's] remarks that Nicaragua is the first domino in Latin America? That since the revolution triumphed here, it will be exported to El Salvador, then Guatemala, then Honduras, then Mexico?" His reply: "This is one historical prophecy of Ronald Reagan's that is absolutely true!"[48]

This was well understood by the new Secretary of State, Alexander Haig, who wrote later that during the early days of the Reagan administration, he had advocated "bringing the overwhelming economic strength and political influence of the United States, together with the reality of its military power, to bear on Cuba in order to treat the problem at its source."[49] This position was not shared by others on the cabinet, however. Although Haig did meet Cuban Vice President Carlos Rafael Rodriguez in Mexico City to clarify U.S. concerns, the United States did not attempt to take decisive action to cut off the arms supplies to Central America.

Haig was frequently criticized for imposing an East-West analysis on El Salvador's "local" problems. It was as though nothing had been learned since July 1979, when President Carter responded to the Sandinista triumph by telling Americans it would be a mistake to worry about "secret, massive Cuban intervention."[50]

That it was anything but a mistake was reflected in the February 1981 State Department White Paper entitled "Communist Interference in El Salvador," a summary of some of the information that had been compiled by U.S. intelligence sources. Cuba and the Soviet Union, it said, were engaged in a "well-coordinated, covert effort to bring about the overthrow of El Salvador's established government and to impose in its place a Communist regime with no popular support." The liberal critics attacked the report with a vengeance, characterizing it as pure propaganda, even accusing the State Department of fabricating its evidence. Oddly, they hadn't paid any attention the previous month, when, during the final offensive, Jimmy Carter's ambassador to El Salvador—no friend of the Reagan team—had said in a press conference that the FMLN objective "is to install a Marxist-Leninist dictatorship in this country. . . . The kind of Government that they would install in this country, in my opinion, would be totally subject to the Soviet Union, along the Cuban style."[51]

Two months after the publication of the White Paper, Hans Jurgen Wischnewski, a representative of the (non-communist) Socialist International, confronted Castro with the State Department evidence. Then, and again in September, Castro confirmed the department's allegations by conceding that Cuba had supplied arms to the Salvadoran guerrillas.[52] Several years later, Haig's successor, George Schultz, gave an accurate assessment of the East-West element: "When Cuban pilots fly Soviet helicopters, it is not the United States that is injecting the East-West conflict into Central America."[53]

Within eight days of the Sandinistas' coming to power, the United States had sent them 732 tons of food and a large supply of medicine.[54] At that very same time, a number of top FSLN leaders were in Havana honoring Castro on the anniversary of the beginning of his revolution.[55] The United States offered to reinstate a Peace Corps program in Nicaragua to help with reconstruction and to provide teachers, but the Sandinistas rejected the offer. They also rejected a Costa Rican offer to send teachers, while gladly accepting a similar offer from Cuba.[56]

By September 1979, the government that the Reagan administration is said to have alienated in 1981 was secretly referring to the United States as the "rabid enemy of all peoples."[57] Two months later, President Carter asked Congress for $75 million in emergency aid "to restore confidence, private initiative, and popular well-being in Nicaragua." Already there were then about two hundred Cubans "performing military and security functions in Nicaragua," according to journalist-author Shirley Christian.[58] Congress approved the aid the following May, but only after requiring the President to certify that Nicaragua was not "aiding, abetting, or supporting acts of violence or terrorism in other countries." This Congressional approval came after the March visit of Sandinista officials to Moscow, where they initiated a military relationship with the USSR and established formal ties between the FSLN and the Soviet Communist Party.[59]

Notwithstanding mounting evidence of Sandinista aid to the Salvadoran rebels, President Carter certified in September 1980 that Nicaragua had met the requirement of nonintervention. Thus, the United States was sending economic assistance to the Sandinistas even as they were arming the Salvadoran guerrillas for the "final offensive," and forging close ties to Moscow as well as Soviet-surrogate Fidel Castro. Of course, they denied any involvement. They even claimed to be intercepting arms shipments to El Salvador (originating, it was said, in Costa Rica). When the United States confronted Nicaragua with the evidence of its sponsorship of airborne supply operations to El Salvador, the Sandinistas insisted they were taking "strong measures" to prevent the "funny business" at the two Nicaraguan airfields involved.[60]

These are the circumstances under which the new Reagan administration informed the Nicaraguan government that U.S. aid would be withheld until there was evidence that Nicaragua had ended its support for subversion. Even when the economic aid was formally suspended on April 1, 1981, the Sandinistas were told that it could be renewed if circumstances improved.

At the time of the aid cut-off, the United States had led the world in providing economic assistance to Nicaragua, contributing over $118 million while encouraging other nations to do likewise. As noted by Christian, "It was the hard-currency help from the United States and other Western nations that kept [the Nicaraguan] government afloat."[61]

The termination of economic assistance did not mean the end of U.S. efforts to find mutually acceptable terms for maintaining a peaceful coexistence with Nicaragua. In August 1981, after the Sandinistas had expressed concerns over a then-hypothetical threat from militant Nicaraguan exiles presumed to be seeking support in the United States, Thomas O. Enders, the Assistant Secretary of State for Inter-American Affairs, presented the Sandinistas with a five-point proposal. Under its terms, both the U.S. and Nicaragua would publicly renounce intervention in Central America. The U.S. would ensure that the activities of Nicaraguan exiles in the United States would not pose a threat to Nicaragua; Nicaragua would cease its military build-up; U.S. economic aid would be renewed. The two countries would also expand cultural ties.

Enders' meeting with the FSLN leadership has been described by subsequent defector Arturo Cruz, who was then serving as Nicaraguan ambassador to the United States:

His message was clear. . . . His government did not intend to interfere in our internal affairs. However, "you should realize that if you behave in a totalitarian fashion, your neighbors might see you as potential aggressors." My perception was that, despite its peremptory nature, the U.S. position vis-a-vis Nicaragua was defined by Mr. Enders with frankness, but also with respect for Nicaragua's right to choose its own destiny. . . . When the conversations concluded, I had the feeling that the

U.S. proposal had not been received by the Sandinistas as an imperialist diktat. However, nothing positive developed.[62]

In October 1981, the proposal was rejected as "sterile." The Sandinistas renewed their claim that the Nicaraguan government was not supporting the FMLN guerrillas in El Salvador. Yet, just a few weeks earlier Comandante Bayardo Arce of the Sandinista National Directorate had said to the U.S. charge d'affaires in Managua that the United States "had better realize that nothing you can say or do will ever stop us from giving our full support to our fellow guerrillas in El Salvador.[63]

Defining the U.S. Role

The war in El Salvador raged on while American leftists proclaimed that Nicaragua was a victim of U.S. bullying. The Salvadoran government clearly needed help. Its economy was in critical condition, its army poorly trained and undisciplined. Meanwhile the guerrillas grew in strength as the arms flow continued. The Reagan administration sent aid: $150 million in fiscal 1981, double the amount of the previous year. Of that, $35 million was military aid, and fifty-five U.S. military advisers were sent to train the Salvadoran army, triggering cries of "another Vietnam!"

This effort to paralyze American foreign policy was epitomized by an April 1983 passage in *Time*:

> If only we were more willing to accept "change," more self-critical of our own past sins in the region, less hung up on communism—if only we could bring ourselves to live with the Sandinistas and encourage a "dialogue" between guerrillas and government in El Salvador. Yes, we would have more leftists running countries in the hemisphere, but those countries are too weak, too poor, too desperate for our help to become

273

genuine Soviet stooges, unless of course we drive them into the Soviets' arms as we did Castro.[64]

Interestingly, American journalists were out of step with their counterparts in Latin America. A study of press treatment of El Salvador in the fall of 1981 shows a wide divergence in outlook between North American and South American newspapers. Political scientist Walter C. Soderlund and journalist Carmen Schmitt write in *Journalism Quarterly* that

> the South American papers portrayed the Salvadorean junta, and especially the United States, positively, while critical of the FDR/FMLN [the guerrillas], Cuba, and Nicaragua. North American papers, on the other hand, were quite negative with regard to the performance of the junta and more positive than negative with regard to the FDR/FMLN.[65]

Their figures are revealing. Press coverage of the Salvadoran guerrillas portrayed them negatively in over 61 percent of the articles in South American papers but in less than 14 percent of those in North American papers. The role of the United States received a favorable press in South American papers over 59 percent of the time; in North American papers the corresponding figure was 2.1 percent.

It is a tribute to the grit of the people of El Salvador—and the determination of the Reagan administration at that time—that a fully functioning democracy would emerge amid the smoke of battle.

One of the more persistent criticisms of Reagan in the press and elsewhere was that he was "militarizing" the Central American situation—or "seeking a military solution." Those claims persisted despite the fact that while Soviet aid to Nicaragua has been overwhelmingly military, most U.S. aid to the region has been of the economic variety. In fact, during fiscal years 1982–85, economic assistance accounted for 78 percent of all U.S. aid to Central America.[66] Most of the military aid has gone to embattled El Salvador, where it eventually helped secure the military defeat of the rebels (reducing them to sabotage and urban terrorism). The remainder of the military assistance went largely to Honduras, defending its long border with Nicaragua.

In Honduras, however, U.S. military aid was less important than the U.S. military presence, which increased dramatically under the Reagan administration. On July 20, 1983, Pentagon officials announced a series of military exercises to be conducted jointly with the armed forces of Honduras. Though the United States had been conducting joint maneuvers with Latin American nations for many years, the new exercises were to be on a larger scale than ever before, clearly indicating to Nicaragua how the United States could be expected to respond to open aggression should the Sandinistas attempt it.

The first major exercises, which began in August 1983 and lasted several months, were followed by others; twenty-four thousand U.S. troops would eventually take part, and about one thousand American troops would remain stationed in Honduras. (A military exercise in May 1987, in which 7,000 American soldiers made a mock landing at the Honduran port of Trujillo, reportedly left the Nicaraguans "nervous." That exercise was cited by some as a factor inducing the Nicaraguans to sign the peace agreement a few months later.)[67]

For Honduras, the military partnership with the U.S. meant the building of airfields and roads, in addition to radar stations and other exclusively defense installations.

About the time the Honduran exercises were announced, the CIA drew up plans to help the anti-communist Nicaraguan resistance fighters increase their strength to twelve thousand or more, while the Pentagon spoke of increasing the number of U.S. advisers in El Salvador. The effects of these announcements were visible within days. The House of Representatives, mesmerized by the argument that to help the *contras* fight for freedom in Nicaragua was to commit American troops in the near future, voted on July 28, 1983 to cut off CIA covert funding to the resistance. The House refused even to make the termination conditional upon Nicaraguan behavior vis-a-vis the Salvadoran rebels. The vote was not binding on the president, but it advertised the unwillingness among Democrats, and a few Republicans, to take a firm stand. Castro's reaction to the Reagan initiatives came one day after the congressional vote, when he declared that he would stop sending military aid and advisers to the region if the United States would reciprocate.[68] Thus the policies that were successful abroad were resisted at home.

In order to reduce the partisan element in the foreign policy debate, President Reagan took yet another step in July 1983: he appointed a National Bipartisan Commission on Central America, chaired by Henry Kissinger, to study the problems of the region and offer long-term policy advice. The commission's report, which appeared in January 1984, called for immediate, dramatic increases in American aid, both military and economic. The president approved, and Congress was persuaded. Annual U.S. economic aid to Central America increased from $186 million in 1980 to over $800 million beginning in 1984. The funds were used for health programs, housing, food and agricultural assistance, employment programs, humanitarian relief, and education. Military aid, on a much smaller scale, was also increased, with the reluctant approval of Congress.

The Kissinger Commission submitted its report just as another assistance program was getting started. The Caribbean Basin Initiative, dubbed a mini-Marshall Plan, offered preferential trade arrangements to the countries of Central America and the Caribbean. Allowing certain products to enter the United States duty-free for twelve years, the program has made some progress in creating jobs and expanding private sector development. By mid-1986, there were twenty-two participating countries.

The Reagan administration's critics who advocated a non-military "solution" were put on the defensive by the bipartisan Kissinger Commission Report as to the source of the violence in Central America:

> Whatever the social and economic conditions that invited insurgency in the region, outside intervention is what gives the conflict its present character. . . .
>
> Propaganda support, money, sanctuary, arms, supplies, training, communications, intelligence, logistics, all are important in both morale and operational terms. Without such support from Cuba, Nicaragua and the Soviet Union, neither in El Salvador nor elsewhere in Central America would such an insurgency pose so severe a threat to the government. With the victory of the Sandinistas in Nicaragua, the levels of violence and counter-violence in Central America rapidly increased, engulfing the entire region.

The commission also saw through the argument that a "good neighbor policy" toward Nicaragua could persuade the Sandinistas to promote democracy as they had promised. "Because the Marxist-Leninist insurgents appeal to often legitimate grievances," wrote the commission,

> a popular school of thought holds that guerrilla leaders are the engines of reform. They characteristically reinforce this by inviting well-meaning democratic leaders to participate in a Popular Front, taking care, however, to retain in their own hands a monopoly of the instruments of force. If the insurgents were in fact the vehicles for democratic and social progress, the entire security issue would be moot; they would no longer be the problem, but rather the solution.
>
> Unfortunately, history offers no basis for such optimism. No Marxist-Leninist "popular front" insurgency has ever turned democratic *after* its victory. Cuba and Nicaragua are striking examples. Regimes created by the victory of Marxist-Leninist

guerrillas become totalitarian. That is their purpose, their nature, their doctrine, and their record.[69]

The Diplomatic Front

The Reagan administration's determination to deal realistically with the Sandinistas' use of armed force did not entail reluctance to pursue a diplomatic settlement. The United States sent no fewer than forty-nine diplomatic missions to Central America between 1981 and the announcement of the Arias peace plan.[70] The United States joined Belize, Colombia, El Salvador, Honduras, and Jamaica at the Costa Rican-sponsored San Jose Conference of October 1982, which formulated a set of guidelines for the promotion of a lasting peace in Central America. The United States also supported the Contadora talks, although not without considerable ambivalence. At the request of the Contadora Group, the United States engaged Nicaragua in nine rounds of talks between June and December, 1984.

The Contadora process, named for the island off the Pacific coast of Panama where the first meetings occurred, was created at the instigation of Mexico in early 1983, but it was not until July that Nicaragua could be persuaded to participate in any multilateral negotiations.

In September 1983, the Contadora participants produced a Document of Objectives, identifying twenty-one essential ingredients for peace. These objectives included the termination of military hostilities, reductions in foreign military advisers and equipment, controls on armaments and troop levels, the termination of support for insurgencies, dialogue between governments and their armed opposition, and open, competitive elections throughout the region. The document also called for procedures to monitor compliance with any agreement that might ensue. The key elements which might have restrained the Sandinistas—reductions in foreign military advisers, controls on armaments, dialogue with armed opposition—all of these would go by the boards by the time the Arias peace plan would be put forth. None survived in that plan.

By mid-1986, the Contadora process had produced several draft treaties but no agreements. The Sandinistas consistently refused to approve any treaty with realistic provisions for verification. They endorsed a draft of September 1984 that lacked such provisions, only to reject every subsequent version that contained them. They also opposed effective provisions to establish arms ceilings or ensure free elections at home. At meetings held in Panama in April 1986, Nicaragua again refused to bargain on arms limits. The frustration of the participants who sought to negotiate in good faith was expressed by Rodolfo Castillo Claramount, the Vice President and Foreign Minister of El Salvador, who said on April 7, "Nicaragua rejected everything, everything that was presented to it. There is nothing left to talk about."[71] Two days later, President Arias of Costa Rica wrote,

> In Panama the true situation was made very clear. Twelve Latin American Foreign Ministers, among them the Foreign Ministers of four Central American countries, supported the prompt signing of the [Contadora] Acta in accordance with international opinion. Only Nicaragua was opposed, thus demonstrating once again that it has neither a true interest in, nor the will for, peace in Central America.[72]

That experience did not cause Arias to lose faith in the Sandinistas. Instead, in crafting the peace plan the presidents finally would sign, he would simply eliminate all the binding features which the Sandinistas had found objectionable.

In February 1986, at the request of the Contadora nations, the United States agreed to resume bilateral talks with Nicaragua on the condition that the Sandinistas open discussions with the Nicaraguan armed resistance. They refused to do so then, as they had before, as they have ever since.

As the Contadora talks were taking place, the Sandinistas were supplying hundreds of tons of arms to the Salvadoran rebels,[73] and mounting guerrilla invasions against Honduras (July 1983 and July 1984), Costa Rica (April 1985),[74] and Colombia (one of the Contadora sponsors—November 1985).[75] In fact, by 1986, Sandinista-sponsored subversion had reached nearly all of Latin America.[76]

The Contras

A great *contra* leader would write the following:

> . . . *After four years of fighting one of the world's great super powers, our only victory has been to escape total defeat.*
>
> *Even if the rest of the world continues to ignore our cause we will fight on. For we are fighting not only for ourselves but for all mankind. We are fighting for freedom and human dignity and the right to worship the God of our choice.*
>
> *I urge you to tell the world of our plight and send whatever help you can.*
>
> *God bless you for caring enough to read my letter.*

That *contra* leader knew the chances of victory were slim. His name was George Washington. He was writing from Valley Forge, in September of 1779.

"Militarization," in the short-hand of the "progressives," means military support to the *contras*. Yet, as Congressman Jack Davis (R-Il), pointed out, "U.S. aid to the *contras* has been truly piddling, averaging only $33.3 million a year over the past six years."

To put that in perspective, for fiscal year 1988, security assistance given by the U.S. to other governments in the region looks like this:

Jamaica, $51.3 million;

Haiti, $34.6 million;

Dominican Republic, $38.0 million.

None of those three countries is, of course, under attack, much less locked in mortal combat to secure the blessings of liberty.

For comparative purposes, the administration has proposed that the three "frontline" states in Central America receive the following amounts in security assistance in fiscal year 1988:

Costa Rica, $92.4 million;

El Salvador, $319 million;

Honduras, $181 million.

"What we are doing now," says an American analyst, "is something very immoral. We are giving the *contras* just enough money to keep on bleeding and dying in the jungles, without giving them enough to win."[77]

He spoke, of course, when the United States was still giving the freedom fighters anything at all. As in Vietnam, a decade before, the crucial battle would be fought not in the jungles of Central America, but in the even more terrifying intellectual jungles of Washington. On the field of battle, at least they knew who the real enemies were.

Beginning in June of 1985, the chief elements of the Nicaraguan forces of armed opposition were united under a single umbrella organization, the Unified Nicaraguan Opposition (UNO). Headed by a three-member civilian directorate. In March of 1987, one of the three—Arturo Cruz—would pull out, blaming political bickering for his decision to return to the Washington, D.C. suburb of Bethesda, Maryland, and a six-figure job with the United Nations. Regrouping, in May of 1987, a 7-member directorate of a unified front, the Nicaraguan Resistance (NR), was democratically elected by members of a 54-member assembly. A single military command—the Nicaraguan Resistance Army (NRA) —

was organized under the authority of the civilian directorate. The main components of the resistance movement:

- Nicaraguan Democratic Force (FDN), with over eighteen thousand members. Formed from three smaller groups in 1982, the FDN is led by its commander in chief, Adolfo Calero. Enrique Bermudez was its original military commander.
- United Villages of the Nicaraguan Atlantic Coast (KISAN), a coalition of Miskito, Sumo, and Rama Indians and English-speaking blacks from the Atlantic Coast, led by Wycliffe Diego, Raul Tobias, and Roger Hermann. KISAN was formed by the unification of three smaller Indian resistance organizations in September 1985. One of those organizations, MISURA, reached a peak of six thousand armed combatants in 1984, but most of its members are now in refugee camps for lack of military supplies. KISAN now has a fighting force of between one thousand and two thousand.[78]
- UNO-Sur ("UNO-South"), led by Fernando "El Negro" Chamorro and numbering about two thousand.
- Nicaraguan Opposition Coordinator (Coordinadora), a nonmilitary coalition of civic organizations. In 1984, the Coordinadora ran former junta member Arturo Cruz as an opposition presidential candidate before withdrawing from the election in protest. Its member groups include the Nicaraguan Private Sector in Exile, the Democratic Nicaraguan Workers' Solidarity, the Union of Nicaraguan Workers and Peasants, the Committee of Nicaraguan Democratic Workers, the Nicaraguan Democratic Movement, and several others.

The alliance of these groups is sometimes strained by their differing objectives. The Indians, for example, seek to recover their culture and their ancestral lands, and to regain their self-determination within a tribal framework. The other groups have a more ambitious objective: to establish democratic institutions throughout Nicaragua. They are united, however, by their desire to overcome the oppression of communism.*

The armed resistance movement can be dated from late 1979, when small groups of former National Guardsmen started launching attacks against Sandinista targets. These raids were insignificant, however, as the Sandinistas themselves have acknowledged. It was in mid-1980 that Nicaraguan dissidents, and even disaffected Sandinistas, began to take up arms against the new regime, and in 1981 the movement was joined by members of the Indian and black Creole communities.[79]

It was in late 1981, after repeated diplomatic efforts to dissuade the Sandinistas from exporting subversion, that the United States finally began to provide covert support for the armed resistance. The role played by the CIA in delivering this assistance was to become by far the most controversial aspect of the Reagan administration's Central America policy. What critics often fail to acknowledge is that the covert involvement of the United States began only *after* Nicaragua itself had initiated a covert war against its neighbors. By mid-1981, the Sandinistas had forged military and party links with the Soviet Union, built the largest military force in Central American history, plotted with the Soviets to provoke war with Honduras, sponsored terrorism in Honduras and Guatemala, and helped launch the "final offensive" to overthrow the government of El Salvador.

All this was done *before* one penny of U.S. government assistance was provided to the *contras*. Nicaragua even rejected the Reagan administration's offer to obstruct *contra* activities in the United States in exchange for more civilized behavior on the part of the Sandinistas.

The resistance forces include peasants, workers, farmers,

---

* Editor's note: Shortly after this was written, the UNO entered what appears to be a process of reorganization. The outcome is not yet clear.

students, shopkeepers, businessmen, and members of the clergy; Indians, mestizos, blacks, and whites; former members of Somoza's National Guard and former Sandinistas. They span the political spectrum from conservative to socialist. Resistance operations expanded from 1982 through 1985, eventually reaching into more than half of Nicaragua's sixteen departments.

With aid from the United States finally flowing by late 1986, the *contras* were able, at last, to carry the fight into Nicaragua itself, instead of operating primarily as a cross-border raiding force. At least 80 percent of their force—a minimum of 10,000 men—moved out of Honduran holding camps into the Nicaraguan countryside.

The stunning reversal was reflected in a *Washington Post* report in early October of 1987:

"BOCAY RIVER, Nicaragua—When five Sandinista helicopters swooped down on a bluff overlooking this river May 14 with about 70 reporters from Managua, the journalists were shown an abandoned rebel post and a couple of bodies as evidence of the success of an offensive to sweep the insurgents out of this jungle wilderness in northern Nicaragua.

"Now the post is back in the hands of the U.S-backed rebels known as counterrevolutionaries or *contras*, who have made it a lookout position in an area they call *el cuartelon*, or roughly, 'the fortress.'

"A trip from Sept. 24 to Sept. 26 with the *contras* along the Honduran-Nicaraguan border and about six miles into Nicaragua suggested that, for the time being at least, the rebels again have the run of a section of the Coco River and the northern swath of the Bocay River that flows into it. Rebel posts and patrols were a common sight, and *contra* boat traffic motored up and down both rivers apparently unimpeded. . . ."[80]

In the first six months of 1987, the *contras* had 1,360 military contacts with the Sandinistas—a total higher than that for all of 1986. Through July of 1987, they had destroyed 55 military posts and temporary bases of the Sandinista army, 15 bridges, 142 poles and transmission line towers, 83 military trucks, five jeeps and nine pick-up trucks. They also shot down at least five Soviet-made helicopters, including two MI-24s—the "devastating" gunships—one MI-17 and one MI-18. By mid-September, the resistance claimed to have destroyed or damaged 14 helicopters in 1987—a handsome pay-off on aid dollars inasmuch as a Stinger anti-aircraft missile costs $100,000 and a helicopter gunship $15 million. At mid-October, another MI-17—commonly used to transport troops and supplies—was downed during what the Sandinistas conceded was some of the heaviest fighting in the six years of the war. As part of that action, a force of 400 *contras* ambushed an Army convoy 110 miles east of Managua, reportedly suffering heavy casualties themselves while killing 22 Sandinista soldiers, wounding 16 and destroying at least two trucks.

As Congressman Davis would put it: "The fact that *contra* units can penetrate so deeply into Nicaragua without being betrayed by farmers and villagers speaks volumes about the public support. . . . Today the *contras* control an area in Nicaragua larger than El Salvador.

". . . Liberals in Congress have shifted the debate from negotiations for aid to no aid at all because 'the *contras* can't win' . . . [but] there are two important groups who think the *contras* can win: the *contras* and the Sandinistas. . . ."[81]

Ollie North described vividly what it was like for the freedom fighters before U.S. aid was resumed in late 1986:

> This weekend's trip to Honduras and El Salvador was the most depressing venture in my four years of working the Central American issue. There is great anxiety that the Congress will not act in time to stave off a major defeat for the resistance. This sense exists in the governments of Honduras and El Salvador, but most alarmingly is now evident in the resistance itself. . . .

As you know, their most pressing need is for anti-aircraft, but the other things are now running short as well. The entire force is back to one meal per day and no more boots, uniforms, packs, ponchos, or weapons are available for the new recruits. New trainees will be turned away, effective today. All hospitalization for wounded in action will cease at the end of the week. Troops returning to Nicaragua this week will carry only 70 to 100 rounds of ammunition, instead of the 500 that they had been carrying. No new radio batteries are available, so there is no way to pass commands or intelligence. . . .

The picture is, in short, very dismal, unless a new source of bridge funding can be identified . . . we need to explore this problem urgently, or there won't be a force to help when the Congress finally acts.

Warm regards—North.[82]

North wrote those lines in 1986. By the fall of 1987, there was no Ollie North to fight, with all his might, to keep that flickering flame of liberty alive.

So long as its military advantage remained immune to serious threat, the Nicaraguan government consistently rejected all attempts at a negotiated settlement to the conflict. The democratic resistance had been on record since December 1983 as willing to lay down its arms for an opportunity to participate in genuinely free elections, and in early 1985 they proposed reconciliation talks to be mediated by the Catholic Church. But—on those terms—the Sandinistas would not talk. When finally, in the fall of 1987, they would agree to talks, they laid down heavy conditions: (1) the talks could be on a cease-fire only—not at all on basic political conditions; (2) the Sandinistas themselves would not take part in the talks, but work only through intermediaries (specifically, Cardinal Obando y Bravo); (3) they would not agree to talks in Nicaragua, but insisted they be held in Washington.

Throughout this period, the Sandinistas were not seriously molested by penetrating, investigative reporting of their behavior by the mainstream press. The attitude of the press has been described by Latin America specialist Robert Leiken:

> A number of correspondents almost feel they have a policy-making role and weigh what they say in terms of its political effect. I think the press has tended to take a position on this issue, and certain stories get coverage and others don't.
>
> What tends to get coverage are those stories which are embarrassing to the administration. But what doesn't get coverage are those aspects of Nicaragua which tend to confirm what the administration is saying.[83]

Congress took a similar tack. As indicated earlier in this chapter, the first of the "Boland Amendments" was passed in late 1982, forbidding the administration to assist the contras "for the purpose of overthrowing the Government of Nicaragua." A 1983 law placed a ceiling of $24 million on new *contra* aid, regardless of its purpose. In October 1984, all U.S. government aid to the Nicaraguan resistance was cut off (though none had been sent since May). Early the next year President Reagan requested renewed funding, but in April the Democratic-controlled House voted to kill even humanitarian aid to the Nicaraguan freedom fighters. The House was mightily embarrassed, however, by Daniel Ortega's tactless response, which was to jet off to the Soviet Union in search of financial support for his expansionist designs. So in July 1985, $27 million in humanitarian aid was finally approved.

The most important of the arguments against freedom fighter aid were:

- *The contras are mercenaries for the CIA with little popular support.* This charge is absurd. Most of the resistance forces are paid far less than the average monthly wage in Nicaragua, and their growing numbers were the result not of CIA recruitment but of Sandinista policies. Furthermore, unlike the Sandinista army—made up overwhelmingly of young men forcibly conscripted into service—the *contras* were 100 percent volunteers, free to leave any time they chose (as—see preceding section—many did).

- *The contras are a band of thugs dominated by Somocistas and ex-National Guardsmen.* This is equally false. Most of the resistance fighters are in their teens or early twenties, making them too young to have belonged to Somoza's National Guard. The three members of the original UNO Directorate were all opponents of Somoza. Two, Adolfo Calero and Arturo Cruz, were actually jailed by Somoza for their opposition. Both Cruz and the third member, Alfonso Robelo, belonged to the Sandinista governing junta before defecting. As of late 1985, the senior military leaders of the FDN (the largest resistance group within UNO) were 53 percent ex-civilian, 27 percent ex-National Guard, and 20 percent ex-Sandinista (see figure 3).

At the regional command level, the figures are 21 percent ex-National Guard and 43 percent ex-Sandinista. Among the rank and file, less than 2 percent are former Guardsmen.[84]

And, as relates to the Guard, three other points need to be made: (1) Following their victory, the Sandinistas went on an indiscriminate (and well-documented) rampage of executions of captured guardsmen, jailing thousands of others without the nicety of charging them with any specific crimes. Inevitably, this drove many guardsmen into armed resistance; (2) mere membership in the guard—the country's army, after all—could no more be equated with criminal behavior than could all German soldiers during World War II be charged with war crimes just because they served in their country's army; (3) it is quite natural, of course, that a guerrilla organization would draw on the skills and experience of men with military training and experience.

It is often pointed out that the top military commander,

Enrique Bermudez, was a colonel in the National Guard. In fact, he served from 1975–79 as Nicaragua's representative to the Inter-American Defense Board in Washington, D.C. He was serving as military attaché at the embassy in Washington when Somoza fell. The Carter administration thought enough of Bermudez to recommend him to Somoza as a suitable candidate to take over the National Guard upon Somoza's departure.

As for the human rights record, the Nicaraguan opposition is the first guerrilla movement in history to have a code of conduct, carry Red Cross manuals, and operate a human rights commission.[85] The commission is run by the former head of the Nicaraguan Red Cross, Ismael Reyes. As in any civil war, the innocent sometimes suffer and even die. But the number of innocent casualties is diminishing, and several members of the resistance have been tried, convicted, and punished for their crimes. Alvaro Baldizon, former Chief Investigator of the Special Investigations Commission of the Sandinista Interior Ministry, has said that *contra* abuses, unlike those committed by the Sandinista government, "cannot be considered abuses under a directed policy. Rather, they are isolated cases in which some contra members are responsible as individuals." Baldizon testified before a congressional subcommittee that government abuses outnumber *contra* abuses by ten to one. The record would likely improve under the influence of U.S. training.

- *The contras can't win.* They can't, of course, if the U.S. pulls the rug on them. But, before the peace process freeze, the Resistance was more than twice the size of the Sandinista guerrilla force that toppled Somoza, and they reached that strength largely without U.S. help. Further, as indicated above, even with a modest amount of U.S. military aid in late 1986 and into 1987, they were able to carry the war vigorously into Nicaragua itself. Although they obviously could not confront a force many times larger and incompartably better-equipped in frontal battle, they could, given the chance, wage a war of attrition in the countryside, gathering popular support along the way, as has been amply demonstrated. In the process, they could exert steady pressure against a financially-troubled regime.

- *Neighboring countries don't support the U.S. policy.* In fact, many leaders of the region's weak democracies told the Kissinger Commission that they would very much like to see the United States get rid of the Sandinistas. They don't say so publicly because a) the strong nationalism at home doesn't reward politicians who appear subservient to U.S. interests, and b) in recent years, the United States has more than once proved to be an unreliable ally; therefore, to openly support U.S. actions against Nicaragua is to set oneself up as an easy target in the event the U.S. should pull out in a spasm of isolationism. Furthermore, as noted in Chapter 5, public opinion in Central America overwhelmingly supported U.S. aid to the resistance, and was as supportive of them as it was skeptical about the Sandinistas.

- *Aid to the contras will lead to the eventual commitment of U.S. troops.* This argument is made by those who favor appeasement at every turn. As history has shown, appeasers end up either by surrendering without a fight or by committing troops only when it is too late. Whether or not the U.S. must eventually send troops to fight in Nicaragua depends on the nature and scope of Nicaraguan aggression, not on the success or failure of the *contras*. There is no better way to encourage Nicaraguan aggression than to demonstrate a lack of will where the contras are concerned. And there is no surer road to U.S. military involvement.

- *U.S. aid to the contras violates international law.* Since 1979, Cuba and Nicaragua have been engaged in an effort to overthrow the now-*elected* government of El Salvador. According to John Norton Moore of the University of Virginia Law School, "Such actions by Cuba and Nicaragua clearly violate Article 18 of the OAS Charter. . . . Under the provisions of Article 51 of the U.N. Charter,

Article 3 of the Rio Treaty and Articles 22, 27, and 28 relating to self-defense and mutual assistance, the United States has both the right and the obligation to assist the government of El Salvador by defending it against Nicaraguan-based aggression."[86] Gonzalo Facio, a man of unimpeachable moral authority—he served as Foreign Minister of Costa Rica, as well as that country's ambassador to the Organization of American States—has written eloquently and persuasively of the *contra*'s legal and moral right to resist tyranny.[87]

In 1986, the issue came up again as President Reagan repeated his request for a renewal of military assistance. This time a new objection was raised: the *contras* were accused of embezzling some of the $27 million in humanitarian aid made available to them the previous year. This was enough to kill the president's proposal in the House by a vote of 222 to 210 on March 20.

The question was not dead, however. In late May of 1986, Congressman Richard Ray (D-Ga.) traveled to Central America to meet with the presidents of the region's democracies, as well as with Daniel Ortega and the leaders of UNO. He also visited *contra* base camps in Honduras. On June 25, he announced his findings on the floor of the House. "First I traveled to Miami," he said, "where I met with the *contra* leaders. . . ." He continued:

I was allowed without restriction to review in depth the accounting and purchasing procedures of the UNO and their military arm, the FDN—their logistics organization, their human rights organization, their press and propaganda organizations. . . .

My colleagues, this is a larger and better coordinated organization than I had imagined. It has a strongly dedicated group of individuals, including many professionals from all walks of life who are dedicating their lives to the organization in exile—many are serving without remuneration. . . .

There is no doubt, in my opinion, that this group is serious and dedicated to a free democracy in Nicaragua. . . . I want to refer to the records which I examined. I was impressed with the meticulous detail of the records. I reviewed the procedures for purchasing and distributing equipment, food, clothing. . . . the accountability and records are not in the poor shape which we have been led to believe.[88]

That day the House voted 221 to 209 to approve $100 million in aid to the *contras,* of which $70 million would be military assistance. The measure later passed the Senate and was signed into law in the fall.

As imperfect people in an imperfect world, we cannot deny wrong-doing, our own as well as that of others, but there is no good, and in fact much evil, in atoning for the wrong sin. Ours lies not in our attempts to keep what remains of the free world free—we have, after all, never held any nation captive against its own will—but in allowing the Soviets to swallow up nations, one by one, and leaving them to work out their enslavement, preferably without ruffling the free world's conscience.

NOTES

1. "Next in Central America, the negotiable revolution," *The Economist,* Sept. 5, 1987, p. 37. Arias quote from Thomas McArdle, "Kemp Leads a 'Mision Libertad' " to Central America, *Human Events,* Sept. 26, 1987, pp. 10–12. Arias was even more specific in an interview with Morton M. Kondracke, who reported that Arias "made it clear in an interview that he does not think the Sandinistas will comply." "I know the nature of the Sandinista government," Arias told Kondracke, "so I am skeptical." Kondracke, "Who Wants Peace? And the price to be paid," *The New Republic,* Sept. 28, 1987, p. 16.

2. The quote is from veteran television commentator Daniel Schorr in his introduction to *Taking the Stand: The Testimony of Lieutenant Colonel Oliver L. North* (New York: Pocket Books, 1987), p. viii.

3. Patrick J. Buchanan, "Will Reagan Make a Comeback—Or Be a Lame Duck?," *Human Events*, Aug. 15, 1987.

4. Associated Press story datelined Washington, "Hearing Cost to Exceed Fund Diversion," *The Los Angeles Times*, Aug. 13, 1987, p. 30. Those costs—$1.95 million by the House, $2 million by the Senate—do not include police overtime, cost of producing hearing transcripts, or needed construction/alteration work. Nor does that figure include the $1.8 million spent in only the first six months of the investigation by independent counsel Lawrence E. Walsh. He was using in that 35 FBI agents, 29 lawyers, 11 Internal Service agents, 6 Customs Service agents and 73 administrative personnel, working out of offices rented at a monthly cost of $59,808.

5. Lou Cannon, "President to Revive Reagan Doctrine on Rebel Aid; Address This Week to Call for Democratic Deeds by Soviets, Sandinistas, Officials Say," Santa Barbara-datelined story, *The Washington Post*, Aug. 23, 1987, p. A-5. Numerous commentators would point out that while the anti-*contra* forces were gathering strength (much as the forces opposed to the Supreme Court nomination of Robert Bork were gathering theirs), not only was the President away from Washington during that eventual month of August—but so, too, were many senior White House staff.

6. The first two headlines are from *The Los Angeles Times*, both on page one. The first story, by *Times* staff writer Michael Wines, and datelined North Platte, Nebraska—then with the president as he traveled west—quoted "a senior Administration official" aboard Air Force One as describing as "a very real option" an Administration request for aid to the freedom fighters even before a Sept. 30 cease-fire was to take effect. The second story flatly contradicted the first; White House spokesman Marlin Fitzwater even said no new support would be sought "even if it means that the rebels are without funds for several weeks or months" (quoting from the *Times* paraphrase of Fitzwater's statement). To add to the confusion, Fitzwater added that the president remained "steadfast," however, in his support of the *contras*; no explanation was offered to reconcile the contradiction between leaving them high-and-dry without funds and "steadfast" support. The second set of headlines are from *The Washington Post*, both also appearing on page one of that newspaper. Once again, it was not a matter of erroneous or slanted reporting; the first story, saying the president planned a "conciliatory" approach to the Arias peace plan in his OAS speech, was leaked to reporters by no less an authority than National Security Adviser Frank Carlucci. Less is known about what caused the president to take a (relatively) hard line when he actually delivered the speech.

7. For example, one such report noted that Mrs. Reagan "was the driving force behind purging hard-line conservatives from the Reagan administration and nudged President Reagan toward his first meeting with Soviet leader Mikhail Gorbachev." Wrote Deaver: "It was Nancy who pushed everybody on the Geneva summit. She felt strongly that it was not only in the interest of world peace but the correct move politically." From an Associated Press story in *The Washington Post*, Dec. 5, 1987, p. A-5. Those accounts were taken from Deaver's book, *Behind the Scenes*, scheduled for February 1988 publication.

8. Henry Kissinger, *Years of Upheavel* (Boston: Little Brown & Company, 1982), p. 370. Kissinger writes that when, on October 16, 1973, an AP news dispatch announcing the award was handed to him during a meeting of the supersecret Washington Special Actions Group (WSAG), "my colleagues read it with astonishment rather than jubilation; they congratulated me but without real passion. For we were all ill at ease . . . I knew that without the ability to enforce the Agreement, the structure of peace for Indochina was unlikely to last. I would have been far happier with recognition for a less precarious achievement . . ." On Nov. 29, 1973, when it was clear there would be no real peace in Vietnam, Kissinger wrote the Nobel Committee returning the Peace Prize and a sum equivalent to the cash award. The committee refused to accept them. North Vietnamese Politburo member Le Duc Tho, named with Kissinger, had already declined the award. It is interesting to observe that, in contrast with the equally flawed Arias "peace plan" which would gain Arias, the 1987 award, the major U.S. media in 1973 roundly roasted Kissinger for his. *The New York Times*, for example, described it in an October 17, 1973, editorial as "the Nobel War Prize." No such skepticism would be displayed vis-à-vis Mr. Arias and his "achievement."

9. *The Washington Post* quoted top White House sources as saying "Gorbachev spoke only about two sentences on the subject [of Nicaragua], and one official considered it 'a rather cryptic statement . . . a casual comment.' No American followed up, and it remains unknown how serious Gorbachev was and exactly what he had in mind . . ." During the exchanges—which took place on the third and last day of the summit, Thursday, December 10—Gorbachev apparently indicated something to the effect that the Soviets might limit themselves in the future to sending Nicaragua only small arms. Yet, according to White House chief of staff Howard Baker Jr., the exchange "only lasted about 15 seconds and I don't know what he [Gorbachev] meant." While Reagan and Gorbachev were taking their eleven-minute stroll in the Rose Garden and later at luncheon, four Americans and two Soviets were working under the pressure of a 2 P.M. deadline—when the two leaders were to say goodbye—laying the groundwork for later arms agreements. When lunch ended with no word from the negotiators, Baker slipped out to check on progress. According to the *Post*: "Baker

was worried. 'I got an antsy president over here and a jumpy general secretary and how much more time do you need?' he asked [National Security Adviser Colin L.] Powell, according to an informed source." Distractedness and anxiety over arms agreement might, then, explain the president's reluctance to press Gorbachev on Nicaragua. "Superpowers' New Words to Live By: 'As Required,' " Dec. 13, 1987, p. A-31, and "U.S. Calls Managua Buildup 'Direct Threat' to Neighbors," Dec. 14, 1987, p. A-32, both in *The Washington Post*.

10. Gerald M. Boyd, in *The New York Times*, May 3, 1987, as quoted in *Conservative Manifesto* of July 1987, pp. 3–4. The article noted that the new policy "reflected the style of the new White House staff, under Howard H. Baker, Jr.," and marked a departure from the policy promoted vigorously by Patrick Buchanan, who by then had resigned his White House post. Carlucci, of course, replaced Poindexter. Both were named over the vocal and bitter protests of conservatives—but their vocal and bitter protests had been ignored by the White House for a very long time already. The Bumpers quote is from an article he authored: "Reagan must refine Nicaraguan peace plan," *The Los Angeles Herald Examiner*, Aug. 11, 1987, p. A 19.

11. Fred Barnes, "White House Errors Cripple Contra Aid," *The Los Angeles Times*, Aug. 18, 1987, pp. II-5, reprinted from *New Republic* magazine.

12. Data on the Duarte compromise, as well as the following quote about his popularity, from Julia Preston, "Duarte Pledges to Fight Pessimism Toward Pact," a San Salvador-datelined story in *The Washington Post*, Aug. 23, 1987, p. A-21. *The Los Angeles Times* story by Marjorie Miller, also datelined San Salvador, Aug. 16, 1987, p. 1. The risk to El Salvador is greatest because the guerrilla insurgency confronting Guatemala is much smaller, and therefore there is little chance that the insurgents there can, in effect, shoot their way into political power-sharing. The Cuban-backed rebels could not hope to win in either of those democratic countries in open elections. But, in El Salvador, there is that risk. By contrast, the one guerrilla force effectively neutralized under the plan is the one fighting the only government in the region which is dictatorial: the one ruling Nicaragua.

13. Timothy Goodman and L. Francis Bouchey, "A Guide to the Arias Peace Plan," Special Brief published by the Council for Inter-American Security, Washington, D.C., October 29, 1987, p. 1. The authors quote Ortega as saying in San Jacinto, Nicaragua, on Sept. 13, 1987: "We are not discovering democracy now. We discovered it on 19 July 1979, and we are developing it in all of its economic, political and social manifestations in our country." As if to reinforce Ortega, Interior Minister Tomas Borge vowed no political retreat. Goodman and Bouchey quote him as saying: "Let no one harbor illusions that we are going to betray the principles of the revolution."

14. Henry Kissinger—who negotiated the agreement ending the Vietnam war and thus knows, first-hand, the difference between words and deeds in the matter of agreements—has written: "To most Americans, it [the agreement] signaled the end of the war. But the millions in Indochina who had suffered and struggled knew that their freedom was precarious. All too soon, the leaders of North Vietnam showed that the cease-fire was merely a tactic, a way station toward their objective of taking over the whole of Indochina by force. Before the ink was dry on the Paris Agreement, they began to dishonor their solemn obligations; in truth, they never gave up the war . . . the violations were not technical; they were flagrant preparations for a new stage of war . . . the United States kept its word throughout . . ." Kissinger, *Years of Upheaval*, p. 302. There was, of course, an International Commission of Control and Supervision, which, as Kissinger observes, "was supposed to" monitor the cease-fire; the North Vietnamese simply—and systematically—blocked it.

15. Cited by Goodman and Bouchey, "A Guide."

16. Stephen S. Rosenfeld, "The Strange Alternative to Intervention," op-ed column, *The Washington Post*, Nov. 13, 1987, P A-23.

17. The administration did finagle $6.7 million from the Congress in non-lethal aid for the *contras*, but beat a steady retreat from the President's repeated assurances that the U.S. would "never" abandon the freedom fighters in the field. By Sept. 8, *The Washington Post* could crow, in a front-page story, that "many administration officials" believed "events are moving so far beyond U.S. control that Reagan soon may find both Congress and U.S. allies in Central America no longer willing to support the Nicaraguan *contras*" (John M. Goshko, "U.S. Seen as Losing Grip on Nicaraguan Situation"). As late as Oct. 10, Secretary of State George P. Shultz was telling a Chicago audience that the President would press ahead with his request for $270 million for the resistance sometime between the Nov. 7 "peace" deadline and the end of November. On Nov. 10, Shultz told the Organization of American States that no further aid would be sought until 1988. By early December, House Republican leaders torpedoed the more modest $30 million request (John M. Goshko and Helen Dewar, "GOP Puts Off Bid for New *Contra* Aid," *The Washington Post*, Dec. 2, 1987, P A-27). When that happened, the administration scaled down its request to $22.8 million in strictly "non-lethal" aid, arguing that as of mid-December, there would be no more money left to disburse to the *contras*. Instead of buying aircraft to drop supplies to the resistance, the scaled-down proposal envisioned leasing helicopters and/or planes for that purpose, as well as supplying the freedom fighters with food and medicines sufficient to keep them alive for a few months more (Joe Pichirallo, "Administration

to Seek $22.8 Million *Contra* Aid," *The Washington Post*, Dec. 10, 1987, p. A-47).

18. For example, on Nov. 3, Paul Fisher, an American affiliated with the left-wing organization Witness for Peace, reported after fourteen days' captivity with the *contras* that the resistance "owned" the central Nicaraguan province of Zelaya (Julia Preston, "Released American Says *Contras* 'Own' Vast Zone," Managua-datelined story, *The Washington Post*, Nov. 3, 1987, p. A-25). *Post* reporter William Branigin wrote, after a two-day trek in the northern province of Jinotega, that "the *contras* have built a network of informers, couriers, lookouts, food suppliers and medical-support personnel in the area . . ." ("Contras Vow To Fight On," Guapinol, Nicaragua story, *The Washington Post*, Nov. 5, 1987). A few days later, Branigin reported from yet another area, "the trip also indicated that, despite evidence of strong popular support in this area and incipient efforts to develop a political base, the *contras* are still a long way from overcoming one of their primary long-term limitations: dependency on U.S. aid" ("*Contras* Draw The Religious," a story datelined Los Planes de Vilan, Nicaragua, in *The Washington Post*, Nov. 11, 1987). It is worth observing that, once the Congress did approve $100 million in funding to the *contras* in August 1986 and the money began flowing in October, the freedom fighters went over to an immediate offensive posture, moving ten-thousand guerrillas into Nicaragua over the months ahead with what a U.S. diplomat called "near impunity." By contrast, in the year preceding, when all their funding had been cut off by Congress, they were forced to spend most of their time hunkered down in neighboring Honduras. Even that option would now be closed to them should the "peace" plan be fully implemented on the non-Communist side. In the early months of the plan, Honduran President Azcona stood fast, however, to the principle that the *contras* would not be expelled until the Sandinistas had complied fully with the peace plan, and that included a comprehensive cease-fire, full amnesty and lifting the state of emergency.

19. Julia Preston, "On Eve of Peace Pact Deadline, Central American Fighting Intensifies," Managua-datelined story, *The Washington Post*, Nov. 5, 1987, p. A-33. The story was accompanied by a detailed chart covering the five major points of the plan: amnesty; cease-fire; national reconciliation and dialogue; democratic reforms; irregular forces, use of national territory for attacks. The chart, and accompanying story, showed very little of substance.

20. I am indebted to the brilliant former assistance defense secretary for his summary of the five Boland amendments, and "tin-cup" quote (Richard Perle, "America's failure of nerve in Nicaragua," *US News and World Report*, Aug. 10, 1987). Buchanan, former director of White House Communications, "Will Reagan Make a Comeback—Or Be a Lame Duck?" *Human Events*, Aug. 15, 1987, p. 17.

21. "Quis custodiet?" *The Economist*, Sept. 12, 1987, p. 29. As of this writing (December 1987), the appeal is still pending.

22. William Branigin, "Outcome Still Uncertain For Winner's Peace Plan; Funding Absent as Truce Deadline Nears," a Mexico City-datelined story in *The Washington Post*, Oct. 14, 1987, p. 1. Branigin observed that, with less than a month to go before a cease-fire would go into effect, "in one of numerous details the plan seems to have glossed over, no provisions have yet been made to finance such endeavors as an international verification commission." The Contadora nations were Mexico, Panama, Colombia, and Venezuela; the four "support" countries Brazil, Argentina, Peru, and Uruguay.

23. Six UN experts left New York Oct. 22 to discuss with officials how the UN could help with the monitoring cease-fires, military aid to rebel groups and the ban on cross-border havens for insurgents—but not the democratization process itself. Pressed on that point, a UN spokesman said that this issue was likely to be discussed as well ("U.N. Readies Plans in Central America," *The Washington Post*, Oct. 22, 1987, p. A-33).

24. Duarte was the first to waffle on time-tables. During a mid-October state visit to Washington, he urged a hold on aid to the *contras* until January. "We have said, 'Give us a chance; give us this opportunity.' And the maximum time we ask from you is 150 days" (John M. Goshko and Helen Dewar, "Duarte Proposes *Contra* Aid Delay; Salvadoran's Remarks Seen as Blow to Administration Request," *The Washington Post*, Oct. 16, 1987, p. A-26). Azcona, before leaving for Washington, criticized the Sandinistas for bad faith in implementing the agreement and made it plain that for Honduras, Nov. 5 was the now-or-never date. But then, in Washington a few days after Duarte had left, he switched his approach. As *The Washington Post* reported: "Nevertheless, he appeared to be backing away from the impression he gave in an interview with *The Washington Post* last week that his government will not consider itself bound by the agreement if Managua has not complied by the Nov. 7 deadline for implementation of the peace machinery. Instead, he focused on Jan. 7, the deadline for the presidents to decide whether the agreement has been effective as the apparent key date in the process." The *Post* offered no clue to explain Azcona's flip-flop (John M. Goshko, "Azcona Suggests Contra Aid Cutoff Until Pact Compliance Is Assessed," *The Washington Post*, Oct. 22, 1987, p. A-36).

25. Kondracke, op. cit., pp. 16–17. By the time he flew to Oslo to receive his Nobel Prize, Arias had hardened his views on the subject to the extreme of saying that he opposed even humanitarian aid to the Nicaraguan freedom fighters. He supported that opinion by claiming that "everything has changed in Central America" since the signing of his plan. "There is," honoree Arias said, "a new attitude, new behavior, a new environment" (Karen DeYong, "Arias Seeks Halt of all *Contra* Aid," Oslo-datelined story in *The Washington Post*, Dec. 10, 1987, p.

A-41). Arias' views on that subject were, from the start, notably one-sided. One of his first official acts as president was to close down a U.S.-built airstrip in northern Costa Rica used for supplying the Nicaraguan resistance. He also refused to allow a plane carrying Rep. Jack Kemp (R-N.Y.) and a delegation of conservative leaders to land in San Jose if *contra* leader Adolfo Calero were on board. But he had no such compunction about Shafik Handal and other leaders of El Salvador's communist guerrilla forces, who flew into Costa Rica for a meeting with him within a day or two of the Kemp mission (Thomas McArdle, *Human Events*, Sept. 26, 1987, op. cit).

26. Karen DeYoung, "Costa Rican President Wins Nobel Peace Prize; Arias Honored for Central America Effort," an Oslo-datelined story in *The Washington Post*, Oct. 14, 1987, pp. 1 and A-26.

27. Reagan-Coelho-Kemp reaction quotes from Karen DeYoung, "Costa Rican President Wins Nobel Peace Prize; Arias Honored for Central American Effort," an Oslo-datelined story in *The Washington Post*, Oct. 14, 1987, pp. 1 and A-26. The August Kemp quote is from a UPI story, datelined Washington, in *The Los Angeles Times*, Aug. 14, 1987, p. 9, Part I.

28. The Sandinistas first succeeded in shifting even their indirect talks with the *contras* to the Dominican Republic. On Dec. 2, the resistance proposed a forty-day truce to begin December 8 as part of a "political negotiating process." After five-and-a-half hours of talks with both sides in Santo Domingo, Cardinal Obando said the Sandinistas had rejected not only the *contra* proposals, but his own as well. The *contras* not only accepted the cardinal's proposals, but agreed to drop their demands for political concessions as a condition for halting the fighting. The Sandinistas demanded, as they had from the beginning, that the *contras* stop receiving aid from the United States and be denied base camps in Honduras, which the *contras* said they would accept only if the Sandinistas showed good faith and would "begin an irreversible process of democratization" in Nicaragua. From two *Washington Post* articles, William Branigin, "Contras Propose Truce; Indirect Talks are Set," a Mexico City-datelined story on Dec. 2 p. A-27, and Richard Boudreaux of *The Los Angeles Times*, a Santo Domingo-datelined story, Dec. 5, 1987, p. A-21.

29. William Branigin, "Sandinista Army Launches Drives Against *Contras*," Managua-datelined story in *The Washington Post*, Nov. 14, 1987 p. A-23. Details of the Ortega maneuvers in Managua and Washington from the following *Washington Post* stories: a Managua dispatch, Nov. 7, "Nicaraguan prelate Weighs Mediation Role," p. A-17 (reporting on Ortega's "surprise visit" to Cardinal Obando y Bravo's office to invite him to act as intermediary); Michael Secter, "Wright Turns Down Latin

The Soviet Assault on America's Southern Flank

Mediation," Nov. 8, 1987, p. A-39; John M. Goshko, "Ortega Backs Indirect Talks With Contras Here," and Goshko, "Ortega Proposes Cease-Fire For a Month, Starting Dec. 5," both page one stories Nov. 13 and Nov. 14, 1987, respectively.

30. Purcell, "Jim Wright Has Made a Mess of Things," op-ed article in *The Washington Post*, Nov. 17, 1987, p. A-27. The "melodrama" and "guerrilla theater" quotes were attributed to an administration "official who declined to be identified but [who] has a major role in planning and executing administration foreign policy" (John M. Goshko, "Diplomacy By Wright, Ortega Hit," *The Washington Post*, Nov. 15, 1987, p. 1).

31. John M. Goshko and Eric Pianin, in front-page stories in *The Washington Post*, Nov. 17 and 18, 1987: "Reagan Hits Wright on Peace Talks," and "Wright, Shultz Say Feud Over," and a John M. Goshko news analysis on Nov. 18, "Wright-Reagan Effort for Nicaraguan Peace Has Backfired on Administration," p. A-016.

32. "Nicaraguan Prelate to Meet With Rebels," UPI story datelined Managua in *The Washington Post*, Nov. 27, 1987, p. A-44.

33. *The Washington Post*, William Branigin, "Salvadoran, Nicaraguan Amnesties to Be in Place Under Pact," datelined San Salvador, Oct. 29, 1987, p. A-35. In it, Branigin wrote that the Salvadoran amnesty law "has come under attack from leftist and human rights groups because it defines political offenses so broadly as to include practically all crimes connected to the civil war except kidnaping, extortion and drug trafficking)."

34. Data on Diaz from Steven Kinzer, "Nicaragua Party Leader Is Key to Pact's Success," a Managua-datelined story in *The New York Times*, Sept. 12, 1987, p. 5.

35. Opposition parties—including even the Communist Party—pulled out of the talks, which had sputtered on and off from Oct. 4—when the Sandinistas rejected altogether a list of seventeen proposed constitutional reforms. (Only the tiny and radical Popular Action Movement sided with the Sandinistas against the reforms.) Those reforms would have included a ban on presidential reelection, voting by members of the military, family succession to the presidency, a limit on presidential power, nonpartisan armed forces, an independent judiciary, and definition of the separation of the military, the government and political parties. (The Sandinistas claim they alone speak for both the military and government.) Coming on the heels of the damaging revelations of secret protocols between the Sandinistas and the Soviet Union to build to gigantic proportions the country's already huge military machine, the collapse of the "reconciliation" talks dealt a heavy blow to those still claiming the Sandinistas were "complying" with the "peace plan" (William Branigin, "Nicaraguan Parties Quit Dialogue," a Managua story in *The Washington Post*, Dec. 16, 1987, p. A-46).

300

36. "Next in Central America, the negotiable revolution," *The Economist,* Sept. 5, 1987, p. 37. In a companion story in the same issue, the magazine noted: "The treaty leaves the three pillars of the Nicaraguan revolution—party, army and state—untouched. It implies no fundamental change in the nature of the Sandinista regime" ("Viva Sandino!," p. 38).

37. "Ortega Reveals Why Peace Plan Is Pipe Dream," *Human Events,* Sept. 12, 1987, pp. 1 & 17. "Wright Says Sandinistas Acting in 'Good Faith'; But Knocks U.S.," *Human Events,* Sept. 19, 1987, p. 3. Wright gave yet another clue as to how understanding he would be during a meeting late in August with *contra* leaders. Wright refused to say when he emerged whether he would go along with their plea for aid funds to be put into an escrow account, to be paid to them if the Sandinistas reneged on their commitments, used for humanitarian purposes if they were to comply. "I'm not ready to spell out exactly what formula Congress might be willing to support. The fundamental concept is we're going to give peace a chance" (Associated Press story datelined Grapevine, Texas, in *The Washington Post,* Aug. 29, 1987, p. A-16).

38. Joe Pichirallo and Terri Shaw, "Top Defector Disillusioned By Marxism," *The Washington Post,* Dec. 13, 1987, p. A-49. In that entire story, which sprawled over three and-a-half full newspaper columns, the *Post*'s reporters could not bring themselves once to indicate that the Soviets had put not millions, or tens of millions—but billions of dollars worth of military hardware into Nicaragua. Nor did any of the other *Post* stories on these new revelations, any more than the *Post* would hint at the enormity of the disparity between piddling U.S. support for the "U.S.-supported *contras*" and massive Soviet support for the Sandinistas in the paper's sprawling coverage of the Washington summit talks. Precise figures for U.S. aid were, however, repeatedly cited in stories which included references to Gorbachev's cryptic and offhanded Washington summit suggestion that the Soviets would consider cutting back on their aid to the Sandinistas if the U.S. would leave the *contras* high and dry. Numerous stories cited that demonstration of brazen cynicism as Gorbachev's "support for the Arias peace plan"(!) Interestingly, the *Post* was given its fist interview with Major Miranda on Dec. 10—the last day of the summit. But the paper held off publishing anything on his stunning revelations until Sunday, Dec. 13, and then only when the Sandinistas themselves, having learned of Miranda's meetings with reporters in Washington, announced the secret deals with the Soviets. The *Post* alibied that it held off while giving the Sandinistas a chance to respond to their questions about the charges— a measure of protectiveness not usual in the handling by the liberal media of stories about persons, nations or causes not to their liking.

39. Julia Preston, "Costa Rica Struggles to Aid Refugees; Record Number of Nicaraguans Flee During Border Opening," a La Cruz, Costa Rica-

datelined story in *The Washington Post*, Oct. 21, 1987, p. 29. The story noted that 636 Nicaraguans had surged across the border the previous Sunday, the largest single-day influx ever into Costa Rica. By then, Costa Rica hosted 25,000 Nicaraguan refugees officially registered with the United Nations, but, as the story added, "tens of thousands of others are living here on their own. Arias has sounded an alarm, saying a total of 100,000 Nicaraguans live in Costa Rica and citing them as a threat to Costa Rica's national integrity." Three weeks after Costa Rica and Nicaragua signed an agreement with the United Nations to repatriate refugees who wish to go home, Ms. Preston reported, a total of 33 decided to return to their Nicaraguan homeland. On Oct. 11, Ms. Preston reported from Quilali, Nicaragua, that peace commissioners venturing into the countryside "discovered that many villages have serious reservations about backing the cease-fire plan" ("Truce Plan Stirs Doubts in Nicaragua; Commissions Hear Complaints From Peasants With *Contra* Ties," Oct. 11, 1987, pp. 1 and A-50). (The reference to "with *contra* ties" appeared entirely gratutious in the context of the story.) "Visa Rumor Spreads in Managua," UPI story datelined Managua, in *The Washington Post*, Nov. 26, 1987, p. A-49.

40. J. Berlin, "U.N. Assembly Acclaims Regional Peace Plan," *The Washington Post*, Oct. 8, 1987, p. A-53. The story noted that "the resolution was timed to precede President Reagan's speech today . . . and Thursday's General Assembly speech by Nicaraguan President Daniel Ortega."

41. Speech quotes from David Hoffman, "Reagan Says Arias Plan Insufficient; President Tells OAS Soviet, Cuban Forces Must Leave Nicaragua," *The Washington Post*, Oct. 8, 1987, pp. 1 and 49; Michael J. Berlin, "Ortega Attacks Reagan, but Urges Talks; Nicaraguan Suggests Opposition Paper Could Be Closed Again," United Nations, N.Y.-datelined story in *The Washington Post*, Oct. 9, 1987, pp. 1 and A-34; John M. Goshko, "Ortega: *Contra* Aid Would Nullify Pact; U.S. Assistance After Nov. 7 Seen as Violation," New York-datelined story in *The Washington Post*, Oct. 8, 1987, p. A-49.

42. John M. Goshko, "Congress May Be Ready to Abandon Reagan's *Contra* Policy," *The Washington Post*, Oct. 13, 1987, p. A-14; Goshko, "Reagan to Ask *Contra* Aid After Nov. 7; 'Appropriate Moment' Awaited, Shultz Says," *The Washington Post*, Oct. 13, 1987, p. A-14.

43. Alfredo Cesar, "The Peace Plan Is Headed Toward Sandinista Victory; Give the resistance nonlethal aid," *The Washington Post*, Oct. 15, 1987, p. A-25. Cesar was by then a member of the directorate of the Nicaraguan Resistance.

44. *Background Paper: Central America*, U.S. Departments of State and Defense, May 27, 1983, pp. 10–11, cited by James R. Whelan and Patricia B. Bozell in *Catastrophe in the Caribbean* (Ottawa, IL: Jameson Books, 1984), p. 104.

45. See *"Revolution Beyond Our Borders": Sandinista Intervention in Central America*, U.S. Department of State, Special Report No. 132, September 1985, pp. 6–9, for selected details on the arms shipments and contemporary intelligence reports.

46. Ibid., p. 9. The emphasis appears in this source.

47. Ibid., p. 3 (secret gathering); and (for the guerrilla commander quotation) Alex Drehsler, "Salvador's Revolution: Just the Beginning," *San Diego Union*, March 1, 1981, p. A1, in Roger Reed, *El Salvador and the Crisis in Central America* (Washington: Council for Inter-American Security, 1984), p. 10.

48. Interview in *Playboy*, September 1983, quoted in Allan C. Brownfeld and J. Michael Waller, *The Revolution Lobby* (Washington: Council for Inter-American Security, 1985), p. 89.

49. Alexander M. Haig, Jr., *Caveat: Realism, Reagan, and Foreign Policy* (New York: MacMillan, 1984), p. 129.

50. See note 2, chapter 4.

51. *The Challenge to Democracy in Central America*, U.S. Departments of State and Defense, June 1986, p. 49. The ambassador quoted here is Robert White, whose antagonism toward Reagan's policies soon became well known.

52. Reed, op. cit., pp. 8–9.

53. Statement before the U.S. Senate Committee on Foreign Relations, February 27, 1986, published by the State Department as "Nicaragua: Will Democracy Prevail?" Current Policy no. 797, March 1986, p. 6.

54. *"Revolution Beyond Our Borders,"* op. cit., p. 20.

55. Shirley Christian, *Nicaragua: Revolution in the Family* (New York: Vintage Books, 1986), pp. 159–60.

56. *"Revolution Beyond Our Borders,"* op. cit., p. 20. This source reports that by the end of 1979, "there were some 1,400 Cuban teachers and medical personnel" in Nicaragua.

57. Bruce Weinrod, "Thirty Myths About Nicaragua," *The Heritage Lectures*, No. 54 (Washington: The Heritage Foundation), 1986, p. 24. The reference occurs in the record of a secret party meeting.

58. *"Revolution Beyond Our Borders,"* op. cit., p. 37 (Carter's request); and Christian, *Nicaragua*, p. 159. She cites the figure as a State Department estimate and writes that "Panamanian military information substantiated that."

59. Joseph G. Whelan and Michael J. Dixon, *The Soviet Union in the Third World: Threat to World Peace?* (Washington: Pergamon-Brassey, 1986),

p. 328 (Joseph G. Whelan is not related to James R. Whelan, author of this book.); and Christian, *Nicaragua*, p. 172.

60. *"Revolution Beyond Our Borders,"* op. cit., pp. 21 (claim of intercepting arms), and 22 ("funny business").

61. Christian, *Nicaragua*, pp. 225–26.

62. Arturo J. Cruz, "Nicaragua's Imperiled Revolution," *Foreign Affairs*, Summer 1983, pp. 1031, 1041–42, in *"Revolution Beyond Our Borders,"* op. cit., p. 23.

63. *"Revolution Beyond Our Borders,"* op. cit., p. 23.

64. *Time*, April 8, 1983, quoted in Whelan and Bozell, *Catastrophe*, p. 90.

65. Walter C. Soderlund and Carmen Schmitt, "El Salvador's Civil War as Seen in North and South American Press," *Journalism Quarterly*, Summer 1986, p. 274. Eight major newspapers were monitored over a 10-week period.

66. *The Soviet-Cuban Connection in Central America and the Caribbean*, U.S. Departments of State and Defense, March 1985, p. 40.

67. "Even now, the killing could go on," *The Economist*, Aug. 15, 1987, p. 32.

68. Whelan and Bozell, *Catastrophe*, pp. 92–93.b Thus the policies that were successful abroad were resisted at home.

69. *Report of the National Bipartisan Commission on Central America*, January 1984, pp. 87, 91, 88.

70. "The Democrats on Nicaragua: Myth-ing the Point, Again," a report of the Republican Study Committee of the U.S. House of Representatives, April 8, 1986, p. 2.

71. Associated Press wire story, April 7, 1986, as quoted in "The Democrats on Nicaragua," p. 7.

72. Two days later, President Arias of Costa Rica wrote,"In Panama the true situation was made very clear. Twelve Latin American Foreign Ministers, among them the Foreign Ministers of four Central American countries, supported the prompt signing of the [Contadora] Acta in accordance with international opinion. Only Nicaragua was opposed, thus demonstrating once again that it has neither a true interest in, or the will for, peace in Central America" (Oscar Arias, "Nicaragua Fears Democracy," *La Nacion*, San Jose, Costa Rica, April 9, 1986, quoted in *The Challenge to Democracy*, p. 67).

73. According to Napoleon Romero, former third-ranking member of the largest guerrilla faction in the FMLN who defected in April 1985, his group alone received up to 50 tons of material every three months from Nicaragua until the supply was reduced after the U.S. liberation of Grenada (*"Revolution Beyond Our Borders,"* op. cit., p. 11).

74. On April 20, 1985, the San Jose paper *La Republica* reported the arrest of terrorists directed and financed by the Sandinistas for the purpose of blowing up several Costa Rican government buildings, including the Legislative Assembly, the offices of the International Department of Security and Intelligence, the Office for the Prevention of Crime, and the police barracks in San Jose (*Turmoil in Central America*, op. cit., p. 32).

75. Nicaragua trained and armed the Colombian "M-19" terrorists who raided the Colombian Palace of National Justice in November 1985, and several Sandinistas probably participated in the attack. In the battle between the terrorists and the army, 115 people were killed, including twelve justices; some of the hostages were apparently murdered by the terrorists. Three days later, Nicaraguan Interior Minister Tomas Borge attended a Mass honoring the M-19; those who died in the attack were eulogized. See Timothy Goodman, "Sandinistas Aid Attack on Contadora Member," *West Watch* (Washington: Council for Inter-American Security), April 1986, p. 3.

76. On page 3 of "Nicaragua: Will Democracy Prevail?" (the statement made by Secretary of State George Schultz before the Senate Committee on Foreign Relations, February 27, 1986) is a map of Latin America indicating the extent of Nicaraguan subversion. Countries where arms originating in Nicaragua have been found: Guatemala, El Salvador, Honduras, Costa Rica, and Colombia; countries from which guerrillas have received military training in Nicaragua: all of the above, plus the Dominican Republic, Venezuela, Ecuador, Brazil, Chile, and Uruguay; countries in which radicals have received other support (such as safe haven, transit, false documentation, etc.) from Nicaragua: all of the above, plus Panama, Bolivia, and Argentina.

77. Rep. Jack Davis, "A New Freedom Fighter Aid Strategy," a lecture given at The Heritage Foundation in Washington, April 30, 1987, reproduced as *#117 The Heritage Lectures*. The bleed-and-die statement was made by Don Simon, foreign relations chairman of the American Legion, who participated in a number of study missions to Central America between June 21 and July 3, 1987, held by the Policy Coordination and Action Group of the American Legion. It appears in "A Search For Consensus," *The American Legion* magazine, October 1987, p. 38.

78. "JUNO Unites Nicaraguans Against Regime."

79. *Turmoil in Central America*, op. cit., p. 80.

80. William Branigin, "*Contras* Back to 'Fortress' In Northern Nicaragua," Oct. 4, 1987, pp. A-29 and 32. Branigin went on to describe as "a major weakness" of the *contras* their "almost total dependence on U.S. aid." Apart from the fact that one wonders where else they might get aid to

fight a Soviet satellite, it is also worth remarking that one never sees the obvious obverse stated: that the Sandinistas, too, would collapse quite rapidly without the far more massive Soviet aid they receive (or, for that matter, so, too, would the Salvadoran guerrillas without the Sandinista-Cuban aid they get).

81. The bulk of the figures on *contra* actions are from Jorge Salaverry, "*Contras* Score Military Gains Inside Nicaragua," Heritage Foundation Executive Memorandum #174, Aug. 31, 1987, p. 1; September figures from Julia Preston, "Rebels Still Seeking a Win," Managua-datelined story in *The Washington Post*, Sept. 8, 1987, pp. 1 and A-16; October actions from "Managua Says Rebels Repulsed," and "*Contras* Said to kill 22 While Losing 91," both in *The Washington Post*, the first Oct. 16, 1987, p. A-26, the second Oct. 19, 1987, p. A-18. The balance from Davis, op. cit., pp. 4 & 2.

82. *Taking the Stand. The Testimony of Lieutenant Colonel Oliver L. North* (New York: Pocket Books, 1987), pp. 551–552. The memo, read into testimony by Col. North on July 13, 1987, was directed to his then-boss, Vice Adm. John Poindexter, the national security adviser.

83. Diana West, "Liberal Converts to Contra Support," *Washington Times*, reprinted in *Campus Review* (P.O. Box 5155, Coralville, IA 52241), September 1986, p. 16.

84. Based on figures in *The Challenge to Democracy*, p. 41.

85. "The Case for the Contras," *The New Republic*, March 24, 1986, p. 8.

86. Paper presented by John Norton Moore at the White House Outreach Program, October 17, 1984, quoted in *The Challenge to Democracy*, p. 43.

87. Gonzalo Facio, "The Nicaraguan Resistance's Right of Rebellion," in a message to the Third Assembly of the Nicaraguan Resistance convened in Guatemala, Sept. 15, 1987, as reprinted in *West Watch*, November 1987, p. 8. While endorsing the peace plan advanced by President Arias of his country, Ambassador Facio says aid to the resistance is reconcilable with that plan because both seek the same end: "To substitute the totalitarian government in Nicaragua for a democratic government, freely elected by all the Nicaraguan people." He noted in his message that "every nation has the right of rebellion against tyrants," and that since the Sandinistas receive "massive military aid from the Soviet Bloc, the Nicaraguan Resistance has every right to search for military support from other nations and peoples." He also chastened the United States for using the *contras* as a mere "instrument of pressure . . . to distance the Sandinistas from the Soviet Bloc," which meant that their soldiers in the field were "sacrificing themselves needlessly. By accepting the advancement of the impression that the CIA or the Pentagon controlled the strategy of the anti-Sandinista insurrection for

that narrow purpose, the false impression was given that the combatants were a tool of the United States instead of, as they really are, genuine patriots that fight for democracy in their much beleaguered country . . ."

88. Richard Ray's floor remarks quoted in "President's Persistence Wins One for the Contras," *Human Events*, July 5, 1986, p. 8.

8

The War in Washington

*We have to win the war inside the United
States.*
—Hector Oqueli, a Salvadoran rebel[1]

THESE words, spoken to *The New York Times* in 1982 by a
political leader of the Salvadoran FDR organization, are
widely understood by proponents of Latin American revolutionary movements. Their message was prominently reinforced almost two years later when Tomas Borge, the
Sandinista Minister of the Interior and head of state security
told *Newsweek*: "The battle for Nicaragua is not being waged
in Nicaragua. It is being fought in the United States."[2]

This idea is another of the "lessons of Vietnam." Revolutionary movements that cannot hope to prevail against the
United States on the field of battle can nevertheless make
great strides within the American political arena. The principle was understood by the communists long before the Vietnam war was over. For it was in a 1970 speech, celebrating
twenty-five years of communist rule in Hanoi, that North
Vietnamese Premier Pham Van Dong said, "The Vietnamese
people are sincerely grateful for the warm sympathy and very
effective support given them by . . . the peace- and democ-
racy-loving people in the World, including the progressive
people in the United States."[3] Similar gratitude was voiced

nine years later by Sandinista Comandante Jaime Wheelock, just after the communist triumph in Nicaragua. In an interview with the *Militant*, a tabloid published by the Trotskyite Socialist Workers Party, Wheelock said:

> I want to use the *Militant* to salute the people of the United States who have understood and been in solidarity with our struggle. Moreover, we have received medical, financial, and material aid from the American people. At the same time they were aiding us, they were protesting the aid given to Somoza. . . . It has also given us confidence that the American people will actively participate in defending those rights and in giving solidarity and aid to those who are struggling for just causes. We are optimistic regarding the future of the struggle in the United States.[4]

The struggle to which Wheelock referred has been carried on in the form of a sophisticated propaganda barrage, directed at American voters and their representatives in Washington. As Wheelock noted, one benefit of the campaign is the direct financial support that many individual Americans can be persuaded to provide to communist causes. But, far more important is the opportunity to influence Congress. Thus, when Salvadoran guerrilla leader Nidia Diaz was captured on April 18, 1985, one of the documents she was carrying was a November 1983 letter to the "Comrades of the National Directorate of the [Nicaraguan] FSLN" in Managua. Signed by members of the FMLN General Command, the letter said that the Salvadoran FMLN leaders "are in agreement that the electoral period in the United States is the appropriate moment to influence the American electorate. . . . We support the current diplomatic initiatives of the FSLN to gain time, to help Reagan's opposition in the United States, and to internationally isolate his aggressive plan toward Nicaragua and El Salvador."[5]

The effort by Latin American communists to "help Reagan's opposition" has taken many forms. Sometimes it involves covert action, as in the case of the "State Department Dissent Paper." This was a document purporting to represent the thoughts of State Department, National Security Council, and CIA staff officers who disapproved of U.S. aid to the government of El Salvador. It was actually a forgery, probably produced by the Soviet KGB, though it was widely accepted as genuine by the media before it was finally exposed.

Often, however, the propaganda activities are open to public view. Sandinista leaders, for example, visited the United States repeatedly during the Carter administration to lobby on behalf of the president's generous Nicaraguan aid proposals. Subsequent visits have involved meetings between top Sandinistas and American political, church, and press groups. To make the most of such opportunities, Daniel Ortega and company have hired the New York public relations firm of Agendas International, which received $500,000 from the Nicaraguan government between 1983 and 1985. Some of the services provided by this firm:

Intensive training for television interviews, including camera practice sessions ... [and] Consultation with Embassy and Permanent Mission press officers on how to manage press conferences and interviews.

Strategy for the release of Nicaragua's peace proposals to the U.S. media (including recommendations for appearances and invitation acceptances by the ambassadors).

Recommendations of stationery and press release designs for the Embassy and Permanent Mission.

Meetings with U.S. support groups to keep advised of and make recommendations for collaboration with them.[6]

While Agendas International was boosting the Sandinistas for a considerable fee, others do it at no charge. Thus when Daniel Ortega visited the United States in August 1986 to lobby against U.S. aid to the *contras,* he was invited to appear in Chicago as a guest of the Reverend Jesse Jackson, who was able to provide him with a large, enthusiastic audience.[7] And this was not Jackson's first effort on behalf of the revolutionary cause. Two years earlier, while he was running for President of the United States, Jackson and his thirty-member entourage had visited Cuba (at the expense of the Cuban and Nicaraguan governments—around $250,000) to attend a Martin Luther King Conference, the purpose of which was to forge ties between Cuba and black churches in the United States.[8] Jackson made his sympathies quite clear by shouting to a large audience in Havana, "Long live President Castro! Long live Martin Luther King! Long live Che Guevarra!"[9] Castro used the occasion to score propaganda points by releasing forty-eight political prisoners, who returned with Jackson to the United States. What was not mentioned was that all of the released prisoners had been held long beyond their sentences. One of them was a black preacher sentenced to twenty years (and tortured) for preaching the gospel.[10] Did Castro's treatment of the church bother the Reverend Jackson? "I felt he ought to be more pronounced in his support of the church," Jackson said.[11]

On September 5, 1987, Rosario Murillo, the wife of Nicaraguan President Daniel Ortega, joined Jackson, Joan Baez and others at a rally saluting "peace" activist S. Brian Willson. Willson lost both legs a few days before when he fell beneath a two-car Navy train carrying explosives, which he was attempting to block in the belief that the munitions were destined for shipment to the Nicaraguan freedom fighters. As part of the rally, demonstrators tore up eight sections of rail and the ties beneath them and erected a six-foot-high barricade at a closed station entry while deputy sheriffs and Marine guards looked on. They were still looking on when the demonstrators built a shanty on the tracks. Meeting with Willson, Mrs. Ortega said "he dreams of having a small house in the mountains of Nicaragua where he can work with the peasants." Said presidential aspirant Jackson: "There's no greater sacrifice than to give up your legs that a nation might walk."[12]

Jesse Jackson is just one of many prominent Americans engaged in propaganda support for revolution in Central America, the acting, entertainment, and intellectual communities being notorious in this regard. Actors Ed Asner, Martin Sheen, and Mike Farrell, for example, have helped raise funds for medical supplies for the communist guerrillas in El Salvador, according to J. Michael Waller of the Council for Inter-American Security. The three actors have signed fund-raising letters for an organization called Medical Aid for El Salvador (MAES). Though the letters speak only of medical aid for the poor, MAES door-to-door canvassers are reminded of "the important contribution you are making to the liberation of the people of El Salvador," while MAES has in fact been used to channel funds to "the people's clinics in El Salvador administered by the FMLN," according to the newsletter of an affiliated organization, the Committee in Solidarity with the People of El Salvador.[13]

It is not clear whether the three sponsors knew that the money they raised would be turned over to the communist guerrillas, but Asner, at least, has been an effective apologist for the radical cause. He has explained, for example, that the Sandinistas shut down La Prensa, the last independent newspaper in Nicaragua, not because "it criticized the government but because it printed lies about potential shortages that sapped the people's morale."[14]

What makes his attitude particularly strange is the fact that Asner reached television stardom playing the role of a hard-boiled newspaper city editor who fought hardest when press freedom was threatened.

By contrast, not only has Congress, over the past 15 years, engaged in a constitutionally suspect (and still Court-untested) attempt to strip away the historic presidential responsibility for the conduct of foreign policy, it has even gone so far as to forbid the Executive Branch from promoting its policies. In 1985, Congress passed a law banning the use of public funds for what it deemed as "unauthorized" publicity and propaganda purposes in support of the administration's Central American policies. A staff member involved in the proceedings wrote, "the Iran/*Contra* committees and their joint hearings represented the pinnacle of that effort. The hearings were clearly calculated to criminalize executive foreign policies carried out without the support or knowledge of Congress. If the committees succeed in their ultimate objective, the revolution in the relations between Congress and the presidency in foreign policy will be legitimized, with profound implications for the future of our national security."

Two months after those hearings, the General Accounting Office (GAO)—an arm of the Congress—issued a report accusing the Reagan administration of "illegal" covert propaganda activities designed to influence the news media and general public in support of its policies. Congressman Jack Brooks (D-TX), chairman of the House Government Operations Committee that released the report, said "this illegal operation represented an important cog in the administration's effort to manipulate public opinion and congressional action." Another veteran congressman reflected the view that only Congress somehow speaks for and represents "the people," a role the president—chosen by direct vote of all the people—somehow cannot pretend to: "It makes me wonder," Congressman Dante B. Fascell (D-FL) said, "what else is still being hidden from Congress and the American people." Fascell is chairman of the House Foreign Affairs Committee.[15]

Inasmuch as the major media shared the same policy objectives in Central America as did the liberal-dominated Congress, there has been no outcry on the editorial pages of the nation's vigilante newspapers against this bizarre gag order against what is, after all, one of the three co-equal branches of government.

Meantime, the major media did enthusiastically support and echo the propaganda messages of the left. While the

313

influence of prominent individuals such as Jackson or Asner is valuable in this one-sided war of ideas, there is another source of support that is also effective, especially in its influence on Congress. This is the network of American think tanks, church groups, charitable organizations, and political fronts and foundations that directly or indirectly, openly or deceitfully, support the revolutionary cause through their continuous lobbying, fundraising, and propaganda activities. Many of these organizations have branches operating across the country, but their headquarters are generally in Washington. Collectively, this network has been variously dubbed the Latin Network, the Latin American Lobby, or the Revolution Lobby. What follows is a sampling of the most important constituents of this lobby, with brief descriptions of their activities.[16]

The Revolution Lobby

Institute for Policy Studies (IPS). One authority on the subject has described the Institute for Policy Studies as "the ideological center and strategic hub for the activist campaigns conducted by the Latin Network."[17] IPS has been promoting radical movements since its founding in 1963 by Richard J. Barnet and Marcus Raskin. According to J. Michael Waller and Allan C. Brownfeld, a journalist and former staff member with the Senate Subcommittee on Internal Security, "IPS fellows and speakers have included members and close friends of a variety of radical organizations, including the Communist Party USA, the Trotskyite Communist Socialist Workers Party, and the radical Students for a Democratic Society."[18] Brian Crozier of London's Institute for the Study of Conflict has called IPS "the perfect intellectual front for Soviet activities which would be rejected if they were to originate openly from the KGB."[19]

The Communist Party's *Daily World* reported in April 1972

that Raskin had recently gone to Paris as part of the "first delegation of prominent Americans to meet with representatives of the liberation forces of Indochina since the U.S. sabotaged the peace talks." While there, he met with several communist officials.[20] Raskin has served as a member of the organization that published *CounterSpy* magazine (now called *National Reporter*), a publication dedicated to exposing and otherwise obstructing the activities of U.S. intelligence agencies.

Other important figures at IPS have included Saul Landau, who has made propaganda films promoting the communist governments of Cuba and Nicaragua; and Orlando Letelier, a former ambassador to the United States for Salvador Allende's Marxist-Leninist government in Chile. When Letelier was killed by a bomb in 1976, he was carrying documents that linked him with Cuban intelligence. According to journalist Virginia Prewett,

> the documents fully unmasked Letelier's work to influence legislation illegally in the U.S. Congress. They confirmed that he was indeed manipulating U.S. Liberals—from whom he took care to conceal his links to totalitarian socialist international networks, activists, and armed terrorists.... Letelier had pulled off a major coup. He had influenced the U.S. Congress to pass legislation startlingly paralleling his undercover mission directive ... imposing mandatory penalties upon nations reputed to violate human rights.[21]

Columnists Rowland Evans and Robert Novak revealed that Letelier had paid part of the travel expenses of Congressman Michael Harrington (D-MA) to a Leftist meeting in Mexico.[22] Senator George McGovern delivered a eulogy at the Cuban agent's funeral.

The chief function of IPS is to provide leftist causes with a veneer of intellectual respectability, without which they would make little headway in Washington. It was to this end that an IPS spinoff, the Transnational Institute, produced the 1977 report: *The Southern Connection: Recommendations for a New Approach to Inter-American Relations.* This report has been described by General Gordon Sumner, Jr., former chairman of the Inter-American Defense Board, as a blueprint for the Carter administration policies. As noted earlier, one member of the "Ad Hoc Working Group on Latin America" that prepared the report—Robert A. Pastor—went on to a key role on the National Security Council under Carter. The report calls upon the United States to accept communism in Latin America and to refrain from acting against it, though not in so many words. Rather, it calls for "the acceptance of ideological pluralism," and insists that the U.S. should "not boycott and isolate (or ultimately invade) any country, however small or near, because of political and economic differences." The report complained of human rights violations in Latin America, though not in Cuba, and called for the U.S. "to phase out gradually public and private military grant aid for arms purchases, and to withdraw U.S. military bases gradually from Latin America."[23]

Five years later, another IPS spinoff issued a much larger report expressing similar views, the *Blueprint for Peace in Central America and the Caribbean,* which was intended, according to IPS, "to be used as an action and organizing document for Congress, the religious community, labor unions, minority and women's groups, community organizations, students," etc. The report was hailed by leaders of the Salvadoran and Guatemalan guerrillas as well as by their American support groups. It characterized the Salvadoran FMLN rebels as a "force composed of left and center elements and a popular resistance led by important church officials," while blaming the United States for the "radicalization of the Cuban revolution."[24]

Because of such work, IPS delegations have been welcomed in Nicaragua by the top leadership of the Sandinistas.[25] Yet that hasn't diminished the Institute's acceptance at home. Thus Senator Mark Hatfield (R-OR) has said of the IPS, "I respect the often thoughtful and scholarly work of these individuals. I have no doubt that theirs is a legitimate and useful role in the formulation of national policy."[26]

North American Congress on Latin America (NACLA). Founded in 1966 as an offshoot of the Students for a Democratic Society, NACLA dedicated its October 1967 newsletter to revolutionary leader Che Guevarra and "the thousands of men and women who have dedicated their lives to the struggle for national liberation."[27] A NACLA statement of the same year declared, "The North American Congress on Latin America seeks the participation and support of men and women, from a variety of organizations and movements, who not only favor revolutionary change in Latin America but also take a revolutionary position toward their own society."[28]

One of the founders of NACLA was Brady Tyson, a Methodist minister and professor who once called the government of Brazil a "front" for the United States.[29] Tyson joined the Carter administration as a close adviser to U.N. Ambassador Andrew Young, from which post he exerted considerable influence over the administration's human rights policy. Other founders were Richard Shaull, who has been a regular contributor to the communist weekly, the *Guardian*,[30] and Michael Locker, who later became involved in the two IPS reports mentioned above.

According to Joan Frawley of the Heritage Foundation, NACLA "provides much of the research used by the Washington-based opposition to the Reagan Administration's policies,"[31] while Brownfeld and Waller write that NACLA "offers some of the best propaganda available on behalf of Fidel Castro, and its writings are widely used by college professors in the classroom, as well as by congressional staffers and the general public."[32]

Frawley reports that NACLA has "repeated and sought to document the official Sandinista party line," as when the Nicaraguan regime's imprisonment of three business leaders was characterized by NACLA as a "reassertion of authority."[33] Rene J. Mijuca, who serves the Cuban government as First Secretary of the Cuban Interests Section in Washington, has said, "NACLA is one of the best organizations in the United States for information on Latin American Affairs."[34]

NACLA receives funding from the National Council of Churches.

The Washington Office on Latin America (WOLA). The Washington Office on Latin America is ostensibly a religious organization concerned with human rights. It was founded in 1974 by the National Council of Churches and the U.S. Catholic Conference; today, much of its $340,000 funding comes from the World and National Councils of Churches, the Maryknoll Order of the Catholic Church, and other religious groups.

WOLA is directed by Joseph Eldridge, a Methodist minister whose salary is paid by the United Methodist Church. Eldridge's Revolution Lobby ties include collaboration with Saul Landau and Isabel Letelier (widow of Cuban agent Orlando Letelier) of IPS. (Mrs. Letelier is a board member.) He has also hosted Cuban delegations to Washington and worked with the Cuban government to facilitate visits of Americans to Cuba. In 1979, when the Cuban mission to the U.N. invited Eldridge to join its celebration of the twentieth anniversary of the Cuban revolution, he replied that he was unable to attend, adding that "I hope that at the next opportunity we can be together ... and that 1979 will be a good year for the continuing struggle of the Cuban regime and its people."[35]

In February of that year, WOLA, IPS, and the U.S. Peace Council (a well-known Communist Party front) jointly sponsored a "National Conference on Nicaragua," for the purpose of generating political support for the Sandinistas. Specifically discussed was the need to lobby Congress and to develop grass roots support, using human rights as a political weapon.[36] Five years later, WOLA's coordinator for Nicaragua, Reggie Norton, attended an international conference of Soviet front organizations held in Portugal for precisely the same purpose. The official conference report indicates that much emphasis was placed on the need to influence the U.S. Congress and to "inform U.S. public opinion, taking into consideration that U.S. public opinion may constitute one of the most important obstacles to the implementation of the Central American policy of the Reagan Administration." The report declared that "a delegation from the Conference should be sent to the USA, with the purpose of explaining its resolutions to the various sectors of USA life, such as Members of Congress, women's groups, religious, young people's, intellectuals', artists' organizations, etc."[37]

Kay Stubbs, a WOLA staff member of long standing, left the organization to accept a full-time position with the Nicaraguan Ministry of Foreign Affairs.[38]

During the late 1970s, WOLA was active in exposing human rights abuses in Nicaragua and arranging for Sandinista spokesmen to testify before Congress. Once Nicaragua fell to the communists, WOLA lost interest in human rights there, turning its critical attention to El Salvador and Guatemala. The organization has provided background briefings for congressional staff and even helped draft legislation. WOLA was among the organizations assisting the Salvadoran communist Farid Handal in setting up the pro-communist network, Committee in Solidarity with the People of El Salvador.

In one of its reports, WOLA has noted that "the media in the United States plays a powerful role in the formulation of foreign policy," and went on to boast that "WOLA serves as an important source of information and analysis for both the print and electronic media. The office maintains working relationships with many domestic and foreign journalists from the wire services, major daily newspapers, radio networks, television and news journals."[39]

The Council on Hemispheric Affairs (COHA). In early 1976, the Cuban operative Orlando Letelier helped pay for Democratic Congressman Michael Harrington and Larry Birns, a Leftist professor of Latin American studies, to attend a meeting in Mexico City of an organization created by the World Peace Council, a front of the Soviet Union. Several months later, as a by-product of that meeting, Birns founded the Council on Hemispheric Affairs, the purpose of which was, he said, "to manipulate the sophisticated political and academic communities."[40] At COHA's initial press conference, Birns expressed the organization's support for Castro's Cuba.[41] The COHA board of trustees has included such Leftist luminaries as Brady Tyson of NACLA, IPS fellows Richard Barnet, Roger Wilkins, and Terry Herndon (who has also been executive director of the National Education Association), and three congressmen, Don Bonker (D-WA), Robert Garcia (D-NY), and Tom Harkin (D-IA).

Birns, who has been quoted by Radio Sandino (a mouthpiece of the Nicaraguan government) as declaring that "the U.S. only seeks a military solution to the Central American conflicts,"[42] says that one of COHA's chief aims is to "cut off from U.S. support" the "vast majority of the nations that make up the Organization of American States."[43] COHA publishes human rights reports with an extreme pro-left bias, and has condemned the free elections in El Salvador while ignoring the injustices of the controlled campaigning in Nicaragua.[44]

Though COHA has been denounced as a "particularly reckless and ill-informed source" of information by former U.S. Ambassador to Nicaragua James D. Theberge[45] it has been quite successful in placing its propaganda in very influential places. One COHA statement claims that:

COHA findings have been cited in official publications of the U.S. government, as well as in national and international publications, such as *Time, Newsweek, The Atlantic Monthly, The New Yorker, New York, The New Statesman, Penthouse, Barron's,* and

Macleans. On almost a daily basis, the results of COHA's work appear in the press of Latin America, the United States, and Europe. COHA has also been cited on numerous occasions in the *New York Times, Washington Post, Los Angeles Times, Christian Science Monitor . . . Baltimore Sun, Miami Herald, Toronto Globe and Mail,* and the *Manchester Guardian.*[46]

As Joan Frawley of the Heritage Foundation notes, "Through Birns's contacts in the White House and the State Department, COHA exerted considerable influence on the Carter Administration's human rights policies."[47] The extent of COHA's continuing influence is suggested by Roger Strickland, advisor to Congressman Tim Valentine (D-NC). Strickland admitted to a lobbyist in 1985 that Central America "is not my area of expertise," and said he got most of his information from COHA.[48]

Committee in Solidarity with the People of El Salvador (CISPES). CISPES is America's leading grassroots pressure group operating on behalf of the Salvadoran FMLN guerrillas. Documents captured in 1981 from a safe house in El Salvador, and later released by the State Department, have provided many details about the founding of CISPES. Those documents belonged to Farid Handal, an FMLN agent whose brother Shafik was chairman of the Salvadoran Communist Party and a member of the FMLN general command.

Farid Handal came to the United States in March 1980 for the purpose of setting up a broad-based solidarity network to support the Salvadoran communist guerrillas. In his efforts to establish a coalition of political, service, and religious groups, Handal met with and received support from WOLA, IPS, the Cuban Mission to the United Nations, the Central Committee of the U.S. Communist Party, and the office of Congressman Ronald Dellums (D-CA).[49] "Monday morning the offices of Congressman Dellums were turned into our offices," wrote Handal, according to the State Department documents. "Everything was done there," he continued. "The meetings with the Black Caucus took place in the liver of the monster itself, nothing less than in the meeting room of the House Foreign Affairs Committee."[50]

Rob Costa of CISPES has conceded that the organization's advisory board included the U.S. Peace Council, a front for the U.S. Communist Party, which is totally subservient to the Soviet Union.[51] Handal understood that if CISPES was to receive broad-based popular support, its communist ties would have to be concealed. "We cannot speak a different language than [sic] those sectors which we hope to incorporate," he said. "The problem should be presented with its human features, without political language and, most importantly, without a political label."[52] CISPES has not always been so discreet, however. Its guest speakers have included diplomats from communist Vietnam, Grenada, and Nicaragua, as well as Rafael Cancel-Miranda, one of the four Puerto Rican terrorists who opened fire on the U.S. House of Representatives in 1954 (three of whom were pardoned by President Carter); and CISPES has distributed fliers saying, "Vietnam has won. El Salvador will win."[53]

While condemning even humanitarian aid to the government of El Salvador, CISPES has used fronts such as People to People Aid and Medical Aid to El Salvador to raise cash, food, and clothing for the FMLN's "liberated zones"—over $450,000–worth in 1983.[54] The organization's 550 nationwide chapters, especially active on college campuses, conduct letter-writing campaigns to lobby Congress. According to Brownfeld and Waller, CISPES has won the support of a number of members of Congress, including Tom Harkin (D-IA), Edward Markey (D-MA), Barbara Mikulski (D-MD), Patricia Schroeder (D-CO), and Gerry Studds (D-MA).

National Network in Solidarity with the Nicaraguan People (*Nicaragua Network*). In 1977, three Sandinista activists began to set up Sandinista solidarity organizations in the United

States, starting at Louisiana State University in Baton Rouge. One of these activists, Miguel Bolanos, became a highly placed Sandinista intelligence officer after the revolution, only to defect to the United States when he later understood the nature of the regime he was serving. Bolanos has explained that he and his two comrades acted on their own when they started their organizing in Louisiana, but says that in 1978 the Sandinista Party realized the value of the American solidarity committees and placed them under the control of the Sandinista National Directorate. What resulted was the National Network in Solidarity with the Nicaraguan People (hereafter referred to by the name it adopted in 1985: the Nicaragua Network). The (communist front) U.S. Peace Council played a major role in building the Nicaragua Network.[55]

According to Bolanos, the Nicaragua Network is "guided by the intelligence organs of Cuba."[56] Its purpose is to distribute propaganda and raise funds and engage in other public relations activities for the Sandinistas. Indeed, people calling the Nicaraguan embassy in Washington seeking information have been referred to the Nicaragua Network by the embassy receptionist.[57] Alvaro Baldizon, a high-ranking official in the Sandinista Interior Ministry who has defected to the United States, reports that as of 1985, the Nicaragua Network's political activities in the United States were directed by the International Relations Department of the Sandinista Party in Managua.[58]

Members of the Nicaragua Network's advisory board have included Saul Landau of IPS, Mrs. Jesse Jackson, actor Ed Asner, and U.S. Representative Pat Schroeder (D-CO). Schroeder has even signed a fundraising letter for the Network. "If you want to change our country's policies toward Nicaragua," she says, "you can join me in the Nicaragua Network."[59]

The Nicaragua Network's activities include producing and distributing written and audio-visual propaganda, lobbying national and local officials, organizing demonstrations and "educational forums" at the national and local levels, raising money through its tax-deductible fund (Humanitarian Aid for Nicaraguan Democracy), and sponsoring tours by Leftist speakers.

In 1984, for example, the Network joined Americans for Democratic Action, Jesse Jackson's Operation PUSH, and several other radical organizations in sponsoring a tour by Gerardo Contreras, who was identified alternatively as a student and a professor. Actually, Contreras belonged to the Costa Rican Communist Party and the International Union of Students, a Soviet front established by Stalin in 1946. He spoke at thirty-six universities and twenty churches, met with four congressmen, and gave thirty radio and television interviews.[60]

Another element of the Network's propaganda strategy is the political tour, whereby Americans are induced to visit Nicaragua for a carefully controlled exposure to the Sandinista utopia. The tours are jointly coordinated by the Nicaragua Network and the Sandinista Interior Ministry, whose director, Tomas Borge, is in charge of the state security police. According to Schroeder's fundraising letter, the Nicaragua Network has helped thousands of Americans to visit Nicaragua.

One episode involving the Nicaragua Network offers a good illustration of the extended influence of the organizations of the Revolution Lobby. On June 26, 1986, viewers of CBS's *Nightwatch*, were given the startling statistic that 42 percent of the people killed by the Nicaraguan contras were children. The person who made that charge was Congressman Peter Kostmayer (D-PA). In an attempt to determine the source of the claim, John Lofton of *The Washington Times* contacted Kostmayer's office, which informed him that Kostmayer had gotten the figure from Congressman Jim Bates (D-CA). Bates, according to one of his assistants, had gotten the statistic from a fundraising letter, signed by Dr. Benjamin Spock, for the Nicaragua Network.

The letter signed by Spock claimed that the Reagan administration's portrayal of Sandinista Nicaragua was "a horrible lie," part of "a relentless campaign to distort the truth." When Lofton contacted Spock's wife, she denounced the letter, saying it contained "many mistakes." She also claimed that, contrary to Spock's insistence, the Nicaragua Network did not allow Spock to see the text of the letter before sending it out over his name. The letter's facts and figures were supplied by the Nicaragua Network, she said.

When the Nicaragua Network was contacted, its national coordinator sought to evade Lofton's question about the 42 percent claim, but finally admitted that it came from the Nicaraguan government's Institute of Social Security and Social Welfare. "It's the equivalent of our Social Security Administration," she said.[61]

The Center for Development Policy (CDP). The Center for Development Policy was formed in 1977 to influence U.S. foreign policy through Congress and the media. Its structure consists of three commissions, one of which is the Commission on U.S.-Central American Relations, whose first director was Fred Branfman, formerly with the editorial board of *CounterSpy* magazine.[62] Commission members have included five IPS fellows and WOLA director Joseph Eldridge.

CDP's influence stems from its success in recruiting the services of former U.S. military and government officials, such as Patricia Derian, the Assistant Secretary of State for Human Rights in the Carter Administration; Ramsey Clark, former Attorney General; Robert Pastor, former member of the National Security Council; Lawrence Pezzullo, former Ambassador to Nicaragua and Argentina; and former U.S. Marine Lieutenant Colonel John Buchanan. Robert E. White, former Ambassador to El Salvador, became the commission's director in 1983.

As an example of the work of this all-star cast, consider the contribution of Lieutenant Colonel John Buchanan, as related by S. Stephen Powell of Boston University's Institute for the Study of Economic Culture:

> In 1982, the Sandinistas gave Buchanan a week-long tour of Nicaraguan military installations. When he arrived back in the United States, CDP arranged for him to testify before Congress and obtain press coverage. On September 21, 1982 he told the House Subcommittee on Inter-American Affairs that the United States posed a greater threat to peace in the region than the Soviet-backed military build-up of Nicaragua.[63]

The New York Times reported that Buchanan "was 'not very impressed with' the Nicaraguan Army and that, in his opinion, Nicaragua is 'not a significant threat to its neighbors.' " [64]

CDP's efforts to distort the facts about Central America were dramatically exposed in early 1984. Seeking to undermine U.S. support for the government of El Salvador, CDP helped arrange for its Central American Commission Director, former Ambassador White, to testify before the House Foreign Affairs Committee on February 2. White asserted that "conditions in most of Central America justify recourse to revolution,"[65] and sought to discredit one of El Salvador's political parties—the ARENA party led by Roberto D'Aubuisson, one of the top two contenders in the March presidential election. White accused ARENA and D'Aubuisson of operating death squads directed by six exiles in Miami. According to White, his source knew that

> central power was exercised by the Miami "six," noting that others among the emigres and their wealthy allies here have some role from time to time but these are the top leadership: Viera Altamirano, Luis Escalante, Arturo Muyshondt, the Salaverria brothers (probably Julio and Juan Ricardo), and Roberto Edgardo Daglio. All are in Miami, hatch plots, hold constant meetings and communicate instructions to D'Aubuisson.[66]

In fact, White's charges were wildly inaccurate. According to Stephen Powell, Viera Altamirano was the pen name of a

Salvadoran publisher who had been dead since 1977, while Luis Escalante had not lived in Miami since May 1, 1983, and Juan Ricardo Salaverria had died in late 1982. When White subsequently testified before the Senate Foreign Relations Committee, Arturo Muyshondt attended, announcing his intention to file a $10 million lawsuit against the former ambassador. White responded, "It appears my source may have been in error." It turned out that CDP had paid White's chief informant $50,000 for his cooperation, a fact that was later admitted by CDP's Executive Director, Lindsay Mattison.[67]

While much of CDP's work has focused on cutting off aid—especially from international lending institutions—to Latin American countries friendly to the United States, the organization has also sponsored propaganda tours to Central America. Two of these, hosted by NACLA Vice President Janet Shenk, involved two Congressmen and seven labor leaders. Both delegations returned with assessments that contradicted the Kissinger Commission. Congressman Edward F. Feighan (D-OH) even accused President Reagan of perpetrating "a gross misrepresentation to the U.S. Congress [and] an indefensible deceit upon the American people."[68]

Witness for Peace (WFP). Organized in 1983, Witness for Peace describes itself as a religiously based, nonviolent group advocating peace and social justice. But, "to call them religious is something of an exaggeration," according to Monsignor Bismarck Carballo, spokesman for the Archbishop of Managua, Cardinal Miguel Obando y Bravo.[69] Founded with the objective of discouraging U.S. aid to the Nicaraguan *contras*, WFP grew out of the idea that the *contras*, because of their reliance on U.S. aid and goodwill, would be reluctant to risk harming any American citizens in Nicaragua's combat zones. The founders therefore set out to create what they call a human "shield of love." According to WFP steering committee member Joyce Hollyday, the organizers took their idea to Sandinista Comandante Sergio Ramirez, who referred them to Interior Minister and State Security Director Tomas Borge (the man who authorizes assassinations and summary executions for the Sandinista regime). Borge, who according to Hollyday has a "Christian conscience," saw the advantages in their proposal and approved the plan to send unarmed Americans into combat zones.[70]

Though WFP activists claim to be politically independent, the organization admits that its purpose is to "deter contra attacks." Peter T. Flaherty, a spokesman for Concerned Catholics for Religious Freedom in Nicaragua, writes that "*Witness for Peace's* independence from the Sandinista regime is suspect, at best. WFP maintains a full-time office in Managua, a privilege denied to many Nicaraguan political organizations." According to Flaherty, "the group's literature reveals enthusiastic support for the Sandinista regime and unyielding opposition to the armed resistance groups," and though WFP speaks in the customary peace jargon, it has opposed peace talks between the Nicaraguan government and the resistance—talks proposed by the contras but rejected by the Sandinistas.[71] WFP activists in Nicaragua have painted street murals conveying an anti-U.S., pro-Sandinista message.[72]

WFP gained instant notoriety in 1985, when it participated in what appears to have been a staged "contra atrocity." The setting was the San Juan River, near the Costa Rican border. In early August, WFP announced plans for a boat trip down the river, where presumably it might come under attack. On August 5, *Barricada*, the official Sandinista newspaper, quoted one of the activists as saying, "I'm very scared, but I want to protest against Reagan," and the next day, as the excursion was departing from El Castillo, a WFP press release declared that the U.S. government would be responsible for any harm that might come to the travelers at the hands of the *contras*.[73]

The group departed with twenty-nine WFP activists and no fewer than fourteen journalists, though a group spokesman denied they were "looking for trouble or publicity."[74] The first half of the two-day journey proceeded without incident, and the group encamped for the night with the Sandinista Army, whom they joined in singing revolutionary songs.[75]

On August 7, however, during the return trip, the WFP activists were forced ashore sixteen miles upstream from La Penca by a band of armed men on the Costa Rican bank. These were said to be the deadly *contras*—although *contra* spokesmen denied any involvement. Furthermore, Nicaraguan exile Alejandro Bolanos-Geyer, director of the Nicaraguan Information Center (St. Charles, MO), pointed out that an assortment of stories in the Sandinista press reveal that the region had been under the "total and absolute control" of Sandinista forces since early June.[76] Shortly after the "capture," a Sandinista helicopter was on the scene with reporters and photographers. The next day, all the travellers were released unharmed. The Sandinistas were organizing "welcome home" rallies before it was known the "captives" would be released.[77]

The Sandinistas generated a great deal of publicity out of the incident, all of it unfavorable to the *contras*. All of this was, however, a mere shadow of what was yet to come. An observor attending a *Witness for Peace* meeting in New York would tell *West Watch*: "*Witness for Peace* leaders privately expressed hope that some of their recruits would get killed or wounded by the Nicaraguan resistance. This way, U.S. public opinion would turn against the freedom fighters. . . ."

At about the same time, a 52-year-old Bangor, Maine, lawyer named Russell Christiansen, a *Witness* activist, told *The Boston Globe*: "Some of us have got to die" in the Nicaraguan war zone.

These death wishes—if that is what they were—would be realized on April 28, 1987, in the tiny hamlet of El Cua, in northern Nicaragua. During a *contra* attack, Benjamin Linder, a 27-year-old American engineer working on a hydroelectric project there, was killed.

Congressman Kostmayer—the same one who told the Nicaraguan dictator Daniel Ortega that "you have to do much less than you could imagine to stop *contra* aid"—hailed Linder as "a national hero, the kind of person of whom our country can be very, very proud."

Congressman Kostmayer—and others who rushed to eulogize Linder as an innocent martyr fallen in the pursuit of peace and help to the downtrodden—did not also say:

(1) Linder was, at the time, part of an armed work crew (four of them in military uniforms) and was, himself, carrying a Kalashnikov AK-47 assault rifle;

(2) that he was so committed to the cause that he shared a house with a Sandinista himself so fanatical that the entire building was painted red and black—the colors of the Sandinista party flag;

(3) a Sandinista army uniform was among his personal effects;

(4) evidence that he was "executed" was cited only after he was buried. While the cameras were rolling and the casket open, it was said he had been killed by a grenade fragment to the back of the head. After burial, a Sandinista military doctor said Linder had been shot in the right temple at point-blank range—executed, in other words;

(5) Linder himself was not only a radical activist, but he had been raised in a family ardently committed to left-wing causes. For months after their son's death, members of the family toured the United States under the auspices of the Socialist Workers Party, a Marxist-Leninist organization of Trotskyite tendency.[78]

Kostmayer was not alone in lionizing Linder. Congressman George Crockett (D-MI), chairman of the House Subcommittee on Western Hemisphere Affairs, gave the Linders a sympathetic national forum as "star witnesses" at a May 13, 1987 congressional hearing; Congressman Les AuCoin (D-OR) launched a campaign to bring the *contras* to "justice" for the "murder" of Linder, and Rep. Don Bonker (D-WA) was quoted as paying "tribute" to Linder for his "courage and commitment."

The Americas Watch Committee (AWC). The Americas Watch Committee, a "human rights" organization, was established in 1981 "in response," it said, "to the Reagan Administration's selective human rights policies which distinguish human rights abuses by 'hostile totalitarian' governments from those committed by 'friendly authoritarian' governments. Americas Watch focuses on abuses in the Americas where authoritarian countries friendly to the United States are in the majority."[79]

Since its founding, AWC has never allowed its concern for human rights to interfere with its political goals. In 1982, AWC collaborated with WOLA, the Center for National Security Studies (an IPS spinoff), and the American Civil Liberties Union to produce a book entitled *Report on Human Rights in El Salvador*, which was widely quoted in the media and had a major impact on Congress. The book's introduction was quite clear about its political motivation:

> This report demonstrates, we believe, that the President's January 28 certification is a fraud.... It is possible ... for Congress to demonstrate that it meant what it said in the foreign assistance act by adopting legislation suspending military aid to El Salvador so long as the gross human rights abuses documented in this report persist. That will happen only if Congress is prompted to act by public outrage. In publishing this report, we hope to provoke that outrage.[80]

The foregoing notwithstanding, the AWC claims it does "not take a position on the U.S. geopolitical strategy in Central America."[81]

The 1984 follow-up to the above report lists civilian casualties by lumping into a single category those killed in military actions and those killed by right-wing terrorists, characterizing the deaths as "government murder of noncombatant civilians" and "political murders."[82] This falsely suggests that the government is responsible for the actions of terrorists, while obscuring the distinction between incidental civilian battlefield deaths and "government murder[s]."

The 1984 election in El Salvador was denigrated by the director of AWC's Washington office, who claimed, "the Left could not participate." On the other hand, "In the Nicaraguan elections the problems appear to have been relatively minor."[83] An AWC report from a trip to Honduras, organized in cooperation with WOLA, completely ignored the enormous military build-up in neighboring Nicaragua while criticizing the Honduran "government's growing preoccupation with national security."[84]

AWC's July 1985 report entitled *Human Rights in Nicaragua: Reagan, Rhetoric and Reality*, found the administration's position to be suspect and often deceitful, according to Stephen Powell, "while expressing trust in the statements and policies of the Sandinistas."[85] Among the findings of the report: "There is not a policy of torture, political murder, or disappearances in Nicaragua. . . . The issue of religious persecution in Nicaragua is without substance." AWC also denied there was any evidence that Nicaragua was involved in a campaign of international terrorism.[86]

Powell reports that by 1985 AWC had published some nine hundred pages of allegations of human rights abuses by the Salvadoran government and military, and less than thirty pages on the violations of the communist guerrillas.

Despite its repeated protestations that it does not take sides in Central America, Americas Watch did just that in a statement issued in connection with the Arias peace process. While tut-tutting the Sandinistas for "sporadic violent abuses" and holding prisoners without due process, AWC reserved its most blistering fire for the *contras*. The 55-page report, issued in November 1987, said the resistance had carried out attacks on civilians and other acts that "have made them an outlaw force." "We see no way for compliance with the plan's requirement for respect for human rights," AMC added, "other than

[by] the dissolution of the *contras* and . . . an end to all aid for them by the United States, Honduras and all others." The Associated Press dispatch on the report referred to America's Watch as "a U.S. based human rights group," and at another point as a "New York group . . . a critic of the Reagan administration's policies in Central America. . . ."[87]

The Revolutionary Churches. With the growth of liberation theology, communist revolutionaries in Latin America have found many sympathetic supporters in North American church groups. The widespread Leftist bias of many such groups has been clearly noticed by Jose Esteban Gonzalez, the exiled coordinator of Nicaragua's independent Permanent Commission for Human Rights. Gonzalez has told journalist Shirley Christian that when he visited Washington in early 1979 to expose the sins of Somoza, he was warmly received by Protestant and Catholic church groups; yet when he returned later to criticize the Sandinistas, his reception was "very cool, even hostile."[88]

One church organization that has played a significant role in supporting communist revolutions is the National Council of Churches (NCC). Documents captured from El Salvador's armed guerrillas show that the NCC has provided funds to that rebel movement, and CBS's "60 Minutes" has reported on an NCC study booklet promoting Castro's regime as a model for other Caribbean countries. A 1982 NCC report claimed there was "no religious repression in Nicaragua" and was followed by a statement by the Rev. Paul McCleary that the Sandinista regime was guilty of only "some mistakes [which] it seems eager to correct." James Tyson notes that McCleary had earlier gained notoriety as executive director of the NCC's Church World Service. In that role, he traveled to North Vietnam to visit one of the infamous "reeducation camps." Returning to the U.S., he reported that he found the food "delicious," and that the communists were doing a better job of "healing the wounds of war" than the United States was. (Those camps were, in other reports, shown to be hovels where political prisoners were worked and starved to death; obviously, the tens of thousands of Vietnamese who gave up everything and risked their very lives to flee would not agree with the Rev. McClearly about the healing qualities of the communist regime).[89]

As we have seen, the Roman Catholic Church is another religious institution that has been active in supporting revolutionary causes. While the Catholic bishops in El Salvador have approved of U.S. aid to the Salvadoran government, their colleagues in the United States have opposed it. One important Latin America specialist at the U.S. Catholic Conference is Thomas E. Quigley, a deputy to the director of the Conference's International Justice and Peace Division. Quigley, who serves on the boards of both the Washington Office on Latin America and the Council on Hemispheric Affairs, has said, "I think many in the church would go farther and say the FDR and FMLN are the embodiment of the legitimate aspirations of El Salvadoran people."[90] He dismisses reports of religious persecution in Nicaragua as "the silly rantings of the right wing."[91]

In November 1987, the National Conference of Catholic Bishops overwhelmingly approved a policy statement calling U.S. support for the *contras* "morally flawed," expressing full support for the Arias peace plan. (The bishops said nothing about Soviet and Cuban aid to the Sandinistas.)[92]

Of specific note is a missionary branch of the Catholic Church, the Maryknoll order. A Maryknoll publication entitled *Communism in the Bible* contains such passages as:

For any Christian to claim to be anti-Communist, without a doubt constitutes the greatest scandal of our century.

For Jesus, whether conservatives like it or not, was in fact a Communist.

Jesus explicitly approves and defends the use of violence.

It is criminal to defend repression by the procedures of quoting to the oppressed about turning the other cheek. Supporters of this official theory will have to be punished for discouraging the struggle against injustice with this verse.[93]

One is compelled to wonder whether the enthusiasms of these religious leaders vis-a-vis communism were not more inflamed and informed more by the 21 commandments of the Second Congress of the Comintern in 1920 than by the 10 commandments which Lenin specifically repudiated. Those 21 points included the obligation to help the Soviet Republic in its struggle against counterrevolution, employing all means legal and illegal to this end as well as the obligation to fight against the government of one's own country. On October 2, 1920, Lenin contrasted communist "ethics" to "bourgeois" ethics which he said were based on God's commandments. "We do not believe in God. . . . We say that our morality is entirely subordinate to the interests of the class struggle." The communists were, in fact, in power less than one year when they issued a decree denying churches all property and legal rights—in effect outlawing their existence. Religious marriage was abolished and the family was declared obsolete. To underscore Lenin's code of "ethics," during 1922, some 8,100 priests, monks and nuns were executed. In 1929, the Soviet constitution was amended making it a crime against the state to propagate religion—"the law on religious cults." Children of priests were forced to renounce their fathers to receive food rations and educational benefits.[94]

Despite their radical views, the Maryknolls have exerted considerable influence in the United States. Tip O'Neill (D-MA), formerly Speaker of the U.S. House of Representatives and one of the most powerful men in the U.S. government, boasted of his "connection with the Maryknoll order."

He adds, "I have great trust in that order. When the nuns and priests come through, I ask them questions about their feelings, what they see, who the enemy is, and I'm sure I get the truth." Of those "coming through," few had greater access than the Maryknoll nun Peggy Healey, an outspoken Sandinista zealot based in Managua.[95] Miguel D'Escoto, the Sandinista Foreign Minister, is a Maryknoll priest was a long-time editor of the Maryknoll magazine before he joined the Marxist government.

One organization that receives funding from the Maryknoll order is the *Instituto Historico Centroamericano* in Managua, though this institute and its sister organization, the Central American Historical Institute (CAHI), located at Georgetown University in Washington, D.C., are more closely affiliated with the Jesuit order than with the Maryknoll. According to Powell, CAHI "was established at the injunction of Alvaro Arguello, a Jesuit priest who headed the Sandinista-controlled Nicaraguan Council of State." He terms the Managua institute a "quasi-official information bureau of the Sandinista regime."[96] CAHI's office space in Washington is donated by Georgetown, a Jesuit University. CAHI claims to be an "independent, non-governmental research center," but its true purpose was made clear in its request for funding from the World Council of Churches. In requesting $36,560 to establish "a channel of communication to and from Nicaragua," CAHI stated:

The news has largely projected a colourless if not distorted image of the ongoing process in Nicaragua, often in the absence of corroborating background information. Moreover, an increasing number of organizations in Europe and America in general in addition to cooperating agencies and solidarity committees have drawn attention to the lack of regular, speedy news, above all at the time when Nicaragua is being criticized by conservative circles throughout the world press.

The government of Nicaragua does not have the necessary resources to meet this challenge.[97]

Therefore, CAHI proposed to set up a telex service to send "news" to various centers in Europe and America.

As for the role of the Nicaraguan branch, the Heritage Foundation's Joan Frawley writes:

In Managua, the *Instituto Historico Centroamericano* is a fixture on pro-Sandinista tours of projects and institutions where the revolution's supporters testify on behalf of its achievements. When foreign journalists visit Nicaragua, the Instituto's staff is on hand to provide party-line answers about the plight of the Miskito Indians on the Atlantic Coast or the conflict between the Nicaraguan Catholic hierarchy and the government.[98]

An example of the party line as CAHI pushes it in Washington: Jorge Salazar, popular leader in Nicaraguan agriculture who was ambushed and assassinated by Sandinista security forces, was, according to CAHI, "killed in a November 1980 dispute with Nicaraguan police."[99]

U.S. church groups have shown a similar tunnel vision on the refugee issue. Church groups have been conspicuous by their absence in support of the one in ten Nicaraguans who have fled their country since the Sandinistas seized power— many to miserable refugee settlements in neighboring Honduras and Costa Rica. But—and again by contrast—church officials have been in the vanguard of those agitating for the rights of pro-communist refugees to return to El Salvador. A delegation of 10 U.S. church men and women—in a glare of admiring publicity—rushed to the Mesa Grande camp in southwestern Honduras in October 1987. Their avowed purpose: to escort many of the 4,500 refugees to "safety" back in the five Salvadoran villages they fled during bitter fighting between 1980 and 1983. The government had balked because it viewed the sudden return of these refugees as an FLMN attempt to rebuild its base camps in the area. Church and refugee officials acknowledged probable ties between the returnees and the communist guerrilla forces but thought they ought to be allowed back. "We see this as the beginning of what we've been looking forward to for a long time—the people being able to go home, plant their crops, build their schools," Lutheran Bishop Gustav H. Schultz, leader of the religious group said. (Apparently the bishop was not aware that five million other Salvadorans had been planting their crops and building their schools throughout the long ordeal of a communist-triggered and communist-sustained war.) Col. Benjamin Canjura, head of the military detachment in the area, said "if they go home and tend to their work, they will be fine. But, if they become collaborators of the terrorists, they will have problems." With that, the Salvadoran officials halted the foreign "escorts" at the border and allowed the returnees in for processing, sending them on their way back to their villages aboard 23 U.N.-provided buses. Looking on were the organizers of the event: the National Committee for Repopulation, a Salvadoran group affiliated with the guerrillas.[100]

Other church organizations have also been in the forefront of the promotion of Sandinista aims in the United States—the leadership of the 1.6-million member United Church of Christ and the central office of the Episcopal Church in New York, importantly among them. The Rev. Jay Lintner, who directs the Washington office of the United Church of Christ, was quoted by James Tyson as saying: "Central America will be the biggest issue, by far, and the key question is whether we could stop American funding to the *contras*. Another big issue is South Africa."[101]

No sooner had the Arias peace plan been signed in Guatemala City than a coalition of 30 religious and peace groups announced a nationwide campaign billed as "the largest effort so far to block aid to Nicaraguan rebel armies and

promote a Central American peace initiative." At press conferences in Washington and Los Angeles, the group said the
campaign would include lobbying of congressional offices,
acts of civil disobedience, a media campaign, and demonstrations. As if to underscore its determination, one of the
groups—the Santa Monica-based Office of the Americas—
invaded the Van Nuys office of the Air National Guard; 30
were arrested. (The office coordinates "educational" tours to
Nicaragua.)[102]

Nor were the foreign policy passions of churchmen limited
to abstract statements. The Roman Catholic bishop presiding
at the 1986 funeral of William Casey, late director of the
Central Intelligence Agency, took advantage of the presence
of the president and other high administration officials to
excoriate U.S. policies in Central America and elsewhere.
And, a group calling itself Disciples Peace Fellowship circu-
lated a letter at the annual General Assembly of the 1.1-
million member Christian Church (Disciples of Christ) blast-
ing the policies of former member Ronald Reagan. Among
the signers of the letter were John Humbert, president and
general minister of the church, and T. J. Liggett, moderator
of the General Assembly. The letter called on Reagan to
"listen to the message of the church, instead of depending
upon advice from the Pentagon and the merchants of war
materials." It also condemned aid to the *contras* and called for
Reagan to support the Arias "peace" plan.[103]

Useful Idiots and Political Pilgrims

As early as his 1902 pamphlet, *What is to be Done?*, Lenin used
the expression "useful idiots" to refer to the naive and gullible
people from all walks of life who could be induced to support
communist aims unwittingly. Since then, millions of well-
meaning people who would never knowingly support Soviet
communism have been duped into doing so just the same.

While they understandably resent being labelled stooges, the fact remains that the Soviet Union operates a sophisticated apparatus for deceiving and manipulating innocent people, and it has been enormously successful. This is affirmed by numerous defectors, many of whom admit to having been duped themselves.

This strategy has been used very effectively by Castro and, more recently, by the Sandinistas, both in the United States and at home. Consider this excerpt from an interview of Alvaro Baldizon Aviles, former Chief Investigator for the Sandinista Interior Ministry's Special Investigations Commission, conducted by journalist Peter Crane:

> ABA: I have heard [Interior Minister] Tomas Borge use the expression in Spanish "idiotas utiles," to refer to people that he says, "these useful idiots are helping us a lot."

> PC: Did Tomas Borge consider Witness for Peace a "useful idiot?"

> ABA: Yes. Tomas Borge has said at different opportunities that these groups of "useful idiots" even though they are of a reactionary essence, because of the religious nature of the groups, these groups can be useful if you know how to use them well, they can be used for the benefit of the propaganda strategy of the Sandinista Front vis-a-vis Western countries.

> PC: But is *Witness for Peace* specifically one of them?

> ABA: Yes. But they act with an honest motivation and with good intentions but the people that are using them are the Sandinistas.

> PC: That is serious because they have a measure of influence over some Christians in the U.S.

> ABA: Tomas Borge has said in some party meetings that there is nothing better to create problems to [sic] the U.S. government than take advantage of U.S. religious figures and take

advantage of the political short-sightedness of the people of the United States.

PC: This is a direct quote from Tomas Borge?

ABA: Yes.[104]

Baldizon has reported that "these groups of 'useful idiots' " have included a variety of foreign delegations from the United States and Europe.

In his book *Political Pilgrims*, University of Massachusetts sociologist Paul Hollander documented the pilgrimages of Westerners—useful idiots—who visited and paid homage to the communist societies of the USSR, China, and Cuba, which many gullible people saw as grand new utopian experiments. Hollander reminds us how, in the 1930s, many brilliant Western intellectuals who visited Soviet Russia were completely duped by the communists' sophisticated propaganda machinery. While Stalin was deliberately starving to death ten million Soviet citizens as part of his agricultural collectivization, political pilgrim and renowned British scientist Julian Huxley claimed that the Soviet people were "not at all undernourished."[105] Likewise, another pilgrim was so thoroughly duped as to claim that "in England a delinquent enters [a prison] as an ordinary man and comes out as a 'criminal type,' whereas in Russia he enters . . . as a criminal type and would come out an ordinary man but for the difficulty of inducing him to come out at all. As far as I could make out they could stay as long as they liked." That was the judgment of no less than George Bernard Shaw.[106]

Because of its far-reaching propaganda value, political tourism plays an important supporting role in the "war in Washington." In one of its manifestations, teams of "true believers" are recruited to perform unpaid manual labor for the communist regime and are given constant indoctrination to reinforce their ideological faith. Such teams began in 1969 in Cuba as the Venceremos Brigades. Managed there by Cuban intelligence, which is thoroughly controlled by the Soviet KGB, the brigades provide Castro with an excellent source of information about the U.S., as well as an opportunity to recruit agents for future use.[107] A similar program is run in Nicaragua by Tomas Borge's Sandinista Directorate for State Security, which puts the pilgrims to work picking coffee or cotton on state farms. A student from the University of Maryland who went there "to work in the fields and pay my dues" reports that he did so as part of a course assignment.[108]

Nor do their "exploits" go unheralded at home. *The Washington Post* gave cover display in its Sunday magazine (circulation one-million-plus) to a story by one of its reporters who spent several weeks in 1985 in Nicaragua reporting on some of the American "brigadistas" (among 1,150 who have gone so far) working in the countryside. What made the story—which rambled over nine pages of the magazine—so remarkable is that the writer reveals (near the very end) that though he ostensibly went in search of the "spirit of Nicaragua," his command of Spanish was so weak that he needed the services of an interpreter. It was remarkable also in that the writer allowed his sources to spew countless propagandistic claims without visible evidence of the usual reportorial diligence in checking or challenging any of them. (But then the author would also reveal his own jejeune prejudices. This, for example, is what he had to say about Ortega's inauguration: "It was an inaugural ball unlike any other, crackling with emotional intensity. There were no tuxedos or evening gowns, just the everyday clothes of the masses, jeans, sweatshirts, skirts and a smattering of military fatigues. . . ."[109]

Quite apart from the work brigades, Castro and the Sandinistas have vigorously promoted political visits by Americans as an important means of influencing U.S. voters and thereby American foreign policy. The tours also generate hard currency for the Nicaraguan government. The itineraries are carefully planned and activities meticulously orchestrated for maximum propaganda impact. Sometimes the sales pitch is aimed at the tourist's vanity, as when Castro puffed sociologist C. Wright Mills by telling him that Mills's *The Power Elite* had been a bedside book of most of the guerrillas in the Sierra Maestra.[110] Often the communists will attempt to "buy off" the guest with extravagant hospitality, as described by journalist Frances Fitzgerald:

> It was embarrassing for us to make demands [regarding itineraries] since the government insisted on treating us as guests and keeping us in a style to which even Cuban officials are not accustomed. Each of us who stayed behind after the Celebrations was given a car and driver, and at the Capri we had air-conditioned rooms, meals with beer and wine and as much meat each day as the Cuban rationing system allows an individual for a week.

Always, the visitors are closely watched. According to one traveler:

> Every taxi journey is logged at a special office inside each major hotel. You are required to give your destination and your name and your hotel room. These are then copied into a log. These logs are openly examined at regular intervals by the police.

> An American business traveller has reported that the cornerstone of all arrangements was the "hot line" telephone in our villa, which seemed to be in constant use, day and night. Via this life-line, Havana could monitor our progress through housing projects, schools, national shrines, cattle-breeding farms and recreational centers. . . .
> Hotel elevator operators . . . function effectively as wardens, checking passengers' room identifications before permitting access to each floor.[111]

In addition to flattery, bribery, and the careful regulation of itineraries, elaborate deceptions are frequently arranged for the benefit of foreign guests. Alvaro Baldizon explains that while Tomas Borge does most of his work in an office decorated with pictures of Marx and Lenin, Borge also maintains an office decorated with pictures of poor children, crucifixes, religious tapestries, and a large wooden statue of Christ. This is where he receives visiting church groups. Borge prepares for such meetings by studying the Bible, for he believes, "There is no more effective way to combat the enemy than with his own weapons."[112] Baldizon also reports that

> Tomas Borge gave me the job of keeping a list of 10 persons with health or economic problems to be available for a "show," whenever a foreign delegation would visit. He would arrange to be attending the person at the hour his guests would arrive in order to impress them. One of these individuals was a blind man who had asked for an accordion to use as a means of supporting his mother and himself. Borge said that he would give him the instrument, and I withdrew money from petty cash to make a down payment. After we gave the blind man his accordion in front of a group of West Germans, I received instructions to take it back.... Borge made a show with this man, just as he did with others.[113]

Another common means of deception is the model prison. Carlos Garcia, a former political prisoner of the Sandinistas, offers his description of such a place:

> When visitors arrive (as was the case of ex-Attorney General Ramsey Clark), they are escorted by well-trained, beautiful, easily seduced translators who take care that the visitor's opinion [will] be favorable.... I happened to be in the infirmary when Clark arrived. As it was, behind a wall where he observed the apparently good medical attention given to the prisoners, there were several punishment cells where 4 female prisoners ... had been confined the previous night.... The female prisoners screamed that night, and the next day they said they had been raped by the guards. Before Mr. Clark's arrival, they had been given a shot of a certain substance that rendered

them unconscious, so the distinguished visitor only saw the bright side.[114]

A different kind of deception, far grander in its scale and its impact on foreigners, is the mass rally, whereby thousands of citizens turn out to honor their exalted leaders and praise their socialist revolution. As one Cuban refugee explains it, "People are always amazed how Castro gets half a million people to show up. . . . Basically when he talks they shut down certain parts of the factories, shut down the schools, bus half a million people to Havana and don't let them leave until he's finished."[115] The procedure is the same in Nicaragua, where anyone not wishing to cooperate is threatened with the loss of his job.[116]

How effective are such propaganda techniques? Well, Senator George McGovern returned from a trip to Cuba saying that "from all indications, Castro has the support and out-right affection of his people."[117] Actor Gary Merrill concluded, after a brief visit to Nicaragua, "This is a beautiful country with a beautiful government, a pure government. The people who run it are the most honest in the world, the last people likely to commit any atrocities. They are just like Jesus." He was so impressed that he agreed to assist the government in producing a propaganda film.[118]

It was a visit to Cuba that prompted a group of Methodist ministers to write in 1981, "We saw . . . a country where the great majority of people believe they are the makers and the beneficiaries of a new society . . . we were inspired. . . . We returned hoping that our communities can lead America in developing humility; we need to learn from Cuba."[119] And when Jim Wright (D-TX), then House Majority Leader, led a delegation of congressmen (sent by President Carter) to Managua in 1980, his reaction to what he saw was that the Sandinista regime "has ideas like our own" on the subject of human rights. He said the FSLN had "good ideas" about "liberty, justice, and human dignity."[120]

Carlos Franqui, a confidant of Castro who later broke with the communists, recalled from his days in Cuba, "On the way back to Havana I passed through Varadero and wondered what sort of Cuba the visitors were seeing while ten minutes away there was a carnival of persecution in full swing. These people saw a stage-set Cuba, not the reality we had to live in every day, and they took the part for the whole."[121]

The Press

Without a doubt, no aspect of the "war in Washington" is more important than the press, for no instrument shapes U.S. public opinion more thoroughly. Understanding this, the revolutionary movements of Latin America have worked very hard to maximize their favorable publicity. A document captured from the Salvadoran guerrillas revealed a plan named *Operacion Aguila* (Operation Eagle) aimed at subverting foreign journalists, and indicated that the FMLN had "advanced the most" with reporters of the Associated Press, United Press International, and the Spanish News Agency EFE.[122] One technique used by the Sandinistas to cultivate friendly reporters, according to Latin America journalist Daniel James, "is to see that the bachelors among them are suitably accompanied by trusted Sandinista females."[123]

Exploiting reporters' biases is another part of the communist game plan. The proportion of U.S. media representatives in Nicaragua who are sympathetic to the Sandinistas may be as high as 90 percent, according to James. As a prime example, he cites John Lantigua, then writing for UPI, *Newsweek*, *The Washington Post*, *The Chicago Tribune*, and *The Dallas Morning News*. Lantigua's enthusiasm for the Nicaraguan government is such that his friends and colleagues call him "Johnny Sandinista."[124] James's assessment of journalistic bias is corroborated by a remark made by the then foreign editor of *The Washington Post*, Karen de Young, who told an audience at the

Institute for Policy Studies, "Most journalists now, most Western journalists at least, are eager to seek out guerrilla groups, leftist groups, because you assume they must be the good guys."[125]

It is striking how far such journalists will go to plant their assumptions in the thinking of their readers. Nora Astorga, who in 1978 admitted her role in the brutal torture and murder of Nicaraguan General Reynaldo Perez Vega, was described six years later by *The Washington Post* in the following language: "She walks down the stairs in Gloria Vanderbilt jeans and a green cashmere sweater. The cheekbones are high, with a wisp of blue shadow about dark brown eyes. Her nails are lacquered pearl and her voice is husky from inhaling too many Marlboros and exhaling revolution. She smiles."[126] This murderess, incidentally, has been aptly chosen by the Sandinistas to represent Nicaragua at the United Nations.

The leftward bias of many American newspapers is affirmed by Jose Esteban Gonzalez of the Nicaraguan Permanent Commission for Human Rights, who reports that in years past, he could call the editors of major U.S. newspapers, and "my statements concerning violations of human rights by the Somoza regime made headlines the following day. Today, they don't even answer my calls."[127]

The approach of the American press to Cuba is similar. Says one Cuban exile: "One can easily imagine the disdain and frustration with which Cubans look upon foreign reporters—often officially escorted and always friendly toward the regime—who stop them to ask naively: 'Amigo, are you happy with the revolution? What do you think of Fidel Castro?' "[128]

Finally, even the most casual reader of newspapers or newsmagazines, radio news listener or television news viewer, must, by now, be familiar with the monotonous ritual: The *contras* are invariably described as "U.S.-backed," or, in even more sinister usage, "the CIA-supported." The democratic government of El Salvador is "the U.S.-backed." By contrast: the Sandinistas are rarely referred to as "Soviet-backed," or

"Cuban-backed," despite the fact that Soviet military aid to the Sandinistas in only the first four months of 1987 was, for example, larger than the total of all U.S. military aid to the *contras* in the entire six years of their existence. Nor are the Salvadoran guerrillas labelled as "communist" (they are), or "Cuban-supported," or "Managua-manipulated" (command-control-communications for them are all in Managua). The effect, obviously, is to produce an image: The People vs. the United States.[129]

The Politics of Human Rights

The failure of the Carter administration's foreign policy is manifest in the turmoil that now plagues Central America, courtesy of Nicaragua. To say simply that this failure resulted from using human rights concerns as the basis for policy is to obscure the important fact that there was never a sincere effort to deal even handedly with the human rights situations in all countries, nor was there any concern shown for the future human rights of populations facing imminent communism. The whole issue was largely an excuse for supporting Leftist movements seeking to overthrow anti-communist regimes friendly to the United States.

Nor, it would appear, did Mr. Carter learn from his own mistakes. When Speaker Wright briefly played surrogate Secretary of State in his November 1987 talks in Washington with Sandinista leader Ortega, Carter jumped in to defend Wright—and take a swipe at the man who had so resoundingly defeated him in 1980, Ronald Reagan. Said Carter: "Had the president and secretary of state been carrying on their duties to try to enhance the peace in Central America rather than being the major obstruction of peace, then I don't think the speaker would have to take the actions he did." That outburst prompted the very liberal (and anti-*contra*) *Washington Post* to observe editorially: "When he [Carter] left office, the sky was darkening in Central America. Now, after a very long night, it may be lightening. For that, Ronald Reagan is 'the major obstruction of peace'?"[130]

Despite improving conditions, the human rights issue has remained at the center of the policy debate on Central America. To be sure, there are still serious abuses occurring in Central American countries whose governments are supported by the United States, and it is essential that we be concerned about them and seek to help those countries improve their records as much as possible. But we should not be fooled by the activists of the Revolution Lobby who continue to exploit the human rights issue to advance their Leftist revolutionary aims.

Caution is in order even when dealing with "respectable" human rights watchdogs, such as Amnesty International. But the lack of balance that characterizes that organization's reports is even more pronounced in the publications of the Revolution Lobby. The sad truth is that the efforts of Latin American leftists and their American collaborators to undermine support, both in Congress and among American voters, for the policies of the Reagan administration, entail the constant trumpeting of exaggerated, and sometimes fabricated, stories of atrocities said to be committed by pro-U.S. governments or democratic freedom fighters. Until 1984, the target was the government of El Salvador, but after the voters there turned out in impressive numbers—despite communist threats—to choose their own leaders, it became more difficult to argue that the people of El Salvador were oppressed by their government. So the Nicaraguan *contras* became the target of opportunity. Though the human rights performance of the Nicaraguan resistance is far from perfect, it does not include the systematic, institutionalized abuse of human rights evidenced by the Sandinista regime, and it is hardly the orgy of torture and murder described by the *contras*' enemies.

The slander campaign waged against the *contras* has been

an important part of the war in Washington, a joint undertaking of the Revolution Lobby and the Sandinista government. The role of the Nicaraguan government is to provide "facts" for its American helpers to disseminate through apparently neutral outlets. A good illustration of this is the aforementioned case in which the Sandinista Institute of Social Security and Social Welfare supplied "information" that the Nicaragua Network was able to inject into the U.S. congressional debate. Additional Nicaraguan disinformation is produced by the government's National Commission for the Protection and Promotion of Human Rights. Founded in 1980 as a propaganda organ, the Commission's board initially included sincere defenders of human rights, but these members were harassed and ultimately replaced by the Sandinistas. Recently the Commission's activities have included threatening or bribing victims of government abuse into claiming they were abused by the *contras*.[131]

In 1987, the *contras* even had to defend themselves against two congressional investigations of charges that they were involved in drug trafficking. Although those charges were garishly publicized, there was little (or no) space given, months later, when Committee investigator Robert A. Birmingham of the Iran-*contra* committee reported: "Our investigation has not developed any corroboration of media-exploited allegations of U.S. government-condoned drug trafficking by *contra* leaders or *contra* organizations or that *contra* leaders or organizations did in fact take part in such activity." Even Congressman Charles Rangel (D-NY), a conspicuous liberal, announced after attending a closed-door briefing that "none of the witnesses gave any evidence that would show the *contra* leadership was involved in drug smuggling."[132]

An organization similar to the Sandinista "human rights" group operates in El Salvador on behalf of the FMLN guerrillas. Nominally independent, the Commission on Human

Rights has been the source of many reports of atrocities attributed to the Salvadoran government forces, reports that have found publication in such papers as *The Washington Post.* Yet a captured guerrilla document refers to "institutions controlled by us, such as the Commission on Human Rights."[133]

Far more sinister than the fabrication of *contra* atrocities is the Nicaraguan government's use of what it calls Special Operations Forces, which terrorize the countryside while disguised as *contras.* Trained in East Germany, they began operations in late 1981, according to Alvaro Baldizon, who reports:

> The soldiers were disguised as counter-revolutionary *guerrilleros.* They were given old clothes and miscellaneous M-16 and Galil weapons.
>
> They went into the bush, and began operations as if they were part of the resistance. They killed about a dozen *campesinos* [peasants] who were known Sandinista collaborators. They burned their houses and set fire to a government cooperative.
>
> A new unit was inaugurated in October 1984, whose mission was distinctly more oriented toward international propaganda. . . . An ex-member of the FDN, Alfredo Lazo Valdivia was assigned as a guide. They began operations near the Honduran border in Chinandega, Madriz, Nueva Segovia, and Jinotega. They also made selective incursions into Honduras. They still operate in that area, and their mission is to pose as FDN combatants [*contras*], ambush civilian vehicles, as well as threaten and beat up local peasants, especially those known to have collaborated with the government. They are one of Interior Minister Borge's greatest treasures.[134]

As the Nicaraguan government stage-manages the human rights drama at home, the Revolution Lobby takes care of the advertising in Washington. While some members of the lobby are content to use the Sandinistas' numbers (as we have seen), many generate their own data, perhaps to avoid too obvious a connection with the communist regime. Excellent examples in this category are the Americas Watch Committee (AWC) and the Washington Office on Latin America (WOLA). On March 5 and 7, 1985, these organizations issued reports ostensibly documenting dozens of bloody crimes by the Nicaraguan *contras*. Each group acknowledged that its timing was planned to produce the maximum impact on Congress, which was then debating the administration's request for $14 million in aid for the freedom fighters.[135] Despite this, an AWC spokesman claimed then—as they would when releasing their 1987 report—that his group "takes no position on the general question of whether the United States should fund the contras."[136]

The two reports received coverage in most of the major media outlets, including all three major networks, *Time*, *Newsweek*, *The New York Times*, *The Washington Post*, and *The Los Angeles Times*. According to *The Boston Globe*, "Democrats said that they will use the charges to fight the administration's request for renewed U.S. aid for the contras,"[137] and indeed they did. Many congressmen placed greater confidence in the sensational claims of the two radical activist organizations than in the more sober appraisals of the State Department. Due in large part to the torrent of accusations, the president's aid request was defeated.

The reliability of Americas Watch reports can be inferred from its transparent pretensions to objectivity. In 1985 as in 1987, it purported to document human rights violations on both sides of the conflict, but charged the Sandinistas with executing only seven Miskito Indians in 1982. As Alvaro Baldizon revealed several months later, even Sandinista government records put the figure at over 250.[138]

WOLA's 1985 report made no pretense of balance, focusing exclusively on *contra* infractions. Its author, American lawyer Reed Brody, described in shocking detail numerous killings, rapes, beatings, and kidnapings, as well as the forced conscription of troops. It was perfect material for whipping up congressional outrage. Brody admitted that his investigation was initiated at the suggestion of the Washington law firm that represented the Sandinista government, but that did not deter Congressman Sam Gejdenson (D-CT) from publicly endorsing the report.

The congressional outrage, however, should have been directed at Reed Brody.[139] In his investigation, Brody relied very heavily on Sandinista sympathizers (including *Witness for Peace*) for testimony, even allowing the government to help him locate witnesses. Brody interviewed only witnesses residing in Nicaragua, that is, those who would be subject to reprisals for providing the "wrong" testimony. Brody set up an office in the government-controlled National Commission for the Protection and Promotion of Human Rights; he never visited the independent Permanent Commission for Human Rights. Brody repeatedly characterized military engagements as attacks on civilians, describing events in great detail while omitting any mention of Sandinista troops. A case in point: His one-page description of an attack on the "Jacinto Hernandez Cooperative," which, he said, "had over 100 people, but was still mostly pastureland and cows,"[140] concealed the fact that the *contras* were attacking a Sandinista Army battalion, which fought them for three days.[141]

Especially suspect were the accounts of "mass kidnapings." On several occasions, large groups of Miskito Indians have escaped from the relocation camps, where they were held by the government, and fled to Honduras, sometimes with the assistance of the *contras*. In such cases, the government invariably claims that the *contras* have kidnaped the Indians.[142] Brody chose to follow the government line. In one case, he described a "mass kidnaping"—two hundred victims marched over rough terrain for two weeks—on the basis of a single witness, who, Brody admitted, was located for him by the government. In another case, 1,230 people were "kidnaped" from Francia Sirpe. According to Brody's witness, the *contras* went "from house to house, taking all the people out with rifle blows, and many old people, women, children and young people were crying out of fear, they didn't want to leave their town." One of the victims was said to be Monsignor Schlaefer, "the Catholic Bishop of Zelaya province."[143]

The first objection to Brody's account is that Francia Sirpe was a resettlement camp, not a town. The second objection is that there was no kidnaping. As Joshua Muravchik wrote in *The New Republic*,

> in one such incident that was widely followed by the Western press, the exodus was more accurately described as a liberation than a kidnapping. The incident was publicized last December because of the presence of American-born Roman Catholic Bishop Salvator Schlaefer. The Nicaraguan government announced that Schlaefer had been kidnapped and then murdered by the rebels. When he and his caravan of hundreds of Miskitos arrived safely in Honduras, it was revealed that the group had been aided in its flight by the "*contras*," and, according to Schlaefer, that it had been bombed and strafed by government forces.[144]

The "last December" referred to by Muravchik was December 1983, nine months before Reed Brody left for Nicaragua.

This is a small sampling of what was wrong with the WOLA report. Nevertheless, the report received uncritical front-page coverage in *The New York Times* and two and a half minutes of prime time on CBS News. When the president's *contra* aid request was defeated, Speaker of the House "Tip" O'Neill (D-MA) and Congressman Michael Barnes (D-MD), then chairman of the House Subcommittee on Western Hemisphere Affairs, both justified their opposition on the basis of the Brody report.[145]

Several days later, Barnes's subcommittee heard testimony from Bayardo de Jesus Payan, the former finance chief of the National Commission for the Protection and Promotion of Human Rights, where Brody had set up his Managua office. Payan, an eyewitness to Brody's ties with the Nicaraguan government, said "I believe and many believe in Nicaragua that the report presented by Mr. Brody is nothing more than a propaganda job directed and financed by the Sandinista government."[146]

Such episodes have not diminished the appetite of big media for such scare stories. For example, on October 17, 1987, *The Washington Post* splashed over virtually the entire top of a page a story claiming a Roman Catholic priest and a Seventh Day Adventist minister had been kidnaped by the *contras*. The story said the report was based on "information received by several religious and human-rights organizations," but deeper in the story it is shown that the original source was *Barricada*, the mouthpiece newspaper of the Sandinistas. The story also acknowledged that should the two be harmed, "it would be a severe blow to the efforts of the *contras* and their backers in the Reagan administration to persuade Congress to approve $270 million in new mlitary aid. . . ." The story also reported that the *contra* leadership not only denied knowledge of the kidnaping, but could state categorically that there was no truth to the "monstrous" claims that two clerics would be executed—even if they had been somehow picked up. None of this prevented the gaudy publication of an unverified story from a tainted source with obvious geopolitical overtones.[147]

In May 1984, Senator Edward Kennedy (D-MA) held a public forum to denounce a *contra* attack on the Nicaraguan "town" of Sumubila. "A total of seven people were killed, fifteen were wounded, and thirty-nine kidnapped during the raid," said the Senator. "It would appear that the only reason for the raid was to kidnap people to go into their army."[148] To document this position, Kennedy provided photographs of the wounded children and a list of the kidnap victims. He also produced three eyewitnesses to describe the atrocities, and an

American priest from Nicaragua, Father Gundrum, who claimed, "There are many other examples [of such raids], almost every day." Background material distributed by Kennedy's office characterized the four witnesses as "totally a-political." One of them assured the audience that no one fired back at the *contras*.

The forum received the desired publicity: *The New York Times*, *The Washington Post*, *The Wall Street Journal*. United Press International wrote, "Poor Miskito Indians from Nicaragua told a Congressional forum Friday that children are being murdered and kidnapped by U.S.-backed '*contra*' rebels. . . . Their stories of tragedy and loss were confirmed by an American Catholic priest."

The three Miskito eyewitnesses began to arouse suspicions, however, when they subsequently claimed not to have heard of any Miskitos being persecuted by the Sandinista government—this at a time when nearly twenty-three thousand Miskitos had fled the country to escape from the Nicaraguan army. Steadman Fagoth, the leader of the Miskito resistance faction implicated by the charges, sent Kennedy a stinging letter denying the allegations.[149]

That Fagoth's anger was justified was revealed by Joshua Muravchik. Writing in *New Republic*, Muravchik noted that a contemporary report in *Barricada*, the official Sandinista newspaper, said of the Sumubila raid that the attacking *contras* were repulsed by seventy defenders, who included policemen and militia. He also revealed that Kennedy's photographs and list of victims were supplied by the Nicaraguan government (not mentioned during the forum, but later admitted by Kennedy's office). Muravchik further revealed that all four of the anti-*contra* witnesses were supplied to Kennedy by that thinly veiled government front, the Instituto Historico Centroamericano (also admitted by Kennedy's office). Finally, it was noted that one month before the forum, the "a-political" Father Gundrum had appeared in a photograph in the *San Francisco Sunday Examiner and Chronicle* posing with a Soviet-made rifle. The accompanying article, entitled "Priest Carries Cross And Rifle," quoted Father Gundrum: "To me it was a day of grace the day the Sandinistas took over, and I really mean it."

Was Senator Kennedy duped?

How, either, to justify the behavior of his then-colleague from Massachusetts, Speaker O'Neill? Richard Perle, the brilliant former assistant secretary of defense, has wondered in print at "the solicitousness with which they [congressmen] sought to protect the Nicaraguan regime."

> While he now denies it, the record shows that former House Speaker "Tip" O'Neill had his own "workaround." After both houses had passed legislation to provide $ 100 million to the *contras,* O'Neill deliberately delayed, for four months, a routine House-Senate conference so that the urgently needed supplies could not be shipped to Central America. In all the talk about frustrating the will of the Congress, O'Neill's manipulation of the legislative process to achieve his agenda somehow has escaped the scrutiny of the select committee.

Perle also adds this insight to what he terms the "needle-threading micromanagement of the anti-*contra* congressional faction."

> And what is one to make of the sordid little encumbrance written into law by Representative Robert J. Mrazek (D-NY) that prohibited the delivery of *contra* aid to locations within 20 miles of the Nicaraguan border? Did Mrazek know (and when did he know it?) that the *contras* had a crucial base just 18 miles from the border? The lengths to which he went to draw the line precisely where he (and a majority of the House) insisted suggest that he understood precisely what he was doing, and why. The result of Mrazek's little legislative ploy was that delivery of urgently needed support to the *contras* was severely impeded.[150]

The Dangers

During the Carter years, the Revolution Lobby was well represented in the administration, for example by NACLA's Brady Tyson at the U.N., or the Transnational Institute's Robert Pastor with the National Security Council. When President Reagan entered the White House, however, the attention of the radical lobby necessarily became focused on Congress. The results, as we have seen, can be spectacular.

Yet more important than the occasional propaganda coup is the steady drumbeat of Leftist cant and Marxist suasion that, maintained by feverish activism, has gradually infiltrated serious political debate. "A perfect Marxist-Leninist analysis," were the words used by Viktor Gonchar, a Third Secretary at the Soviet embassy, to describe a speech presented by Democratic Senator Christopher Dodd.[151] Taking the form of a rebuttal to President Reagan's emergency address to the nation on April 27, 1983, Dodd's nationally televised speech defined the official position of the Democratic Party.

It is through its friends in Congress that the Revolution Lobby projects its influence most effectively. And when WOLA, NACLA, and the National Council of Churches joined the National Lawyers Guild (widely regarded as a Soviet front) and the U.S. Peace Council (a well-known communist front) in holding a National Conference on Nicaragua in 1979, they had the formal endorsement of five members of Congress. Congressmen Ronald Dellums (D-CA), Tom Harkin (D-IA), and Walter Fauntroy (D-DC), and Senators Mark Hatfield (R-OR) and Edward Kennedy (D-MA) thus lent their prestige to proceedings that included resolutions favoring financial support for the Sandinista guerrillas.[152]

Far more deplorable, however, was the solo performance by Congressman Dellums on behalf of the communist government of Grenada. As a member of the House Armed Services

Committee (with access to military secrets, incidentally), and as chairman of its Subcommittee on Military Installations and Facilities, Dellums had the responsibility for investigating the Point Salines airfield under construction in Grenada to determine whether its purpose was military, as the Reagan administration claimed, or strictly civilian, as was claimed by Maurice Bishop's regime. At stake was the possibility of the Soviet Union's acquiring landing rights to the airstrip, a matter with major strategic implications.

Ron Dellums and his staff prepared a sixty-six page report based on a "fact-finding" tour to Grenada *and Cuba*. In June 1982, Dellums presented the report to the Armed Services Committee with the words, "This report is intended to give . . . an objective assessment of factual information regarding Grenada and the building of the new international airport," adding that he hoped that "every member of the Committee will consider this material valuable and will refer to it as a precedent to seek the truth and present constructive arguments against many misconceptions regarding our relationship with Grenada." The report's conclusion was that "nothing being done in Grenada constitutes a threat to the United States or her allies."[153]

A very different picture was brought to light by the documents captured during the 1983 liberation of Grenada by U.S.-Caribbean forces. One document contained this notation, dated March 22, 1980, by Lieutenant Colonel Liam James, a deputy to Grenadian General Hudson Austin and a member of the New JEWEL Movement Central Committee: "The Revo[lution] has been able to crush the Counterrevolution internationally, airport will be used for Cuban and Soviet Military."[154] This, of course is what the Reagan administration had said all along. Another document, however, was remarkable for its revelations concerning Congressman Dellums. It consisted of a letter from Carlottia Scott, one of Dellums' congressional aides, to Grenadian Prime Minister Maurice Bishop, and it contained the following passages:

Ron has become truly committed to Grenada and has some very positive political thinking to share with you. He feels that he can best be of assistance in a counseling manner and hopes to be able to discuss these thoughts in the near future. He just has to get all to [sic] his thoughts in order as to how your interests can best be served. Ron, as a political thinker, is the best around and Fidel will verify that in no uncertain terms. . . .
We are now in the process of pulling together the report for the Armed Services Committee. . . . We hope that this report will serve as a basis for a clear understanding and direct counter to the Administration's policy . . . . However, the specifics need to be mapped out very carefull [sic] This is only part of what Ron needs to discuss with you in a much as [sic] this has to be a team effort. . . . Like I said, he's really hooked on you and Grenada and doesn't want anything to happen to building the Revo and making it strong.[155]

Miss Scott went on to say she knew of no one Dellums admired as much as he did Bishop, except for "Fidel."

There was yet another document found in Grenada that is pertinent to this episode, the minutes of a meeting of the New JEWEL Movement. They recorded the presence of Barbara Lee, a Dellums aide, who "had brought with her a report on the International Airport that was done by Ron Dellums. They have requested that we look at the document and suggest any changes we deem necessary. They will be willing to make the changes."[156]

Ron Dellums still sits on the Armed Services Committee.

Disraeli, in one of his novels, wrote that few ideas are certain, and fewer yet know which they are. But, the great British statesman of a century ago would add, what is certain is that it is with words that we govern men. Lenin understood that, as has every Soviet ruler since. Lenin also believed that he and those who accompanied him on his march to world conquest had a franchise to lie. "For Communists," he would proclaim in 1920, "morality consists entirely of compact united discipline and conscious mass struggle against the exploiters." Deceit, dissembling—anything and everything that would advance the cause of the revolution—all these were legitimate weapons to be brandished against those who stood in the way. "We must"—Lenin told his disciples—"resort to all sorts of stratagems, maneuvers, illegal methods, evasions and subterfuge . . . to carry on Communist work." A year later, Lenin told Foreign Affairs Commissar Grigory Chicherin: "Telling the truth is a bourgeois prejudice. Deception, on the other hand, is often justified by the goal."

So, too, from the beginning, was mass murder. On September 5, 1918, the Soviet cabinet authorized the Cheka—the forerunner of today's KGB, an agency such western "intelligentsia" as the media, the professorate, routinely, carelessly, mindlessly equate with the CIA—to carry out "merciless mass terror." Four months later, on January 24, 1919, new orders: "In view of experience with the Cossacks in civil war . . . wage the most ruthless possible war against all Cossack upper elements, exterminating them to the last man. . . ."

There was a central place, too, for murder's evil twins, terror and terrorism. "The questioning of Stalin's terror," Nikita Khrushchev told the Twentieth Party Congress, "may lead to the questioning of terror in general. But Bolshevism believes in the use of terror. Lenin held that no one was worthy of the name Communist who did not believe in terror."

Nothing was beyond the pale, not even nuclear annihilation. Writing in 1968, a Soviet analyst concluded: "On the Communist side, nuclear war will be lawful and just . . . the natural right and sacred duty of progressive mankind to destroy imperialism. . . ."

And so it was, as early as 1920, the Soviets would begin their systematic mugging of the world around them, training Indian terrorists at Tashkent, and so it was that Lenin would order terrorist bombing in Britain.

And so it was that they would use terror at home on a scale

the world had never before seen, to liquidate not only those who opposed them, but even those who might oppose them, or those thought to be thinking of opposing them. By 1922, at least 15 million of their fellow citizens had been put to death. These would be followed to their graves by millions more—literally millions—victims of cruelly contrived famine, mass executions, purges; lobotomies even; surgery no sane doctor would have prescribed, no real doctor would botch; torture; journeys into exile on railroad cars so cold the bodies stuck to the metal floors; Siberia.

And so it was, from the very beginning of their long night of Kafkaesque rule, they would paper the world with worthless agreements. The very first act of the Bolshevik government was, in fact, an act of international betrayal: with the war in Europe at its murderous peak, the new Russian rulers abandoned their western allies and sued for a separate peace with the Germans, so as to consolidate their fragile and fraudulent claim to power at home. That 1917 Decree of Peace proposal, written by Lenin himself, contains this passage that—as a gullible world would later learn (or never learn?)—has, for cynicism, few rivals in the annals of written language:

> If any people is held by force within the borders of a given state, if such a people in defiance of its expressed wish—whether this wish be expressed in the press, in meetings of the populace, in the decisions of a party, or in uprisings against the national yoke—is not given the right of deciding, free of every form of duress, by free elections, without the presence of the armed forces of the incorporating state or any more powerful state, what forms of national existence it wishes to have—if these circumstances prevail, then the incorporation of such a state should be called annexation, i.e., an act of seizure and force.[157]

There are no new ideas, only new debates.

Give peace a chance. Not—give freedom or liberty or hu-

man dignity a chance. Not—give me liberty or give me death.
Give peace a chance. Give peace a chance by signing an
agreement with a client state of a nation that has elevated
treachery and terror to the level of revolutionary principles,
with a government—the Sandinistas—that, itself, gained
power by promising to do what it never would do, what it
never had any intention of doing.

Given the fact that—in the crucial first months of the Central American peace process there was no real mechanism to
monitor compliance—nobody talked much about verification. Probably just as well. The memory of Vietnam, and then
the murder of that gentle land, Cambodia (Kampuchea, in
later usage) may be too uncomfortably fresh even for those
eternally eager for peace, any kind of peace, at any price.
There was, after all, an international verification commission
in Vietnam. That would not prevent the North Vietnamese
from breaking their pledge to remove 145,000 troops already
garrisoned on South Vietnamese soil—and then, infiltrate
30,000 more in just the first three months after the accord was
signed, adding, for good measure, 400 tanks and 300 pieces
of heavy artillery. These were, as peace plan architect Henry
Kissinger would later and ruefully write, "violations not technical [but] flagrant preparations for a new stage of war." The
United States protested to the Soviet Union, the source of the
arms. The Soviets shrugged. As for the International Commission of Control and Supervision—it was flawed from the
start—two of the four members were Soviet satrapies (Poland
and Hungary), effectively nullifying the work of the other two
(Indonesia and Canada). But when the commission did
become too curious, the North Vietnamese simply refused to
allow it into convoy areas, and even shot down one of its
observation aircraft.[158]

So it was, as weeks became months with nothing of real
consequence to show for the Arias peace process, the argument centered not on verification, not on past performance.

It centered on faith. To take an eloquent example: Stephen S. Rosenfeld, a member of *The Washington Post*'s editorial board, argued thus, in a thoughtful article written after he had a chance to meet with all four democratically elected Central American presidents:

> Sometimes the Latins are dismissed as frivolous for thinking they can wield moral pressure on the Nicaraguan Sandinistas, whose Marxism and hunger for power appear to distance them from conventional moral appeals. But what I hear from the Central American presidents is that they count on Daniel Ortega to do just what he solemnly undertook to do in the peace plan—to put aside dogma and start down a road leading to democracy.
>
> Why would Ortega do that? In the presidents' collective view, because he is under heavy pressure, from the *contras* and from the Nicaraguan people. Because he owes it to his fellow Latins who in the peace plan gave his regime a precious measure of security and legitimacy and the political space in which to make its way toward a common regional destination of democracy. And because the democratic idea is transcendent, unstoppable, the idea of the age. . . .[159]

Perhaps. Perhaps the Congress may yet give the *contras* the money they must have if they are to continue to bring that heavy pressure to bear. Perhaps the Soviets, for their own reasons, will tire of subsidizing yet another incompetent puppet. Perhaps a totalitarian government will respond to heavy pressure from its own people. Perhaps a committed Marxist-Leninist state will do what none has ever done before: voluntarily yield to that transcendent idea called democracy.

Perhaps.

NOTES

1. Philip Taubman, "Salvadorans' U.S. Campaign: Selling of Revolution," *The New York Times*, February 26, 1982, p. A-10.

2. *Newsweek*, November 14, 1983, p. 44.

3. Hanoi Radio, September 1, 1970, in J. Michael Waller, *Consolidating the Revolution: How the Sandinistas' Support Apparatus Operates in the United States* (Washington: Council for Inter-American Security, 1986), p. 12.

4. *Militant*, August, 1979, p. 28, in Waller, *Consolidating*, p. 24.

5. *The Challenge to Democracy in Central America*, U.S. Departments of State and Defense, June 1986, p. 52.

6. Waller, *Consolidating*, pp. 36–37.

7. Kevin Klose, "Ortega Seeks New Talks With U.S. Aides, Vatican: Jesse Jackson Hosts Nicaraguan in Chicago," *The Washington Post*, August 3, 1986, p. A-14. Note that the *Post* doesn't consider Jackson's sponsorship of a communist dictator to be front page material.

8. Diego A. Abich, "Fidel Castro's Role Behind Jesse Jackson's Cuba Tour," *The Wall Street Journal*, November 2, 1984, p. 29. The final declaration of the conference called for a closer association with black churches.

9. Allan C. Brownfeld and J. Michael Waller, *The Revolution Lobby* (Washington: Council for Inter-American Security, 1985), p. 94.

10. Abich, "Fidel Castro's role."

11. Ed Magnuson, "Stirring Up New Storms," *Time*, July 9, 1984, p. 9.

12. Carrick Leavitt, United Press International, "Ortega's Wife Praises Peace Activist; Thousands Rally at Site Where Protester Was Hit by Train," *The Washington Post*, Sept. 6, 1987, p. 7-A.

13. J. Michael Waller, "Celebrities Raise Money for El Salvador's Marxist Guerrillas," *West Watch* (Council for Inter-American Security), June–July 1986, p. 5.

14. *National Review*, September 26, 1986, p. 11.

15. The first quote is from Dennis Teti, "The Coup That Failed; An Insider's Account of the Iran/*Contra* Hearings," in *Policy Review*, #42, Fall 1987, p. 24. Teti was an associate staff member of the select committee investigating the Iran/*Contra* affair. The GAO material is

from Don Oberdorfer, "GAO Accuses Administration of Illegal Latin Propaganda," *The Washington Post*, Oct. 5, 1987, p. 1.

16. For more detailed information than is presented here, three excellent sources are Brownfeld and Waller, *The Revolution Lobby*; Waller, *Consolidating the Revolution* (both cited above); and S. Steven Powell, *Second Front: Advancing Latin American Revolution in Washington* (Washington: Capital Research Center, 1986).

17. Powell, *Second Front*, p. 6.

18. Brownfeld and Waller, *The Revolution Lobby*, p. 16.

19. Ibid.

20. Ibid., p. 17.

21. Virginia Prewett, "The Mysterious Letelier Affair: Another Rush to Judgement?" Special Report of the Council for Inter-American Security, September 1978, pp. 13–14, quoted in Brownfeld and Waller, *The Revolution Lobby*, p. 18.

22. Brownfeld and Waller, *The Revolution Lobby*, p. 18.

23. *The Southern Connection*, quoted in Brownfeld and Waller, ibid., pp. 21–22. Robert Pastor contributed to the report in 1976. He did not, however, participate in preparing the final draft which came out after he joined the Carter administration in eary 1977.

24. Brownfeld and Waller, *The Revolution Lobby*, pp. 23, 25.

25. Powell, *Second Front*, p. 20.

26. Brownfeld and Waller, *The Revolution Lobby*, p. 23.

27. Ibid., pp. 9, 11.

28. Draft Statement on ideology by the North American Congress on Latin America, May 1967, in Powell, *Second Front*, pp. 22–23.

29. Brownfeld and Waller, *The Revolution Lobby*, p. 11.

30. Ibid., p. 10.

31. Joan Frawley, "The Left's Latin American Lobby," Heritage Foundation *Institution Analysis* No. 31 (October 11, 1984), p. 2.

32. Brownfeld and Waller, *The Revolution Lobby*, p. 13.

33. Frawley, "The Left's," p. 4. She cites George Black and Judy Butler, "Target Nicaragua," *NACLA Report on the Americas*, January–February 1982, p. 29.

34. Powell, *Second Front*, p. 24.

35. Ibid., pp. 26, 27.

36. Ibid., p. 27.

37. Conference report, as quoted to the authors by J. Michael Waller of the Council for Inter-American Security.

38. Powell, *Second Front*, p. 27.

39. Ibid., p. 30.

40. Ibid., p. 34.

41. Brownfeld and Waller, *The Revolution Lobby*, p. 15.

42. Radio Sandino, June 5, 1984, in Brownfeld and Waller, ibid., p. 16.

43. Brownfeld and Waller, *The Revolution Lobby*, p. 15.

44. Frawley, "The Left's," pp. 9–10.

45. Brownfeld and Waller, *The Revolution Lobby*, p. 15.

46. "Human Rights in Latin America," a 1983 report by the Council on Hemispheric Affairs, p. 58, in Powell, p. 35.

47. Frawley, "The Left's," p. 9.

48. Waller, *Consolidating*, p. 51.

49. Brownfeld and Waller, *The Revolution Lobby*, pp. 31, 33.

50. "Report of Farid Handel's [sic] Trip to the United States," U.S. State Department, p. 11, in Powell, *Second Front*, p. 45. (Handal's name is misspelled throughout the report.)

51. Terri Shaw, "Mimeographs Roar in Propaganda War," *The Washington Post*, March 7, 1982, p. A22.

52. "Report of Farid Handal's Trip to the United States," pp. 20–21, in Powell, *Second Front*, p. 44.

53. Brownfeld and Waller, *The Revolution Lobby*, p. 34.

54. Ibid.

55. J. Michael Waller, "How Pat Schroeder Helps the Sandinistas," *Human Events*, May 10, 1986, p. 6. Waller writes that "the Feb. 8, 1979, CPUSA [U.S. Communist party] paper, *Daily World*, reported that the founding conference of what became the Nicaragua Network was initiated by the United States Peace Council (USPC), the American branch of the Soviet-controlled World Peace Council. . . . Sandy Pollack, a member of the CPUSA National Council and the International Solidarity Coordinator of the USPC, 'helped sow the seeds' of the Nicaragua Network, according to her official USPC biography published in 1985."

56. Brownfeld and Waller, *The Revolution Lobby*, p. 36.

57. Ibid., p. 37.

58. Waller, "How Pat Schroeder."

59. Schroeder's undated letter for a 1985 fundraising effort. Reproduced in Waller, *Consolidating*, p. 67.

60. Waller, *Consolidating*, p. 41.

61. John Lofton, "Without First Considering the Source . . ." *The Washington Times*, July 16, 1986, p. D1.

62. Powell, *Second Front*, p. 37.

63. Ibid., p. 38.

64. *The New York Times*, September 10, 1982, p. A4.

65. Robert White, prepared statement before the House Subcommittee on Western Hemisphere Affairs, February 2, 1984, p. 2, in Powell, *Second Front*, p. 38.

66. White testimony, p. 5, in Powell, ibid., p. 39.

67. Powell, *Second Front*, p. 39. For the quotation, Powell cites *Wall Street Journal* editorial, "Guerrilla PR," March 22, 1984.

68. Powell, *Second Front*, p. 37.

69. Stephen Kinzer, "29 U.S. Activists Reportedly Freed in Nicaragua," *The New York Times*, August 9, 1985, p. 4A.

70. L. Francis Bouchey, "Bearing False Witness . . . for 'Peace'," *West Watch*, September–October, 1985, p. 5. Hollyday's description is from *Sojourners* magazine, cited by Bouchey.

71. Peter T. Flaherty, "A Closer Look at 'Witness for Peace'," *The Presbyterian Layman*, November/December, 1985, p. 9.

72. Lawrence W. Reed, "Nicaragua's 'Army of Useful Idiots'," *Human Events*, June 7, 1986, p. 13 (photo caption).

73. " 'Siento mucho miedo, pero quiero protestar contra Reagan'," *Barricada*, August 5, p. 5; and (press release) "Cristianos norteamericanos rechazan amenaza del traidor," *El Nuevo Diario*, August 6, p. 7; both cited in Alejandro Bolanos-Geyer, "Taken for a Ride Down the San Juan River," *Voice of Nicaragua* (newsletter of the Nicaraguan Information Center, P.O. Box 607, St. Charles, MO 63302), November 1985, p. 2.

74. Bouchey, "Bearing False Witness" (entourage); and Flaherty (quotation).

75. "Crónica del secuestro," *Barricada*, August 12, p. 4, cited in Bolanos-Geyer, "Taken for a Ride."

76. Bolanos-Geyer, "Taken for a Ride."

77. Bouchey, "Bearing False Witness;" and Flaherty.

78. Data on Linder from: "Some Sandinista Supporters Want More American Deaths;" J. Michael Waller, "Benjamin Linder: A Casualty of his Parents;" "Linder Family Touring With Communist Group," all in *West Watch*, the first two p. 4, June 1987, the third from p. 3, October 1987; "Linder Falls Short Of Martyrdom; But Kostmayer Calls Him 'Hero,'" *Human Events*, May 30, 1987, p. 3. *West Watch* notes that Benjamin's mother, Elisabeth, is a local leader of the Women's International League for Peace and Freedom, which a 1982 State Department report describes as one of several "nominally independent organizations that are controlled by the Soviets . . ." (October 1987); his brother, John, first joined the youth branch of the Socialist Workers Party at age 15, and his father was active in the anti-war movement of the 1960s, and was quoted by *The Washington Post* magazine as saying, "in our house, socialism was not a dirty word, and freedom was not equated with capitalism." In San Francisco's Haight and Ashbury district—hot-bed of radicalism where the family lived during the 1960s—they were sufficiently conspicuous in the radical community to host at dinner such radical activists as Stokely Carmichael and Julian Bond. At the University of Washington in Seattle, Benjamin founded a chapter of the Committee in Solidarity with the People of El Salvador, and on arrival in Managua in 1984, worked for a time for the Sandinista government. A well-known picture showed him in a clown outfit, arms suspended by strings like a marionette, controlled by a "puppeteer" wearing an Uncle Sam hat. Around his neck was a sign marked "Honduras." *Human Events* quotes both *The Washington Post* and *The Los Angeles Times* as the sources of its report on the shooting incident in which Linder was killed.

79. "Helsinki Watch" brochure, Americas Watch, in Powell, *Second Front*, p. 31.

80. The Americas Watch Committee and the American Civil Liberties Union, *Report on Human Rights in El Salvador* (New York: Vintage Books, 1982), pp. v-vi, in Powell, *Second Front*, p. 31.

81. Fred Barnes, "The Sandinista Lobby: 'Human rights' groups with a double standard," *The New Republic*, January 20, 1986, p. 13.

82. Cynthia Arnson, Aryeh Neier, and Susan Benda, *As Bad as Ever: A Report on Human Rights in El Salvador*, Fourth Supplement (Washington: Americas Watch Committee and American Civil Liberties Union, January 31, 1984), pp. 7–8.

83. Juan Mendez, director of the Washington Office of the Americas Watch Committee, interview, March 13, 1985, in Powell, *Second Front*, p. 32.

84. Americas Watch, Lawyers Committee for International Human Rights, Washington Office on Latin America, *Honduras: On the Brink*

(Washington: Washington Office on Latin America, 1983), p. 7, in Powell, *Second Front*, p. 32.

85. Powell, *Second Front*, p. 32.

86. *Human Rights in Nicaragua*, pp. 14–15, 91, in Powell, *Second Front*, p. 33.

87. Rights Group Says *Contras* Are an 'Outlaw Force,'" Managua-datelined Associated Press story in *The Washington Post*, Nov. 6, 1987, p. A30.

88. Shirley Christian, *Nicaragua: Revolution in the Family* (New York: Vintage Books, 1986), p. 327.

89. Brownfeld and Waller, *The Revolution Lobby*, p. 42. The "60 Minutes" program aired on January 23, 1983. Source for the 1982 report and Rev. McCleary: Allan C. Brownfeld, "How U.S. Church Groups Further Soviet Goals in Central America," *Human Events*, June 6, 1987, pp. 10–11, commenting on a study done by James L. Tyson, *Prophets Or Useful Idiots? Church Organizations Attacking U.S. Central American Policy* (Washington: Council for the Defense of Freedom, 1987).

90. "Catholic Church is a Major Influence on U.S. Policies Toward El Salvador," *Congressional Quarterly Weekly Report*, April 24, 1982, p. 899.

91. Lawrence W. Reed, "Nicaragua's Army of Useful Idiots," *Human Events*, June 7, 1986, p. 13.

92. Marjorie Hyer, "Catholic Bishops Call Support for *Contras* 'Morally Flawed,' " in *The Washington Post*, Nov. 20, 1987, p. A 30.

93. Patrick Buchanan, "Get this—'Jesus was the first Sandinista'," syndicated column appearing in *The Washington Times*, June 3, 1983, quoted in Brownfeld and Waller, *The Revolution Lobby*, p. 45.

94. One would also contrast the enthusiasm of these clerics for communism with the message of Yosyp Terelia, a Catholic lay leader in the Ukraine, which he scribbled on March 6, 1977, to Pope Paul VI on a scrap of cloth: "Our priests groan in labor camps and psychiatric wards . . . I live in a country in which it is a crime to be a Christian. Never before have the faithful of the Church of Christ been exposed to such persecutions as today." Or, late in 1986, under the ostensibly "liberal" Gorbachev regime, the attitude displayed by Anatoly Shcharansky, on the day he was moved from a labor camp where he had already served eight years of a 13-year sentence back to Moscow for "recovery" prior to his much-ballyhooed pre-Summit release. Guards spotted Shcharansky's little book of psalms and confiscated it. Shcharansky said he would not leave without it, and when the guards still refused, he threw himself to the snow-covered ground and said: "Not another step." Later, when Shcharansky was carried by the crowd to the Temple Wall in Jerusalem, he was clutching that book of Psalms, from which he said he had drawn so much faith and strength. There

are, of course, those who say executions and decrees were part of the errors and excesses of the first days of "revolution." After rolling into Austria in 1945, Soviet secret police arrested the entire hierarchy of the Catholic Church, plus hundreds of clergy and lay leaders; of 3,600 priests and monks, only 216 survived. In 1950, in Czechoslovakia, 6,174 monks and nuns were imprisoned, a number of priests accused of "deception" simply disappeared. One wonders, too, how those clerics could reconcile their enthusiasm for communism with this, from May 15, 1931, signaling the start of a new campaign against the church: "By the first of May 1937 not a single house of prayer will be needed any longer in the territory of the Soviet Union, and the very notion of God will be expunged as a survival of the Middle Ages and an instrument for holding down the working masses." Six years after amending the constitution to make the teaching of religion a crime against the state and compelling children to renounce their cleric parents, Stalin introduced (on April 8, 1935) yet another "law on children," holding children twelve and older accountable for failure to denounce "treason" by their parents—forerunner of a similar Nazi law. For the bulk of this data, see Michael Johns, "Seventy Years of Evil; Soviet Crimes from Lenin to Gorbachev," in *Policy Review*, #42, Fall of 1987, pp. 10–23. The Shcharansky anecdote is from the same issue, Rabbi Joshua O. Haberman, "The Bible Belt Is America's Safety Belt; Why The Holocaust Couldn't Happen Here," pp. 41–42.

95. Philip Taubman, "The Speaker and His Sources on Latin America," *The New York Times*, September 12, 1984, p. B10. Tyson notes that O'Neill's late aunt Eunice was a Maryknoll nun—presumably the person providing him with his initial introductions to the order.

96. Powell, *Second Front*, p. 46.

97. *World Council of Churches 1983 Resource Sharing Book*, pp. 279–80, in Frawley, "The Left's," p. 16.

98. Frawley, "The Left's," p. 17.

99. *Update*, a publication of the Central American Historical Institute, quoted by Fred Barnes, op. cit. The Salazar assassination is described in Christian, *Nicaragua*, pp. 210–211. Her version is corroborated by Alvaro Baldizon, former Chief Investigator of the Special Investigations Commission of the Nicaraguan Ministry of the Interior; see *Inside the Sandinista Regime: A Special Investigator's Perspective*, U.S. Department of State, February 1986, p. 5.

100. "U.S. Clerics Extend Hand To Salvadoran Returnees"; "El Salvador Says Refugees May Return," the first a Religious News Service story, the second by William Branigin in San Salvador, El Salvador, both in *The Washington Post*, Oct. 10, 1987; "Thousands of Refugees Return to El Salvador," Branigin, in El Poy, Salvador, Oct. 11, 1987, p. A 51.

101. As reported by Brownfeld in his review of the study, op. cit., p. 10. Reference to the activity of the Episcopal Church—in this instance, in support of a hunted Puerto Rican terrorist—is on pp. 10–11.

102. Laurie Becklund, "Group Starts Nationwide Drive to Halt *Contra* Aid," *The Los Angeles Times*, Aug. 15, 1987, Part II p. 3. The story quoted David Reed, executive director of a Washington based group called Coalition for a New Foreign Policy, as telling of a $250,000 media campaign planned for the fall of 1987.

103. UPI story datelined Louisville, "Disciples of Christ Letter Challenges Ex-Member Reagan's Peace Policies," *The Washington Post*, Oct. 24, 1987.

104. Interview with Alvaro Baldizon Aviles, conducted by journalist Peter Crane, at the U.S. State Department, September 30, 1985, with the translation assistance of Lillian Nigaleoni, Translator Services, U.S. State Department.

105. Paul Hollander, *Political Pilgrims* (Oxford University Press, 1981), p. 118, in *Turmoil in Central America*, p. 92.

106. George Bernard Shaw, *The Rationalization of Russia* (Bloomington, Indiana: Indiana University Press, 1964), p. 91. Shaw wrote this in 1932, on the basis of a brief visit to Russia the previous year.

107. Waller, *Consolidating*, p. 11. Waller quotes Gerardo Peraza, a former Cuban intelligence agent, as saying, "The Venceremos Brigade brought the first great quantity of information through American citizens that was obtained in the United States, because up to the moment when the brigades came into existence . . . the amount of information that we had on American citizens came from public sources, and it was confusing."

108. Reed, "Nicaragua's 'Army of Useful Idiots'."

109. Neil, Henry, "Inside The Revolution; A reporter's search for the spirit of Nicaragua," *Washington Post Magazine*, Sept. 29, 1985.

110. Paul Hollander, "Political Tourism in Cuba and Nicaragua," *Society*, May–June, 1986, p. 32.

111. Frances Fitzgerald writing in *The New Yorker*; Ian Mather, writing in *Business Traveller*; and an unnamed American businessman writing in *Freedom at Issue*; all quoted in Hollander, "Political Tourism in Cuba and Nicaragua," pp. 30–32.

112. Borge, quoted by Baldizon, *Inside the Sandinista Regime: A Special Investigator's Perspective*, U.S. Department of State, February 1986, pp. 11–12.

113. *In Their Own Words: Testimony of Nicaraguan Exiles*, U.S. Department of State, March 1986, p. 5.

114. Statement made to the White House Outreach Working Group on Central America, March 27, 1985, quoted in *Turmoil in Central America*, p. 50.

115. Hollander, "Political Tourism in Cuba and Nicaragua," p. 33.

116. A good example is documented in Glenn Garvin's "Sandinistas boost crowds for rallies with job threats," *The Washington Times*, July 15, 1986.

117. Hollander, "Political Tourism in Cuba and Nicaragua," p. 32.

118. Reed, "Nicaragua's 'Army of Useful Idiots'."

119. Hollander, "Political Tourism in Cuba and Nicaragua," p. 29.

120. "Opina Congresista Wright que el Gobierno de Nicaragua Tiene Ideales como EEUU . . ." *Diario Las Americas*, June 11, 1980, in Waller, *Consolidating*, pp. 26–27.

121. Carlos Franqui, *Family Portrait with Fidel*, trans. Alfred MacAdam (New York: Vintage Books, 1985), pp. 143–44.

122. Brownfeld and Waller, *The Revolution Lobby*, p. 49.

123. Daniel James, "Whose News from Nicaragua?" *AIM Report* (Washington: Accuracy in Media), July 1985, in Waller, *Consolidating*, p. 39.

124. Ibid.

125. *AIM Report*, September 1983.

126. *The Washington Post*, quoted by Kirk Kidwell in "The Battle Over Contra Aid: The Untold Story of the Revolution Lobby," *The New American*, March 24, 1986.

127. Richard Araujo, Heritage Foundation *Backgrounder*, July 19, 1983, p. 3, in James R. Whelan and Patricia B. Bozell, *Catastrophe in the Caribbean* (Ottawa, IL: Jameson Books, 1984), p. 60.

128. Hollander, "Political Tourism in Cuba and Nicaragua," p. 30.

129. Examples are as close at hand as your morning newspaper or the next network newscast, so to cite even one—pulled at random—may be redundant. Nonetheless, a single paragraph: "The two main arenas of fighting in Central America are El Salvador, where leftist guerrillas are trying to overthrow Duarte's U.S.-backed government, and Nicaragua, where the United States supports rebels trying to oust the leftist Sandinista government." Julia Preston, "Duarte Pledges to Fight Pessimism Toward Pact," *The Washington Post*, Aug. 23, 1987, p. A-21. Or this, from self-professed Sandinista enthusiast Karen DeYoung, reporting on Arias' Nobel Peace Prize: "Although it is considered to have drawbacks, the Arias plan is seen as the first optimistic sign that Central America's various wars can be resolved at

a regional diplomatic level, without direct outside military intervention." "Costa Rica President Wins Nobel For Central American Peace Plan," *The Washington Post*, Oct. 14, 1987, p. A 26. Ms. Preston sets up a perfect symmetry: "leftist" guerrillas, a "leftist" government. No distinction is made between one which shot its way into power and maintains power at the point of a gun and one which is democratic; nor is the tidy equation sullied by a reference to the Soviets or the Cubans. Ms. DeYoung manages a more extraordinary feat in a single paragraph. We are not told who those optimistic onlookers are; we are persuaded that all of Central America's wars were, apparently, born equally and equal in value, merit and meaning (or lack thereof); we are asked to believe that the withdrawal of U.S. aid (the only outside military aid contemplated by the plan) would mean "regional diplomatic" solutions "without outside military intervention," even though there is neither hint in the plan nor in Ms. DeYoung's reportage what is to become of those thousands of Soviet bloc people ensconced in Nicaragua, nor the immense arsenal already in place, bolstered by daily Soviet bloc shipments. But, again, examples abound, and these are but two.

130. "Jimmy Carter and Nicaragua," *The Washington Post*, Nov. 24, 1987, p. A-22.

131. This account of the National Commission for the Protection and Promotion of Human Rights is based on the revelations of Mateo Guerrero Flores, former executive director of the Commission, and Bayardo de Jesus Payan Hidalgo, former Chief of the Commission's Office of Budget and Finance. Guerrero's account is summarized in "Inside the Sandinista Regime: Revelations by the Executive Director of the Government's Human Rights Commission," a report produced by the State Department's Office of Public Diplomacy for Latin America and the Caribbean (no date, possibly October 1985); his testimony to the State Department is excerpted in *In Their Own Words: Testimony of Nicaraguan Exiles*, U.S. Department of State, March 1986, pp. 6–7. Payan's account is given in his testimony before the House Subcommittee on Western Hemisphere Affairs, April 18, 1985. In that testimony, Payan said: "They [the Commission] identify some leading member of the FSLN organizations in key areas to 'help' the victims of abuses and to prepare their stories. In some cases they threaten or try to bribe the victims of abuses by the government so that these will say that it was the rebels who harmed them. . . . They try to convince the people through their communications network that the only thing the Contra do [sic] is massacre the people. . . . They organize press conferences for foreign delegations to tell them that the conditions in Nicaragua are wonderful, and to demonstrate that the only ones who commit abuses are the rebels."

132. *The Washington Post*, for example, splashed a story across all eight

columns of the top of a page in its A section: "2 Hill Panels Probing Alleged Links Between *Contras* and Drug Trafficking," by David S. Hilzenrath, Aug. 8, 1987, p. A-16. In October 1987, *West Watch* ran a lengthy story: *"Contras* Cleared of Drug Smuggling Charges," p. 4.

133. Brownfeld and Waller, *The Revolution Lobby*, p. 49.

134. Public statement, entitled "Sandinistas Disguised as *Contras*," made by Alvaro Baldizon, February 27, 1986. A nearly identical statement by Baldizon appears in *In Their Own Words*, p. 5.

135. According to *Newsweek*, "Americas Watch Vice Chairman Aryeh Neier admitted that the release of his group's report was timed to influence Congress" ("Playing Propaganda Games," *Newsweek*, March 18, 1985, p. 32). The author of the other report acknowledged that its release during the *contra* aid debate was "not unintentional" (Larry Rohter, "Nicaragua Rebels Accused of Abuses," *The New York Times*, March 7, 1985, p. A12).

136. Aryeh Neier, quoted by Joel Brinkley, "Rights Report on Nicaragua Cites Recent Rebel Atrocities," *The New York Times*, March 6, 1985, p. A10.

137. *The Boston Globe* (from *The Los Angeles Times* wire), March 10, 1985, p. 17, in Powell, *Second Front*, p. 55.

138. Brinkley "Rights Report" (only seven executed); *Inside the Sandinista Regime: A special Investigator's Perspective*, pp. 7–8 (Baldizon figure).

139. The discussion that follows, except where noted otherwise, is based on research done by the Council for Inter-American Security.

140. Reed Brody, *Contra Terror in Nicaragua: Report of a Fact-Finding Mission, September 1984—January 1985* (Boston: South End Press, 1985), p. 67.

141. This comes from detailed battle records of the resistance fighters. Another example was the attack on the "state farm" at La Sorpresa. Brody made no mention of the sixty Sandinista troops who were there, nor the forty-eight rifles and 11,500 rounds of ammunition captured by the *contras*.

142. The reaction of one escaped Miskito to this Sandinista claim: "Them that you call the contra is us, my brother, my uncle, my grandfather, and my son" (*Dispossessed: The Miskito Indians in Sandinista Nicaragua*, U.S. Department of State, June 1986, p. 13).

143. Brody, *Contra Terror*, pp. 100, 107, 108, 115. Brody spells the bishop's name "Schlaeffer"; most other writers use Schlaefer.

144. Joshua Muravchik, "Manipulating the Miskitos: The Sandinista propaganda war comes to the Senate," *The New Republic*, August 6, 1984, p. 24.

145. Powell, *Second Front*, p. 5.

146. Testimony of Bayardo de Jesus Payan before the House Subcommittee on Western Hemisphere Affairs, April 18, 1985. Payan provided evidence of close ties between Brody and Nicaraguan President Daniel Ortega, and claimed to have witnessed Brody's selective transcribing of tape-recorded testimony. The Commission's former executive director, Mateo Jose Guerrero, later told the State Department that the Commission "paid all the bills incurred during their [the Brody team's] visit" ("Inside the Sandinista Regime: Revelations by the Executive Director of the Government's Human Rights Commission," a report produced by the State Department's Office of Public Diplomacy for Latin America and the Caribbean; no date, possibly October 1985; p. 3).

147. John M. Goshko, "Contras Accused of Seizing, Threatening 2 Clergymen," *The Washington Post*, Oct. 17, 1987, p. 19-A.

148. Except where noted otherwise, this account of the Kennedy forum is based on the article by Muravchik, "Manipulating the Miskitos."

149. *Dispossessed*, op. cit., p. 13 (twenty-three thousand Miskitos); the Fagoth letter is reprinted in Brownfeld and Waller, *The Revolution Lobby*, p. 114.

150. Richard Perle, "America's failure of nerve in Nicaragua," *US News and World Report*, Aug. 3, 1987.

151. Andrew Cherry, "Soviets seeking 'nuclear parity' with West," *GW Hatchet* (the student newspaper of George Washington University, Washington, DC), April 5, 1984, p. 8. Gonchar addressed his remarks to a group of students at George Washington University.

152. Brownfeld and Waller, *The Revolution Lobby*, p. 77.

153. Ibid., pp. 71, 159.

154. Document No. 23, *Grenada Documents: An Overview and Selection*, U.S. Department of State, September 1984.

155. Letter from Carlottia Scott to Maurice Bishop, reprinted in Brownfeld and Waller, *The Revolution Lobby*, p. 116.

156. Brownfeld and Waller, *The Revolution Lobby*, p. 71.

157. Citations concerning deceit and terrorism from Michael Johns, "Seventy Years of Evil," op. cit. Data on the Decree of Peace from George F. Kennan, *Russia and the West: Under Lenin and Stalin* (New York: Mentor, 1960), pp. 37 and 39.

158. Kissinger, *Years of Upheaval* (Boston: Little Brown & Company, 1982), pp. 302–303.

159. Stephen S. Rosenfeld, "True Believers in Democracy," *The Washington Post*, Oct. 25, 1987, p. C-7.

APPENDIX I

From "Salvation" to Ruin—Economic Update

TABLE 1
**Percentage Increases in Gross Domestic Product and
Per Capita Income, 1985 and 1986***

	GDP		Per Capita	
	1985	1986	1985	1986
Costa Rica	1.0	3.0	−1.6	2.7
El Salvador	2.0	1.0	0.8	−0.9
Guatemala	1.0	0.0	−3.7	−2.8
Honduras	2.7	3.0	−0.5	−0.3
Nicaragua	−4.1	−0.4	−7.3	−3.7
(Mexico)	2.8	−3.8	0.0	−6.4
Latin America	3.7	3.8	1.3	1.4

Source: *Economic and Social Progress in Latin America, 1987 Report,* Inter-American Development Bank (Washington, D.C., 1987), p. 17 (hereafter referred to as *1987 Economic and Social Progress Report*).
(*1986 figures are preliminary estimates)

TABLE 2
Gross Domestic Product
(In Millions, 1986 Dollars)

	1984	1985	1986*	% Change, 1984–1986
Costa Rica	4,797	4,843	4,987	3.9
El Salvador	4,215	4,298	4,343	3.0
Guatemala	10,601	10,499	10,503	−0.1
Honduras	3,326	3,416	3,520	5.8
Nicaragua	3,052	2,928	2,915	−4.4
(Mexico)	193,592	198,976	191,506	−1.0
Latin America	783,381	812,298	842,997	7.6

Source: *1987 Economic and Social Progress Report*, p. 426. Percentages extrapolated from that table.
(* Preliminary figures)

TABLE 3
The five Central American countries and Mexico as measured against the pacesetters* among 12 selected Latin American Countries on Basis of Improvement in Key Health Indicators, from late 1970s to Mid- or Late-1980s (see details in Table 4)

Life Expectancy[a]	Infant Mortality[b]	Death Rates
1. HONDURAS	Chile	Mexico
2. Chile	Argentina	EL SALVADOR
3. Haiti	Brazil	Colombia
4. NICARAGUA	COSTA RICA	Haiti
5. GUATEMALA	5. Mexico	NICARAGUA
	5. EL SALVADOR	
6. Uruguay	7. GUATEMALA	GUATEMALA
7. Mexico		8. COSTA RICA
9. COSTA RICA		10. Mexico
10. EL SALVADOR		11. HONDURAS

* Selected among the most advanced and the most underdeveloped countries of the region; English-language countries were not included in the sample.

[a] Comparative figures not available for Brazil, so ranking is from one to 11.

[b] Late 1970s figures for both Nicaragua and Honduras were computed on a different basis, so as to make meaningless comparisons between those figures and more recent ones.

TABLE 4
Key Health Indicators

	Life Expectancy (number years at year of birth)			Infant Mortality (per 1,000 live births)			Death Rates (per 1,000 inhabitants)		
	Year^a '75-'80*	Year^b	Years of Change	Year^a	Year^b	% Change	Year^a	Year^b	% Change
Argentina	68.2	1985 69.7	+1.5	60.1	1970 32.2	1985 +46.4	'75-'80 8.8	1985 8.6	+ 6.8
Brazil	63.4	n.a.	—	1977 95-100	1980 68.1	approx. +43.2	'75-'80 7.9	1980 6.8	+ 1.9
Chile	64.4	'80-'85 70.9	+6.5	1978 39.7	1985 19.5	+50.9	1979 6.8	1985 6.1	+10.3
Colombia	63.4	1981 62.1	-1.3	1976 59.6	1981 60.9	- 2.1	1976 7.4	1982 5.8	+21.6
COSTA RICA	71.8	'80-'85 73.1	+1.3	1977 27.8	1984 18.8	+32.4	1977 4.2	1984 3.9	+ 7.0
EL SALVADOR	62.2	1984 63.3	+1.1	1977 59.5	1984 35.1	+41.0	1977 10.8	1986 8.9	+17.6
GUATEMALA	57.8	1982 62.0	+4.2	1977 76.0	1986 57.1	+24.9	1977 7.8	1984 6.0	+23.0
Haiti	52.2	'85-'90 (est.) 57.0	+5.2	1978 141.1	'80-'85 12.4	+12.1	1978 14.5	'85-'90 (est.) 11.5	+20.6
HONDURAS	1978 54.1	1983 62.0	+7.9	c	1983 78.6	n.a.	1978 5.5	1983 8.3	-50.9
Mexico	64.0	1985 66.1	+2.1	1976 56.0	1984 33.0	+41.0	'75-'80 8.5	1984 5.4	+36.0
NICARAGUA	55.2	1985 59.8	+4.6	1976 c	1985 76.4	n.a.	1978 12.2	1985 9.7	+20.9
Uruguay	66.4	'80-'85 70.3	+3.9	1977 43.0	1984 30.3	+29.5	1977 6.0	1984 10.2	-70.0

ᵃ James R. Whelan and Patricia B. Bozell, *Catastrophe in the Caribbean* (Ottawa, IL.: Jameson Books, 1984), pp. 13–14.
ᵇ Individual country reports, *1987 Economic and Social Progress Report*, op. cit.
ᶜ Earlier figures computed differently, and thus not comparable.
* For years 1975–1980 except where indicated

379

TABLE 5
Comparative Literacy Rates

	(a)	(b)
Costa Rica	89.8% in 1977	89.9% in 1981
El Salvador	59.5% in 1977	66.9% in 1985
Guatemala	45.4% in 1977	56.6% in 1986
Honduras	59.5% in 1978	59.7% in 1982
Nicaragua	53.6% in 1977	72.3% in 1986
Mexico	82.4% in 1978c	87.9% in 1985

a Whelan and Bozell, op. cit., p. 15.
b *1987 Economic and Social Progress Report,* op. cit.
c *1978 Economic and Social Progress Report,* p. 322.

TABLE 6
Central Government Expenditure on Education 1980–1985
(percentage of Gross Domestic Product)

Country	1980	1981	1982	1983	1984	1985
Costa Rica	6.2	5.0	4.3	4.6	4.3	4.2
El Salvador	3.4	3.7	3.6	3.1	3.1	2.8
Guatemala	1.8	1.8	1.6	1.4	1.4	1.2
Honduras	3.0	3.5	3.7	3.8	3.9	4.7
Nicaragua	3.5	4.2	4.2	5.5	6.3	6.6
Mexico	3.3	3.8	3.6	2.7	2.6	2.7

Source: *1987 Economic and Social Progress Report,* p. 64.

TABLE 7
Central Government Expenditure on Health 1980–1985
(percentage of GDP)

Country	1980	1981	1982	1983	1984	1985
Costa Rica	1.6	1.1	1.1	1.0	1.2	0.5
El Salvador	1.5	1.6	1.4	1.4	1.5	1.2
Guatemala	1.6	1.1	1.4	1.4	1.5	1.2
Honduras	1.4	1.5	1.6	1.5	1.6	2.0
Nicaragua	4.4	4.6	4.4	4.8	4.3	5.0
Mexico	0.5	0.5	0.3	0.2	0.3	0.3

Source: Ibid., p. 68.

From "Salvation" to Ruin—Economic Update

TABLE 8
Agricultural Growth Rates, 1961–1986
(Percentages)

Country	Average[a] 1961–1970	1971–1980	Annual 1980	1981	1982	1983	1984	1985	1986*
Costa Rica	5.1	2.6	−0.5	5.1	−4.7	4.0	10.1	−2.9	0.0
El Salvador	3.9	3.0	−5.2	−6.4	−4.7	−3.2	3.3	−1.1	−2.1
Guatemala	4.4	4.7	1.6	1.2	−3.0	−1.7	1.6	−0.8	−0.2
Honduras	5.5	2.9	0.8	0.1	−1.7	2.1	1.1	1.9	1.6
Nicaragua	6.7	0.0	−19.0	9.5	2.8	5.8	−5.3	−4.8	−5.4
(Mexico)	3.9	3.4	7.1	6.1	−0.6	2.9	2.5	3.8	−2.1

a Compound growth.
* Preliminary estimate.
Source: *1987 Economic and Social Progress Report*, p. 42.
(Note: Though not directly comparable to Table 9 in Whelan and Bozell ("Indices of Per Capita Food Production"), absent that data this table does give a sense of overall farm—and thus food—output.)

TABLE 9
Per Capita Supply of Calories

	1971–1973[a]	% Change, 1961–1973	1985[b]	% Change, 1973–1985
Costa Rica	2,576	11.2	2,803	8.8
El Salvador	1,916	1.9	2,514	12.4
Guatemala	2,155	11.7	2,514	16.6
Honduras	2,102	11.3	2,224	5.8
Nicaragua	2,467	15.3	2,514	11.6
(Mexico)	2,772	4.8c	3,126	12.7

a Whelan and Bozell, p. 19.

b Individual country reports, *Social Indicators of Development—1987* (Washington: The World Bank, 1987). The report describes this data as "most recent estimate," noting (p. 3) that these are mainly for 1985.

c Ibid. The first figure for Mexico is 1965, so that the comparison is somewhat skewed.

TABLE 10
Central American Common Market: Intraregional Trade
(1985–1986[a]; millions of dollars)

Importing Countries	Central America	C.R.	Exporting Countries			
			El Sal.	Guat.	Hon.	Nic.
Costa Rica						
1985	99.8		33.0	49.3	7.8	9.6
1986	95.0		33.4	50.6	5.6	5.3
El Salvador						
1985	216.7	54.1		149.6	10.5	2.3
1986	145.3	33.6		101.6	8.2	1.7
Guatemala						
1985	99.4	37.2	49.4		5.1	7.6
1986	98.4	39.8	51.7		4.5	2.2
Honduras						
1985	74.8	33.0	7.0	32.7		1.9
1986	53.6	21.9	6.6	23.6		1.3
Nicaragua						
1985	56.7	15.1	9.0	25.5	7.0	
1986	28.4	11.7	5.8	8.3	2.5	
Central America						
1985	547.6	139.5	98.6	257.2	30.5	21.5
1986	420.9	107.2	97.6	184.3	21.0	10.6

[a] Estimated.

Source: *1987 Economic and Social Progress Report*, p. 75.

Appendix II:

The Sandinista Program

THE HISTORIC PROGRAM OF THE FSLN
By the Sandinista National Liberation Front (FSLN)*

The Sandinista National Liberation Front (FSLN) arose out of the Nicaraguan people's need to have a "vanguard organization" capable of taking political power through direct struggle against its enemies and establishing a social system that wipes out the exploitation and poverty that our people have been subjected to in past history.

The FSLN is a politico-military organization, whose strategic objective is to take political power by destroying the military and bureaucratic apparatus of the dictatorship and to establish a revolutionary government based on the worker-peasant alliance and the convergence of the patriotic anti-imperialist and anti-oligarchic forces in the country.

The people of Nicaragua suffer under subjugation to a reactionary and fascist clique imposed by Yankee imperialism in 1932, the year Anastasio Somoza Garcia was named commander in chief of the so-called National Guard (GN).

The Somocista clique has reduced Nicaragua to the status of a neocolony exploited by the Yankee monopolies and the country's oligarchic group.

* From the Spanish, Frente Sandinista de Liberacion Nacional; the initials "GN" for National Guard are from the Spanish, Guardia Nacional.

The present regime is politically unpopular and juridically illegal. The recognition and aid it gets from the North Americans is irrefutable proof of foreign interference in the affairs of Nicaragua.

The FSLN has seriously and with great responsibility analyzed the national reality and has resolved to confront the dictatorship with arms in hand. We have concluded that the triumph of the Sandinista people's revolution and the overthrow of the regime that is an enemy of the people will take place through the development of a hard-fought and prolonged people's war.

Whatever maneuvers and resources Yankee imperialism deploys, the Somocista dictatorship is condemned to total failure in the face of the rapid advance and development of the people's forces, headed by the Sandinista National Liberation Front.

Given this historic conjuncture the FSLN has worked out this political program with an eye to strengthening and developing our organization, inspiring and stimulating the people of Nicaragua to march forward with the resolve to fight until the dictatorship is overthrown and to resist the intervention of Yankee imperialism, in order to forge a free, prosperous and revolutionary homeland.

I. A REVOLUTIONARY GOVERNMENT

The Sandinista people's revolution will establish a revolutionary government that will eliminate the reactionary structure that arose from rigged elections and military coups, and the people's power will create a Nicaragua that is free of exploitation, backwardness, a free, progressive and independent country.

The revolutionary government will apply the following measures of a political character:

A. It will endow revolutionary power with a structure that allows the full participation of the entire people, on the national level as well as the local level (departmental, municipal, neighborhood).
B. It will guarantee that all citizens can fully exercise all individual freedoms and it will respect human rights.
C. It will guarantee the free exchange of ideas, which above all

leads to vigorously broadening the people's rights and national rights.

D. It will guarantee freedom for the worker-union movements to organize in the city and countryside; and freedom to organize peasant, youth, student, women's cultural, sporting, and similar groups.

E. It will guarantee the right of emigrant and exiled Nicaraguans to return to their native soil.

F. It will guarantee the right to asylum for citizens of other countries who are persecuted for participation in the revolutionary struggle.

G. It will severely punish the gangsters who are guilty of persecuting, informing on, abusing, torturing, or murdering revolutionaries and the people.

H. Those invididuals who occupy high political posts as a result of rigged elections and military coups will be stripped of their political rights.

The revolutionary government will apply the following measures of an economic character:

A. It will expropriate the landed estates, factories, companies, buildings, means of transportation, and other wealth usurped by the Somoza family and accumulated through the misappropriation and plunder of the nation's wealth.

B. It will expropriate the landed estates, factories, companies, means of transportation, and other wealth usurped by the politicians and military officers, and all other accomplices, who have taken advantage of the present regime's administrative corruption.

C. It will nationalize the wealth of all the foreign companies that exploit the mineral, forest, maritime, and other kinds of resources.

D. It will establish workers' control over the administrative management of the factories and other wealth that are expropriated and nationalized.

E. It will centralize the mass transit services.

F. It will nationalize the banking system, which will be placed at the exclusive service of the country's economic development.

G. It will establish an independent currency.

H. It will refuse to honor the loans imposed on the country by the Yankee monopolies or any other power.

I. It will establish commercial relations with all countries, whatever their system, to benefit the country's economic development.

J. It will establish a suitable taxation policy, which will be applied with strict justice.

K. It will prohibit usury. This prohibition will apply to Nicaraguan nationals, as well as foreigners.

L. It will protect the small and medium-size owners (producers, merchants) while restricting the excesses that lead to the exploitation of the workers.

M. It will establish state control over foreign trade, with an eye to diversifying it and making it independent.

N. It will rigorously restrict the importation of luxury items.

O. It will plan the national economy, putting an end to the anarchy characteristic of the capitalist system of production. An important part of this planning will focus on the industrialization and electrification of the country.

II. THE AGRARIAN REVOLUTION

The Sandinista people's revolution will work out an agrarian policy that achieves an authentic agrarian reform: a reform that will, in the immediate term, carry out massive distribution of the land, eliminating the land grabs by the large landlords in favor of the workers (small producers) who labor on the land.

A. It will expropriate and eliminate the capitalist and feudal estates.

B. It will turn over the land to the peasants, free of charge, in accordance with the principle that the land should belong to those who work it.

C. It will carry out a development plan for livestock raising aimed at diversifying and increasing the productivity of that sector.

D. It will guarantee the peasants the following rights:
   1. Timely and adequate agricultural credit.
   2. Marketability (a guaranteed market for their production).
   3. Technical assistance.

E. It will protect the patriotic landowners who collaborate with the guerrilla struggle, by paying them for their landholdings that exceed the limit established by the revolutionary government.
F. It will stimulate and encourage the peasants to organize themselves in cooperatives, so they can take their destiny into their own hands and directly participate in the development of their country.
G. It will abolish the debts the peasantry incurred to the landlord and any type of usurer.
H. It will eliminate the forced idleness that exists for most of the year in the countryside, and it will be attentive to creating sources of jobs for the present population.

III. REVOLUTION IN CULTURE AND EDUCATION

The Sandinista people's revolution will establish the basis for the development of the national culture, the people's education, and university reform.

A. It will push forward a massive campaign to immediately wipe out "illiteracy." (sic)
B. It will develop the national culture and will root out the neo-colonial penetration in our culture.
C. It will rescue the progressive intellectuals, and their works that have arisen throughout our history, from the neglect in which they have been maintained by the anti-people's regimes.
D. It will give attention to the development and progress of education at the various levels (primary, intermediate, technical, university, etc.) and education will be free at all levels and obligatory at some.
E. It will grant scholarships at various levels of education to students who have limited economic resources. The scholarships will include housing, food, clothing, books, and transportation.
F. It will train more and better teachers who have the scientific knowledge that the present era requires, to satisfy the needs of our entire student population.
G. It will nationalize the centers of private education that have been immorally turned into industries by merchants who hypocritically invoke religious principles.
H. It will adapt the teaching programs to the needs of the country:

it will apply teaching methods to the scientific and research needs of the country.

I. It will carry out a university reform that will include, among other things, the following measures:

1. It will rescue the university from the domination of the exploiting classes, so it can serve the real creators and shapers of our culture: the people. The university must be oriented around man, around the people. The university must stop being a breeding ground for bureaucratic egotists.

2. Eliminate the discrimination in access to university classes suffered by youth from the working class and peasantry.

3. Increase the state budget for the university so there are the economic resources to solve the various problems confronting it.

4. Majority student representation on the boards of departments, keeping in mind that the student body is the main segment of the university population.

5. Eliminate the neo-colonial penetration of the university, especially the penetration by the North American monopolies through the charity donations of the pseudo-philanthropic foundations.

6. Promotion of free, experimental, scientific investigation that must contribute to dealing with national and universal questions.

7. Strengthen the unity of the students, faculty, and investigators with the whole people, by perpetuating the selfless example of the students and intellectuals who have offered their lives for the sake of the patriotic ideal.

IV. LABOR LEGISLATION AND SOCIAL SECURITY

The Sandinista people's revolution will eliminate the injustice of the living and working conditions suffered by the working class under the brutal exploitation, and will institute labor legislation and social assistance.

A. It will enact a labor code that will regulate, among other things, the following rights:

1. It will adopt the principle that "those who don't work don't eat," of course making exceptions for those who are unable

to participate in the process of production due to age (children, old people), medical condition, or other reasons beyond their control.

2. Strict enforcement of the eight-hour work day.
3. The income of the workers (wages and other benefits) must be sufficient to satisfy their daily needs.
4. Respect for the dignity of the worker, prohibiting and punishing unjust treatment of workers in the course of their labor.
5. Abolition of unjustified firings.
6. Obligation to pay wages in the period required by law.
7. Right of all workers to periodic vacations.

B. It will eliminate the scourge of unemployment.
C. It will extend the scope of the social security system to all the workers and public employees of the country. The scope will include coverage for illness, physical incapacity, and retirement.
D. It will provide free medical assistance to the entire population. It will set up clinics and hospitals throughout the national territory.
E. It will undertake massive campaigns to eradicate endemic illnesses and prevent epidemics.
F. It will carry out urban reform, which will provide each family with adequate shelter. It will put an end to profiteering speculation in urban land (subdivisions, urban construction, rental housing), that exploits the need that working families in the cities have for an adequate roof over their heads in order to live.
G. It will initiate and expand the construction of adequate housing for the peasant population.
H. It will reduce the charges for water, light, sewer, urban beautification; it will apply programs to extend all these services to the entire urban and rural population.
I. It will encourage participation in sports of all types and categories.
J. It will eliminate the humiliation of begging by putting the above mentioned practices into practice.

V. ADMINISTRATIVE HONESTY

The Sandinista people's revolution will root out administrative governmental corruption, and will establish strict administrative honesty.

A. It will abolish the criminal vice industry (prostitution, gambling, drug use, etc.) which the privileged sector of the National Guard and the foreign parasites exploit.
B. It will establish strict control over the collection of taxes to prevent government functionaries from profiting, putting an end to the normal practice of the present regime's official agencies.
C. It will end the arbitrary actions of the members of the GN, who plunder the population through the subterfuge of local taxes.
D. It will put an end to the situation wherein military commanders appropriate the budget that is supposed to go to take care of common prisoners, and it will establish centers designed to rehabilitate these wrongdoers.
E. It will abolish the smuggling that is practiced on a large scale by the gang of politicians, officers, and foreigners who are the regime's accomplices.
F. It will severely punish persons who engage in crimes against adminsitrative honesty (embezzlement, smuggling, trafficking in vices, etc.), using greatest severity when it involves elements active in the revolutionary movement.

VI. REINCORPORATION OF THE ATLANTIC COAST

The Sandinista people's revolution will put into practice a special plan for the Atlantic Coast, which has been abandoned to total neglect, in order to incorporate this area into the nation's life.

A. It will end the unjust exploitation the Atlantic Coast has suffered throughout history by the foreign monopolies, especially Yankee imperialism.
B. It will prepare suitable lands in the zone for the development of agriculture and ranching.
C. It will establish conditions that encourage the development of the fishing and forest industries.
D. It will encourage the flourishing of this region's local cultural values, which flow from the specific aspects of its historic tradition.
E. It will wipe out the odious discrimination to which the indigenous Miskitos, Sumos, Ramas and Blacks of this region are subjected.

VII. THE EMANCIPATION OF WOMEN

The Sandinista people's revolution will abolish the odious discrimination that women have been subjected to compared to men; it will establish economic, political, and cultural equality between woman and man.

A. It will pay special attention to the mother and child.
B. It will eliminate prostitution and other social vices, through which the dignity of women will be raised.
C. It will put an end to the system of servitude that women suffer, which is reflected in the tragedy of the abandoned working mother.
D. It will establish for children born out of wedlock the right to equal protection by the revolution's institutions.
E. It will establish day-care centers for the care and attention of the children of working women.
F. It will establish a two-month maternity leave before and after birth for women who work.
G. It will raise women's political, cultural, and vocational levels through their participation in the revolutionary process.

VIII. RESPECT FOR RELIGIOUS BELIEFS

The Sandinista people's revolution will guarantee the population of believers the freedom to profess any religion.

A. It will respect the right of citizens to profess and practice any religion.
B. It will support the work of priests and other religious figures who defend the working people.

IX. INDEPENDENT FOREIGN POLICY

The Sandinista people's revolution will eliminate the foreign policy of submission to Yankee imperialism, and will establish a patriotic foreign policy of absolute national independence and one that is for authentic universal peace.

A. It will put an end to the Yankee interference in the internal problems of Nicaragua and will practice a policy of mutual respect with other countries and fraternal collaboration between peoples.

B. It will expel the Yankee military mission, the so-called Peace Corps (spies in the guise of technicians), and military and similar political elements which constitute a bare-faced intervention in the country.

C. It will accept economic and technical aid from any country, but always and only when this does not involve political compromises.

D. Together with other peoples of the world it will promote a campaign in favor of authentic universal peace.

E. It will abrogate all treaties, signed with any foreign power, that damage national sovereignty.

X. CENTRAL AMERICAN PEOPLE'S UNITY

The Sandinista people's revolution is for the true union of the Central American peoples in a single country.

A. It will support authentic unity with the fraternal peoples of Central America. The unity will lead the way to coordinating the efforts to achieve national liberation and establish a new system without imperialist domination or national betrayal.

B. It will eliminate the so-called integration, whose aim is to increase Central America's submission to the North American monopolies and the local reactionary forces.

XI. SOLIDARITY AMONG PEOPLES

The Sandinista people's revolution will put an end to the use of the national territory as a base for Yankee aggression against other fraternal peoples and will put into practice militant solidarity with fraternal peoples fighting for liberation.

A. It will actively support the struggles of the peoples of Asia, Africa, and Latin America against the new and old colonialism and against the common enemy: Yankee imperialism.

B. It will support the struggle of the Black people and all the people of the United States for an authentic democracy and equal rights.

C. It will support the struggle of all peoples against the establishment of Yankee military bases in foreign countries.

XII. PEOPLE'S PATRIOTIC ARMY

The Sandinista people's revolution will abolish the armed forces called the National Guard, which is an enemy of the people, and will create a patriotic, revolutionary, and people's army.

A. It will abolish the National Guard, a force that is an enemy of the people, created by the North American occupation forces in 1927 to pursue, torture, and murder the Sandinista patriots.
B. In the new people's army, professional soldiers who are members of the old army will be able to play a role providing they have observed the following conduct:
   1. They have supported the guerrilla struggle.
   2. They have not participated in murder, plunder, torture, and persecution of the people and the revolutionary activists.
   3. They have rebelled against the despotic and dynastic regime of the Somozas.
C. It will strengthen the new people's army, raising its fighting ability and its tactical and technical level.
D. It will inculcate in the consciousness of the members of the people's army the principle of basing themselves on their own forces in the fulfillment of their duties and the development of all their creative activity.
E. It will deepen the revolutonary ideals of the members of the people's army with an eye toward strengthening their patriotic spirit and their firm conviction to fight until victory is achieved, overcoming obstacles and correcting errors.
F. It will forge a conscious discipline in the ranks of the people's army and will encourage the close ties that must exist between the combatants and the people.
G. It will establish obligatory military service and will arm the students, workers, and farmers, who—organized in people's militias—will defend the rights won against the inevitable attack by the reactionary forces of the country and Yankee imperialism.

XIII. VENERATION OF OUR MARTYRS

The Sandinista people's revolution will maintain eternal gratitude to and veneration of our homeland's martyrs and will continue the shining example of heroism and selflessness they have bequeathed to us.

A. It will educate the new generations in eternal gratitude and veneration toward those who have fallen in the struggle to make Nicaragua a free homeland.
B. It will establish a secondary school to educate the children of our people's martyrs.
C. It will inculcate in the entire people the imperishable example of our martyrs, defending the revolutionary ideal: Ever onward to victory!

Source: *Congressional Record*, June 15, 1987, p. H-4950, taken from Peter Rosset and John Vandermeer, *The Nicaragua Reader: Documents of a Revolution Under Fire.*

BIBLIOGRAPHY

Agency for International Development. *Summary Economic and Social Indicators, 18 Latin American Countries: 1960–1970*. Washington: AID Bureau for Latin America, Office of Development Programs, April 1971.

————*U.S. Overseas Loans and Grants and Assistance from International Organizations; Obligations and Loan Authorizations, July 1, 1945–Sept. 30, 1978*. Washington: AID Bureau for Program and Policy Coordination, Office of Planning and Budgeting.

Alisky, Marvin. "Revolutionary Mystique: Central America's Big Brother." *National Review*, June 28, 1985, p. 29.

Arce, Bayardo. Speech published as *Comandante Bayardo Arce's Secret Speech before the Nicaraguan Socialist Party (PSN)*. Washington: U.S. Department of State, March 1985.

Arnson, Cynthia; Neier, Aryeh; and Benda, Susan. *As Bad as Ever: A Report on Human Rights in El Salvador*, Fourth Supplement. Washington: Americas Watch Committee and American Civil Liberties Union, January 31, 1984.

Ashby, Timothy. "Honduras' Role in U.S. Policy for Central America," *Backgrounder* No. 412. Washington: The Heritage Foundation, February 1985.

Bibliography

————"The Grenada Rescue Mission Is Not Over," *Backgrounder* No. 380. Washington: The Heritage Foundation, September 1984.

Baldizon, Alvaro. Transcript of interview with journalist Peter Crane, conducted at the Office of Latin America Diplomacy, U.S. Department of State, September 30, 1985. Mimeographed.

Barnes, Fred. "The Sandinista Lobby: 'Human rights' groups with a double standard." *The New Republic*, January 20, 1986, p. 13.

Belli, Humberto. *Breaking Faith*. Westchester, IL: Crossway Books, 1985.

Bolanos-Geyer, Alejandro. "Taken for a Ride Down the San Juan River." *Voice of Nicaragua* (newsletter of the Nicaraguan Information Center, P.O. Box 607, St. Charles, MO 63302), November 1985, pp. 2–3.

Bouchey, L. Francis. "Bearing False Witness . . . for 'Peace.' " *West Watch*, September-October, 1985, p. 5.

Bouchey, L. Francis, and Piedra, Alberto M. *Guatemala: A Promise in Peril*. Washington: Council for Inter-American Security, 1980.

Brody, Reed. *Contra Terror in Nicaragua: Report of a Fact-Finding Mission, September 1984–January 1985*. Boston: South End Press, 1985.

Brooks, David. "Latin America Is Not East of Here." *National Review*, March 14, 1986, p. 32.

Brownfeld, Allan C. "How Nicaragua Fell to Communism." *Human Events*, May 31, 1986, pp. 12–14.

————"How U.S. Church Groups Further Soviet Goals in Central America." *Human Events*, June 6, 1987, p. 10.

Brownfeld, Allan C., and Waller, J. Michael. *The Revolution Lobby*. Washington: Council for Inter-American Security, 1985.

Buchanan, Patrick J. "Will Reagan Make a Comeback—Or Be a Lame Duck?" *Human Events*, August 15, 1987.

Christian, Shirley. *Nicaragua: Revolution in the Family*. New York: Vintage Books, 1986.

Cirincione, Joseph, and Hunter, Leslie C. "Military Threats, Actual and Potential." In *Central America: Anatomy of Conflict*, edited by Robert S. Leiden. New York: Pergamon Press, 1984.

Cline, Ray S. *World Power Trends and U.S. Foreign Policy for the 1980's*. Boulder, CO: Westview Press, 1980.

Council for Inter-American Security. *Mexico 2000: A Look at the Problems and Potential of Modern Mexico*. Washington: CIS, 1980.

Bibliography

Cruz, Arturo J. "Nicaragua's Imperiled Revolution." *Foreign Affairs.* Summer 1983.

Davis, Rep. Jack Davis. "A New Freedom Fighter Aid Strategy," *The Heritage Lectures* No. 117. Washington: The Heritage Foundation, 1987.

Devine, Frank J. *El Salvador: Embassy Under Attack.* New York: Vantage Press, 1981.

Dickey, Christopher. *With the Contras: A Reporter in the Wilds of Nicaragua.* New York: Simon and Schuster, 1985.

Elliot, Michael. "The shadow of the past." *The Economist: A Survey of Mexico*, September 5, 1987, p. 3.

English, Adrian J. *Armed Forces of Latin America: Their Histories, Development, Present Strength and Military Potential.* London: Jane's, 1984.

Evans, M. Stanton. "Who Are the Contras?" *Human Events*, June 28, 1986, p. 7.

Fallows, James. "The Passionless Presidency." *Atlantic Monthly*, May 1979.

Fehrenbach, T. R. *Fire and Blood: A History of Mexico.* New York: Macmillan, 1973.

Feinberg, Richard E., and Pastor, Robert A. "Far From Hopeless: An Economic Program for Post-War Central America." In *Central America: Anatomy of Conflict*, edited by Robert S. Leiken, pp. 193–217. New York: Pergamon Press, 1984.

Fisk, Daniel W. *Violence and Oppression in Nicaragua,* hearing before the Task Force on Central America of the Republican Study Committee, U.S. House of Representatives. Washington: American Conservative Union, June 1984.

Flaherty, Peter T. "A Closer Look at 'Witness for Peace.' " *The Presbyterian Laymen*, November–December, 1985, p. 9.

Franqui, Carlos. *Family Portrait with Fidel.* Translated by Alfred MacAdam. New York: Vintage, 1985.

Frawley, Joan. "The Left's Latin American Lobby," *Institution Analysis* No. 31. Washington; The Heritage Foundation, October 1984.

Fulbright, J. William. *Arrogance of Power.* New York: Random House, 1966.

Gomez, Leonel. "Feet People." In *Central America: Anatomy of Conflict*, edited by Robert S. Leiken. New York: Pergamon Press, 1984.

Goodman, Timothy. "Sandinistas Aid Attack on Contadora Member." *West Watch* (Washington: Council for Inter-American Security), April 1986.

Bibliography

Haig, Alexander M., Jr. *Caveat: Realism, Reagan, and Foreign Policy.* New York: MacMillan, 1984.

Hannon, Esther Wilson. "Why Mexico's Foreign Policy Still Irritates the U.S.," *Backgrounder* No. 383. Washington: The Heritage Foundation, September 1984.

Hollander, Paul. "Tourism in Cuba and Nicaragua." *Society*, May–June 1986, pp. 28–37.

Inter-American Development Bank. *Economic and Social Progress in Latin America, 1986 Report.* Washington: IADB, 1987.

International Institute for Strategic Studies. *The Military Balance, 1986–87.* London: IISS, 1986.

James, Daniel. *Red Design for the Americas: Guatemalan Prelude.* New York: John Day, 1954.

Johns, Michael. "Seventy Years of Evil." *Policy Review*, Fall 1987, pp. 10–23.

Kennan, George F. *Russia and the West: Under Lenin and Stalin.* New York: Mentor, 1960.

Kirkpatrick, Jeane J. "U.S. Security and Latin America." *Rift and Revolution: The Central American Imbroglio*, edited by Howard J. Wiarda, pp. 329–359. Washington: American Enterprise Institute for Public Policy Studies, 1984.

Kissinger, Henry. *Years of Upheaval.* Boston: Little, Brown & Company, 1982.

Kondracke, Morton. "Who Wants Peace (And The Price To Be Paid)." *The New Republic*, Sept. 28, 1987, pp. 16–19.

Leiken, Robert S. "Fantasies and Facts: The Soviet Union and Nicaragua." *Current History*, October 1984, p. 314.

———"Nicaragua's Untold Stories." *The New Rupublic*, Oct. 8, 1984.

McArdle, Thomas. "Kemp Leads a 'Mision Libertad' to Central America." *Human Events*, September 26, 1987, pp. 10–12.

McColm, R. Bruce. "Revolution's End." *American Spectator*, May 1980, pp. 7–10.

Muravchik, Joshua. "Manipulating the Miskitos: The Sandinista propaganda war comes to the Senate." *The New Republic*, August 6, 1984, p. 21.

Murdock, Deroy. "ARENA: Strong Second Party Emerging in El Salvador." *Human Events*, August 22, 1987, pp. 10–11.

Nelson, Lowry. *Cuba: The Measure of Revolution.* Minneapolis: University of Minnesota Press, 1972.

Bibliography

North, Lt. Col. Oliver L. *Taking the Stand: The Testimony of Lieutenant Colonel Oliver L. North.* New York: Pocket Books, 1987.

Perlmutter, Amos. *The Military and Politics in Modern Times.* New Haven: Yale University Press, 1977.

Polk, Virginia. "The New Guatemala Deserves U.S. Support," *Backgrounder* No. 435. Washington: The Heritage Foundation, May 1985.

———"Why Costa Rica Needs U.S. Help," *Backgrounder* No. 371. Washington: The Heritage Foundation, August 1984.

Powell, S. Steven. *Second Front: Advancing Latin American Revolution in Washington.* Washington: Capital Research Center, 1986.

Prewett, Virginia. *Washington's Instant Socialism in El Salvador.* Washington: Council for Inter-American Security, 1981.

Reed, Lawrence W. "Nicaragua's 'Army of Useful Idiots.' " *Human Events,* June 7, 1986, p. 13.

Reed, Roger. *El Salvador and the Crisis in Central America.* Washington: Council for Inter-American Security, 1984.

Republican Policy Committee, U.S. Senate. *Turmoil in Central America.* Golden, CO: Independence Institute, 1986.

Rosett, Claudia. "Economic Paralysis in El Salvador." *Policy Review,* Fall 1984, pp. 44–47.

Rothenberg, Morris. "The Soviets and Central America." *Central America: Anatomy of Conflict,* edited by Robert S. Leiken. New York : Pergamon Press, 1984.

Salaverry, Jorge. "Contras Score Military Gains Inside Nicaragua," *Executive Memorandum* No. 174. Washington: The Heritage Foundation, August 1987.

Samuel, Peter. "Defector Describes 'Bloody,' 'Corrupt' Regime." *Human Events,* October 12, 1985, pp. 12–13.

Sanders, Sol. *Mexico: Chaos on Our Doorstep.* Lanham, MD: Madison Books, 1986.

Sandford, Gregory. *The New JEWEL Movement: Grenada's Revolution.* Washington: Foreign Service Institute, U.S. Department of State, 1985.

Shea, Nina H. "Human Rights in Nicaragua." *The New Republic,* September 1, 1986, pp. 21–23.

Soderlund, Walter C., and Schmitt, Carmen. "El Salvador's Civil War as Seen in North and South American Press." *Journalism Quarterly,* Summer 1986.

Bibliography

Somoza, Anastasio, and Cox, Jack. *Nicaragua Betrayed.* Boston: Western Islands Publishers, 1980.

Tammen, Melanie. "Deja Vue of Policy Failure: The New $14 Billion Mexican Debt Bailout," *Backgrounder* No. 588. Washington: The Heritage Foundation, June 1987.

Teti, Dennis. "The Coup That Failed: An Insider's Account of the Iran/*Contra* Hearings." *Policy Review,* Fall 1987, pp. 24–31.

Tierney, John J., Jr. *Somozas and Sandinistas: The U.S. and Nicaragua in the Twentieth Century.* Washington: Council for Inter-American Security, 1982.

U.S. Department of Defense. *Background Paper: Nicaragua's Military Build-Up and Support for Central American Subversion.* July 1984.

U.S. Department of State. *Attack on the Church: Persecution of the Catholic Church in Nicaragua.* July 1986.

———*Dispossessed: The Miskito Indians in Sandinista Nicaragua.* June 1986.

———"El Salvador: Revolution or Reform?" Current Policy No. 546, February 1984.

———*Grenada Documents: An Overview and Selection.* September 1984.

———*Inside the Sandinista Regime: A Special Investigator's Perspective.* February 1986.

———"Inside the Sandinista Regime: Revelations by the Executive Director of the Government's Human Rights Commission," a report by the Office of Public Diplomacy for Latin America and the Caribbean (no date). Mimeographed.

———*In Their Own Words: Testimony of Nicaraguan Exiles.* March 1986.

———*Lessons of Grenada.* February 1986.

———*"Revolution Beyond Our Borders": Sandinista Intervention in Central America.* September 1985.

———*Selected Articles Censored from La Prensa.* June 1986.

———*Sustaining a Consistent Policy in Central America: One Year After the National Bipartisan Commission Report,* Special Report No. 124. April 1985.

U.S. Departments of State and Defense. *Background Paper: Nicaragua's Military Build-Up and Support for Central American Subversion.* July 1984.

———*The Challenge to Democracy in Central America.* June 1986.

Bibliography

————*The Soviet-Cuban Connection in Central America and the Caribbean.* April 1985.

U.S. National Bipartisan Commission on Central America. Report. January 1984.

Valenta, Jiri and Virginia. "Soviet Strategy and Policies in the Caribbean Basin." *Rift and Revolution: The Central American Imbroglio*, edited by Howard J. Wiarda, pp. 197–252. Washington: American Enterprise Institute for Public Policy Studies, 1984.

Valladares, Armando. *Against All Hope: The Prison Memoirs of Armando Valladares.* Translated by Andrew Hurley. New York: Alfred A. Knopf, 1986.

Waller, J. Michael. "Celebrities Raise Money for El Salvador's Marxist Guerrillas." *West Watch* (Council for Inter-American Security), June-July 1986, p. 5.

————*Consolidating the Revolution: How the Sandinistas' Support Apparatus Operates in the United States.* Washington: Council for Inter-American Security, 1986.

————"Guatemala's Marxist Guerrillas Nearly Defeated." *West Watch,* October 1987, p. 1.

————"How Pat Schroeder Helps the Sandinistas." *Human Events,* May 10, 1986, p. 6.

————"Mexico: The Achilles Heel of NATO." *West Watch* (Washington: Council for Inter-American Security), April 1986, p. 8.

————"Soviet Policy in Middle America, 1919–1964: A Coherent Agenda Succeeds." Unpublished study. Washington: George Washington University, December 1984.

Washington Institute for Values in Public Policy. *Central America in Crisis: Washington Institute Task Force Report,* rev. ed., 1984.

Weinrod, W. Bruce. "Thirty Myths About Nicaragua," *The Heritage Lectures* No. 54. Washington: The Heritage Foundation, 1986.

Whalen, Christopher. "The Soviet Military Build-Up in Cuba," *Backgrounder* No. 189. Washington: The Heritage Foundation, June 1982.

Whelan, James R., and Bozell, Patricia B. *Catastrophe in the Caribbean: The Failure of America's Human Rights Policy in Central America.* Ottawa, IL: Jameson Books, 1984.

Whelan, Joseph G., and Dixon, Michael J. *The Soviet Union in the Third World: Threat to World Peace?* Washington: Pergamon-Brassey, 1986.

Bibliography

Wiarda, Howard J. "The Origins of the Crisis in Central America." *Rift and Revolution: The Central American Imbroglio,* edited by Howard J. Wiarda, pp. 3–23. Washington: American Enterprise Institute for Public Policy Studies, 1984.

Wisgerhof, Paula R. "Mexico's Many Faces," *Backgrounder* No. 581. Washington: The Heritage Foundation, May 1987.

INDEX

Index

Index

Index

Index

Index

Index

Pollack, Sandy, 367
"popular fronts," 11–12
Powell, S. Stephen, 325–26, 332, 336
Prensa Latina, 26
Presbyterian Church of U.S.A., 89
Preston, Julia, 196, 197, 206, 297, 302, 374
Prewett, Virginia, 152, 154, 315
production, gross domestic product, 53
"progressive" (word), 54
protectorate status, 69
public health expenditures, 61
public opinion, aid to Resistance Forces, 145
Puebla Conference (1979), 90
Puerto Rico, 89
Punta Huete airfield, 4
Purcell, Susan Kaufman, 251, 259–60

Q

Quigley, Thomas E., 334

R

Rama Indians of Nicaragua, 132
Rangel, Charles, 350
Raskin, Marcus, 314
Ratzinger, Joseph, 91
Ray, Richard, 291
Reagan, Nancy, 244, 294
Reagan, Ronald, 7, 125, 243–47, 248, 254, 258, 264–69, 276, 287, 291, 293, 294–95, 309, 339, 348–49, 358
Reconciliatio et Paenitentia (papal exhortation), 91
reconciliation theology, 93
reconnaissance aircraft, 4–5
Reed, David, 137, 200

Reed, Roger, 161
reform politics, 63
refugees from Central America, 7, 21–22
religion and moral values, 66, 87–94, 140–47
Reston, James, 22
revolution: change and modernization theory, 75–76; Grenadan revolution, 34–35; human rights and revolution, 78; pre-emptive revolution, 84; religion and revolution, 87–94
Reyes, Ismael, 289
Ribas Montes, Mario, 170–71
Riding, Alan, 155, 230
Rios Montt, Efrain Jose, 173
Rivera y Damas, Arturo, 163
Robelo, Alfonso, 116, 119
Robertson, Pat, 244
Rodriguez, Carlos Rafael, 12, 269
Romero, Carlos Humberto, 147–48, 151, 162
Romero, Napoleon, 305
Romero, Oscar Arnulfo, 92, 167
Romero, President, 162
Roosevelt, Theodore, 69
Rosa Chavez, Gregorio, 93
Rosenfeld, Stephen S., 207, 251–52, 364
Rosett, Claudia, 203
Rositzke, Harry, 218
Rothenberg, Morris, 24–25, 102, 205

S

Saborio, Alberto, 195
Salaverria, Juan Ricardo, 327
Salazar, Jorge, 337
Salinas de Gortari, Carlos, 232–33, 239

411

Index

About the Authors

JAMES R. WHELAN has been observing and writing about Latin American affairs since he was posted to Buenos Aires in 1958 to begin a ten-year career as a foreign correspondent for United Press International. His performance earned him a coveted Nieman Fellowship at Harvard University, 1966–1967. Later, Whelan returned to the Latin beat with the Scripps-Howard Newspaper Alliance, winning the Certificate of Excellence of the Overseas Press Club of America in the category, best reporting on Latin America, any medium, 1971. Though he would rise through the ranks of newspaper management in the ensuing years—managing editor of *The Miami News*, editor of *The Sacramento Union*, founding editor and publisher of *The Washington Times*—he would never lose his interest in Latin America, authoring four books on Latin American affairs.

FRANKLIN A. JAECKLE graduated Phi Beta Kappa from Cornell University in 1975, and earned his M.A. and D.M.A. (Doctor of Musical Arts) degrees at the University of Iowa. He has taught music at Troy State University in Alabama, and at the Universities of Iowa, Tennessee, and Wisconsin.

Dr. Jaeckle began writing on public affairs at the University of Iowa, where he helped launch the *Campus Review*. Since moving to the Washington area, he has written for the *American Education Report* and served as an editorial assistant at the Council for Inter-American Security. He is presently on the staff of the Congressional Information Service in Bethesda, Md.